Kotlan

herb ruud

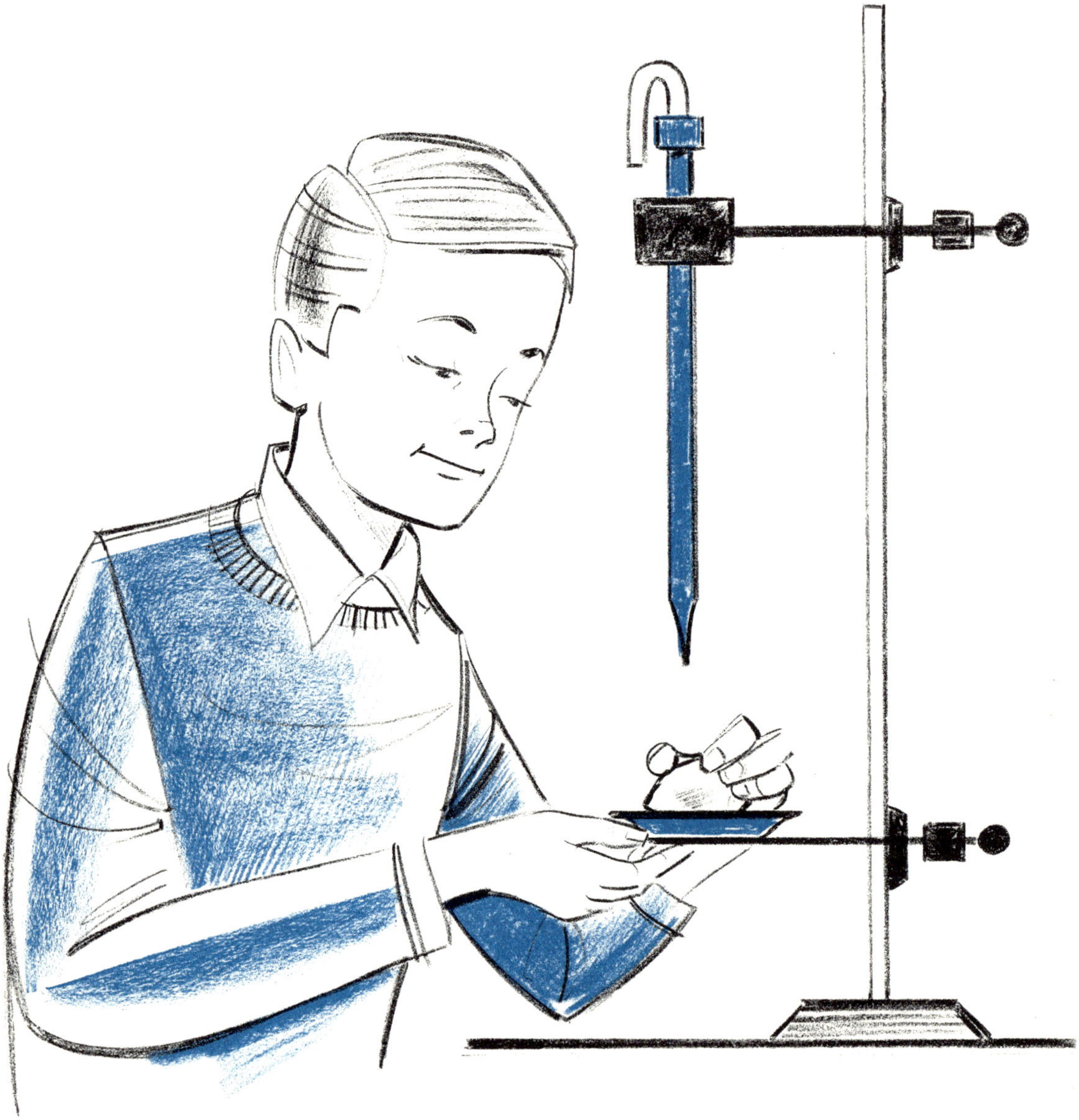

SCIENCE ACTIVITIES FROM A TO Z

by
Helen J. Challand
and
Elizabeth R. Brandt

illustrated by
Herb Ruud

in cooperation with
The Science Center
National College of Education

Grosset & Dunlap • New York

A Childrens Press Book

TABLE OF CONTENTS

INTRODUCTION . . 8	Blood 46	Day and night . . . 73
SETTING UP YOUR OWN LABORATORY . . 10	Blueprinting 47	Diffusion 73
	Boiling point 48	Dip net 74
	Bones 48	Distillation 74
BASIC EQUIPMENT . 12	Botanical press . . . 50	Dogs 75
SOURCES OF EQUIPMENT . . . 13	Buoyancy 50	Dry ice 76
	Camera 51	Dyes 77
SAFETY SUGGESTIONS . . 14	Capillarity 53	Ears 78
	Carbon dioxide . . . 54	Earthworms 78
SCIENCE ACTIVITIES	Catalyst 54	Electrical wiring . . . 80
Absorption 16	Caterpillars 55	Electricity 82
Acids and bases . . . 16	Cats 56	Electrolytes 83
Air 17	Cells 57	Electromagnet . . . 84
Air pressure 18	Centrifugal force . . 58	Electroscope 84
Airplane 19	Charcoal 58	Embryology 85
Amphibians 22	Chemical change . . 59	Enzymes 86
Anemometer 24	Chicken brooder . . 60	Equilibrium 86
Animals 24	Chlorophyll 61	Erosion 87
Annual rings 29	Circulation 61	Evaporation 87
Antenna 29	Cleavage 62	Expansion 88
Antiseptics 30	Clouds 62	Eyes 89
Ants 30	Color 64	Ferns 90
Aquarium 31	Compass 66	Fingerprints 91
Arachnids 33	Compost 66	Fire extinguisher . . 91
Atoms 33	Condensation . . . 67	Flowers 92
Baby animals 35	Conduction 67	Fog 92
Bacteria 36	Constellations . . . 68	Footprints 92
Barometer 38	Convection 70	Fossils 93
Battery 40	Crystal radio 71	Friction 94
Birds 41	Crystals 72	Fruit flies 94

Library of Congress Catalog Card No. 63-17439

Copyright, 1963, Childrens Press
Printed in the U.S.A.

Fungus 96	Moss 141	Soil 176
Fuse 96	Motor 142	Sound 179
Galvanometer . . . 97	Musical instruments .144	Spectrum 183
Gardening 98	Nature trail 145	Spider webs 183
Gas 100	Nervous system . . .145	Spores 184
Germination 101	Optical illusions . . .146	Stalactites 184
Grafting 102	Oscillation 147	Static electricity . . .185
Gravity 103	Osmosis 148	Steam 186
Guinea pigs 104	Oxidation 149	Stethoscope 187
Guppies 104	Parakeets 149	Sundial 187
Hardness scale . . .105	Paramecia 150	Surface tension . . .188
Heat 105	Periscope 151	Switch 188
Heredity 107	Photometer 151	Tadpole 189
Hibernation 107	Photosynthesis . . .152	Taste 189
Hydrometer 108	Planaria 152	Taxidermy 190
Hydroponics 109	Planets 153	Telegraph 191
Hygrometer 110	Plants 154	Telephone 192
Ice 112	Plasmolysis 155	Telescope 193
Inclined plane . . .112	Pollen 156	Terrarium 194
Incubator 113	Precipitates 157	Thermometer 196
Indicator 114	Protein 157	Transpiration 196
Insects 115	Protoplasm 158	Trap 197
Jet propulsion . . .117	Protozoa 158	Trees 198
Kaleidoscope 118	Pulley 159	Tropisms 198
Leaves 119	Pulse 159	Turtles 200
Lever 121	Quiz board 160	Undershot water wheel 201
Lift pump 122	Rabbits 161	Vegetables 201
Light 123	Radioactivity 162	Volcano 202
Lightning 126	Rain 162	Water purification . .203
Machines 126	Reactions 163	Water wheel 205
Magnetic dip circle. .127	Respiratory system . .164	Weather 206
Magnetism 128	Rheostat 165	Wind 207
Matches 132	Rocks 165	Wind tunnel 210
Mealworms 132	Roots 169	Windlass 211
Metals 133	Scale 170	Wood 212
Mice 133	Screw 170	Xylophone 212
Microphotography . .134	Seeds 171	Yeast 214
Microscope 134	Short circuit 173	Zones of time . . .215
Mixture 139	Silkworms 173	Zoo 216
Mold 140	Skeleton 174	Zygote 217
Momentum 140	Snakes 175	INDEX 218
Moon 141	Snow 176	

INTRODUCTION

Most books of this sort start by saying, "This is a book for young scientists." This, too, is a book for young scientists; but it isn't just that. It is also a book for boys and girls who love animals; but it isn't just that either. It is a book for everyone and anyone who is curious about why and how things happen. That includes all of us. The best thing about this book is that it doesn't just tell you how things work; it gives you a chance to find out for yourself.

Have you ever really understood why an airplane, as heavy as it is, is able to leave the ground and stay up in the air? Perhaps you have read the explanation and it still doesn't make sense. Teachers know that the way people learn best is by doing. We can almost guarantee that after you have done the experiment called "Discovering what keeps an airplane up," you'll know the answer. And not only that—you'll be able to show other people what keeps an airplane up.

This is a book of experiments and activities. The experiments are going to help you find out about the fascinating world around you. The materials you will need are listed at the beginning of each activity so that you can gather everything before you start. There may be some questions at the end of the experiment. They will be asking you what you think happened and why. It is very important for you to be able to explain the "why"—the reasons for what happened. Nothing happens in our world without a reason. This is called "cause and effect." Everything that happens has been caused by something else, and part of the scientist's job is to try to understand this relation.

A scientist keeps very detailed and accurate records when he does an experiment so that he can do it over again the very same way and compare the results. When he finds out what caused the results, his problem is well on the way to being solved. It would be a good idea for you, too, to keep a record of each thing you do. You might use a form something like this:

    Materials used:

    Procedure *(what you did):*

    Results *(what happened):*

    Conclusions *(why what you did caused that particular thing to happen):*

Repeat the experiments. You want to be sure that an experiment will work the same way every time you do it. You'll probably think of better or easier ways to use the same materials and get the same results. This is part of the fun of experimenting.

There are many activities in the book which are not experiments. They are not experiments because you know exactly what is going to happen and because they do not follow the scientific method. You can learn how to trap animals, build cages for them, feed and care for them, and build a backyard zoo. Have you ever asked on a summer day: "What can I do?" Try building a weather station, constructing a microscope or telescope, setting up a nature trail, or making musical instruments. Many winning projects in school science fairs were started the summer before.

This is meant to be a real do-it-yourself book for boys and girls. Most of the activities can be done without help from adults. Occasionally it is suggested that you ask for help in using tools or chemicals which could be dangerous to handle. The materials are mostly things you can find around your house or in someone's junk pile. Boxes, scrap lumber, old electrical equipment can be collected by explaining what you are doing to local storekeepers. The chemicals and other new equipment you'll need to buy are reasonably priced and can usually be paid for out of a babysitter's or lawn mower's pay.

Whenever you are working in your laboratory on science experiments and activities, remember to:

1. Be neat. Be careful about spilling and cleaning up after yourself.

2. Be sensible. Observe the safety suggestions on page 14.

3. Be courteous. Ask permission before using other people's possessions.

4. Be persistent. Don't give up after trying something just once. The longer and harder you work on a project, the prouder you'll be when it is done.

5. Be inventive. Use the experiments and projects in this book as a springboard to more difficult and complicated projects of your own.

Helen J. Challand, Ph.D.
Elizabeth R. Brandt, M.A.
Science Department
National College of Education
Evanston, Illinois

SETTING UP YOUR OWN LABORATORY

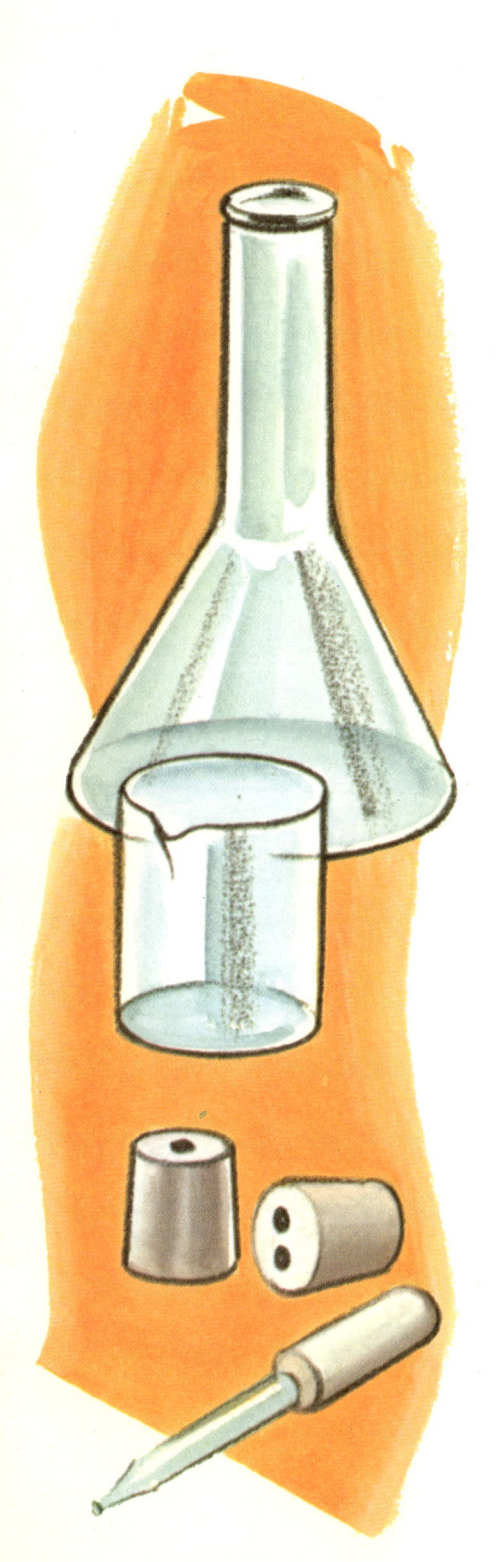

A scientist needs supplies, equipment, and a place to work. If you are seriously interested in performing many of the experiments and activities in this book, you will want to collect many of the items listed on page 12. A large number of the materials can be found around your home, in the garage, or from friends. Chemicals can be purchased at the local drugstore or supply houses. Hardware stores, lumber yards, hobby shops, and dime stores will offer many others.

Before you set out to find or buy science equipment, ask permission to use a corner of the basement, garage, or utility room for a work and storage area for your laboratory. It will be helpful if you can easily get to water—many experiments call for it and all equipment must be cleaned after use.

An old dresser, bookcase, table and sheet of pegboard would give enough storage and work space. Since you don't care how old-fashioned or pretty the furniture is, you may find the pieces at a second-hand shop for just a few dollars. The bookcase can serve as the chemical and glassware closet. The drawers in the dresser can be divided into neat sections to hold many of the other supplies. All tools and instruments can be hung on the pegboard. A durable finish on the work table would be desirable but is not necessary. Since you will be using candles, an alcohol lamp, and a hot plate for sources of heat, you will not have to use the kitchen stove.

As you collect equipment be sure that all chemicals are clearly labeled. Put a "CAUTION" sign on the ones that should be used very carefully. Each shelf and drawer should have the inventory of its contents taped to the outside. Print the safety rules on a poster board and hang it on your pegboard as a daily reminder.

Take good care of all equipment. Clean and dry glassware, tools, and instruments each time you use them. Put tops back on chemicals to keep them from evaporating or collecting dust.

All scientists keep careful records. You may do this in a notebook or on cards. Record the date, experiment, procedures, results and your ideas about what happened. Remember to be thorough and accurate.

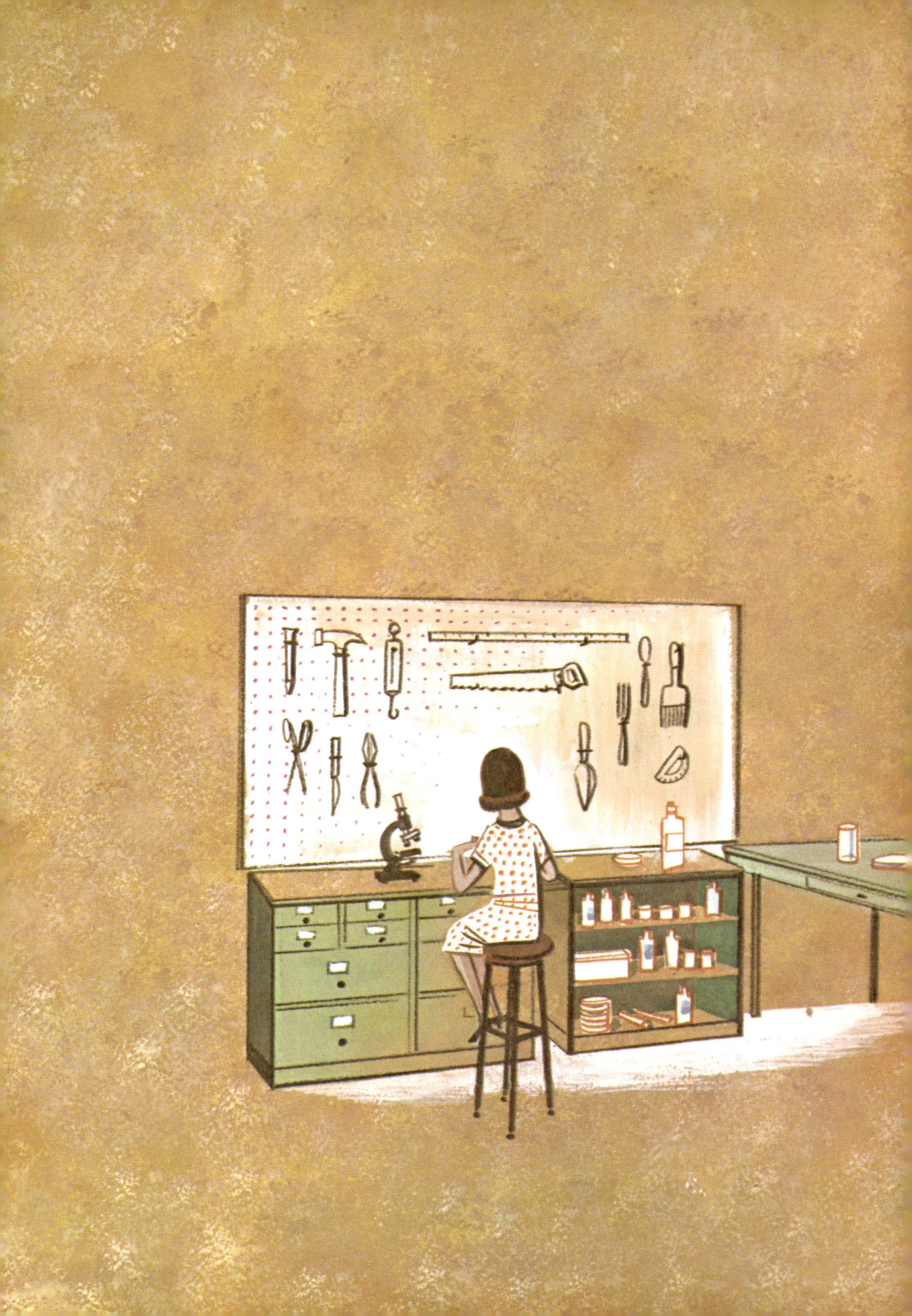

BASIC EQUIPMENT

GLASSWARE AND CONTAINERS
beakers
chimneys
clay flower pots
cover glasses (microscopic)
cups
flasks
funnel
glass rod
glass sheets
glass slides (microscopic)
glass tubing
ink bottle
jars with lids
petri dishes
pie pans
plastic containers
pop bottles
saucers
teakettle
test tubes
tin cans
water glasses
Y-tube

HEAT SOURCES
alcohol lamp
Bunsen burner
candles
electric hot plate

CHEMICALS AND RELATED MATERIALS
alcohol
alum
ammonia
ammonium chloride
aquarium cement
aspirin
baking soda
balsam
bleach
borax
boric acid
bouillon cubes
bluing
carbon tetrachloride
carmine
chalk
charcoal
clay
copper sulfate
cornmeal
crystal violet
detergent
distilled water
eosin
Epsom salts
ferric ammonium citrate
fertilizer
formaldehyde
gelatin
glue
hydrochloric acid
India ink
iodine crystals
lemon juice
lighter fluid
lime
limewater tablets
magnesium chloride
magnesium ribbon
mercury
methylene blue
paraffin
phosphorus
plaster of Paris
Plasticine
potassium ferricyanide
powdered paint
rock salt
rubber cement
salt
shellac
sugar
sulfur powder
tempera paint
turpentine
vegetable dyes
vinegar
xylol
yeast

PAPER AND CLOTH
cardboard boxes
cardboard cylinders
cardboard sheets
cellophane
cloth (black and white)
construction paper
cotton
filter paper
foil
gauze
index cards
litmus paper
milk cartons
newspapers
paper towels
photographic film
plastic envelopes
rope
sandpaper
sawdust
soda straws
string
tagboard
thread
tissue paper

INSTRUMENTS
atomizer
bicycle pump
bulbs (electric)
camera
chisel
clamps
clock
compass
door bell
drill
dry cells
earphones
electric fan
eye dropper
flashlight
hammer
hand lens
knife
lamp
lenses
magnets (bar & horseshoe)
magnifying glass
measuring cup
measuring spoons
microscope
mirrors
paint brush
pencils
pliers
prism
protracter
pulleys (single & double)
razor blades
receptacles
ring stand and clamps
ruler
saw
scissors
screwdriver
spring scale
stop watch
switch (knife)
tape measure
thermometers (C & F.)
tweezers
weights (1 to 5 pounds)

HARDWARE
bell wire (#22 & #26)
brads
chicken wire
cookie sheet
copper strips
hardware cloth
hinges
hook and eye
iron filings
L-hooks
lead strips
nails
nuts and bolts
pins
screw eyes
screws
sheet metal
steel wool
tacks
thumbtacks
wire
zinc strips

MISCELLANEOUS
adhesive tape
balloons
balsa wood
carbon rod
cellophane tape
coat hangers
corks
crayons
dowels
electrician's tape
inner tube
lumber
matches
plywood
rubber balls
rubber bands
rubber tubing
sand
seed assortment
sponge
spools
stoppers (1 & 2-holed)
tennis balls
tooth picks

SOURCES OF EQUIPMENT

Most of the materials needed for the activities in this book can be obtained around the home or from local shops at very little cost. These sources include the drugstore, grocery market, five-and-ten, greenhouse, hardware store, hobby shop, photography shop, lumber yard, second-hand shop, electrical appliance store, pet shop and farms.

A few pieces of equipment will need to be purchased from a scientific supply house. From the list below, select the one nearest you. Write to the company for a catalog. In a few cases, they will request that the order be signed by an adult.

Allied Radio Corporation, 833 North Jefferson Blvd., Chicago 7, Illinois
American Science Center, 5700 Northwest Highway, Chicago 46, Illinois
Cambosco Scientific Company, 37 Antwerp, Brighton Station, Boston, Massachusetts
Carolina Biological Supply Company, Elon College, North Carolina
Central Scientific Company, 1700 Irving Park Road, Chicago 13, Illinois
                6446 Telegraph Road, Los Angeles 22, California
                79 Amherst Street, Cambridge 42, Massachusetts
Coe-Palm Biological Supply House, 1130 Milwaukee Avenue, Chicago 22, Illinois
Difco Laboratories, Inc., Detroit 1, Michigan
Edmund Scientific Company, Barrington, New Jersey (for lenses)
Eimer and Amend Company, Greenwich and Morton Streets, New York 14, New York
Fisher Scientific Company, 635 Greenwich Street, New York 14, New York
                717 Forbes Street, Pittsburgh 19, Pennsylvania
General Biological Supply House, 8200 South Hoyne Avenue, Chicago 20, Illinois
Los Angeles Biological Laboratories, 2977 West 14th Street, Los Angeles, California
New York Scientific Supply Company, 28 West 13th Street, New York 1, New York
Pacific Laboratory Apparatus Company, 3555 Whittier Blvd., Los Angeles 23, California
Harry Ross, 70 West Broadway, New York 7, New York
E. H. Sargent and Company, 155 East Superior Street, Chicago 11, Illinois
Science Materials Center, 59 Fourth Avenue, New York 3, New York
Scientific Apparatus Makers of America, Inc., 20 North Wacker Drive, Chicago 6, Illinois
Standard Scientific Supply Corporation, 34-38 West Fourth Street, New York 12, New York
Taylor Instrument Company, Rochester, New York
Ward's Natural Science Establishment, Inc., P.O. Box 24, Beechwood Station,
                Rochester 9, New York
Ward's of California, P.O. Box 1749, Monterey, California
W. M. Welch Scientific Company, 1515 North Sedgwick Street, Chicago 10, Illinois

SAFETY SUGGESTIONS

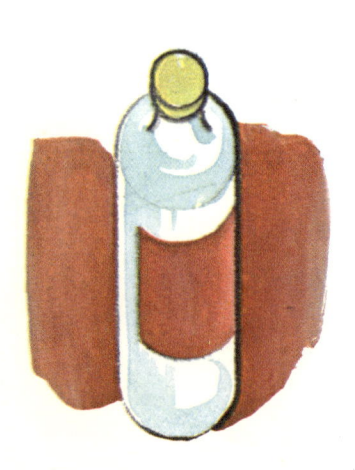

In general, work slowly and carefully. Follow directions with care. Whenever you see the CAUTION! sign, work even more carefully. Remember the following simple suggestions and you can have great fun in your laboratory.

GLASSWARE

Occasionally there is breakage when the directions call for glass tubing to be inserted in a cork or one-holed stopper. The tubing will go into the stopper easily if you wet the tube with soap and water or grease it with vaseline. Hold a folded handkerchief in the hand you use to push the tubing. If it does break, it won't cut you. Push the tubing in with a twisting motion.

Whenever directions call for glass to be cut, fire polish or tape the cut edge. To fire polish, hold the cut edge in a flame until it melts and rounds off.

ELECTRICITY

All of the activities involving electricity call for dry cells as the source of power. Use 1½-volt dry cells. They have such low voltage that there is no danger of receiving a shock from one or even from two or three in series. The only danger is in short circuiting a dry cell—that is, wiring a circuit without some type of resistence, such as a lamp or bell, or connecting the terminals on one cell. This may cause the wires to become so hot they cause a minor burn. When using bell wire, remove the insulation only at connecting points.

CHEMICALS

Label all bottles containing chemicals. Use adhesive tape for the labels.

The acids called for in this book are all weak acids, such as vinegar. If you decide to use hydrochloric acid (which isn't necessary because vinegar can always be used in place of it), take care in handling the acid. If you get some on your hands, wash immediately.

Never heat alcohol or any other volatile (quickly evaporating) liquid directly. A beaker of alcohol should be placed in a larger container of water and the water heated. Do not let the alcohol boil.

Be sure to use carbon tetrachloride in a well-ventilated place—preferably outdoors. Its fumes can be dangerous.

The rest of the chemicals called for in the experiments are harmless if used as directed. However, it is always a good idea to wear old clothes or a smock or apron over your clothes when you are working with chemicals.

When you have finished an experiment, you must get rid of used chemicals. Liquids can be washed down a drain with lots of water to dilute them. Solids, such as iron sulfide and various precipitates should be emptied into the trash.

BACTERIA

When culturing or experimenting with bacteria, handle the culture carefully. Be sure to wash your hands well with soap and water when you are through. Flush the bacterial culture down a toilet and sterilize the dishes and instruments used after washing them in soap and water. Most of the bacteria you will be working with are harmless, but disease-producing ones may accidentally have contaminated the culture.

ANIMALS

You can make pets of all baby turtles and most adult turtles. Adult snapping turtles and soft-shelled turtles, however, grow very large and become savage, so they don't make good pets.

Before you go collecting snakes, find out what poisonous ones are in your area and study their descriptions and pictures. If you are suspicious that a snake may be poisonous, don't gamble. Avoid it! Always handle pet snakes with one hand firmly around the neck and the other hand supporting the rest of the body. It is best not to handle a snake after it has been fed or while it is shedding its skin. It is inclined to be irritable.

Handle small mammals regularly but for short periods of time to accustom them to people. If you should be bitten, get medical attention. Allow only experienced people to handle small mammal pets. A frightened animal may scratch or bite.

Squirrels, chipmunks, woodchucks and beavers do not adjust well to captivity. Don't try to make pets of them. They can inflict serious bites.

Before adding any wild mammal (rabbit, flying squirrel, etc.) to your collection of pets, take it to your veterinarian to make sure it is not diseased. He may suggest that the animal be given an anti-rabies shot.

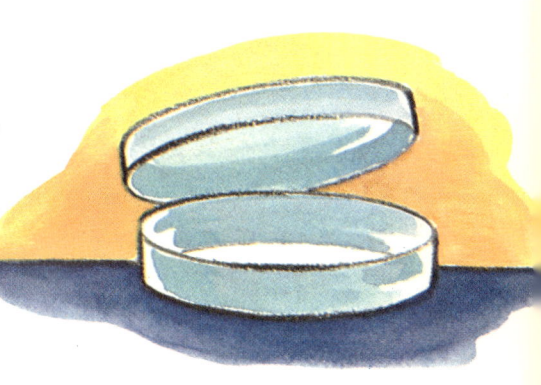

ABSORPTION

TESTING LIGHT ABSORPTION

Materials you'll need:
2 weather thermometers, a black and a white cloth, 2 plastic containers, black and white paint, heat lamp

Cover one thermometer with a black cloth. Cover the other thermometer with a white cloth. Set both covered thermometers in the sun for one-half hour. Which one then registers a higher temperature? Does the black or the white cloth absorb more light and therefore more heat?

If you can get hold of two plastic containers (like the ones used to hold leftover food in the refrigerator), you can do an even more dramatic experiment. Paint one container black and one white. Place both under a strong light, preferably a heat lamp. After a few minutes you will see a change occur in one of the containers. What happens? Why?

ACIDS AND BASES

TESTING FOR ACIDS AND BASES

Materials you'll need:
litmus paper, substances mentioned below

The scientist uses litmus paper to find out whether a substance is acid or alkaline. Blue litmus turns pink in the presence of an acid and pink litmus paper turns blue in the presence of a base (alkaline substance). Using both the pink and the blue strips, test some of these substances: soap, baking powder, ammonia, orange, raw potato, vinegar, washing soda, salt, bicarbonate of soda, rhubarb and sugar. The substance to be tested must be wet or in a solution. Try making your own indicator (page 114).

AIR

TESTING FOR AIR

Materials you'll need:
  glass of water, soil, brick, source of heat

In order to discover whether there is air in soil, put a handful of soil in a glass of water. What rises to the surface? When a brick is placed in a pan of water, what do you observe? What does this prove? The water is pushing the air out of the spaces in the brick.

To find out whether there is air in water, heat the water (but not to boiling) and watch the air bubbles rise to the surface. Test other materials as you did the soil and brick.

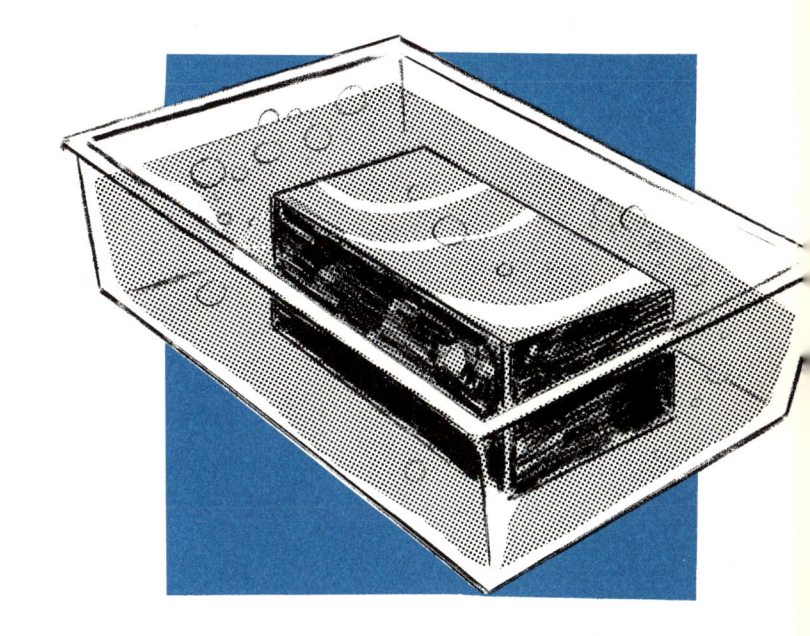

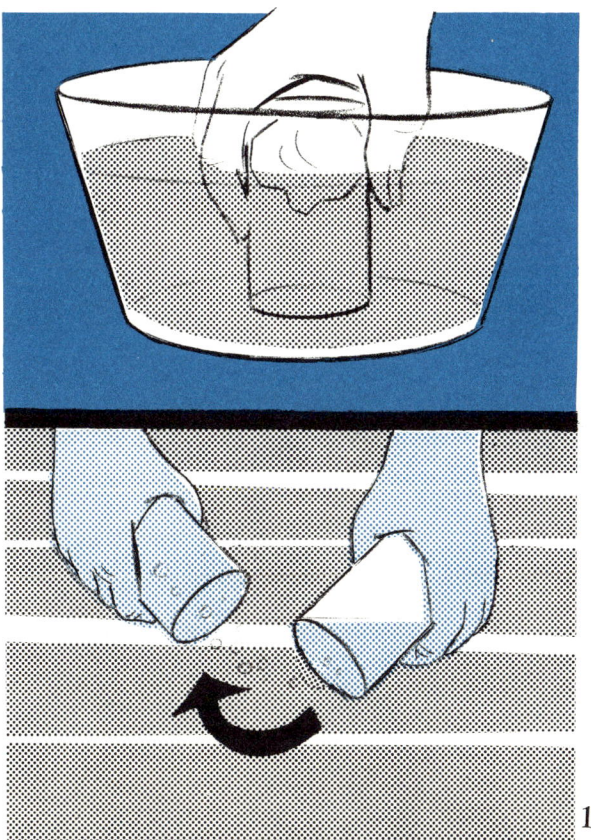

FINDING THAT AIR TAKES UP SPACE

Materials you'll need:
  glass, paper, jar of water, aquarium filled with water

Crumple a piece of dry paper and push it into the bottom of a glass so that it stays there when the glass is turned upside down. Now invert the glass and push it straight down into a large jar of water. The paper will be dry when you remove the glass. Why?

Now invert two empty glasses in an aquarium of water. Tilt one to allow it to fill with water. Hold it slightly above the one which is still filled with air. Tip the air-filled glass and allow the bubbles of air to escape. Catch them in the water-filled glass. What happens to the water in that glass?

AIR

AIR PRESSURE

FINDING THAT AIR HAS WEIGHT

Materials you'll need:
  yardstick, string, 2 footballs or basketballs

Suspend a yardstick by a string so that it hangs parallel to the ground and fasten it to a support. Blow up two footballs of the same size so that they are equally firm. Tie one to each end of the yardstick so that they balance. Carefully let the air out of one but don't let the sides collapse. Why does the other end of the yardstick go down?

SHOWING THAT AIR EXERTS PRESSURE

Materials you'll need:
  milk bottle, hard-boiled egg with shell removed, match, paper, glass of water, cardboard square, tin can with screw top (such as cleaned turpentine can)

Crumple a sheet of paper and drop it into a milk bottle. Light the end of a paper straw. Hold the burning end of the straw in the bottle to light the paper. Hold the bottle horizontally until the paper is burning. When the flame goes out set the hard-boiled egg in the opening of the bottle. Watch what happens to the egg. What is pushing the egg into the bottle? Why? Can you figure out a way to get the egg back out of the bottle without breaking it?

Fill a glass with water. Place the cardboard over the top of the glass. Hold it in place and turn the glass upside down. Carefully take your hand away. Does the cardboard stay in place? How many pounds of pressure are pushing against the bottom of the cardboard in order to keep the water from coming out of the glass? Would this experiment work if the glass were filled only half full? Try it and see.

Pour half a cup of water in the tin can without capping it. Place the can over a source of heat such as a hot plate. Boil the water for several minutes. Using a pot holder, remove the can from the heat and put the cap on tightly at once. Watch what happens to the sides of the can. What happens to the air pressure inside the can as it cools? What force is pushing from the outside of the can?

CAUTION!

AIR PRESSURE

TESTING BERNOULLI'S PRINCIPLE

Materials you'll need:
   2 tennis balls, string, bicycle pump

Bernoulli, a famous 18th-century scientist, discovered a principle which has been very important in the field of aviation. Try this experiment and see if you can explain his contribution to science. It has to do with air pressure.

Suspend two tennis balls on long string from a door frame or other firm support. Using a bicycle pump, direct a blast of air between the two balls. What happens to the position of the balls? What is happening to the air that is similar to the principle involved in flight?

AIRPLANE

DISCOVERING WHAT KEEPS AN AIRPLANE UP

Materials you'll need:
   piece of paper 9" by 2", another paper 10" x 2", glue

Hold the shorter strip of paper by one end. Blow across the top of it. The paper will rise. This happens because the faster-moving air over the top of the paper exerts less pressure than the slower-moving air underneath the paper. This is called *lift*.

A cross section of an airplane wing which has a front, or *leading*, edge thicker than the back edge is called an *airfoil*. Air moving over an airfoil lifts it even against the pull of gravity. You can make an airfoil by folding and gluing the larger strip of paper as shown. Place it over a ruler and blow so that the air strikes the thick leading edge. Does it rise?

19

AIRPLANE

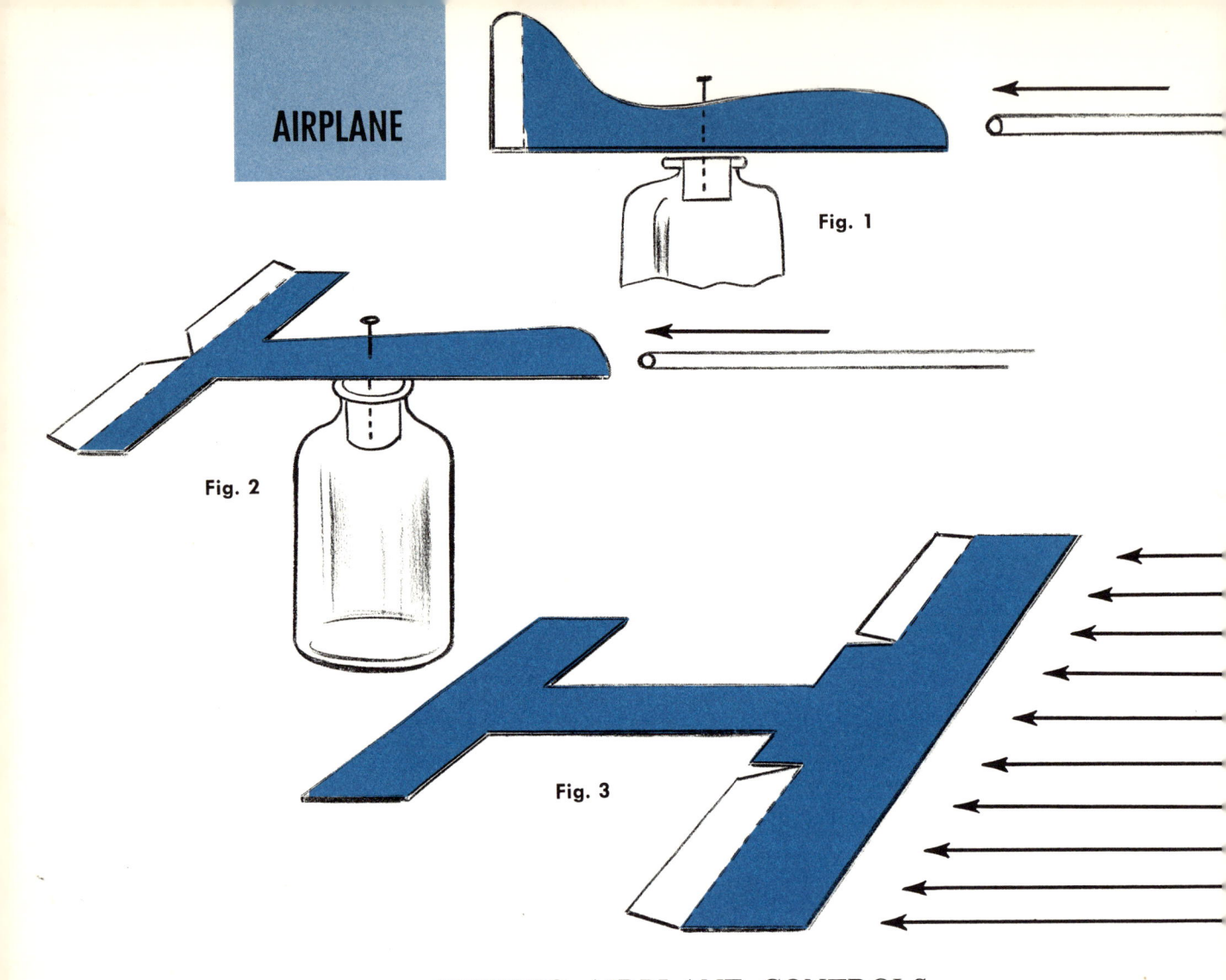

Fig. 1

Fig. 2

Fig. 3

TESTING AIRPLANE CONTROLS

Materials you'll need:
   piece of tagboard, bottle with cork, pin, soda straw

Make a crude model airplane out of tagboard. Cut it as shown in Figure 1 in the illustration. Make a crease in the tail to form a rudder. Find the balancing point of the plane (the point where your finger touches when it balances on it). Stick a pin through it and into the cork in the jar. Now bend the rudder to one side and blow at the plane through a straw. Bend the rudder the other way and blow. You will be able to see how the rudder controls the plane.

Now make a second airplane without the upright section of the tail but with the elevators which can be folded up or down (Figure 2). Balance it on the jar and blow at it in order to discover what effect the elevators have on control of the plane.

For the experiment with the ailerons (Figure 3), you will need a wind tunnel (see page 210) to produce a fast-moving stream of air. Fashion a flat tagboard plane with cuts and folds as in the illustration to imitate ailerons. Bend the left aileron up and the right down and hold the plane in front of the wind tunnel. You will see it bank to the left. Reverse the bank by adjusting the ailerons. Almost all airplanes are controlled by movable surfaces such as these.

AIRPLANE

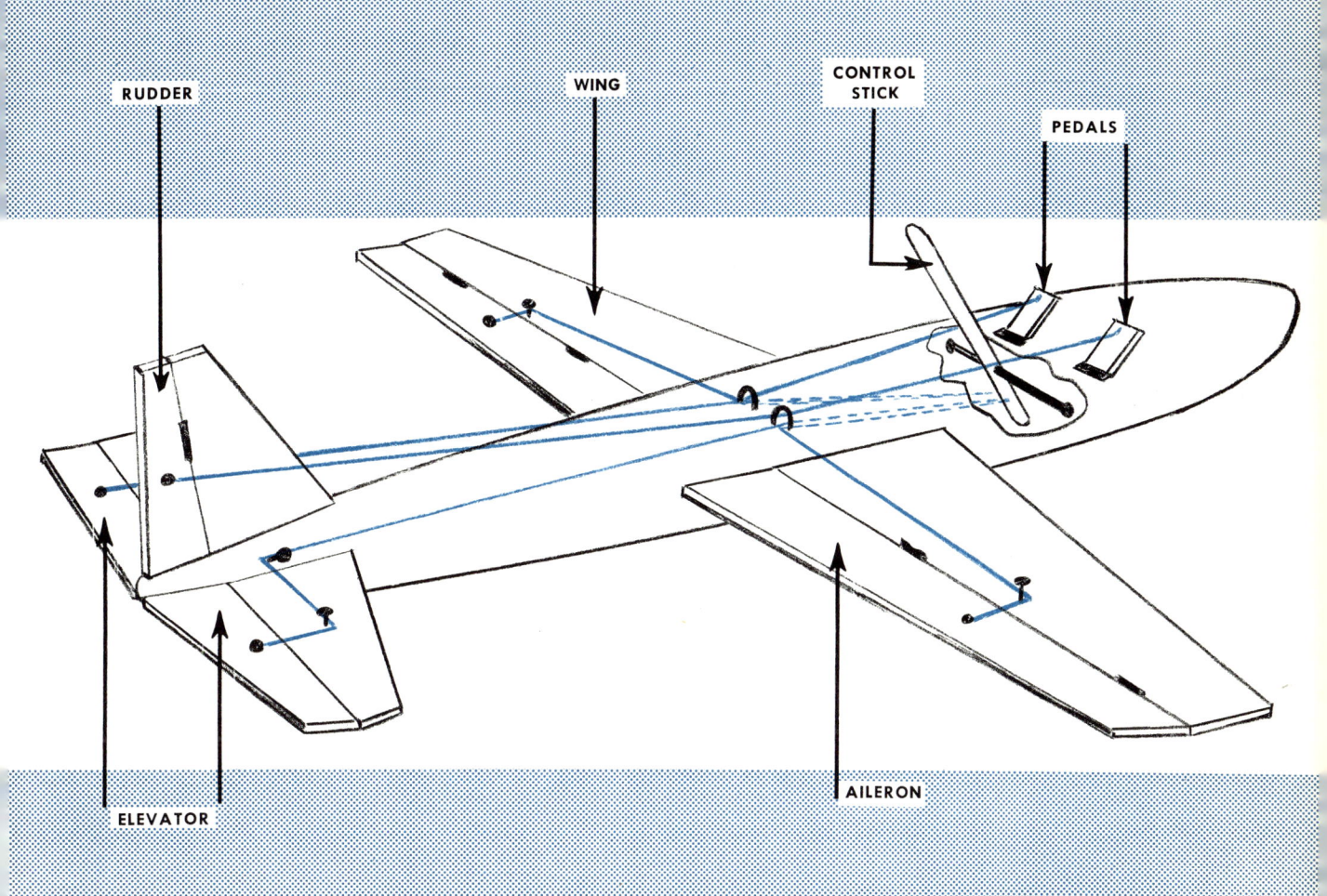

RUDDER · WING · CONTROL STICK · PEDALS · AILERON · ELEVATOR

MAKING A MODEL AIRPLANE

Materials you'll need:
  balsa wood, wire, screws, hinges, stick, wooden pedals

Assemble an airplane by following the labeled illustration. The elevators, rudder, and ailerons are fastened to the body of the plane with little metal hinges. With a stiff wire connect the right pedal to the right side of the rudder. Do the same on the left side. Fasten wire from the control stick to each aileron and elevator. When the stick is pulled back the elevators are pulled up. The plane begins to climb. When the stick is moved to the right, the right aileron turns up and the left one goes down. The airplane banks to the right. Experiment with the model airplane to understand how a pilot can use the single control stick to climb, nose-dive, bank to the right and to the left.

AMPHIBIANS

FROG

TOAD

SALAMANDER

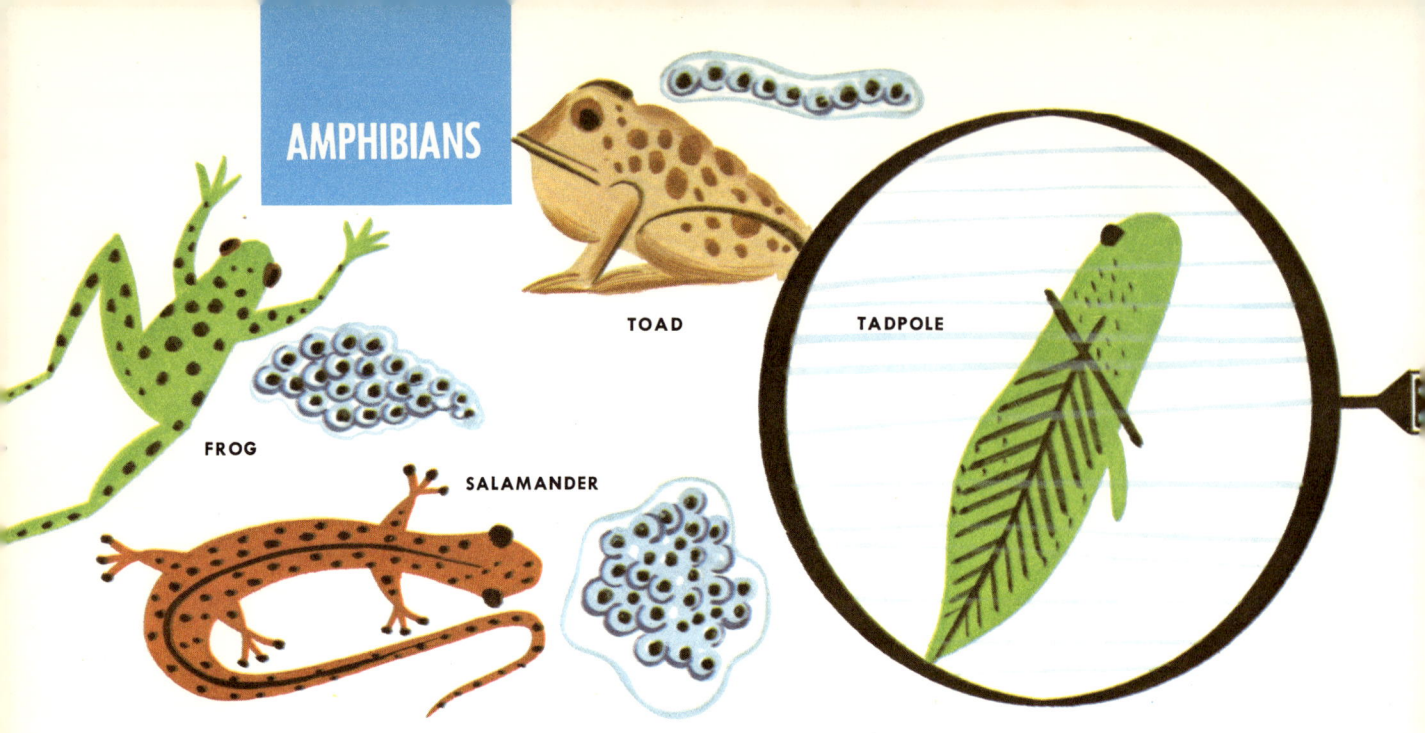

TADPOLE

RAISING AMPHIBIANS FROM EGGS

Materials you'll need:
glass jar, semi-aquatic terrarium (with water and a land area), thermometer, screen

The best eggs for watching the development of the embryo are those of the amphibians—toads, frogs and salamanders. The eggs are large and have rather transparent coverings. In early spring go to a pond or similar body of water and search for eggs. The salamanders lay their eggs first, often before the pond is free of ice. The salamander egg clusters may be attached to sticks and plants under water. Frog eggs may be in jellylike masses which float on the surface of the water. Collect about 20 eggs in a jar filled with pond water. Keep the different species in separate containers in a cool place. Maintain the water temperature between 55 and 75 degrees Fahrenheit.

Clumps of floating plants of the type often found in ponds of greenish water should be added to the containers of amphibian eggs. Tadpoles feed on the algae which surround these plants.

The tadpoles will develop within the jelly mass and, when fully developed, will swim free of the mass. The length of the incubation period depends on the variety of frog or salamander. Separate the tiny tadpoles into several containers to avoid crowding. Feed them bits of leafy vegetables and the yellow of a hard-boiled egg. Avoid overfeeding. Change the water frequently. Observe the tadpole as its legs are developed and its tail is absorbed.

Construct a semi-aquatic terrarium by placing a bowl of water in one end of an aquarium. On the other half build a land environment of sand, soil, and plants. As the tadpoles develop lungs they will leave the water environment and seek the land. You will need to cover the aquarium with a wire screen top as the amphibians mature. Adult frogs like live insects for food. If you have trouble catching live insects with a net (page 74), try pressing a bit of raw hamburger on the end of a thread and dangling it in front of the frog. If the frog refuses to eat, let it go. Do not be impatient—it may take months for some species to develop.

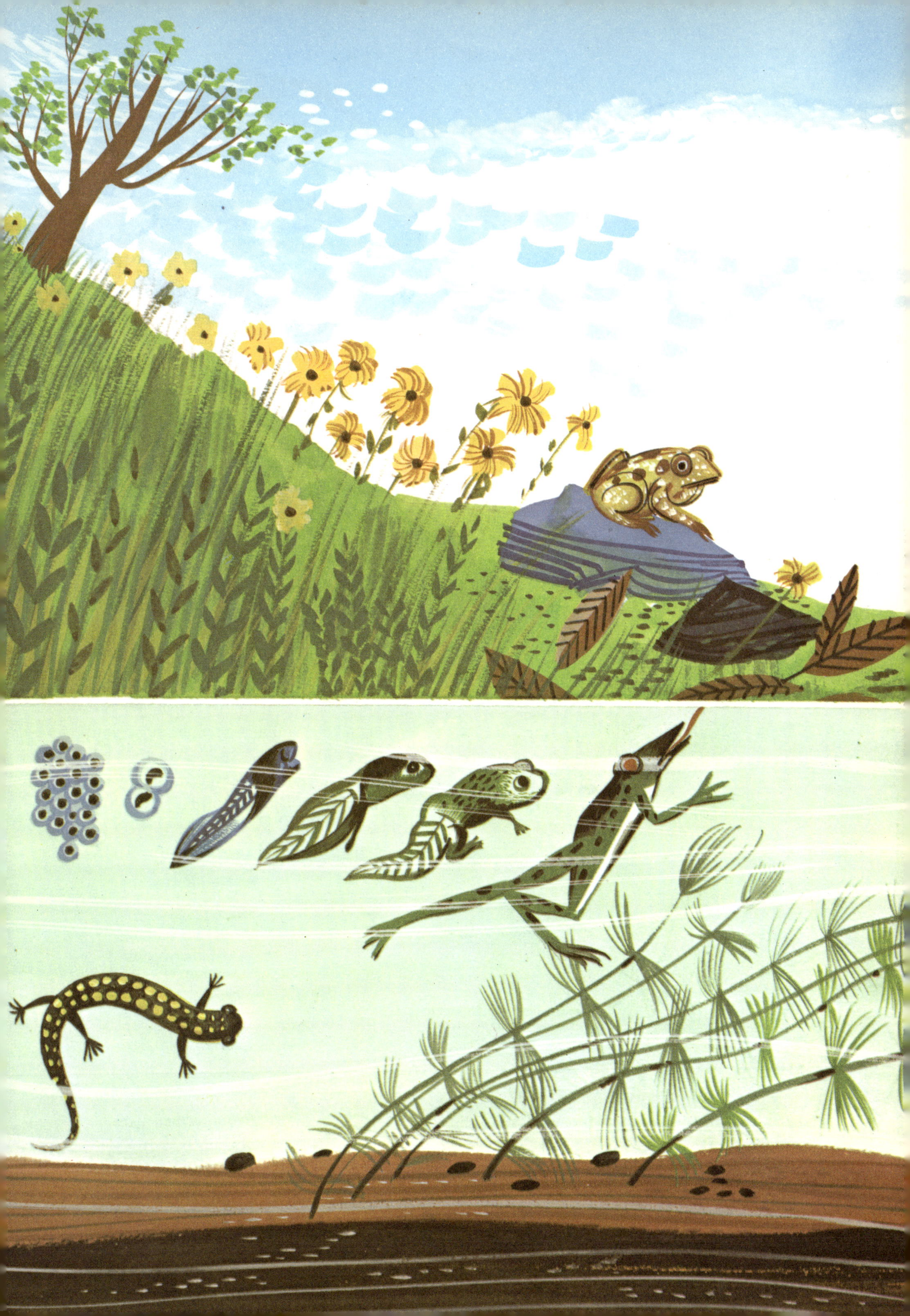

ANEMOMETER

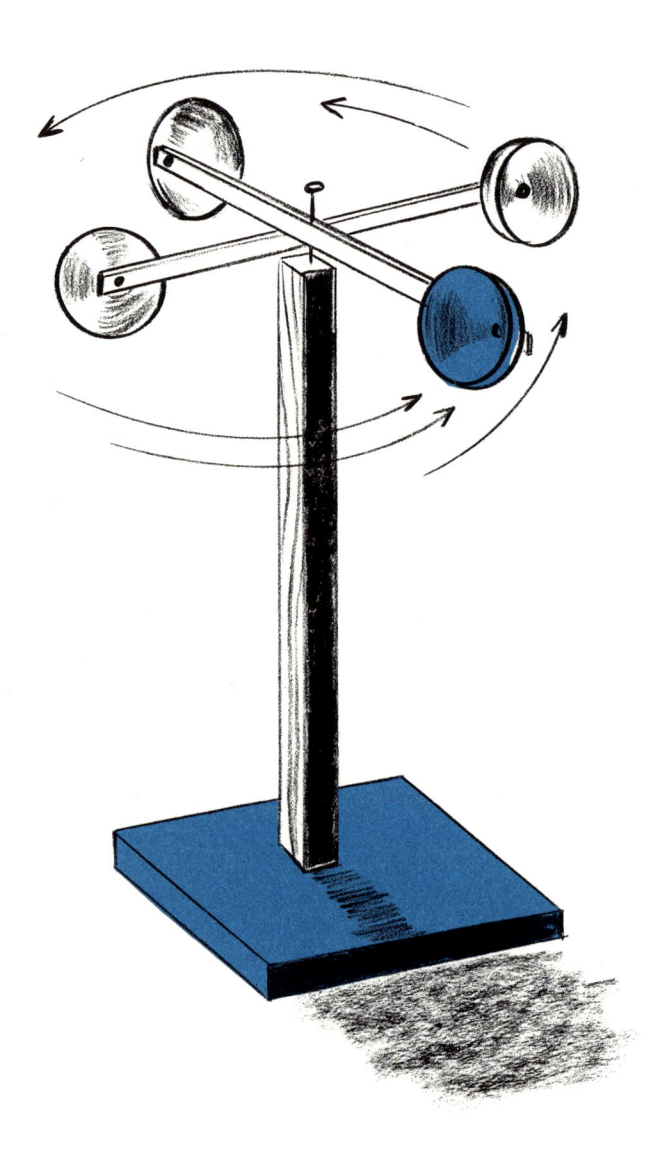

ANIMALS

FINDING THE SPEED OF MOVING AIR

Materials you'll need:
2 rubber balls cut in half, 2 sticks 18 inches long with a 1-inch diameter, wooden support, long nail, several short nails, wax

Assemble these materials according to the illustration. Nail the halves of the balls on the ends of the two sticks. Fasten the two sticks in the center at right angles. Paint one cup a different color to make counting the number of revolutions easier. In the end of the support, drill a hole a little larger than the nail used in the cross arms. Wax the inside of the hole to cut down on friction. Set the nail of the arms in the hole.

To determine the wind velocity in miles per hour with a homemade anemometer, count the number of revolutions in thirty seconds and divide by five. A more accurate method is to hold the instrument outside the window of a moving car and check the revolutions with the speedometer.

FEEDING PET ANIMALS

Animals, like boys and girls, eat a wide variety of foods. Your pet might be one of the animals in the list on the next page. The foods suggested, the amount, and time of feeding, should be followed closely. Remember that animals, like people, are not exactly alike, so your pet may need a little more or less than the amount listed. Just be sure that you do not overfeed or leave leftover food in the cage to decay. Keep your pet's "table" as neat and sanitary as you would your own. Most commercial pet food contains the proper balance of vitamins, proteins, minerals, and other basic foods. If you use table scraps for food, you may have to give the larger animals a vitamin supplement. Be sure to give all of your pets fresh water every day.

ANIMAL DIETS

ANIMAL	FOOD	HOW OFTEN	HOW MUCH
Alligator	earthworms, mealworms, raw hamburger	2 weekly	*
Ants	honey, bread crumbs, sugar water	daily	unlimited
Bat	biscuits, meats, cottage cheese, hard-boiled eggs, bananas	daily	small portion of each
Birds	suet, seeds, grains, unsalted nuts, raisins, currants	daily	unlimited if wild
Canary	canary and rape seed, apple, lettuce, chickweed, dandelion leaves, water cress, cuttlefish, gravel	daily	1 teaspoon
Caterpillars	plant leaves on which it was crawling when captured	daily	unlimited
Chameleon	raw hamburger, leafy vegetables, live insects	3 weekly	*
Chipmunk	meat, nuts, seeds, bread, hard-boiled eggs	daily	5 ounces
Crickets	leafy vegetables, bits of apple and bread	daily	unlimited
Crayfish	raw hamburger, fish	daily	*
Crow	meat scraps, puppy meal, grapes, live insects, grains, cereals, nuts, cuttlefish, gravel	2 daily	3 tablespoons
Earthworms	humus, soil, cornmeal	weekly	unlimited
Finch	millet, canary seed, clover, apple, orange, flower seeds, cuttlefish, gravel	daily	1 teaspoon
Fish (tropical)	Daphnia, brine shrimp, crab, shrimp, clam, fish eggs, commercial food	daily	amount eaten in 5 minutes
(others)	worms, insects, raw hamburger	"	"
Frogs, Toads	raw meat, hard cheese, spiders, live insects, fish, shellfish, earthworms, mealworms	2 weekly	*
Gophers	potatoes, bulbs, cereal, insects, meat	daily	5 ounces
Grasshoppers	leafy vegetables, moist bread, apple	daily	unlimited
Guinea pigs	barley, corn, oats, wheat, leafy vegetables, ripe apples, beets, liver meal, clover, cereal	2 daily	*
Guppies	commercial guppy food	daily	amount eaten in 5 minutes
Hamsters	pellets, grains, fruits, puppy biscuits, leafy vegetables, beet tops	daily	1 ounce dry plus greens
Hydra	Daphnia (water fleas)	3 weekly	1 water flea
Lizards	raw meat, insects, mealworms, earthworms	2 weekly	*
Mice	grains, dog biscuits, leafy vegetables, peanut butter, carrots, rat food, bread soaked in milk	daily	1 ounce
Myna	chick starter, grated carrot, nuts, puppy meal, berries, mealworms, celery leaves, cuttlefish, gravel	3 daily	2 tablespoons
Newt	earthworms, raw hamburger, fish	2 weekly	*
Parakeet	millet, oats, canary seed, lettuce, chickweed, cottage cheese, cuttlefish, gravel, bread	daily	1 teaspoon
Parrot	raw peanuts, sunflower seeds, cornmeal, leafy vegetables, berries, bananas, corn, cuttlefish, gravel	2 daily	2 tablespoons
Planaria	raw heart or liver	daily	*
Rabbit	grains, peanuts, leafy vegetables, clover, cauliflower, parsnips, pellets, carrots, salt	daily	6 ounces
Raccoon	corn, meat, fruit, table scraps	daily	5 ounces
Salamanders	raw meat, snails, slugs, insects, spiders, earthworms, mealworms	2 weekly	*
Silkworm moth	mulberry leaves, osage-orange leaves	daily	unlimited
Skunk	table scraps, fruit, corn, oats, meat	daily	6 ounces
Snails	fish food, Elodea, bits of lettuce	daily	unlimited
Snakes	frogs, fish, tadpoles, earthworms, slugs, raw egg, insects, raw liver, caterpillars, spiders	2 weekly	*
Squirrel	bread, cookies, seeds, nuts, hard-boiled egg	daily	6 ounces
Tadpoles	lettuce, water cress, hard-boiled eggs, algae	daily	*
Turtles (land)	fleshy fruit, leafy vegetables, fish, insects, eggs	2 weekly	*
(water)	earthworms, ground beef, insects, leafy vegetables	"	*

*as much food as the animal can consume in one feeding for 15 minutes or, in the case of larger animals, until they refuse to take more

ANIMALS

BREEDING PET ANIMALS

Breeding animals is usually done for a definite purpose. The purpose ordinarily has something to do with improving certain qualities of appearance or special abilities in the animals. For example, fast race horses are bred by selecting the best male runners and the best female runners and allowing them to mate only with each other.

You may be interested in finding out how this selective breeding works. If you are, select animals which represent the qualities you want to see in the offspring and allow them to mate with each other. Keep careful records of appearance of parents and of the offspring—observing how traits are passed on from one generation to another.

Of course there are other reasons for breeding animals. You may want to raise and sell rabbits or guinea pigs. Or perhaps you simply like baby animals and want to watch them grow and develop.

Don't breed animals which you don't intend to take care of if they can't be released near your home. Pets such as hamsters and guinea pigs shouldn't be released from captivity. Of course you can turn loose large numbers of frogs, salamanders and snakes if you live in the country but it will be difficult for you if you live in the city.

It is interesting to note that some of the animals care for their young while others forget and ignore offspring. Notice differences in the ways the young can care for themselves.

PET ANIMAL BREEDING

ANIMAL	READY TO BREED FOR FIRST TIME	BABIES INDEPENDENT	GESTATION OR INCUBATION	NUMBER IN LITTER	READY TO REBREED
Hamster	2 months	weaned at 2 to 3 weeks	16 days	2-15	4 to 6 days after delivery (then return to babies)
Rabbit	8 months	weaned at 2 months	30–33 days	5-18	several days after litter is weaned
Mice	2-3 months	weaned at 4 wks.	20 days	5-15	after litter is weaned
Guinea pig	5-6 months	weaned at 3 wks.	63-70 days	1-6	after litter is weaned
Canary	1 year	3 weeks	13 days	4-5 eggs	3 weeks after hatching
Parakeet	11 months	5 weeks	18 days	3-7 eggs	4 mos. after hatching
Turtles					
painted	spring after birth	immediately	70-84 days	4-8 eggs	the following spring
spotted	"	"	82 days	2-4 eggs	"
box	"	"	89 days	3-8 eggs	"
Snakes					
live-bearers	spring after birth	immediately	several months		the following spring
egg-layers	"	"	2-3 months		"
Frogs					
leopard	2 to 4 years	immediately	4 days—3 wks.	5000 eggs	early each spring
pickerel	"	"	6 days—2 wks.	2-3000 eggs	"
spring peeper	"	"	5 days—2 wks.	1300 eggs	"
green	"	"	3 to 5 days	several thousand	late each spring
bull	"	"	4 days	10-12,000 eggs	"
Salamanders					
newt	spring after birth	immediately	3-5 weeks	200 eggs	each spring
spotted	"	"	4-7 weeks	100 eggs	"
marbled	fall after birth	"	all winter	100 eggs	each fall

ANIMALS

ATTRACTING WILDLIFE

Materials you'll need:
feeding pans, variety of grains, seeds, table scraps

If you live near a wooded area or forest preserve or spend summers at camps, you will find it most rewarding to feed and watch animals in their wild state. So many animals are harmed by captivity that one should try to set up feeding stations in the woods instead of in cages.

Select a rather secluded spot, away from human traffic, to set up the feeding grounds. Place the food in metal pans staked to the ground. A heavy crock or jar can serve as a water bowl if a stream is not near. Deer are attracted to a variety of grains and a salt lick, if you are permitted in your state to set it out for animals. Skunks and raccoons will come to eat after dark. Even when a light is on they will continue to return once they are adjusted. See page 25 in order to learn the favorite foods of birds, chipmunks, gophers, rabbits, raccoons, skunks, and squirrels. Let the wild animals eat for a week or so before you get within range of their sight. Then slowly each day get closer as they learn to trust you. Soon some of them will eat out of your hand. Any quick movement or loud noise will frighten them away. Enjoy your wild friends.

ANIMALS

MAKING ANIMAL CAGES

Materials you'll need:
A—an 11" by 30" piece of ¼-inch mesh hardware cloth, 9" round cake pan, 9" pot cover, 18-gauge copper wire; B—wooden framework of 1" square posts, ¼" mesh hardware cloth, wood staples, two pieces of sheet metal, hinges

A good cage suitable for large insects, mice or hamsters can be made using the materials listed under "A" above. Roll the hardware cloth into a cylinder nine inches in diameter and eleven inches high. Lace the sides with copper wire. Drill holes at three-inch intervals around the pot cover and lace it to the top of the cylinder. Set the cylinder over the upside-down cake tin. The cage is ready for use.

Larger animals such as chipmunks and guinea pigs will live comfortably in a cage made with the materials listed in "B." Construct the cage according to the illustration. It can be made any size that is convenient as long as it is large enough for the animals to have room to move. Use one piece of sheet metal as a hinged roof and the other as a floor which can be pulled out for regular cleaning.

Wire small tin cans to the inside of the cage for food and water containers. Provide a small shelter made of a wooden box filled with shredded paper so that the animal can hide.

PRESERVING ANIMAL TRACKS

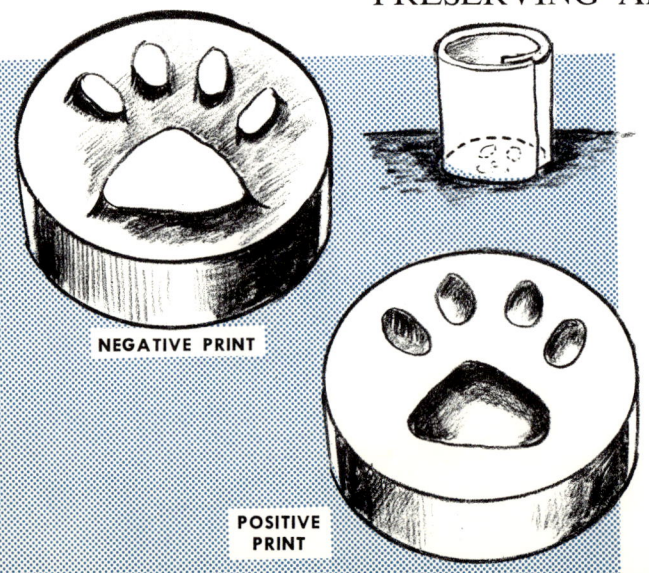

NEGATIVE PRINT

POSITIVE PRINT

Materials you'll need:
cardboard, plaster of Paris, grease, pan, spoon, grease

Take a hike to the woods with a sack of plaster of Paris, pan, water, spoon, and cardboard cylinders. When a footprint of some animal is discovered on the ground place the circle of cardboard around it. Mix some water in the plaster of Paris to the thickness of thin pudding. Pour this mixture over

ANNUAL RINGS

the animal track and let the plaster harden. Remove the cardboard, clean the soil off the surface, and grease the raised print with grease or petroleum jelly. This is the *negative print*.

Place another circle of cardboard around this mold so it extends a little above the level of the negative print. Pour another mixture of plaster of Paris on top of the first mold. When this hardens, separate the two pieces. The second casting is a *positive print*—depression—of the animal's footprint.

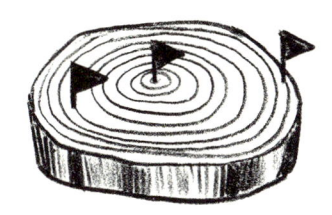

FIGURING THE AGE OF A TREE

Materials you'll need:
thin cross section of tree, clear shellac varnish, sandpaper

Following a storm, or at any time someone around your home is removing a tree, ask the men to saw a thin (three to five inch) cross section for you. Sand the surface until it is very smooth. Brush on clear shellac varnish to bring out the "grain" in the wood. Starting from the center (the first year's growth) count a light and dark band as one year. Notice how some bands are wider than others. What would cause the wider bands? How old was the tree when you were born, when you started to school, now? Place little markers on the annual ring which grew the same year that historical events happened.

ANTENNA

FINDING HOW AN ANTENNA AFFECTS WAVES

Materials you'll need:
pan of water, paper towels, coffee can rim, objects of different shapes

Set up a pan of water with paper towels at one end to absorb waves so they won't bounce back. Start small ripples moving with a ruler or stick, until regular waves are made. These are "sound waves." Use a "dish-type" antenna bent from the rim of a coffee can. The waves will be collected and reflected to a point where they are concentrated, bigger and easier to notice. Try other shapes to see which reflect and concentrate waves best. The principle here is the same as with sound waves.

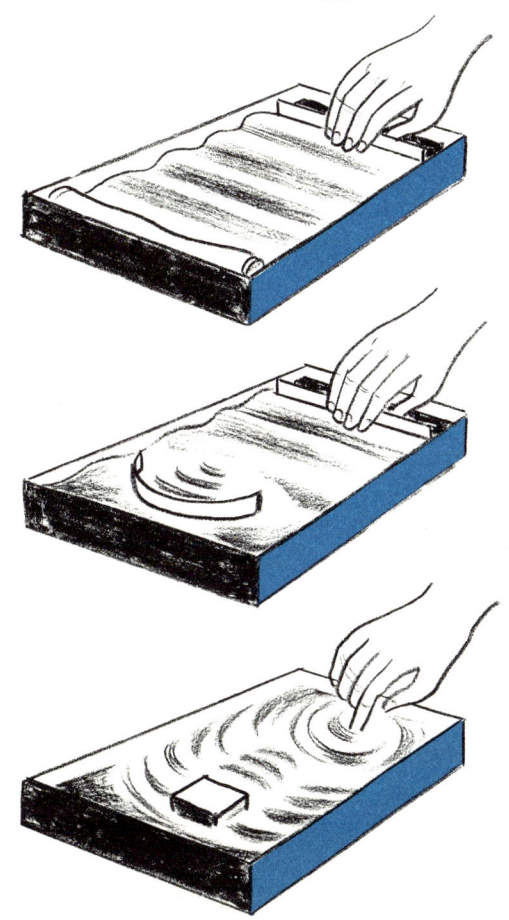

29

ANTISEPTICS

USING ANTISEPTICS TO DESTROY GERMS

Materials you'll need:
  agar-agar culture, cotton, 70% rubbing alcohol, flat dishes

Make a bacterial culture by contaminating agar which has been prepared (see page 37) in sterilized petri dishes or saucers. Let the bacteria grow for several days in a warm dark place. Take a piece of cotton which has been soaked in alcohol (an antiseptic) and rub it across part of the bacteria culture. What happens to the whitish patches (bacteria colonies) that were touched by the antiseptic?

ANTS

PREPARING YOUR OWN ANT COLONY

Materials you'll need:
  2 sheets of glass 12" by 18", 2 wooden strips 1" by 1" by 12", 2 wood strips 17" long, dark paper, spade, white cloth

A highly-organized ant colony is fun to observe. By building and maintaining your own ant colony, you can obtain first-hand knowledge of ant life. Build the ant home according to the illustration. Drill a hole in the top piece of wood through which food and water may be put. A cotton plug in the hole will keep ants inside. Keep the top piece movable for stocking the colony. Tape the other edges.

Locate an ant hill. Dig up one square foot of soil around it. Place the soil and ants on a piece of white cloth. Examine the contents until the queen is located. It can be identified by the picture below. Transfer the colony and soil to the new home through a large funnel made of newspaper.

Cover the glass with dark paper for two weeks to encourage the ants to make tunnels and rooms close to the sides for observation. Ants need honey, sugar water, and a wet sponge placed on top of the soil line. Keep the soil damp so it never becomes dry and caked.

QUEEN

WORKER

MALE

AQUARIUM

MAKING A FRESH-WATER AQUARIUM

Materials you'll need:
5 pieces of glass, board, waterproof tape, aquarium cement, sand, gravel

Building and maintaining an aquarium of interesting plants and animals can be a long-term interesting project. The large commercial fish tanks suitable for extensive study are expensive compared to the cost of building your own.

Plan your aquarium according to the size and number of fish you are going to house in it. Remember it is wise to allow one gallon of water per inch of fish if you do not have a mechanical apparatus to put air into the water. A tank, measuring 10″ by 10″ by 18″, will hold approximately eight gallons of water. Using this dimension, secure a thick board which is 12″ wide and 20″ long. Do not paint or varnish the board. Saw grooves one inch in from the edge on all four sides and about ¼″ deep. The saw teeth should cut a groove a fraction wider than the thickness of the glass. The larger the aquarium the heavier the glass needed.

Glass cutting requires adult help. You will need two pieces 10″ by 10″, two pieces 10″ by 18″, and a glass cover measuring 11″ by 19″. Tape the four pieces of glass to form a rectangular box. Squeeze aquarium cement into the grooves. Push the glass box into this. If you have been careless measuring you will soon find it out. Now apply cement up the inside corners and all around the bottom where

CAUTION!

31

AQUARIUM

the glass meets the wooden floor. Let the aquarium set for two days.

Now stock the water home. Put two inches of well-washed sand and gravel on the bottom. Next, plants that need rooting should be anchored inside the sand bed. When filling, pour the water on to a paper laid over the sand. Let the water stand overnight before putting in the animal life (it must stand a week for tropical fish). This permits the chemicals to escape.

Goldfish, minnows, and tadpoles should have a water temperature ranging from 55° to 72° Fahrenheit. Tropical fish thrive in a temperature maintained between 72° and 80°F. A thermostatic heating unit will be necessary for guppies, platys, tetras, zebras, mallies, and other tropical fish.

Several snails added to this home will help keep it clean. Avoid overcrowding and do not put together animals which are not naturally compatible. Observe your tank carefully to see that all animals and plants are living in a balanced environment.

Aquarium plants will thrive in reflected light, so keep the aquarium out of direct sunlight which speeds algae growth and increases the need for cleaning. Don't overfeed your fish. What they don't eat in twenty minutes is excess food and should be removed.

MAKING A SALT-WATER AQUARIUM

Materials you'll need:
salt (sodium chloride), potassium sulfate, magnesium chloride, magnesium sulfate, aquarium, water, sand

A salt-water aquarium should have a wide open top to permit a large surface of water to be exposed to oxygen in the air. The bottom of the tank should be covered with two inches of clean sand. Make sea water as follows: to each gallon of water to be used add three ounces of salt (sodium chloride) and a few grains each of potassium sulfate, magnesium chloride and magnesium sulfate. Fill the tank with water to a depth of three inches. Root live seaweed, Irish moss, water grass, and other plants in the sand. By placing a paper over the plants when you finish filling the tank you will keep from uprooting the plants and stirring up the sand bed.

Now the ocean home is ready for some inhabitants. If you happen to live near a salt-water coast you may capture your own mollusks and shellfish. Inland, one must purchase them from a pet shop or supply house. Interesting salt-water animals to raise are mussels, limpets, snails, and scallops. You will soon learn which animals live well together.

ARACHNIDS

ATOMS

KEEPING ARACHNIDS AS PETS

Materials you'll need:
2 cake pans, fine wire mesh, plaster of Paris, branching sticks, piece of sponge, wire

Construct a cage by putting a cylinder of fine wire mesh upright in a cake pan of wet plaster of Paris. Sew the cylinder together with wire. Allow it to harden. Use the other cake pan as a removable cover. Insert several sticks to which spiders can attach their webs.

Many species of spiders and other arachnids may be found in the grass of open fields and under logs or rocks. Capture them in a jar and transport them to their new home. In fall the spider egg cases may also be collected.

Spiders need water daily but may go for weeks without food. Keep a wet sponge in the cage and occasionally drop in live, soft-bodied insects or meal-worms for food. Arachnids are fascinating animals to observe. They will live and reproduce in captivity.

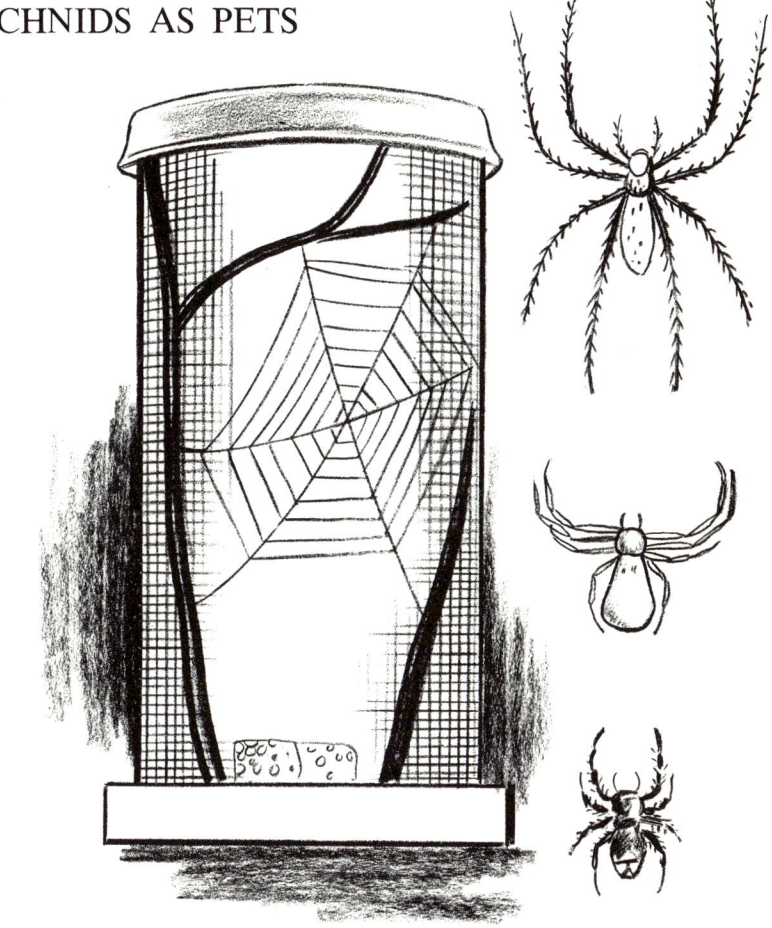

WATCHING ATOMS SPLIT

Materials you'll need:
a watch or clock with a luminous dial (it shines in the dark),
a strong magnifying glass

The first thing to do is to make sure you have a strong enough magnifying glass to see what you want to see. Hold the glass up and look through it at your finger. If your finger is in clear focus when it is less than one inch from the glass, the glass is strong enough.

Wait until after dark for this activity. Turn out the lights in your room and wait ten minutes for your eyes to adjust. Hold the magnifying glass near your eye and look at the clock. Move the glass around until the dial of the clock is in clear focus. You will see sparks or flashes from the dial. The luminous paint contains *radiothorium* (radioactive thorium). Atoms of radiothorium are constantly splitting and particles are shooting out from them. When the particles strike the zinc sulfide in the paint, they light up. You are actually watching atoms split, although you cannot see the tiny atoms themselves.

ATOMS

MAKING MODELS OF ATOMS

Materials you'll need:
  soft wood base, wire from coat hangers, Plasticine (3 colors)

If you wish to build a model of a fairly simple atom, you can plan to attach it to a wooden base. If your model is complicated and heavy, you probably will not be able to balance it on a base.

Atoms contain electrons in orbits and protons and neutrons in the nucleus. Use the following set of rules to determine the atomic structure of the element you choose to model. The *atomic number* of the element indicates the number of electrons in the orbit and the number of protons in the nucleus. The difference between the *atomic weight* and the atomic number tells you the number of neutrons in the nucleus. Some of the more common elements are listed in the table.

For example, the atomic number of sodium is 11, which means it has 11 electrons and 11 protons. The electrons are arranged in three rings or orbits with two electrons in the inner ring, eight in the middle ring and one in the outer ring. The atomic weight is 23 so there are 12 neutrons in the nucleus (23 minus 11).

Cut wire from coat hangers to form the orbits. First cut a straight piece which goes into the base and to which the orbits are attached. You might use red Plasticine for the protons, blue for electrons and green for neutrons. Form the Plasticine into balls—the large balls in the center representing several neutrons and protons—and stick them onto the wire.

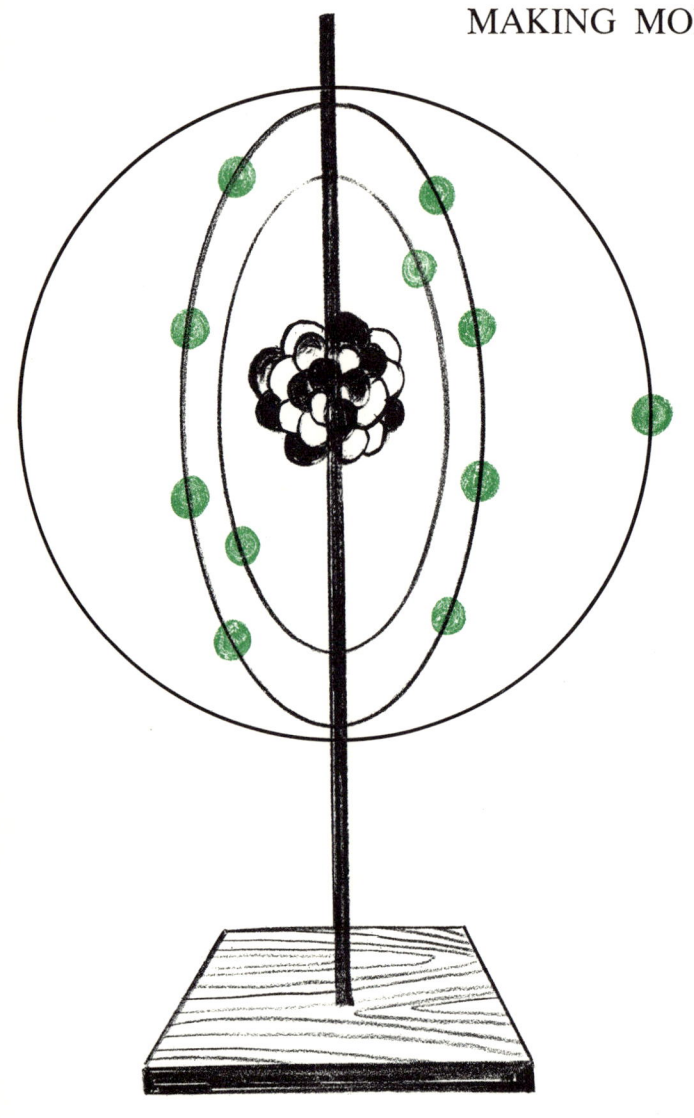

ELEMENTS	ATOMIC NUMBER	APPROXIMATE ATOMIC WEIGHT	NUMBER OF ELECTRONS IN RINGS
Hydrogen (H)	1	1	1 (only one ring)
Helium (He)	2	4	2
Carbon (C)	6	12	2, 4
Oxygen (O)	8	16	2, 6
Fluorine (F)	9	19	2, 7
Sodium (Na)	11	23	2, 8, 1
Sulfur (S)	16	32	2, 8, 6
Calcium (Ca)	20	40	2, 8, 8, 2
Iron (Fe)	26	56	2, 8, 14, 2
Uranium (U)	92	238	2,8,18,32,21,9,2

BABY ANIMALS

CARING FOR BABY BIRDS AND MAMMALS

Materials you'll need:
zwieback, carrot, egg yolk, water, box lined with dried grass or newspaper, doll's nursing bottle, milk, tweezers

Occasionally you will find a wild baby bird or baby mammal too young to care for itself. Take it in only if it is injured or you're sure it has been deserted by its mother. Wild animals are unhappy in captivity and should be kept only until they are old enough to care for themselves.

Keep either a bird or a mammal in a box lined with dried grass or bits of paper. It should be able to hide and keep warm. Do not handle it too often.

You must watch the diet of a baby animal very carefully. For a bird, mix crumbled zwieback or crackers with grated carrot and hard-boiled egg yolk. Add a few drops of water to make the mixture moist. Roll it into soft balls and feed the bird using rounded tweezers. Add pieces of grape, cherry, insects, seeds, or earthworms, depending on whether the bird is an insect-eater or seed-eater.

Baby mammals, such as squirrels or rabbits, may be so young they require milk from a doll's nursing bottle, or they may be able to drink from a medicine dropper. Experiment to find out. Dilute cow's milk half and half with water. If the milk seems to agree with the baby, add a little Pablum to it after a few days. Cod-liver oil can also be added. As the baby animal grows older, add greens and other vegetables to its diet so it has a variety of foods.

35

BACTERIA

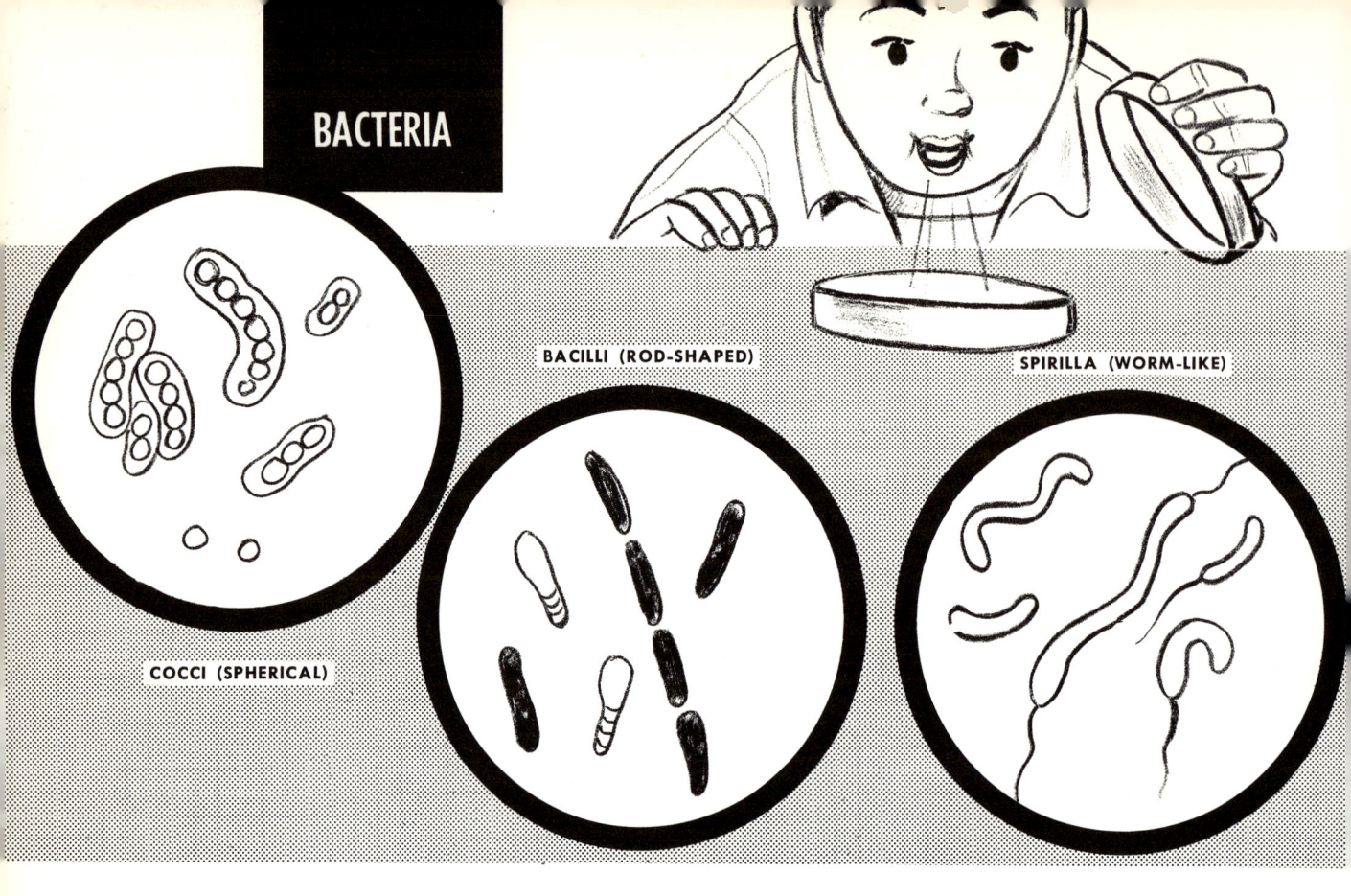

COCCI (SPHERICAL)

BACILLI (ROD-SHAPED)

SPIRILLA (WORM-LIKE)

GROWING BACTERIAL CULTURES

Materials you'll need:

agar-agar (purchased at a biological supply house) or gelatin and bouillon cube, boiling water, flat dishes with tight covers

It is difficult to see bacteria because they are so very small. However, it is important to know where they are found. To do this, we can try to grow them in large numbers, called *colonies,* which are visible without a microscope.

They will grow only if they have the right kind of food. The food in which bacteria will grow is called a *medium*. Agar-agar is a good medium.

Bring one-half cup of water to a boil. Stir in one teaspoon of powdered agar-agar and boil for five minutes. If you can't get agar-agar, substitute one-half tablespoon gelatin and add one half bouillon cube. When this is dissolved, pour a thin layer of it in each of several flat dishes. The liquid will harden as it cools. The dishes should first be sterilized by boiling them for fifteen minutes. Everything used, including the measuring spoon, should be boiled.

Now contaminate the plates with bacteria in several different ways. Roll a pencil over one. Rub a dirty finger over one plate and the same finger washed with soap and water over another. Roll a soiled fork over one plate. Leave one dish untouched as a control. Cover it quickly. Cover all the plates immediately after contaminating them so bacteria cannot settle on them from the air.

Place the plates in a warm—not hot—place for two days. At the end of this time, one to several white spots should be visible. These are colonies of bacteria. Find out whether bacteria grow the same way if the dishes are put in a cold place. Try the experiment on page 30 to see the effect of antiseptic.

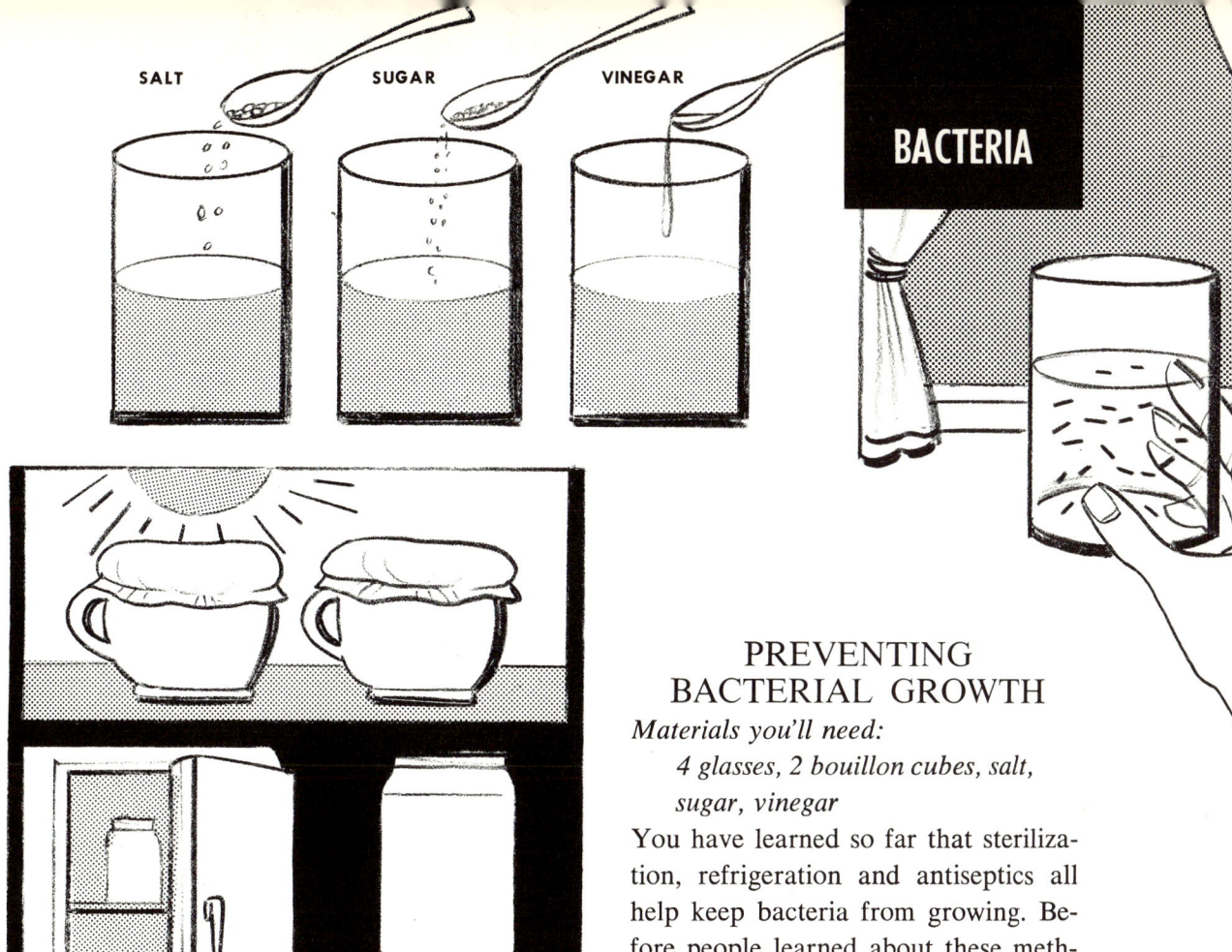

OBSERVING THE ACTION OF BACTERIA IN MILK

Materials you'll need:
  pasteurized milk, raw milk, 4 glass jars with tight covers

Fill two jars with boiling water and set them aside for ten minutes. This will sterilize them. Fill one jar with pasteurized milk and the other with raw or unpasteurized milk. Cover both jars tightly to prevent contamination by bacteria in the air and leave them in a warm place for several days. Does the raw milk or pasteurized milk sour first?

Fill two glass jars with raw milk. Cover them tightly. Place one in the refrigerator and leave the other in a warm place. Which jar of milk sours first? Does this show us how to keep bacteria from growing?

BACTERIA

PREVENTING BACTERIAL GROWTH

Materials you'll need:
  4 glasses, 2 bouillon cubes, salt, sugar, vinegar

You have learned so far that sterilization, refrigeration and antiseptics all help keep bacteria from growing. Before people learned about these methods, they treated their food in another way so that bacteria would not grow in it and spoil it. They added *preservatives*. Some of the same preservatives are still used in making pickles, jams and jellies, and many other things. Here is a chance to try a few yourself and see how they work.

Mix two bouillon cubes with a pint of hot water. Partly fill four clean glasses with the bouillon stock. Add one teaspoon of salt to one glass, one teaspoon of sugar to one, three teaspoons of vinegar to one and nothing to the last glass. Put all four glasses in the same warm place and look at them after two days. You will find the "soup" to which you added nothing is cloudy, indicating that there are bacteria and other microbes growing in it. The rest of the solutions should be clear because the preservatives you added prevented the growth of bacteria.

BAROMETER

ASSEMBLING BAROMETERS

Materials you'll need:
  A—rubber from balloon, milk bottle, broom or soda straw, cardboard;
  B—mercury, dish, support, 36" glass tube

A simple aneroid barometer from the materials listed in "A" will show increase or decrease in air pressure. Fasten a circle of rubber from a balloon over the top of a bottle. Tape it securely in place. Glue one end of a broom straw to the center of the rubber cap. Place a cardboard or posterboard scale by the free end of the straw so that it is close but doesn't touch. Choose a clear day and find out the air pressure from the newspaper. Use this pressure reading as a starting point to make your scale.

As the air pressure increases, the rubber is pushed down into the bottle and the other end of the straw goes up. This is an indication of a change in pressure. Temperature, too, has an effect on the rubber top, so keep the instrument in a place that has a fairly steady temperature.

In a regular commercial aneroid barometer, a thin metal case is around the instrument. Part of the air is removed from inside the case. As air pressure changes the walls of the case move in or out and the internal instruments indicate the changes on a dial. *Aneroid* means that no liquid is involved.

BAROMETER

You can construct a mercurial barometer from the materials in "B". First seal the end of a three-foot glass tube by rotating it over a flame. Slowly fill the tube with mercury. Shake the tube gently or run a fine wire down the tube if bubbles of air separate the column of mercury. Place one finger over the open end, invert the tube and submerge the end in a small dish of mercury. Follow the illustration in designing a support to hold the barometer.

Air pressure is 14.7 pounds per square inch at sea level. This amount of pressure is called one *atmosphere*. The mercury column will stay about thirty inches high. General weather changes can be predicted by watching the level of the mercury rise and fall from a starting point marked on the tube. If water were used, the tube would have to be thirty-two feet long to obtain the reactions to air pressure. Water is about thirteen times lighter than mercury.

An increase in air pressure means the approach of fair weather. As the pressure of the air increases, the level of mercury in the tube rises. When bad weather is approaching, the pressure of the air is less and the mercury level in the tube goes down. Even though the change in pressure may be so slight that it is hard to see a change in the mercury level in the dish, the small changes are magnified in the narrow tube. They can be very important to meteorologists in predicting weather. See if you can predict weather using these barometers and other weather instruments (see page 207).

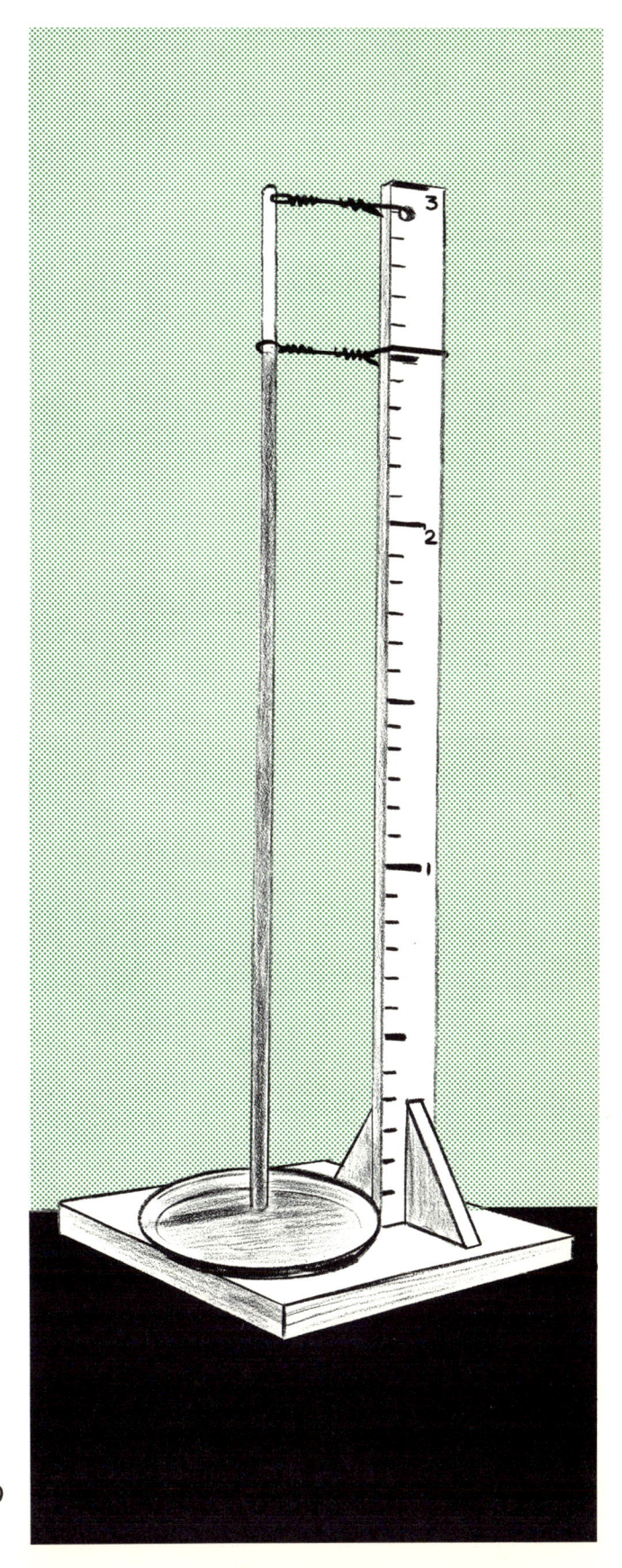

BATTERY

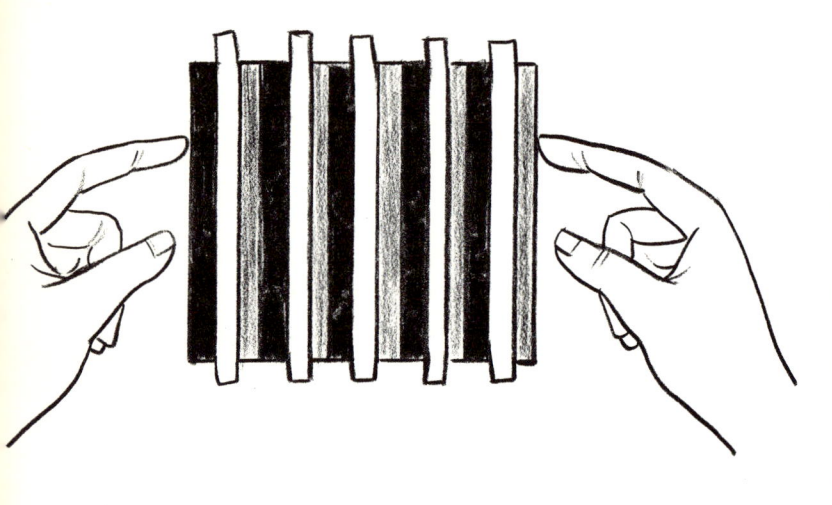

MAKING A SIMPLE ELECTRIC BATTERY

Materials you'll need:
> 5 zinc strips, 5 copper strips, 5 strips of filter paper, water, ammonium chloride

You can make a simple battery which will produce a slight current. First soak five strips of filter paper or other absorbent paper in a solution of ammonium chloride. Ammonium chloride dissolved in water can carry a current of electricity.

Build a stack of materials as follows: a strip of zinc, a piece of wet paper, a strip of copper. Repeat this until all the material has been used. End with a piece of metal. Wet the tips of your fingers and put one finger on each end of the stack. You'll feel a slight tingle which indicates a current of electricity. Placing the unlike metals together has produced this flow of electricity. This is the basis of a battery.

MAKING A STORAGE BATTERY

Materials you'll need:
> 3 dry cells, lead strips, wood, bell wire, small bulb, light receptacle, baking soda, glass

Batteries come in all shapes and sizes, but each must contain three necessary parts. These are the *anode* (active metal strip), the *cathode* (less active metal strip), and the *electrolyte* (solution which is a chemical conductor).

Nail two sheets of lead strips to a piece of wood. Expose one end on each of two pieces of bell wire and attach the exposed ends to the lead strips. Connect three dry cells in series (see page 80) to the other ends of the bell wire. Set the lead strips in a glass of baking soda solution. Make this by combining one tablespoon of baking soda to one cup of water. Let this stand for ten minutes. Remove the dry cells from the circuit and substitute a small light. The bulb will glow for several minutes.

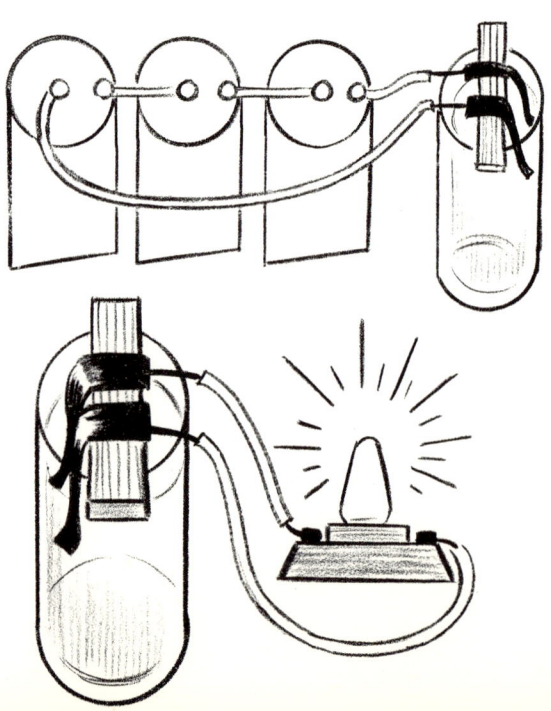

BIRDS

MAKING HOUSES FOR BIRDS

Materials you'll need:
½" and ¼" lumber, finishing nails, small wooden box, supporting poles, log with bark on, sawdust, hammer

Each variety of bird prefers a somewhat different type of house. The house you build must meet the specifications of the particular bird you want to attract. Remember, you must be sure that: (1) the interior size is correct, (2) the entry hole is not too large or too small, (3) the interior is unpainted, (4) it is placed where the bird will use it, (5) it is located the proper distance from the ground.

Following are some important things to consider when building the houses.

1. *Martin house:* Because of a definite sociable nature, martins will live together in a two or three-story house of considerable size. The house must be on a pole at least fifteen feet in the air, preferably higher. An open location, not too near trees, is best.

The martin "apartment" should consist of a number of separate rooms approximately six inches square with a separate 2" entry hole for each room. You can build a good one with used ½" lumber. The hole should be one inch above floor level. In building, remember to leave a little space between several of the walls to provide for air circulation throughout the house. Also, remember that martins should have clean houses. To make the annual cleaning job easier, build the post in two halves bolted together so that the top half can be lowered.

2. *Wren house:* Wrens will build a nest in almost any old abandoned receptacle. Place it about ten feet above the ground. Hang an old teakettle, hollowed out coconut shell, or tin can in a tree and a wren will probably make it a home. If you build a home of wood, its dimensions should be 4" by 4" by 6" with an entrance hole ⅞" in diameter.

BIRDS

3. Robin house: A robin likes a somewhat open, shady place for its home. The house of ½″ or ¼″ lumber may have one or two sides open to the weather. The height of the shelter is not important since robins will nest high in trees or low in a bush. The illustration above shows an adequate robin house.

4. Bluebird house: If you live in one of the northern states, get your bluebird house ready in early spring. The house, also of ¼″ lumber, should measure about 5″ by 5″ by 8″ with an entrance 1½″ in diameter. Paint the outside dull green, gray or brown. The bluebird house should be from five to ten feet from the ground.

5. Tree swallow house: Tree swallows need a house about 6″ square. The entrance hole should be 1½″ in diameter. Paint the house a dark color or use natural, weathered wood. Hang the house about ten to fifteen feet up in a tree. Swallows like to be near water, so provide a large birdbath for them.

6. Screech owl house: Screech owls can easily be attracted to a house if it resembles a tree. A section of a log with the bark still on can be chiseled out or sections cut and nailed together. Nail the log home to a wooden base and a back support which will be used to anchor it to a tree. A roof made of a split log should be hinged in back to the foundation, and a hook and eye used to hold it down in front. A 3¼″ hole can be cut for the doorway. Pour an inch or two of sawdust in the house to serve as a carpet and nesting place. Nail the entire structure on a tree in an open stand of trees. It may be placed from 12 to 30 feet above the ground. Owls will do a good job of keeping the area free of small rodents.

BIRDS

7. *Chickadee house:* These little birds are fun to watch as they hang upside down while searching for larvae in the bark of trees. You can even train them to come to your doorstep for seeds and crusts of bread.

Chickadees need a house of seasoned wood, preferably ¼" lumber with a doorway measuring 1⅛". Nail it to a tree or post about eight to fourteen feet up from the ground. Since these birds stay around all winter, furnish a seed diet, though insects are their favorite food when available.

8. *Nuthatch house:* This small bird appears to spend more time upside down than looking at the world the way we do. It walks down trees and under branches looking for insects, larvae and eggs. It will be a vegetarian in the winter, so seeds, berries, and nuts should be supplied at that time.

Select well-seasoned ¼" lumber for the house. The doorway should be 1¼" in diameter. Fasten the new house about fifteen feet up on a tree along the edge of a wooded area.

9. *Titmouse house:* The tufted titmouse spends much of its life looking for and eating insects. For this reason it is helpful to man though people may tire of its constant cry ringing through the woods. A weathered house of ¼" lumber should be placed in a grove of trees. A titmouse avoids wide open spaces since the food supply there is limited. The house should be fastened on a tree from eight to fourteen feet up in the air. Make a door measuring 1¼" in diameter.

BIRDS

MAKING BIRD-FEEDING STATIONS

Materials you'll need:
discarded Christmas tree, aluminum foil pie pan, wooden stake, wooden box, bread board, large jar, birdseed, pine cones or shallow box and chicken wire, wood, suet-seed mixture, log

If you live in a northern area, you must begin feeding birds in October before they go to other places to eat. Remember, once you begin this project, the birds are now depending on you for food all winter. Continue supplying their diet until spring.

Bird feeders are easy to make. Use old unpainted lumber since birds don't like the smell of fresh lumber or paint. Here are the directions for six different types of feeding stations.

1. Fasten suet (hard animal fat) and crusts of bread to a discarded Christmas tree after you have removed all the ornaments. Chisel a hole in the frozen ground and set the tree up outside.

2. Make a very simple feeder by nailing a pie pan to a stake and filling it with various kinds of food (grains, pieces of boiled potatoes, chopped hard-boiled eggs, lettuce, celery leaves, crumbled dog biscuit, oatmeal, peanut butter, and suet). Drive the stake into the ground. Make the stake high enough so that other animals can't reach the food.

3. The box can be the tray of a feeder, so it should be large enough to permit the birds to hop around on it while they are feeding. Nail the bread board to one side of the box so that it

BIRDS

serves as the back of the feeder. Make a hole at the top of the bread board so that the feeder can be hung from a nail on a tree. Do not fasten it permanently to the tree.

Wire the jar to the back of the feeder to prevent its full weight from resting on the tray, yet put it close enough to the tray to allow the seeds to escape slowly. One heavy wire around the middle of the jar and one around the neck will be enough. To fill the feeder, turn the whole unit upside down and slide the jar out. Fill it with seed mixture, put it back in the wire holder and invert the unit. You may add berries, nuts, and apples to the tray after it is on the tree.

4. Birds in cold climates need heat-producing foods such as suet. The piece of suet may be nailed or tied to a tree, or a pine cone can be stuffed with suet and hung from a tree. Another method is to place the suet in a shallow box, cover it with wire and fasten it to a tree trunk.

5. An inverted feeder protects the food in bad weather. Nail two-inch sides on a board one by two feet long. Fasten two narrow strips of wood along the length of the tray for perches. Mix melted suet and sand, bird seed and bread crumbs and pour it into the tray. After it has hardened, tack it down in several places. Invert the tray and fasten it to a tree with a bracket.

6. Bore several two-inch holes in a small log. Fill them with suet-seed mixture. Run a wire between two trees or fence posts and fasten the log at the center of the wire. This will prevent rodents from using the feeder.

BLOOD

STUDYING FRESH BLOOD

Materials you'll need:

microscope, glass slide, cover glass, alcohol, cotton, salt solution, candle, needle

Which are larger—red or white corpuscles? You can look at your own blood but be sure to have an adult supervise this experiment.

First, put a drop of water on a glass slide. Drop six to eight grains of salt into it and carefully stir with the needle to dissolve the salt. Do not spread the drop all around. Saturate a piece of cotton with alcohol and wipe a finger of your left hand (if you are right-handed). The alcohol will kill bacteria. Put the bottle of alcohol away from you—preferably in another room—since it is now necessary to light the candle. You know how explosive alcohol is.

CAUTION!

Sterilize the needle in the flame of a candle. Using the thumb of the left hand to put pressure on the end of the finger you are going to prick, give that finger a slight jab with the needle. It feels a little like a mosquito biting you. Continue pressing the finger until a small drop of blood collects. Touch the drop of blood to the drop of salt solution. Place a cover glass over this.

Focus your specimen under low power of the microscope first. Are the red corpuscles really red? Remembering that there are about 800 red to one white corpuscle, can you figure out which cells are which? As soon as you have, swing to high power and study each one more closely. Do they have nuclei? Are their shapes, as well as their sizes, different?

BLUEPRINTING

MAKING AND USING BLUEPRINT PAPER

Materials you'll need:
 potassium ferricyanide, ferric ammonium citrate, water, heavy, white writing paper

Blueprint paper is heavy, white paper that has been coated with certain chemicals. To make your own, prepare two solutions in an almost dark room. For solution #1 mix 10 grains of potassium ferricyanide with 50 milliliters of water. Mix 10 grams of ferric ammonium citrate with 50 milliliters of water for solution #2. Pour equal parts of these two solutions in a pan. Let the sheet of paper float in this solution for several seconds. Hang the paper in a dark room to dry. It is now coated.

When light strikes the chemicals on blueprint paper it changes the chemicals to a blue color which will not dissolve in water. The areas not exposed to light will dissolve away leaving the white print of the object.

Do the blueprinting on a day with bright sunshine and no wind. Any object which has a distinctive shape is a good one to blueprint. Grasses, leaves, flowers, shells and some insects all make good specimens.

Place the specimen on a piece of blueprint paper and do not expose it to any light until you are ready to make the print. Next, expose it to direct sunlight. The length of time it must be exposed depends on the directness of the sun's rays. In the winter, several minutes may be necessary. In the summer as little as 30 seconds in the sun will produce a print. Do one or two test prints first.

Have a pan of water ready so that the print can be rinsed immediately after exposure. Press and dry the print between paper towels.

BOILING POINT

FINDING THAT AIR PRESSURE AFFECTS BOILING

Materials you'll need:
   heat-resistant bottle, water, source of heat, cork

Try this experiment to see if you can discover why cooks may take longer to prepare a meal in a high mountain resort than down near sea level.

Put an inch of water into a Pyrex bottle. Place the bottle in a pan of water on the stove. Heat it until the water in the bottle has boiled for at least five minutes. Turn off or remove the source of heat. The water will stop boiling. Immediately cap the bottle and turn it upside down in the pan of water. Slowly pour a glass of ice water over the bottle. Does the water start to boil again? Why?

BONES

TESTING THE STRUCTURE OF BONE

Materials you'll need:
   leg bones of chicken, vinegar, tin can, bottle

Bone tissue is made in such a way that it supports and protects the body. About two-thirds of it is hard mineral matter, most of which is calcium phosphate. The other one-third of the bone is soft animal matter in the form of gelatin.

Heat one of the chicken bones in a large tin can for an hour and the animal matter will be destroyed. The bone will be whitish and brittle and the ash will consist of mineral compounds.

Drop another bone in undiluted vinegar so the bone is covered. Leave it for a couple of days. Remove it and rinse it thoroughly. Notice that the bone is no longer stiff. The mineral matter has been dissolved away by the acid, leaving only the animal matter.

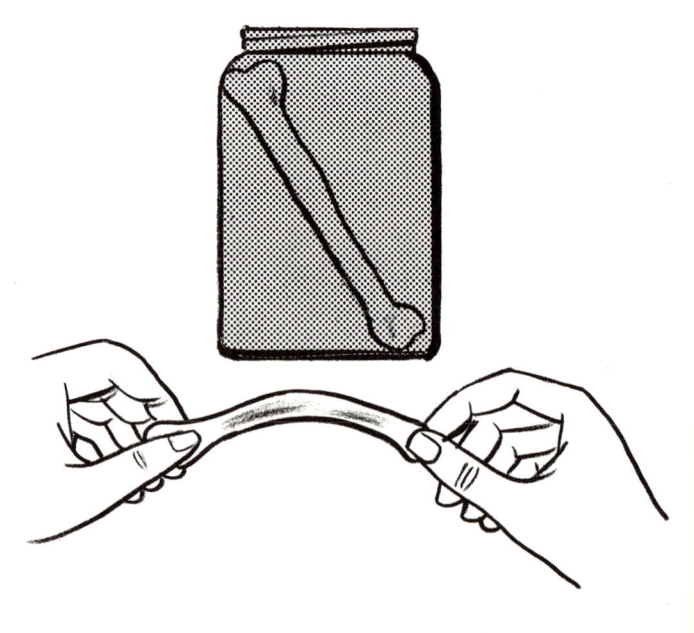

BONES

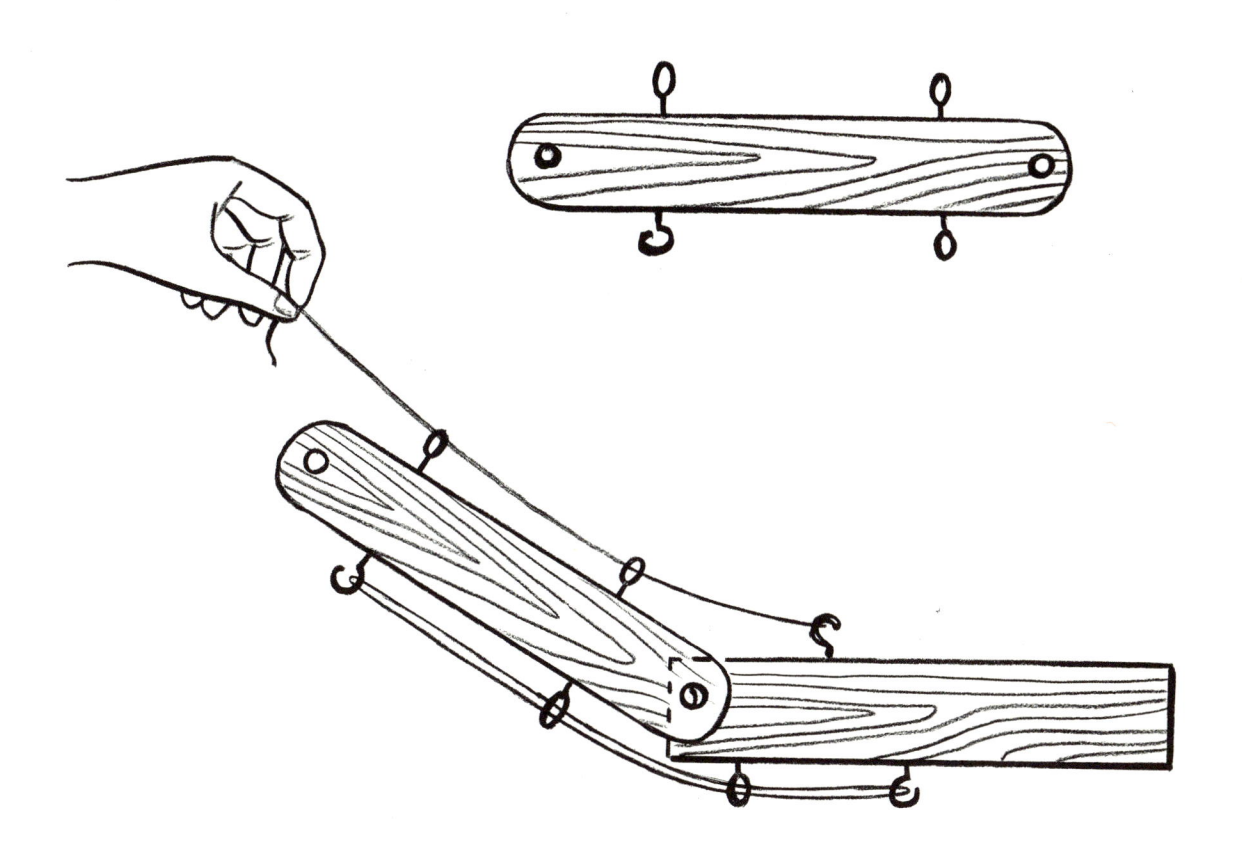

MAKING A MODEL TO SHOW HOW BONES AND MUSCLES WORK

Materials you'll need:
2 pieces of plywood—each 2" by 12", strip of rubber cut from inner tube, 4 screw eyes, 3 cup hooks, short nut and bolt, length of cord, tools

Sometimes it is hard to imagine what happens to the muscles of an arm or leg when we are exercising. Here is a working model which you can use to show yourself and others how the muscles move and control the bones.

Drill a hole in one corner of one piece of plywood. Round the ends of the other piece and drill a hole in each end. Put in the screw eyes and cup hooks as shown in the illustration and use a bolt and nut to fasten the two pieces of wood together.

Now cut a thin strip of rubber from all the way around a small inner tube. Thread it through the screw eyes and around the cup hooks. It may have to be cut and tied together if it does not fit tightly.

The last step is to thread a strong cord from the cup hook on the top of the model through the screw eyes.

Pull on the cord and you can make the model work in much the same way as the muscles and bones of your arm work when you bend your elbow.

BOTANICAL PRESS

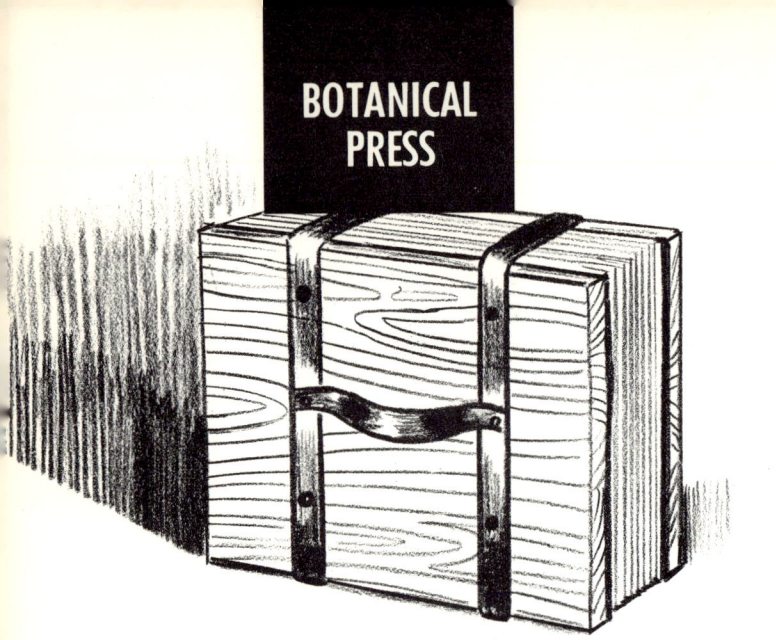

CONSTRUCTING A PRESS TO USE ON NATURE TRIPS

Materials you'll need:
  cardboard, newspaper, 2 pieces of wood, leather straps

A botanical press is useful to take along on nature hikes so that specimens such as wild flowers, which wilt rapidly, can be pressed on the spot. Take careful notes on the habitat of each specimen.

A botanical press is easy to make. You need two pieces of wood for the outside. The ends of orange crates are a good size and usually are free for the asking. Nail the centers of two leather straps, or old belts, to the bottom of one of the boards. Place sheets of newspaper and cardboard between the two boards. When a specimen is found, carefully spread it out in between the papers. Tie the straps to hold the press tight. A small handle makes the press easier to carry on your journey through the woods and meadows.

Since some wild flowers are rapidly disappearing from our nature haunts, there are rules about picking them. Be sure you are familiar with the laws of your state and then pick only those specimens which are numerous.

BUOYANCY

FINDING OUT ABOUT BUOYANCY

Materials you'll need:
  rock, spring scale, jar of water, cork, small bottle

Archimedes was a Greek scientist who experimented with the problem of buoyancy. After you have done these two experiments, try to state the principle which explains the results.

1. Weigh a rock with a spring scale. Put the rock in a jar of water with the spring scale still attached. How much does the rock weigh now? What is the buoyant force on the rock?

2. Fill a jar ¾ full of water. Invert a small empty (filled with air) bottle inside the large jar. Put a cork in the opening of the jar and push it down as far as you can. What happens to the little bottle inside?

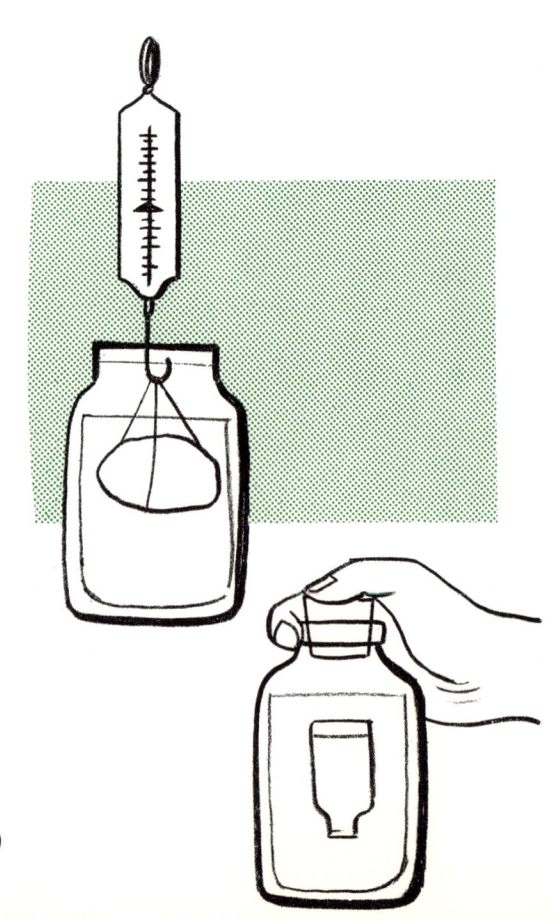

CAMERA

MAKING A CAMERA

Materials you'll need:
cigar box, cork, metal foil, photographic film, drill

Recording pictures on light-sensitive paper is a fascinating hobby for many people. It is relatively easy to take pictures with a commercial camera. What will really tax your scientific skill is constructing a homemade camera that works. Try this one.

Drill a half-inch hole in one end of a cigar box. Find a cork that fits tightly into this hole. On the inside of the box tape a one-inch by one-inch piece of metal foil over the hole. With a needle punch a clean hole exactly in the center of the foil.

In a dark room tape a piece of photographic film on the end of the box directly opposite the needle hole. Fasten the lid of the box tightly and be certain the cork is in before going out in the daylight.

Outdoors, point the camera at an object. Rest it on something to keep it from jiggling and distorting the picture. Remove the cork for one or two seconds depending on the brightness of the day (the darker the day, the longer the time required). Have the film developed. Test different times of exposure and a variety of light conditions.

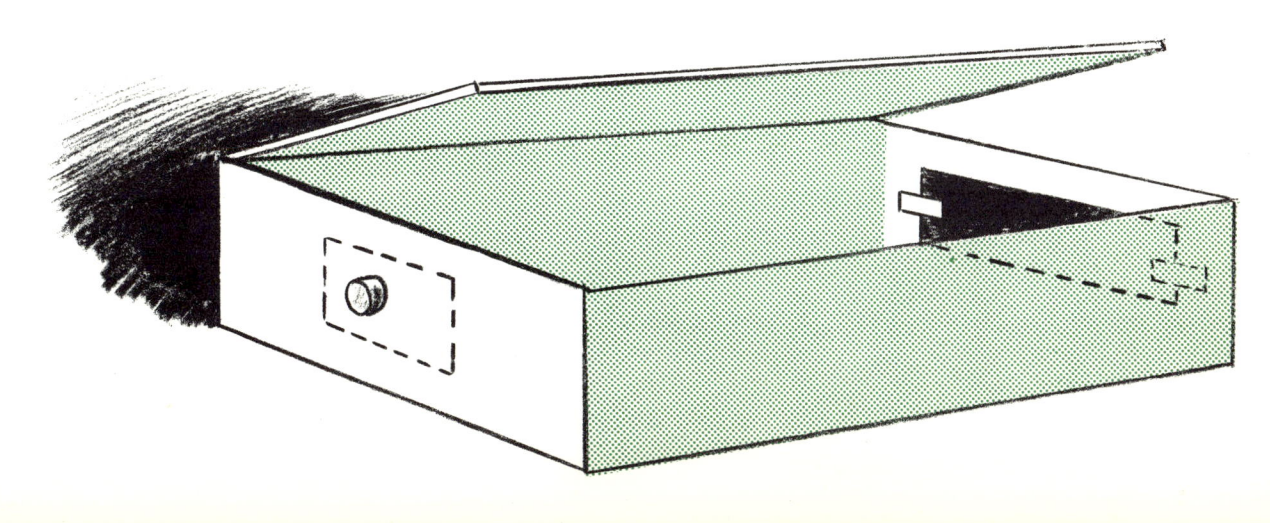

FIGURING OUT HOW A CAMERA WORKS

Materials you'll need:
cracker box, tissue paper, candle, tape

Cut one end off a cracker box and cover it with tissue paper. Tape the paper securely in place so it doesn't wrinkle. Make a pinhole in the center of the closed end of the box. Take the "camera" into a dark room. Set a lighted candle two feet in front of the pinhole. Stand behind the camera and observe the pattern on the tissue paper. What does the image look like? What causes this?

CAMERA

BUILDING A CAMERA TRAP

Materials you'll need:
camera with shutter-release lever and synchronized flash gun, spool of strong black thread, snap mousetrap, wooden peg, adhesive tape, screw, eye, bait

This is an activity which will teach you about the fascinating art of photography and help acquaint you with night-prowling, or *nocturnal,* animals at the same time.

Find a tree with a large branch that leans out from the main trunk at an angle. Tape the camera securely to the branch, wedging it so that it points downward. Tape the mousetrap to the trunk below the camera with the bait hook pointed downward.

Put the screw eye into the top of the wooden peg and hammer the peg into the ground close to the tree. Decide on the bait you want to use. It depends on what animal you are hoping to attract. Deer are attracted by a salt block made from one-half pound of table salt that is put in a box, dampened and allowed to harden. Skunks come for either vegetables or meat. They, along with the raccoons and opossums, will be drawn by corn on the cob and bones.

Place the bait so that the camera is aiming at it. Tie the black thread around the bait, running it through the screw eye and up to the bait hook of the trap. Run another tight thread from the mousetrap's spring to the camera's shutter-release lever. Set the trap and test the action by pulling on the bait so that you are sure the arrangement works. Load the camera with film and a flash bulb. Have patience in waiting for the animals.

52

CAPILLARITY

EXPERIMENTING WITH CAPILLARITY

Materials you'll need:
  sponge, salt, alcohol lamp, glass tubes of various widths, white flower, vegetable dyes

Set a bathroom sponge in a flat dish. Pour a cup of water in the dish and observe what happens. Where did the water go?

Pile a mound of table salt in the center of a saucer. Pour a small amount of vegetable dye in the bottom around the salt. What happens and why?

Study an alcohol lamp closely. Notice that the upper part of the wick is not down in the bottle of liquid. Light the wick. What is burning? How did it get up to the top?

Set the ends of several glass tubes of varying widths in a solution of colored liquid. Does the liquid rise to the same height in all tubes?

Place the stem of a white flower in a glass of colored water. After an hour or two cut a cross-section of the stem which is above the water line. Notice the colored areas.

53

CARBON DIOXIDE

CATALYST

PRODUCING CARBON DIOXIDE

Materials you'll need:
baking soda, vinegar, chalk, lemon juice, yeast, sugar water, limewater, candle, matches, straw

Accepting the fact that fire will not burn in air which is highly concentrated with carbon dioxide, one can test the combustion of two materials which release carbon dioxide.

Combine baking soda and vinegar in a cup. Light a match and hold it over the solution. What happens to the flame? Repeat the experiment above, substituting lemon juice and either lime chips, chalk, or egg shells for the two materials to be combined.

Mix yeast in warm sugar water. This plant feeds on the sugar, releasing carbon dioxide and alcohol. Hold a lighted match over the mixture to test for this release.

Limewater becomes cloudy when combined with carbon dioxide. Using a straw, blow air into a glass of limewater. Notice the color before and after. We exhale carbon dioxide along with other gases.

Burning will produce carbon dioxide. Burn a candle which has been placed in a jar with a small amount of limewater. After several minutes extinguish the flame, cover the jar, and shake lightly. What happens to the color of the limewater?

USING A CATALYST

Materials you'll need:
tongs, tablespoon, sugar, ashes, source of heat

A catalyst is a material which will speed up or slow down a chemical reaction. It does this without itself being changed. This experiment will show you how a catalyst works.

Using tongs for protection, hold a tablespoon of sugar over a flame. Let the sugar burn. It will melt and turn brown but will not blaze up. Repeat the experiment, only this time mix ashes with the sugar. The ash is a catalyst. What did it do to the process of oxidation?

CAUTION!

CATERPILLARS

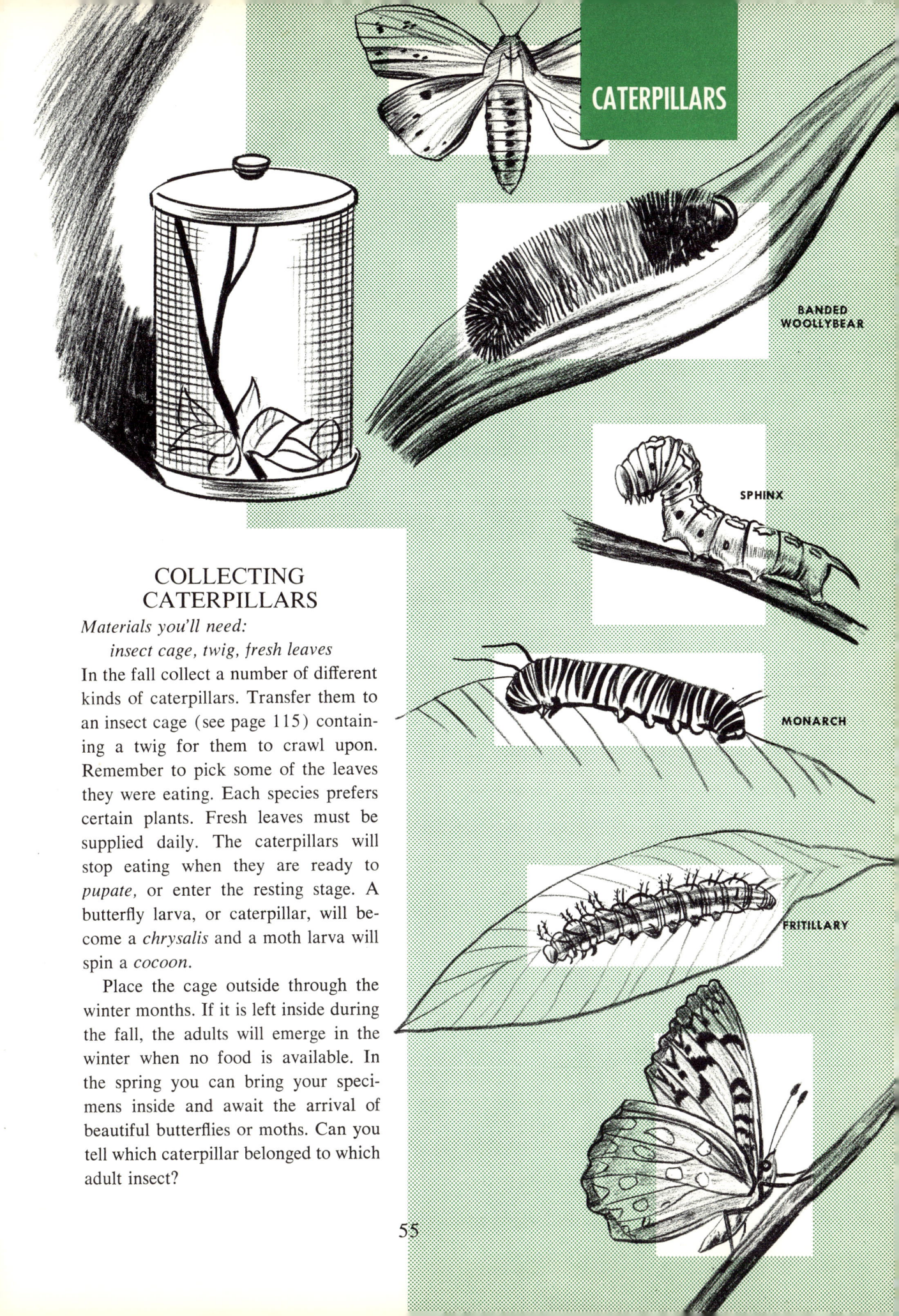

BANDED WOOLLYBEAR

SPHINX

MONARCH

FRITILLARY

COLLECTING CATERPILLARS

Materials you'll need:
insect cage, twig, fresh leaves

In the fall collect a number of different kinds of caterpillars. Transfer them to an insect cage (see page 115) containing a twig for them to crawl upon. Remember to pick some of the leaves they were eating. Each species prefers certain plants. Fresh leaves must be supplied daily. The caterpillars will stop eating when they are ready to *pupate,* or enter the resting stage. A butterfly larva, or caterpillar, will become a *chrysalis* and a moth larva will spin a *cocoon.*

Place the cage outside through the winter months. If it is left inside during the fall, the adults will emerge in the winter when no food is available. In the spring you can bring your specimens inside and await the arrival of beautiful butterflies or moths. Can you tell which caterpillar belonged to which adult insect?

CATS

CARING FOR KITTENS AND CATS

A kitten should not be separated from its mother until it is six to eight weeks old. Then it will require four to five meals each day. Three of these meals can be milk and cooked cereal, one can be a tablespoon of raw hamburger or commercial cat food and then just milk during the late evening. When your kitten is over three months old you can give it three larger meals, and finally one or two feedings when it is full grown. Cats need daily servings of good meat, some fish and fresh water.

A box which is lined with a soft blanket and kept in a warm dry place makes good sleeping quarters. If you live in an apartment and cannot let your pet out daily, provide a box of sand or sawdust in a permanent corner of a room for its use.

Cats should be groomed daily even though they appear to be doing the job for themselves. Long-haired cats especially require brushing to remove loose hairs. The constant licking forms hair balls in the digestive tract and can be fatal. Avoid bathing cats. Your pet can be trained to use a scratching post so it won't scratch the rugs and upholstered furniture.

Cats are very inquisitive and get on to places and into things that dogs do not. Be careful of pans of boiling liquid and sharp objects such as pins and needles when your pet is around. Never put a collar or ribbon on your pet unless you train it to go walking outside with a leash. Leave it off indoors because it may get caught on objects as the cat leaps from place to place.

Watch your pet for skin diseases, parasites, or signs of illness. Always consult a veterinarian before home treatment is given.

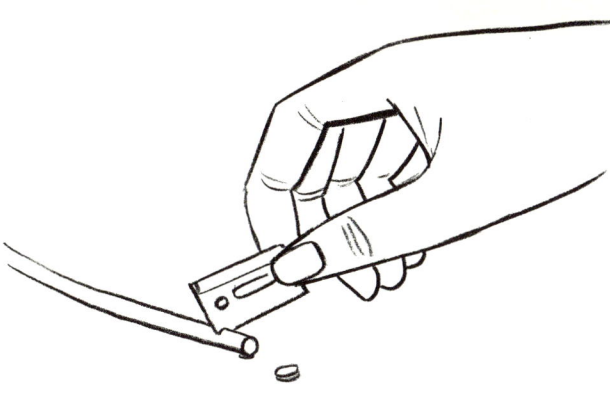

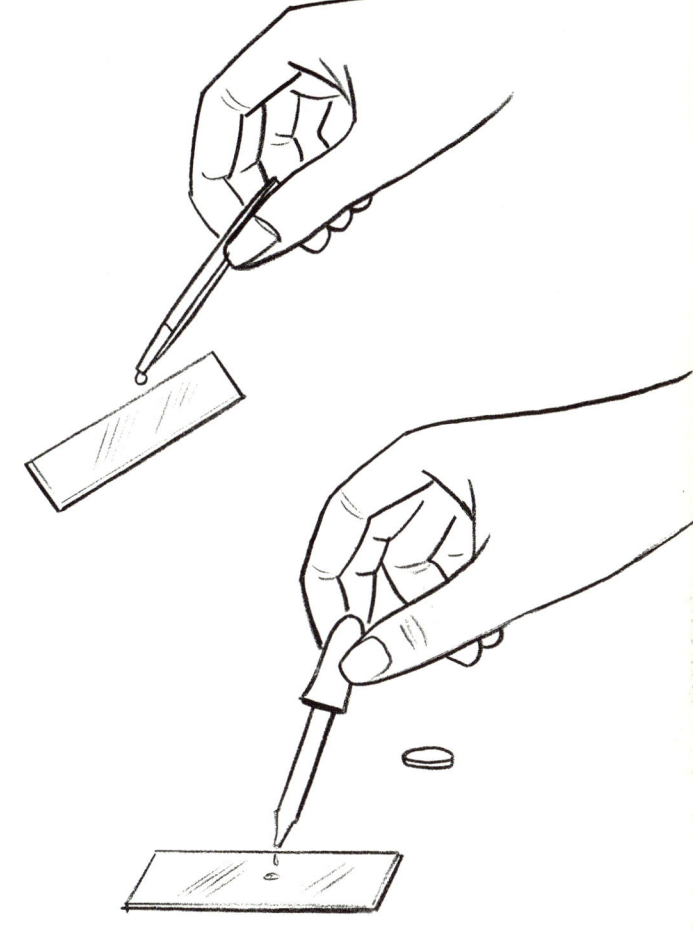

CELLS

MAKING TISSUE SLIDES TO OBSERVE CELLS

Materials you'll need:
microscope, glass slides, cover glasses, sharp knife or razor blade, a variety of dyes (methylene blue, eosin, crystal violet)

A group of cells working together in the same function is called a *tissue*. Commercial tissue slides are rather expensive for the young amateur histologist, so try making your own.

Animal tissue may be cut from fresh chicken, fish, or beef organs. With a sharp razor, slice as thin a section as possible from different parts of the animal. Cut slices from glands, tendons, epidermis, muscle, intestine, blood vessel, and brain.

Tissue slides of plants may be made by cutting thin sections from roots, stems, leaves, fruits, flowers, and seeds. Cellular samples from the lower plant groups (algae, fungi, mosses, ferns) may be prepared in the same manner.

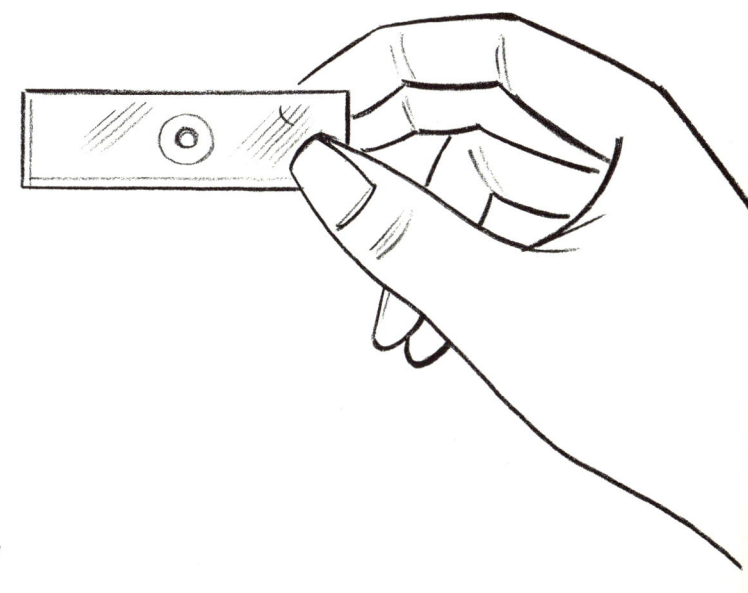

Place the tissue specimen on a slide. Add a drop of dye. Blot it carefully to remove excess liquid. Now put a drop of distilled water on the tissue and cover it with a cover glass. Observe your specimen in the microscope under low power first and then swing to high power for more detailed observation of cellular contents. See page 134 for working with a microscope.

CENTRIFUGAL FORCE

TESTING CENTRIFUGAL FORCE

Materials you'll need:
   pail, water, 1-pound weight, 5-pound weight, string

Centrifugal force keeps an object moving in a circle as far as possible away from the center of revolution. Increasing the weight and speed of the object will increase the centrifugal force.

Fill a pail one-third full of water. Swing it quickly over your head and down in a circle. The water clings to the bottom of the pail and does not spill out.

Fasten a one-pound weight to the end of a strong string. Holding the other end of the string, start swinging the weight in a circle. Swing it as fast as possible. Feel the pull on your arm. Replace the small weight with a five-pound one. Repeat the circular motion. Is the pull greater on your arm? Try it outside away from people and houses and see what happens when you release the string.

CHARCOAL

MAKING CHARCOAL

Materials you'll need:
   tin can, hardwood—such as oak or maple, source of heat

Man makes charcoal by partially burning plant or animal material. It is almost pure carbon. Try making some of your own with the help of an adult friend. Do this outdoors.

Puncture a hole in the lid of a tin can. Place several small sticks of hardwood in the can. Replace the lid. Heat the can over a source of heat to drive out the water vapor in the wood. As wood gas escapes from the hole light a match to it until the gas is all burned up. Remove the can from the heat and allow it to cool. The sticks of wood are now charcoal.

CAUTION!

CHEMICAL CHANGE

CAUSING CHEMICAL CHANGES

A chemical change occurs when materials are combined to make a product which has properties entirely different from the original materials.

1. Chew a dry soda cracker until it becomes sweet. What happened to the starch?

2. Dip a silver spoon into a jar of salad dressing. What caused it to become tarnished?

3. Burn a sheet of paper. Is this a physical or chemical change? How can you tell?

4. Combine small amounts of white vinegar (that clean iron nails have been soaked in for several days to make iron acetate), tannic acid (very strong tea) and glue, to make ink.

5. Put a handful of carpet tacks in a jar. Sprinkle them with water. Cover the jar and let it stand for several days. In the presence of moisture, iron combines with oxygen to form rust, iron oxide.

6. Keep a glass of milk out of the refrigerator for several days in a warm room. What happened to it? Can you name the plant that brought this about?

7. Heat a slice of bread in a toaster until it is black. What changed?

8. Heat sugar until it is brown and turns to caramel.

9. Cover a silver coin with sulfur until the coin is black. Sulfur and silver combine to form silver sulfide.

Chemical changes are going on constantly all around you. How many more can you name?

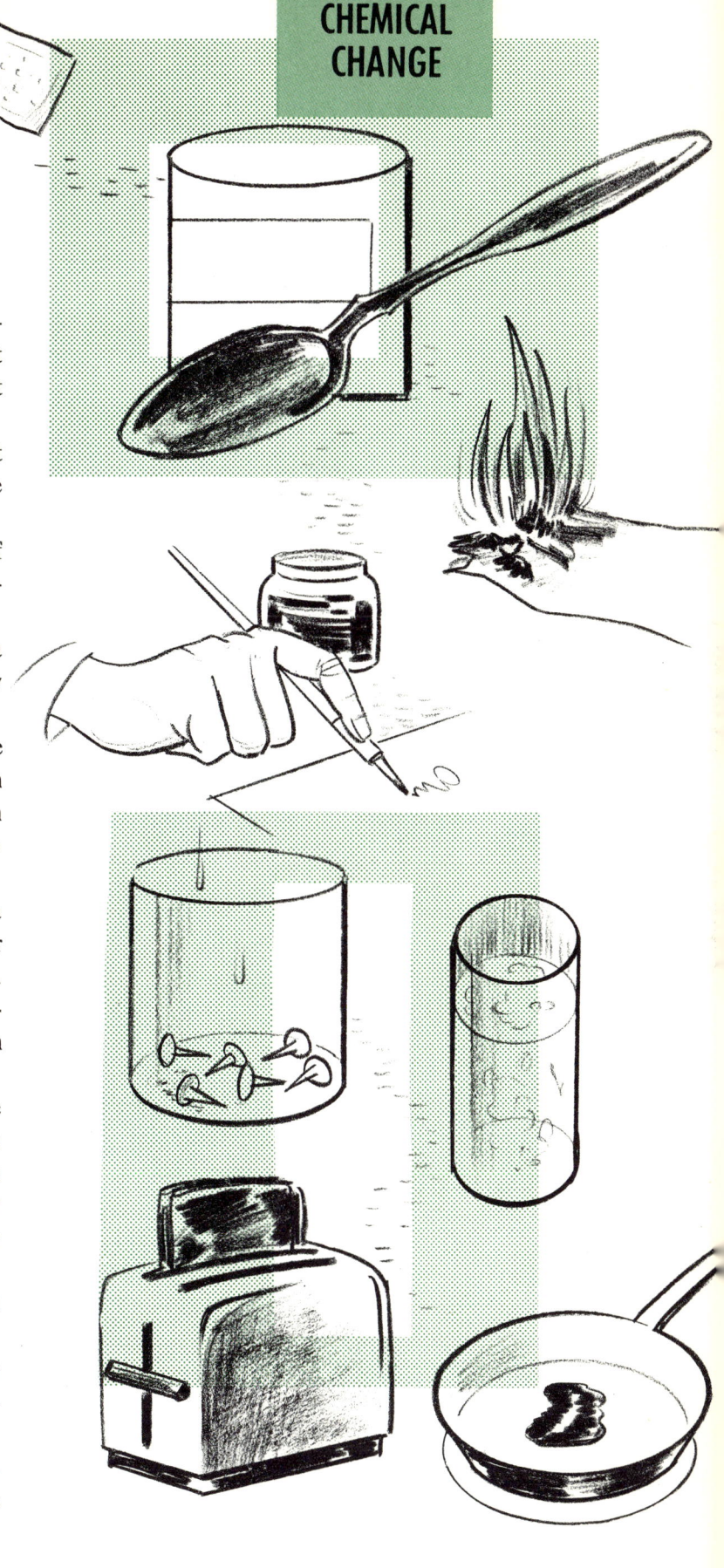

CHICKEN BROODER

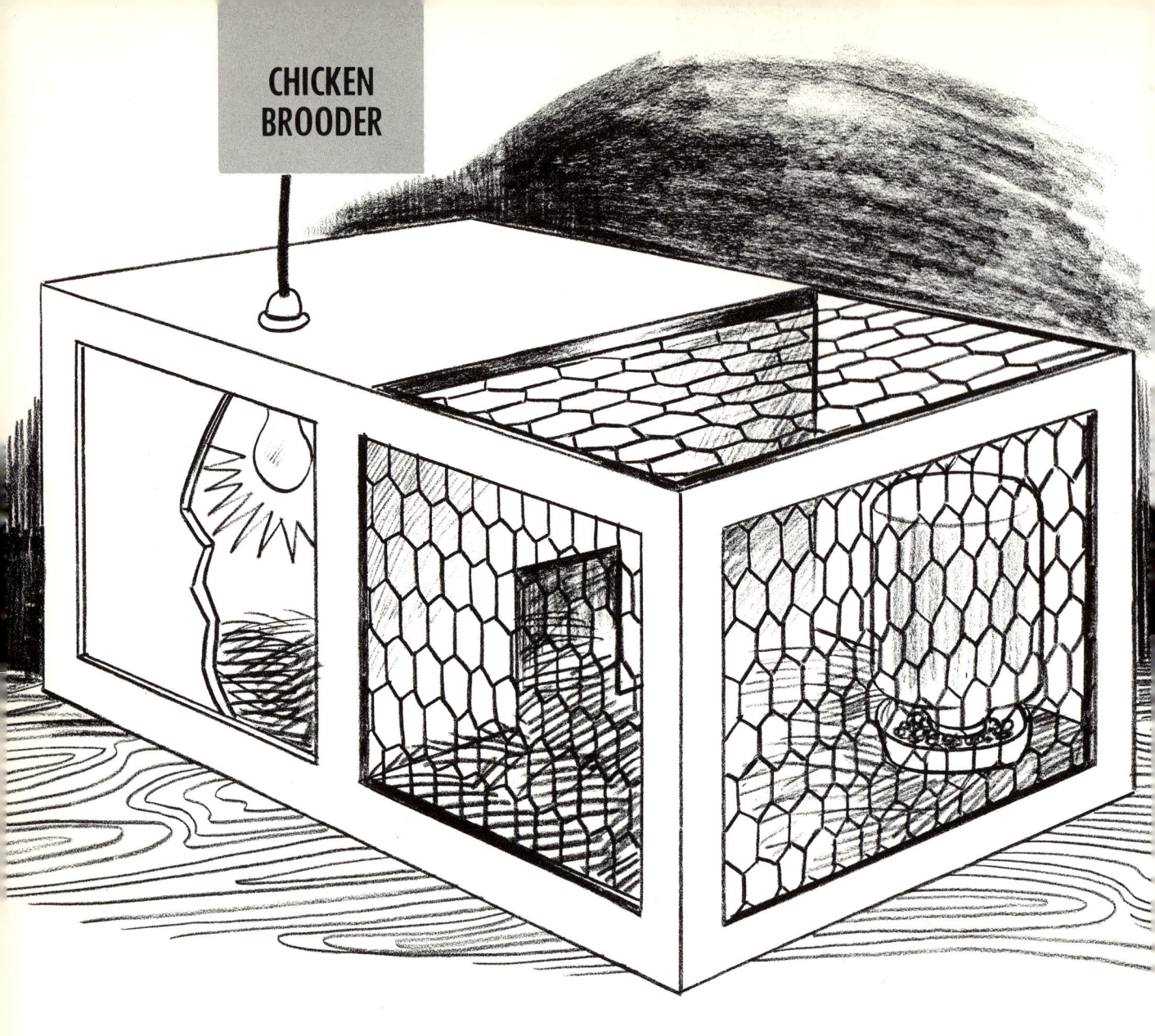

CONSTRUCTING A CHICKEN BROODER

Materials you'll need:
orange crate, 12 feet of chicken wire, heavy cardboard, water jug, hanging lamp, mash, straw, scratch

Perhaps you looked up this activity because your baby chicks have just hatched and you need to build them a house. An old orange crate will work fine since it is naturally divided into two "rooms."

Cover the sides and top with chicken wire. Remember to make an opening on top for a door through which you can furnish the chicks food and water daily. Box in one room with cardboard. Put the hanging light in it with a 25-watt bulb for heat when the room temperature goes down at night. Cut a little doorway in the middle partition to permit the chickens to go from one room to the other. In the exposed room or yard, place an upside-down feeder, mash and scratch. The mash and scratch will have to be purchased at a local feed store. A little straw scattered on the floor in both rooms will add to the comfort of your young birds.

CHLOROPHYLL

EXPERIMENTING WITH CHLOROPHYLL

Materials you'll need:
broad-leafed plant, alcohol, iodine, aluminum foil, two pans or beakers

You can accept the statement that a plant needs chlorophyll to manufacture food or you can do this experiment and prove it to yourself.

There are two ways of removing chlorophyll from green plants:

1. Put a green leaf in a small beaker of alcohol. Set this in a larger beaker of boiling water. Never boil alcohol directly over a flame. After several minutes the alcohol will become green and the leaf white. Test for the presence of starch by applying a few drops of iodine to the leaf. It will turn a dark blue if starch is present.

2. Cover an entire leaf on a plant with foil. Permit it to continue growing on the plant for three days. Remove the leaf and foil. The leaf has lost its green coloring. Repeat the test for starch. Which experiment showed that starch (the plant's food) was being manufactured? See page 152 to find out more about photosynthesis.

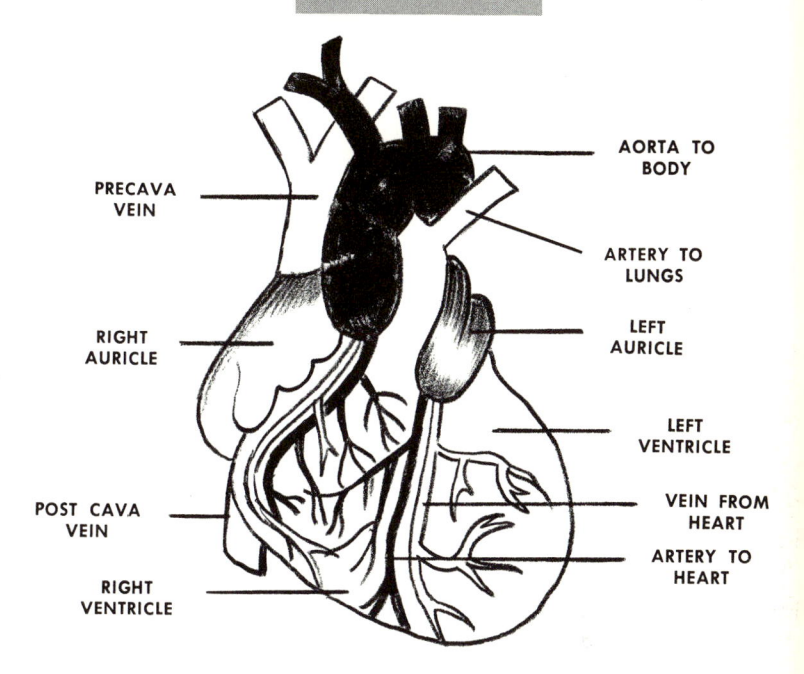

CAUTION!

CIRCULATION

TRACING THE FLOW OF BLOOD THROUGH THE HEART

Materials you'll need:
scissors, razor blade, string, fresh beef or sheep's heart from butcher

Study the outside of the heart before you do any cutting. Find the two ventricles and two auricles. Notice the two large vessels leading into the right auricle and the pulmonary veins leading into the left auricle. The large vessel from the left ventricle going up and over the auricles is the aorta. The pulmonary artery takes blood from the right ventricle to the lungs.

Now with sharp scissors or razor blade, carefully cut the sides from all four chambers. Notice how thick the walls of the ventricles are. Can you find the valves between the right and left sides? Cut open the vessels leading to each chamber. Do they also have valves? With a piece of string trace the flow of blood through the heart.

CLEAVAGE

MAKING CLEAVAGE MODELS

Materials you'll need:
   Plasticine, dowels, wooden bases

Have you ever wondered how a fertilized egg becomes a new individual? It goes through a series of divisions called *cleavage*. Models of these stages may be molded out of Plasticine clay. Insert a dowel stick into each one and attach it firmly to a wooden base. Label your models—*first cleavage, second cleavage, . . . blastula, gastrula,* etc., in order of division, as in the illustration.

This activity may accompany the hatching of eggs. Crack them open periodically and study the progressive development of the chick embryo (see page 85). Compare the early stages with your models.

CLOUDS

MAKING CLOUDS FORM

Materials you'll need:
   large glass jar, cork, glass tube, chalk dust, water, alcohol

When air is compressed the temperature goes up. Warm air holds more moisture than cool air. When air expands it becomes cooler. Droplets are formed and a cloud appears.

Drill a hole in the center of a cork which fits snugly into the mouth of a large glass jar. Insert a glass tube into the hole in the cork. Rinse the inside of the jar with water mixed with a small amount of alcohol. Pour out the water, leaving the inside of the jar wet. Add several pinches of finely-crushed blackboard chalk. Put the cork and tube into the neck of the jar. Blow through the tube to scatter the chalk and compress the air, then suck very hard and suddenly on the tube. This will allow the air to expand. Did a cloud form?

62

CLOUDS

DESIGNING A CLOUD CHART

Materials you'll need:
large sheet of tagboard, blue paint, cotton, felt pen or crayon, rubber cement, construction paper

Clouds appear in different shapes, sizes, and colors. Charting the clouds will help you classify them into their types and to recognize their relationship to each other in the atmosphere. Follow this guide: high clouds (cirrus, cirro-cumulus, cirro-stratus)—20,000 feet; middle clouds (alto-cumulus, alto-stratus)—6500 at lower level; low clouds (strato-cumulus, stratus, nimbo-stratus)—6500 at upper level; clouds with verticle development (cumulus, cumulo-nimbus)—lower level about 1650 feet.

Paint the tagboard blue so that it looks like the sky. Draw an altitude scale in feet at one side of the chart. Cut from black construction paper silhouettes or shapes of well-known mountains and the tallest buildings. Paste these silhouettes on the bottom of the chart, making sure that they extend to the proper heights.

Unroll a fresh pack of cotton. Cut the different shapes or forms of clouds out of the cotton. Spray a little black paint on the thunderclouds. Use rubber cement to attach the clouds to the chart at their proper altitudes or heights. Label the clouds either by printing the name of each cloud directly under it or on a slip of paper which is glued over the cloud. It is easy to identify clouds using the chart.

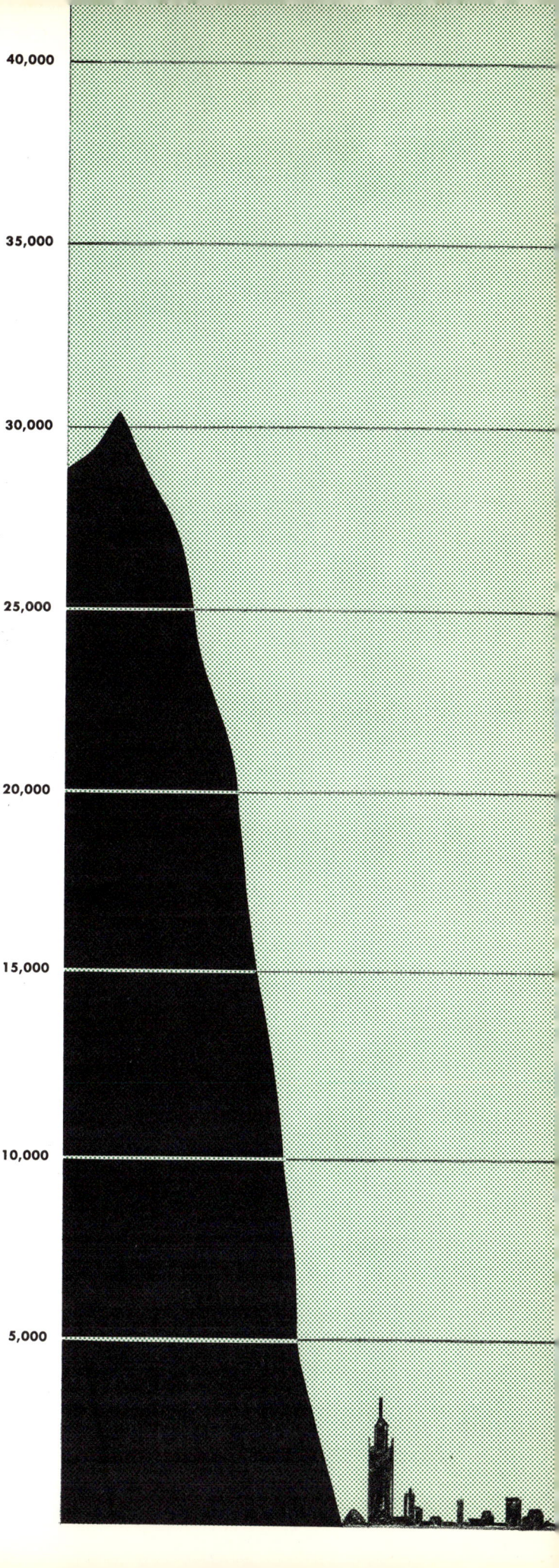

COLOR

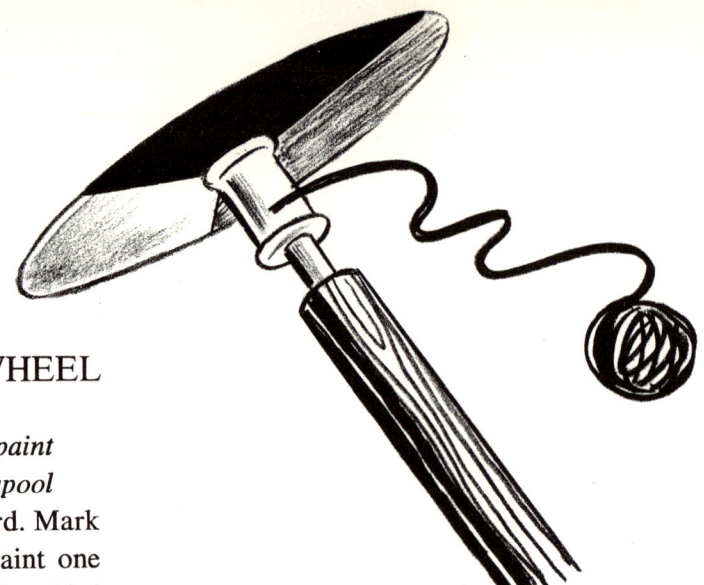

MAKING A COLOR WHEEL
Materials you'll need:
   cardboard, dowel, cord, paint (red, green, blue), thread, spool

Cut a six-inch disk of cardboard. Mark off three pie-shaped pieces. Paint one section red, one green, and the third blue. Glue the cardboard disk onto the end of an empty spool. Mount a short piece of dowel on a square piece of wood. Put the dowel into the hole in the spool. Wind a piece of cord tightly around the spool. Pull hard on the loose end of cord. This will make the disk spin rapidly. What color does it appear to be?

EXPERIMENTING WITH COLOR
Materials you'll need:
   3 flashlights, pieces of colored cellophane

Do you think that mixing colored lights will produce the same combinations as when you combine the same pigment colors? Try this experiment and see if you were right.

Obtain three flashlights and cover the front end of each with a different colored piece of cellophane. Tape it securely in place. Project each beam of light on a white cardboard or the wall in a darkened room. Let the inside circles of light overlap slightly. What colors did you get? The primary colors in light are red, green and blue. In pigment they are red, yellow and blue.

TESTING COLOR ABSORPTION
Materials you'll need:
   water or oil paints, water, brush, containers

A color gets its name according to the rays of light which it will *reflect*. All other colors in a beam of light are *absorbed* by it.

Water colors or oil paints may be used for this experiment. The object is to mix two different colors to determine the color of the resulting mixture. Mix a small amount of yellow pigment with the same amount of blue pigment. What color is it now?

Try a combination of red and blue pigments, then red and yellow. Save each mixture. Blend a small quantity of two of these mixtures together to obtain still another color. Record the results each time and draw conclusions. Does there seem to be a pattern to pigment combinations? You will find that, unlike combining colored lights, pigment colors are *subtracted* by others.

Think about the principles of reflection and absorption of colors and then find out what causes white and black.

64

COLOR

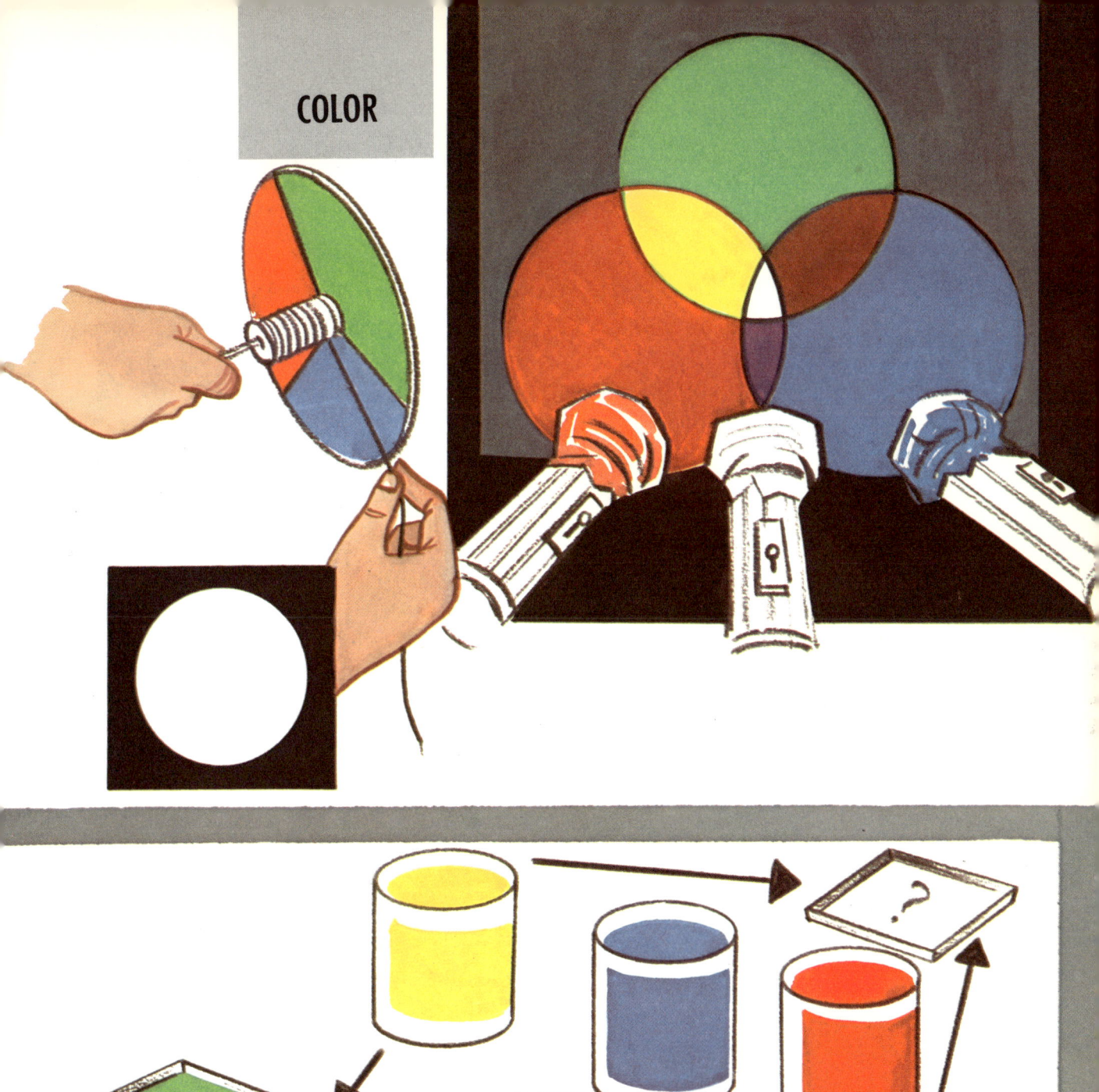

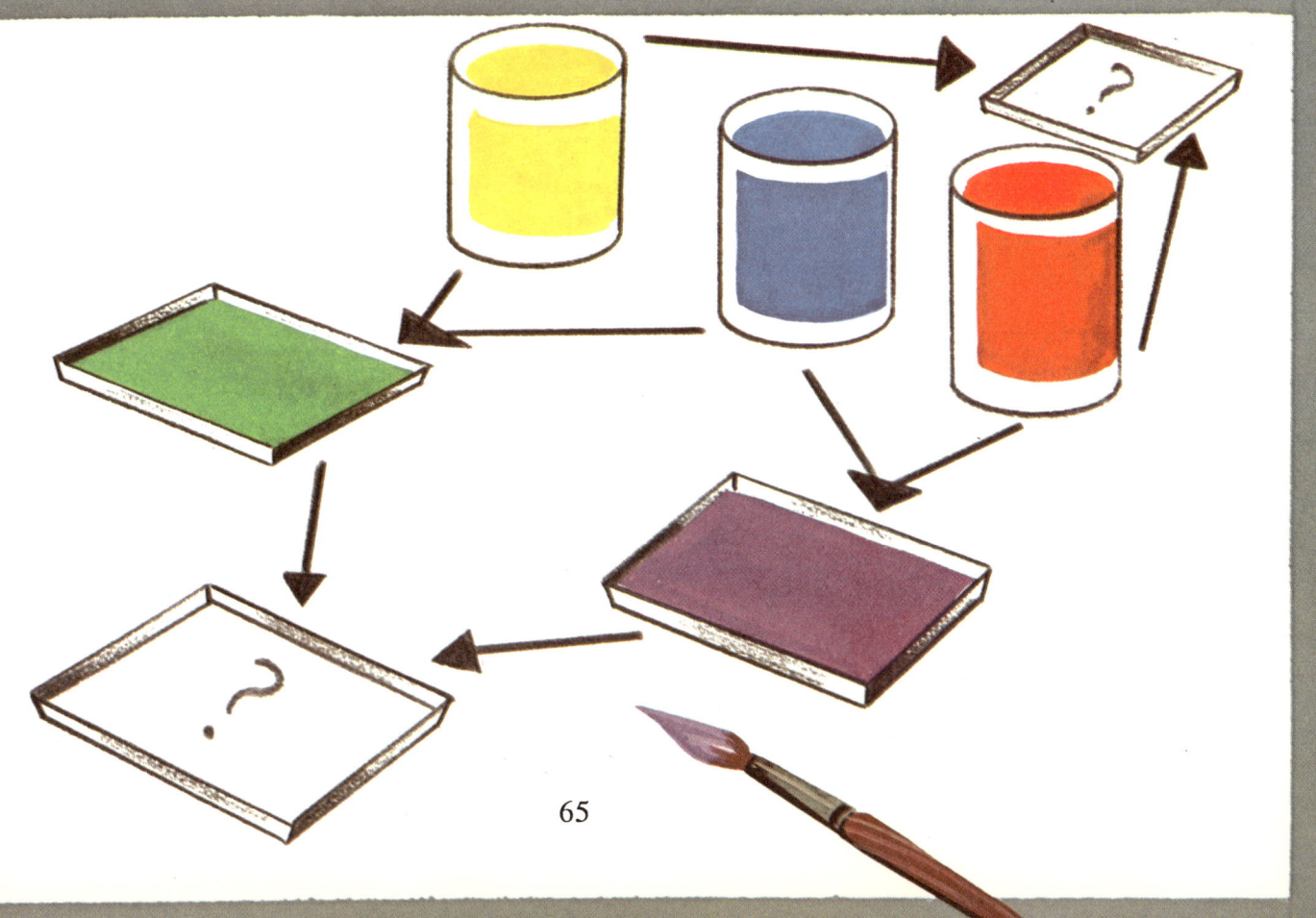

65

COMPASS

COMPOST

MAKING A COMPASS
Materials you'll need:
¼" slice of cork, saucer, detergent, magnet, needle, bottle with cork, thread, paper

Add a small amount of detergent to a dish of water. This will permit an object to float freely in the center of the saucer.

Magnetize the needle by stroking it with the magnet. Stroke from the middle of the needle toward one end with one pole of the magnet and from the middle toward the other end with the other pole. Stroke from the middle to the end only. Run the needle through the slice of cork. Float the cork in the dish of water. It will turn so that the needle points north and south. The apparatus is now a compass.

To make another kind of compass, fold a small piece of paper, tie a thread around it, and stick a magnetized needle through it so that both ends are visible. Fasten the thread with a thumbtack to the bottom of a cork in a bottle. This permits the paper and needle to hang down inside the bottle and swing freely. The needle will swing around to a north and south position.

MAKING YOUR OWN COMPOST FERTILIZER
Materials you'll need:
wire fencing, grass, leaves, garbage, ashes

If you are a serious gardener, you will find that a compost pile provides the most satisfactory fertilizer. It is necessary to start the pile the year before you will want to use it.

Choose a hidden, shady corner of the yard. Dig a pit which is about four feet by six feet and two feet deep. Around the hole, erect a wire fence. It should not be too high for you to reach over comfortably to turn over the rotting material occasionally.

Fill the hole with grass cuttings, a little kitchen garbage, sifted wood ashes from a fireplace, dead leaves, cornstalks, or any other organic material available. Wet it down with a sprinkler. When the contents of the pile have disintegrated into fine pieces (after several months), the compost is ready to be worked into the soil. You are returning to the soil the elements necessary for the growth of your plants. The compost will supply lime, phosphorus, potassium, nitrogen and calcium.

CONDENSATION

GETTING WATER OUT OF AIR

Materials you'll need:
  pitcher of ice water, tray of ice cubes

When air is cooled it cannot hold as much moisture as when the air is warm. The water is released in the form of droplets—*condensation*. This process can be seen.

Place a pitcher of ice water in a warm room. Observe what happens on the outside of the pitcher. Would covering the pitcher prove that the droplets on the outside did not come from within the container?

Why do cold water pipes drip in the summer? Would the amount of moisture that accumulates depend upon the amount of humidity on a particular day? What happens when one blows hot air on a cold window pane? What does this condensation process have to do with rain (see page 162)?

CONDUCTION

TESTING ELECTRICAL CONDUCTION

Materials you'll need:
  2 dry cells, small bulb and receptacle, paper clips, cardboard, tin, nail, coil, glass, salt solution, baking soda, bell wire

Can electricity be conducted through all materials? Collect a number of items to experiment with and determine which ones will permit an electric current to flow through them. Connect a light socket to two dry cells in series (see page 80). Cut one of the pieces of wire in the middle and remove the insulation from both cut ends. Attach paper clips to both bare wire ends. Then slip the paper clips onto the ends of a piece of cardboard 1″ by 3″ long. Lay different objects so they touch both clips. Try tin, a nail, piece of cloth, flat stone, safety pin, etc. Which ones close the circuit and cause the bulb to light?

Remove the wires from the clips. Place both ends in a glass of salt solution. Don't let the wire ends touch each other. What happens? Do the same thing in a baking soda solution and in vinegar. If the current going through the solution isn't strong enough to cause a bulb to light, try wiring a homemade galvanometer (see page 97) into the circuit. The galvanometer is a more sensitive current detector than a light bulb.

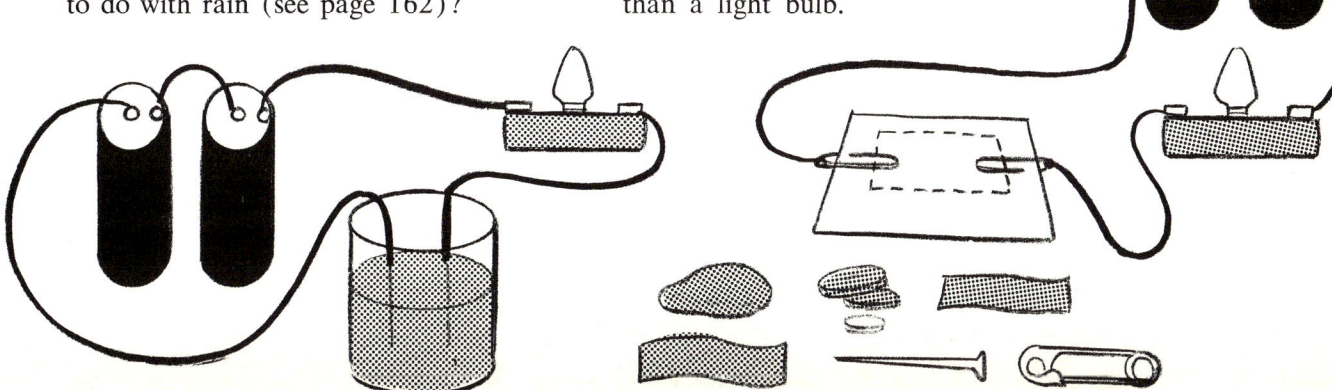

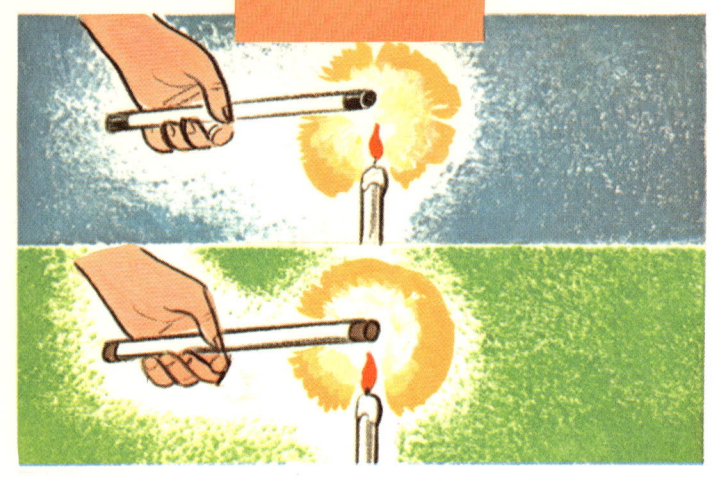

CONDUCTION

TESTING HEAT CONDUCTION

Materials you'll need:
  metal pipe, wooden dowel,
  sheet of paper, candles, tape

Wrap a piece of paper around a metal pipe and tape it securely in place. Do the same with a length of wooden dowel. Hold both the pipe and the dowel over (not in) the flames of two candles while you count to ten. Observe the paper where it was in contact with the fire on each object. Which one was scorched the most? One of the materials conducted the heat away from the paper so fast the paper did not reach the kindling temperature.

CONSTELLATIONS

ASSEMBLING A CONSTELLARIUM

Materials you'll need:
  cardboard carton (oatmeal box
  or round ice cream carton),
  cardboard disks, flashlight

A star projector is an interesting way to study individual constellations or show them to friends.

Cut out the center of the carton lid so that there is a ¼″ frame left around the edges of the top. Cut several cardboard disks so that they fit tightly into the lid. Punch out a pattern of one constellation in each disk. Make larger holes for the brighter stars in each group. Cut a hole in the bottom of the carton just large enough so that the large bulb end of a flashlight fits into it exactly. Put one of the circles with the punched-out pattern of the constellation on it into the lid of the carton and place the lid on the carton. Go into a dark room. Turn the flashlight on and the constellation can be projected onto a dark surface.

Have each of your friends make a constellarium. Get together in a dark room where each person can project a different constellation on the ceiling at the same time. Can you make the pattern of the night sky as it is normally seen around the North Star?

CONSTELLATIONS

FOLLOWING CONSTELLATIONS ACROSS THE SKY

Materials you'll need:
dark, plain-colored umbrella, chalk, large circle of black paper, white ink

Open a dark umbrella. The handle of the umbrella represents the axis of the earth which points toward the North Star. With chalk, draw in the stars and names of the constellations on the underside of the umbrella.

With a star circle you can show the constellations in their relative positions in the sky as they appear to move from month to month.

Draw the constellations on black paper using white ink. At night, face the northern sky. Hold the chart so that the constellations on it are in the same positions as the constellations you can see in the sky. Write the name of the current month on the uppermost or northernmost part of the circle. A month later, repeat the process. The star groups will seem to move across the sky although it is really the earth which is moving rather than the stars. You can make a sky chart for the whole year on the one paper.

CONVECTION

SHOWING CONVECTION CURRENTS IN AIR

Materials you'll need:
chalk box, piece of glass, two chimneys, ice water, pan, lighter fluid, candle, paper towel, string

As air is heated the molecules move farther away from each other, making the air lighter, or less dense. The cold air is heavier and moves in to push the warm air up. If you construct the following apparatus, you can make your own convection currents.

Assemble a convection box from a wooden chalk box, piece of glass, and two glass chimneys. Turn the box on one side and cut out two holes on the top side over which the chimneys will be placed. Substitute a piece of glass for the sliding box cover. Place a lighted candle inside the box under one hole. Slide the glass door closed. Ignite a dampened rolled paper towel so that it smolders. Hold it over the chimney which is not over the candle. Observe the path of smoke.

Commercial chimneys are fragile and expensive. There are a number of times when young scientists need a bottomless glass jar. Try this only with adult supervision. Select a Mason jar, olive bottle, or other rather thin glass container. Milk bottles are too heavy. Saturate a piece of string with lighter fluid. Tie it tightly around the jar about one inch up from the bottom. Holding it away from you, ignite the string. The instant the string stops blazing dip the bottle in a pan of ice water. The bottom will drop off where the string was tied. Tape the raw edge.

CAUTION!

SHOWING CONVECTION CURRENTS IN LIQUID

Materials you'll need:
2 glass jars, food coloring, piece of cardboard, hot and cold water

Fill two jars, one with hot water and one with cold water. Be sure the necks of the jars are exactly the same diameter. Put a few drops of food coloring in the hot water in order to detect the movement of currents. Hold a piece of cardboard over the mouth of the cold water jar and turn it upside down over the other jar. Carefully slide the cardboard out from between the jars. Observe the fluid action in both jars.

Cold water is heavier than hot water. It descends into the lower bottle pushing the hot water up in small currents.

MAKING A CRYSTAL RADIO SET

Materials you'll need:

60 feet of fine, enameled wire (#26 or #30), a paper tissue tube for the cylinder, earphone with connections, 35 feet of antenna wire and insulator mountings, a germanium crystal diode (from radio store), tuning strip cut from tin, clips (Fahnstock type), small screws or nails, a mounting board

The construction of crystal sets has changed little in the last fifty years. They are simple to assemble, inexpensive, and they work.

Wrap 50 feet of the enameled wire neatly on the tube, providing connecting ends. Fasten tube to board and position tuning strip outside to rub along length of wire coil. Remove enamel from wire with sandpaper at points where tuner rubs. Connect the antenna to the coil and tuner. Attach the ground wire (connected to a water pipe or other firm metal piece) to the other end of the coil and one side of the crystal diode. Follow the illustration in mounting it all to a board.

Attach the earphone wires to the antenna side and to the diode. Check all connections to be sure they are right. Gently slide the tuner back and forth until a strong radio station in your area is heard.

CRYSTALS

GROWING CRYSTALS

Materials you'll need:
brick or charcoal brickettes, table salt, ammonia, bluing, hammer, cereal bowl, medicine dropper, water, food coloring

Break brick or charcoal into small pieces. Place several pieces in the center of a bowl. Mix ¼ cup salt, ¼ cup liquid bluing, ¼ cup water and one tablespoon ammonia together.

Pour the solution over the pieces of coal or brick. Fill the medicine dropper with food coloring and drop small amounts over the brick pile. Leave the dish alone now and let the crystals grow. The crystals will crumble easily so don't move the dish around much.

Watch and note when the first crystals appeared and how fast they developed. Crystals are formed because water is drawn into the brick leaving the solids behind. The ammonia, bluing and salt form a complex crystal. Use a hand lens to observe the shape.

OBSERVING CRYSTAL SHAPES

Materials you'll need:
water glasses, boiling water, salt, sugar, alum, string, borax, Epsom salts, copper sulfate, sodium hyposulfite, hand lens

Crystals take various shapes and sizes, but the angles of corresponding faces are always the same. For example, table salt crystallizes with its atoms as the points of a cube. Experiment with growing different crystal shapes from a variety of solutions.

Use half a glass of boiling water for each kind. Mix as much powdered alum in the hot water as it will hold. Tie a weight to the end of a string. Drop the weight in the glass of alum solution. Let the other end hang over the top of the glass. Permit it to cool slowly. Observe the diamond-shaped crystals clinging to the string.

Repeat the experiment using colored salt and sugar solutions. Also try using borax, Epsom salts, copper sulfate and sodium hyposulfite. Can you see the differences among the kinds of crystals?

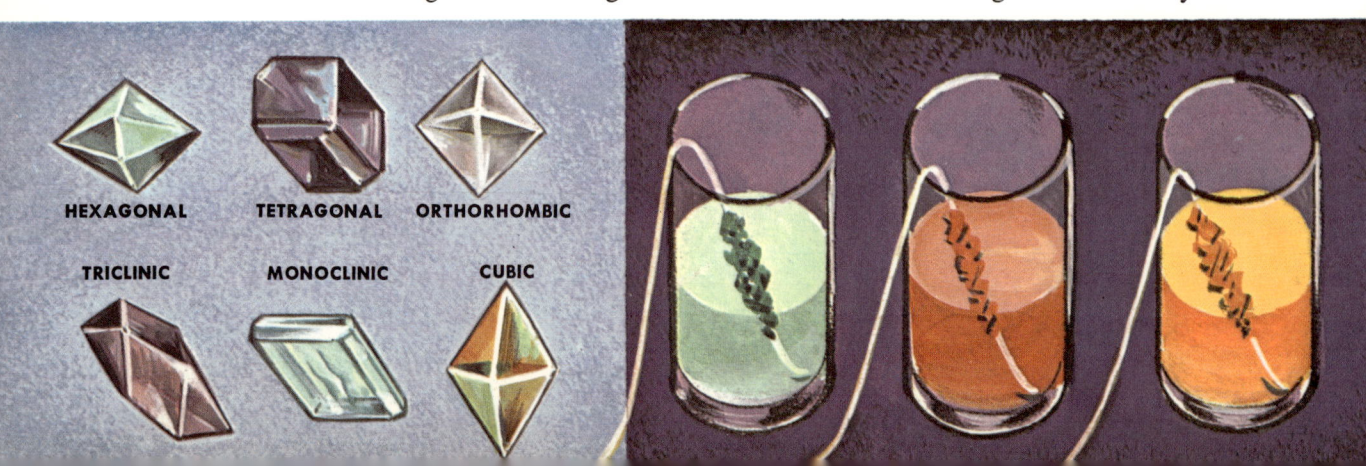

HEXAGONAL   **TETRAGONAL**   **ORTHORHOMBIC**

TRICLINIC   **MONOCLINIC**   **CUBIC**

DAY AND NIGHT

DIFFUSION

SHOWING DAY AND NIGHT ON A GLOBE

Materials you'll need:
   flashlight, globe, partner, dark room

The movement of the earth on its axis is called *rotation*. It is this turning toward and away from the sun that gives us days and nights. Do this demonstration with another person so you can see how this happens.

Have your partner stand several feet away from you with a flashlight—the "sun." You hold the globe—the "earth"—with the axis pointing at 23 degrees in the northerly direction. Be sure the light of the flashlight strikes the globe. Which continents are on the lighted side? Which countries are having night? Now slowly turn the globe counter-clockwise. Watch the circle of light fall on other places while the ones on the opposite side are going into the dark side away from the sun. Do you see why the sun appears to rise in the east and set in the west? Continue to experiment and figure out why some places have longer days or nights than other countries.

TESTING DIFFUSION

Materials you'll need:
   glasses of water, cube of sugar, piece of rock salt, crystal of potassium dichromate, ball of hard candy, perfume, ink, vegetable dye

The molecules of liquids, gases and solids are constantly moving around. Any solid which will dissolve in a liquid is soon spread by diffusion.

Set an open bottle of perfume or vanilla extract in one part of the room. Go to the other corner and wait until you can detect the odor. How did it get to you?

Put a few drops of different liquids (iodine, ink, vegetable dye) into glasses half full of water. Do not stir the solutions. What happens to the color of the water?

Place several glasses of water on a table where they may remain for two days without being moved. Put a cube of sugar in one, a piece of rock salt in another, a crystal of potassium dichromate in a third, and a ball of hard candy in the last. Do not stir them. What happens to each material?

DIP NET

MAKING A DIP NET

Materials you'll need:
  broom handle, coat hanger, cheese cloth, wire

Shape the coat hanger into a twelve-inch hoop. Make the cotton mesh into a bag with a twelve-inch opening. It should be six inches deep. Hem the bag around the hoop. Groove the sides of the broom handle. Insert the ends of the hoop into the grooves and bind them tightly with wire.

Use the net to catch small fish and aquatic insects for an aquarium. Hold it still in a rapidly moving stream and sweep it in still water. Insects can be caught by sweeping the net over weeds growing near the edge of the body of water. By making the net bag 20 inches deep you can use it to catch insects in the air.

DISTILLATION

PURIFYING WATER

Materials you'll need:
  glass tube, 1-holed stopper, Pyrex bottle, candle, hot plate

Heat is required to change a liquid into a gas. Collecting and cooling the gas turns it back to a liquid. This total process is called *distillation*. See if you can make enough distilled water to use in a steam iron.

Hold a piece of glass tubing over a flame and gently bend an elbow near one end. Grease the short arm and insert it carefully into a one-holed stopper. Put the stopper on a Pyrex bottle or flask partly full of water. Direct the other end of the tube into a sterilized container. Don't plug up the tube. Boil the water in the bottle. Soon water will drip from the tube into the container. This is distilled water. The steam given off by the boiling water will condense in the glass tube. The impurities are left behind.

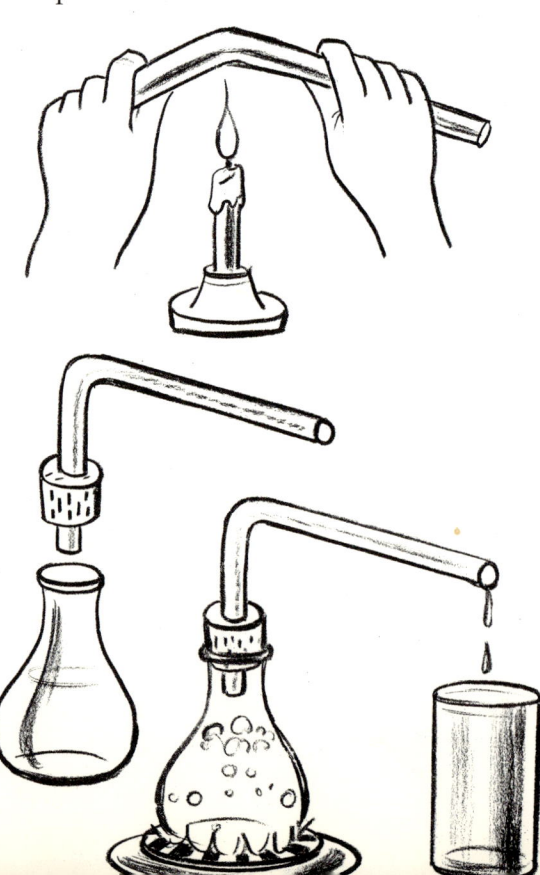

DOGS

CARING FOR PUPPIES AND DOGS

Before you buy or accept a puppy for a pet, be sure that you are willing to take all the responsibility that a dog involves. To raise a well-behaved, friendly animal requires considerable care, expense and devotion.

A puppy needs its own sleeping quarters. A box or a small doghouse lined with a warm blanket will be fine. Large, long-haired dogs may be kept in an outside kennel if it is protected and dry. A puppy (up to two months old) should have four meals a day: cereal and milk for breakfast, three to four tablespoons of raw hamburger for lunch and dinner, and milk for a bedtime snack. Change its drinking water daily. As your pup grows you can gradually leave out the bedtime milk and the noon feeding. By the time it is a year old, the pet can be on one large meal a day or two smaller ones. The total amount of food for a 20-pound dog is one cup each of meat, cereal and vegetables. An adult dog should not become fat. As your dog ages, watch its weight and feed it accordingly. Obesity in animals is just as dangerous as it is in human beings.

Plenty of fresh air and exercise will keep your pet in good condition. If you are unable to walk and run your dog daily, provide an overhead running line in the yard. The line should be 30 feet long and have a shady spot within reach for your dog to get out of the sun. Fresh water should be near if the dog is left alone for any time.

You must groom your pet. Be sure to brush and comb it daily. In the summer watch for fleas, ticks, lice and other pests. Consult your veterinarian for treatment of parasites. Any time your dog refuses to eat for a couple of meals, is listless, or displays other unusual symptoms, take it to a veterinarian immediately. The dog cannot tell you its ailments, so be sensitive to its needs.

Training your dog to follow simple commands will make it more secure and also more acceptable to the neighbors. Always praise the dog when praise has been earned.

DRY ICE

EXPERIMENTING WITH DRY ICE

Materials you'll need:

dry ice, mercury, ink, molasses, glass tube, tongs, 1-holed stopper, bottle, pitcher, candle

Dry ice is interesting to watch because it is a solid which changes directly to a gas. Dry ice is *solid carbon dioxide*. Remember two precautions when working with dry ice. *Never touch it with your bare hands* and *never confine it in a closed container*. The temperature of dry ice is minus 110° Fahrenheit.

CAUTION!

With a pair of tongs place a piece of dry ice on several thicknesses of newspaper. Dig out little cavities on the surface. Put mercury in one, ink in another, molasses in a third. Observe what happens. Do all of the materials turn to solids? Try other liquids and record the time it takes for them to freeze. Compare.

Is pressure exerted when solid dry ice changes to a gas? To find out, insert a glass tube carefully in a one-holed stopper which fits tightly in the mouth of a small-necked bottle containing a few inches of warm water. Hammer the dry ice into pieces. Drop them into the bottle of warm water. Insert the stopper. Can you see the escaping gas exerting pressure?

Will dry ice snuff out a burning candle? Put several pieces of dry ice in a pitcher with a few inches of water. A cloud will form since carbon dioxide gas is so cold it causes the water vapor in the air to condense. Now tilt the pitcher over a burning candle. Did the flame go out? The gas is heavier than air, tumbles over the side, and down to the blaze, driving oxygen away.

76

BLUEBERRIES

ONION SKINS

DYES

BEETS

RED SUMAC LEAVES

BLACK WALNUT HULL

GOLDENROD

COLORING CLOTH WITH NATURAL DYES

Materials you'll need:
  variety of white fabric, samples of fruits, vegetables, parts of trees, pan, strainer, stove

It was everyday work for Indians and pioneers to dye material with vegetable and fruit juices. You can dye fabric the same way.

Wash well and cut to uniform size, one piece each of white cotton, white rayon, white linen, white wool, and white nylon.

Chop leaves, grind roots and stems, or crush berries (see the suggestions below). Soak the plant pieces overnight in enough water to cover. Boil slowly for one hour. Strain dye, removing the plant material. Dip cloth samples in water and wring them out. Put them in the dye bath and cover. Simmer slowly until material is the desired color. The color will lighten up as it dries. Let the cloth almost dry and then iron it smooth.

Some natural dyes that can be obtained are: light brown, yellow, and orange from onion skins, roots of white mulberry, wood from sumac, roots from osage orange hedge, and carrots; green from spinach; rose from beets, pokeweed berries, and roots from dogwood; gold from goldenrod flowers; brown from coffee and hulls of black walnut; red from red sumac berries, bloodroot roots, and red raspberries; black from red sumac leaves; blue from red maple and blue ash bark, and blueberries; purple from red cedar roots.

EARS

USING BOTH EARS

Find a partner to experiment with. Stand in one place and close your eyes so you are unable to see where your partner is in the room. Hold your hand tightly over one ear. Have your partner make noises on different sides of you—in front, back, above, and below head level. Can you tell from which direction the sound is coming? Repeat again while you listen with both ears. What does this tell you about how sound travels?

MAKING A WORMERY

Materials you'll need:
 old aquarium or large glass jar, soil, decaying leaves, sand, cornmeal, black construction paper

EARTHWORMS

Earthworms are easy to raise and they will reproduce in captivity. The worms will furnish you with a ready supply of food for pet amphibians and reptiles or for bait during the fishing season.

Fill an old aquarium with alternate layers of garden soil, leaf mold (decaying leaves), and sand. Sprinkle each layer with a little water. On top of the last layer place small pieces of leafy vegetable and a handful of cornmeal. Dig up several earthworms from the backyard or off the sidewalk after an especially heavy rainfall. Transfer them to their new home. Cover the sides of the aquarium with dark paper for a week or two to encourage the worms to tunnel near the glass. As the earthworms consume the decayed vegetation they will keep turning the soil.

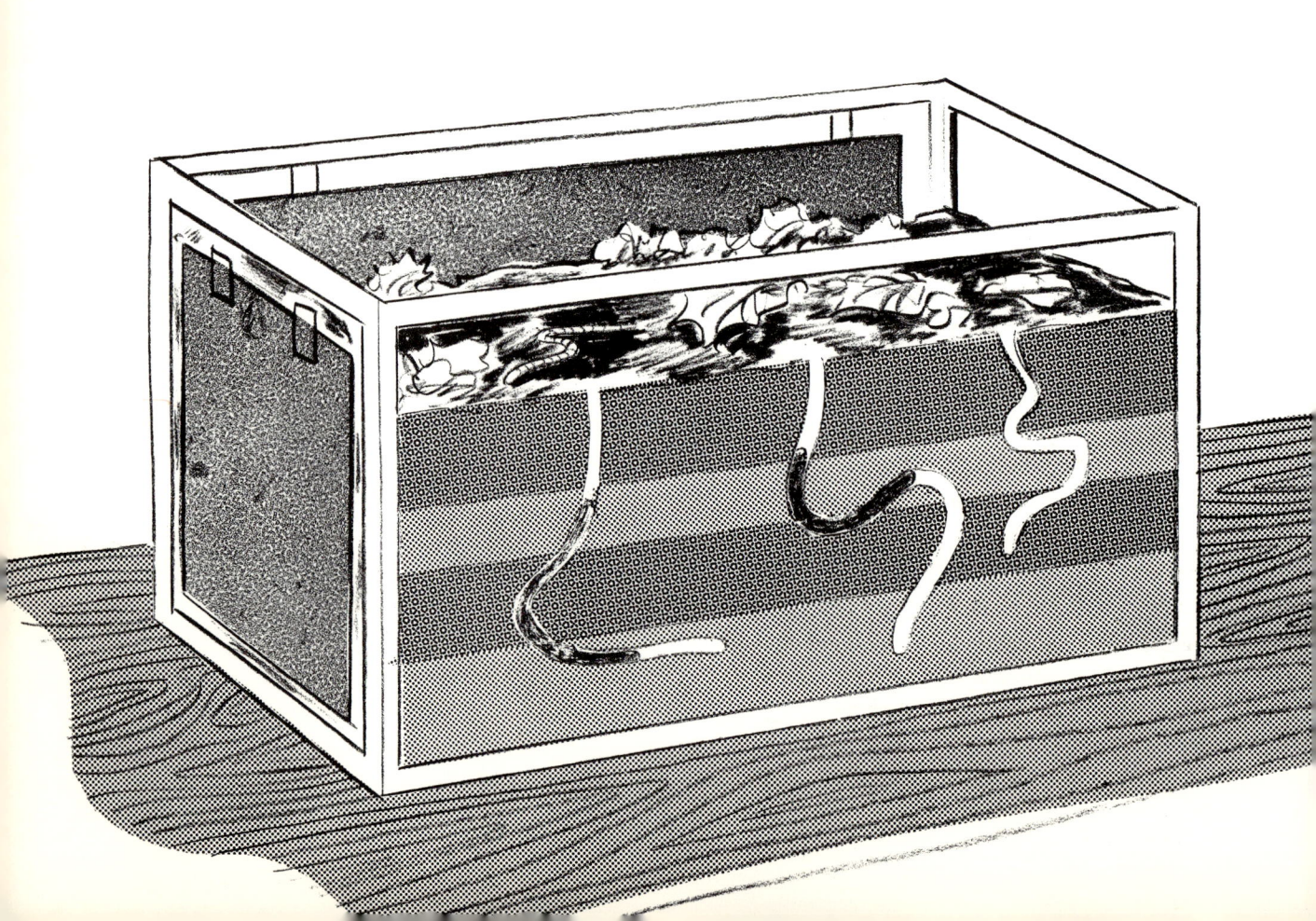

EARTHWORMS

STUDYING AN EARTHWORM

Materials you'll need:
 supply of worms, lemon juice,
 2 dry cells, bell wire, paper

The earthworm crawls with the help of the bristles, called *setae*, on its ventral surface. These appendages also help the worm hold fast inside its burrow.

Turn the earthworm over and stroke it carefully on its ventral (under) side. You should be able to feel the bristles.

Watch it crawl. Notice how the body alternately stretches and contracts. Try to imagine how the bristles help.

Turn the worm over on its back. Does it stay there? How does it move?

It is somewhat surprising to find that even such a lowly animal as a worm reacts to stimuli such as light and electricity.

Touch the forward or anterior end of the earthworm. What happens?

Dip a small piece of paper into lemon juice or vinegar and, without touching the worm, bring it close to its anterior end. The anterior end will contract. Do you get the same reaction from the posterior end?

Connect the two dry cells in series as shown, with a piece of wire extending from each. Place the worm on a piece of wet paper. Place the wire from the positive (center) pole down on the paper about an inch from the anterior end of the worm and, at the same time, place the other bare wire an inch from the worm's posterior end. What happens? Now reverse the wires, placing the negative tip near the head and the positive tip near the tail. Last, place the bare tips about an inch away from the sides of the worm, touching the paper. What is the worm's response?

ELECTRICAL WIRING

WIRING A SERIES CIRCUIT

Materials you'll need:
3 dry cells, bell wire, 2 miniature lamps

There are three ways to wire in series. You can wire dry cells in series or you can wire lamps in series, or both.

To wire dry cells in series, attach the outside terminal of one cell to the inside terminal of the next and so on. The total voltage supplied to the circuit is the combined voltage of all three cells. If the cells are one and a half volts, the total in this diagram is four and a half volts. Notice the difference in brightness in a lamp when it is connected to one cell and then to two or three. It is often recommended in projects like the Telegraph Set (page 191) that you use several dry cells in series.

To connect lamps in series, run a short piece of wire from one screw on a lamp to a screw on the next and so on. Run a long wire from the second screw on the last lamp to the dry cell.

Unscrew one of the bulbs in the series. Do they all go out? Why? Trace the circuit from one terminal of the dry cell back to the other terminal.

WIRING A PARALLEL CIRCUIT

Materials you'll need:
3 dry cells, 3 miniature lamps, bell wire

You can also do three kinds of parallel wiring. You can wire either lamps or dry cells in parallel, or both.

When dry cells are wired in parallel, the voltage being supplied to the circuit is no more than would be supplied by a single dry cell.

Connect three dry cells in parallel by attaching all three of the center terminals to one wire (be sure to scrape off insulation at places of attachment), and all outside terminals to another wire. Connect the ends of the wires to a lamp. Notice that you can disconnect any one or two of the cells without changing the brightness of the lamp.

Wire lamps in parallel by running one wire down the side of all three sockets and a second wire down the other three. Unscrew one bulb. Do the others go out? Why not? Can you trace a complete circuit through each lamp independent of the others?

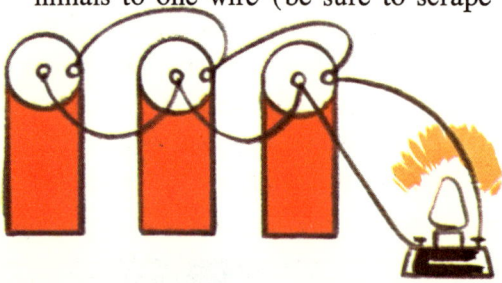

ELECTRICAL WIRING

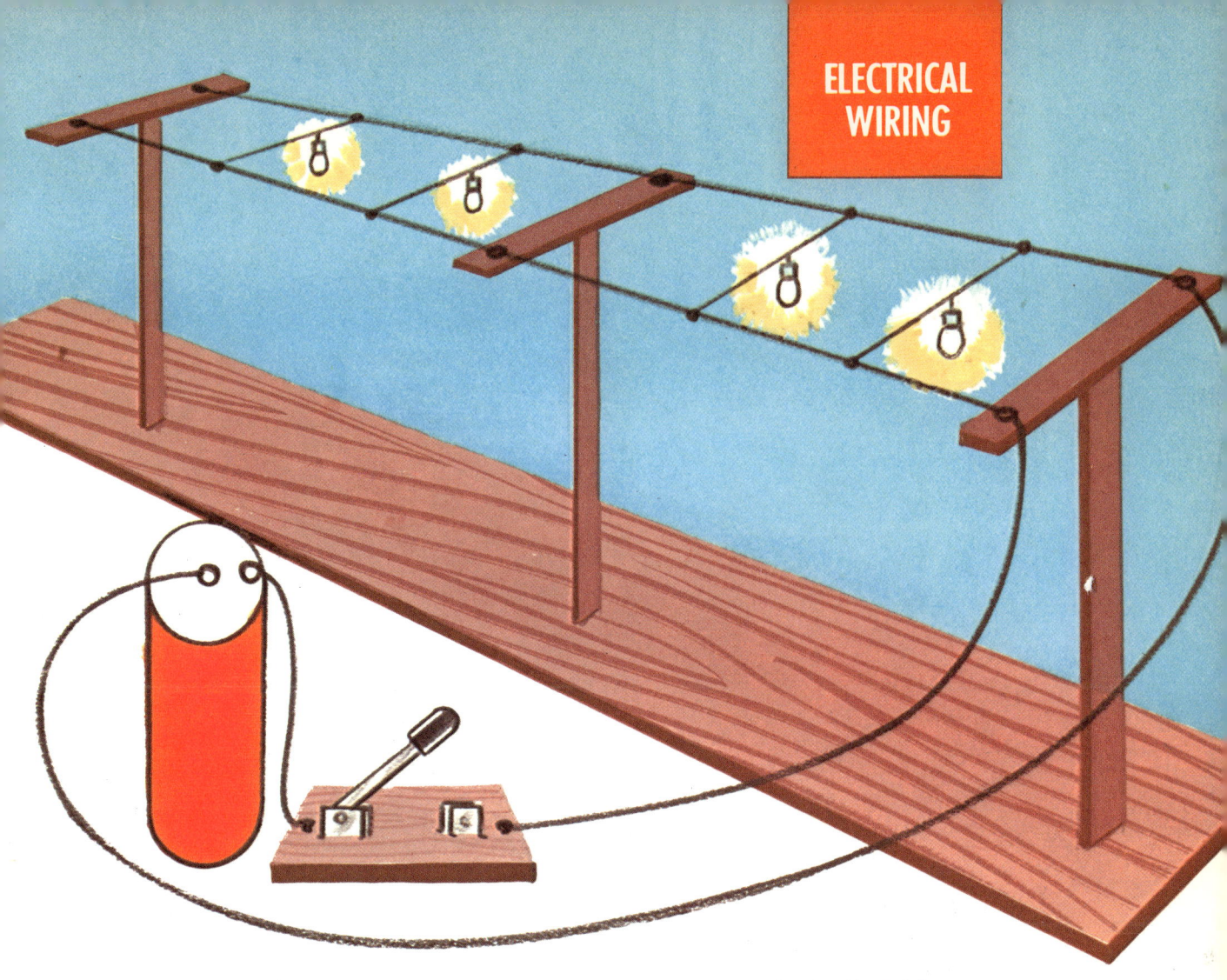

MAKING A MODEL STREET LIGHTING SYSTEM

Materials you'll need:
dry cell battery, simple electric switch, bell wire, small metal screws, Christmas tree light sockets and bulbs, ½-inch square sticks, electrician's tape

A model train lay-out or miniature town will be more realistic with a lighting system on its streets. If you are lighting a model town, be certain the system is in proper proportion to your houses, stores, etc. (Utility poles are usually about as high as a two-story house.) You will achieve more realism by using round dowels instead of square ones but attaching the cross bars is somewhat more difficult with round than square material.

If you are simply making a demonstration model, tack a stick about two and one-half to four inches long to the top of a piece six to ten inches long forming a "T". Put two screws near the tips of the cross bar for use in holding the wires. Now, following the diagram, string your poles with bell wire from one dry cell pole back to the switch (see page 188) and to the other pole. Using short pieces of wire attached to Christmas tree light sockets, remove the insulation from the lines at even intervals and tape bare ends of the socket wires at each of these points. Throw the switch when you have finished wiring and putting in the bulbs. Your model system is complete.

ELECTRICITY

MAKING A SIMPLE ELECTRIC CELL FROM A LIME

Materials you'll need:
  1 lime, 1 strip of zinc, 1 strip of copper

This is one of the simplest electric cells. An electric cell actually produces a current. The basic parts of an electric cell are strips of two different metals and a chemical (called an *electrolyte*) which conducts a current. The lime juice, since it is an acid, is an electrolyte.

You can buy the metal strips at any toy or hobby shop which sells chemicals. Roll the lime in order to make it juicy inside. Insert the two strips, making sure they do not touch inside the lime. Now touch the ends of both strips at the same time with your tongue. You should be able to feel a slight tingling sensation which means a current is flowing. It is probably not enough current to be detected by a galvanometer.

MAKING A STRONGER ELECTRIC CELL

Materials you'll need:
  glass of water, ammonium chloride, zinc strip, wire, carbon rod, galvanometer

Chemical energy producing an electrical force similar to that of a flashlight battery can be easily demonstrated. Mix a tablespoon of ammonium chloride in a glass of water. Attach one wire from a homemade galvanometer (see page 97) to the zinc strip and the other to the carbon rod. An excess of electrons results from the chemical reaction of the salt solution and the zinc strip. These electrons leave the zinc strip and travel over the wire. They form a current of electricity which can be detected by the galvanometer. It is not strong enough to light a small lamp.

82

ELECTRICITY

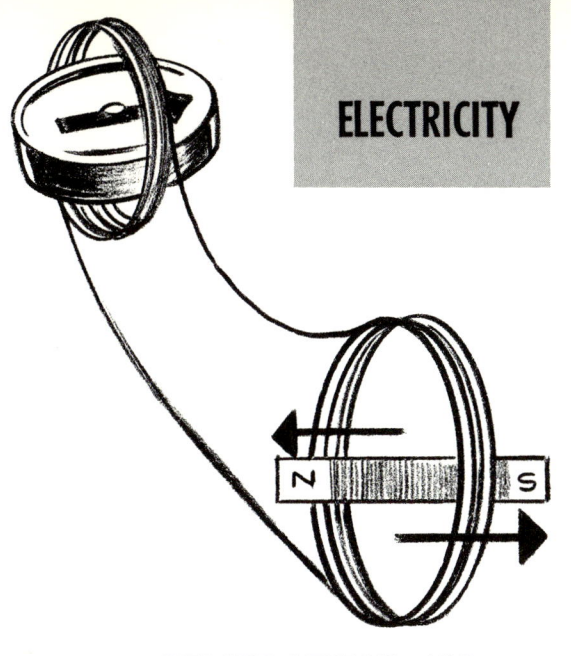

GENERATING AN ELECTRIC CURRENT

Materials you'll need:
homemade galvanometer, coil of bell wire, bar magnet

Whenever magnetic lines of force (a magnetic field) are cut by a coil of wire, a current is set up in the coil.

You will need a very sensitive instrument to detect the small amount of current produced by your generator. You can make a galvanometer (a current detector) by following the instructions on page 97. You will have to put a compass inside a coil of bell wire on this galvanometer.

Attach another coil of wire to the coil around the compass. The connecting wires should be at least five feet long so that the magnet isn't close enough to the compass to affect it directly.

Move a magnet rapidly in and out of the coil while you watch the current detector. Does the needle move? If it does, it indicates that you are generating a current in the coil by moving the magnet in and out of it. Does the same thing happen when you hold the magnet still and move the coil on and off the pole of the magnet?

ELECTROLYTES

DISCOVERING ELECTROLYTES

Materials you'll need:
dry cells, light receptacle, bell wire, glass, salt, sugar, baking powder, soda, vinegar, ink, lemon juice, apple juice

When certain materials dissolve in water they will dissociate (separate) into positively and negatively charged ions. The solution—an electrolyte—will now conduct an electric current.

Follow the diagram in connecting three or four dry cells and the light receptacle. Remove the insulation from the free ends of the bell wire. These will be placed into a glass to test the conductivity of several solutions. If the solution is an electrolyte the bulb will light up. Make a solution of each of these materials: salt, sugar, baking powder, soda, vinegar, ink, lemon juice, and apple juice. Test them separately in the circuit arrangement. Which ones are electrolytes?

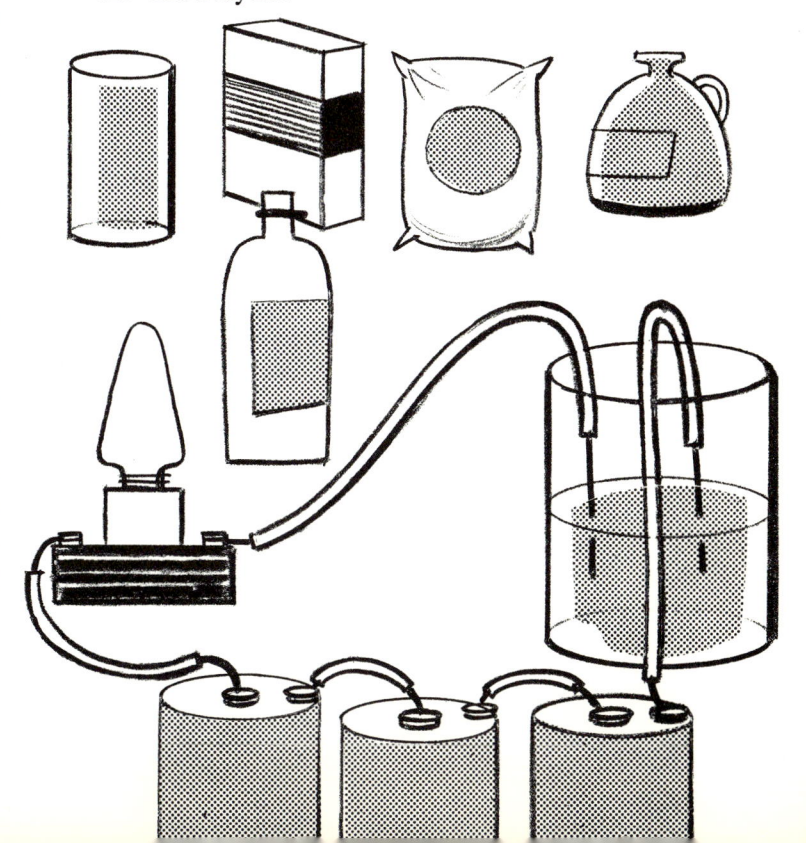

ELECTROMAGNET

MAKING A SIMPLE ELECTROMAGNET

Materials you'll need:
  dry cell, large nail or bolt, 3 or 4 feet of bell wire

You can make a piece of iron into a temporary magnet by wrapping bell wire tightly around it and connecting the wire ends to a dry cell. When both ends are connected current flows through the wire and the iron will act like a magnet—picking up paper clips or tacks. If one end is disconnected, the bolt is no longer magnetic.

Increasing the number of turns of wire around the spike increases its magnetic force. It will pick up more tacks. Test the spike to see if it has magnetic poles (see page 131). Then send the current through the coil in the opposite direction by reversing the wire connections on the dry cell. What happens to the polarity?

ELECTROSCOPE

DETECTING AN ELECTRICAL CHARGE

Materials you'll need:
  3" by 10" strip of newspaper, ruler, piece of fur or wool, comb, jar, waxed cork, copper wire, aluminum foil

An electroscope is an instrument which detects an electrical charge on an object. You can make your own in either of the following ways. Crease the newspaper and then spread it out on the floor—crease up—and rub the surface hard with the piece of fur. Insert a ruler in the crease and hold up the paper. The ends will fly apart, showing that they have like negative charges. Now rub a rubber or plastic comb with the fur and hold it between the leaves of the paper. What kind of a charge does the comb have?

A more complex electroscope requires a large glass jar and a cork soaked with wax which fits the jar exactly. Make a hook on the end of the copper wire large enough to hold a strip of foil. The foil from a stick of gum (if separated from the paper) works best because it is thin and light. Push the straight end of the wire through the cork so that it is outside of the bottle. When a charged body is brought near the upper end of the wire, the foil leaves will fly apart.

EMBRYOLOGY

WATCHING CHANGES IN CHICK EMBRYOS

Materials you'll need:
homemade incubator, fertile chicken eggs, alcohol, capped jars

If you want to observe the changes that take place in the development of an animal, this project will be very exciting. One and a half days after fertilization the chick's heart is formed and beating. In two and a half days the head is almost developed. In four days the eyes and limb buds can be seen. Every day for 21 days the animal develops further until it is ready to hatch. Incubate some chicken eggs and see for yourself.

Place two dozen fertile chicken eggs in a commercial incubator or a homemade one (see page 113 for directions). Secure a bottle of rubbing alcohol to be used as a preservative for the chick embryos. Starting on the third day of incubation, carefully break open an egg. Gently remove the embryo from the yolk and put it in a small bottle of preservative. Continue breaking one every day for eighteen days. Observe the changes that occur in the embryonic development from egg to chick. Record what you see. Take care of the chicks that hatch.

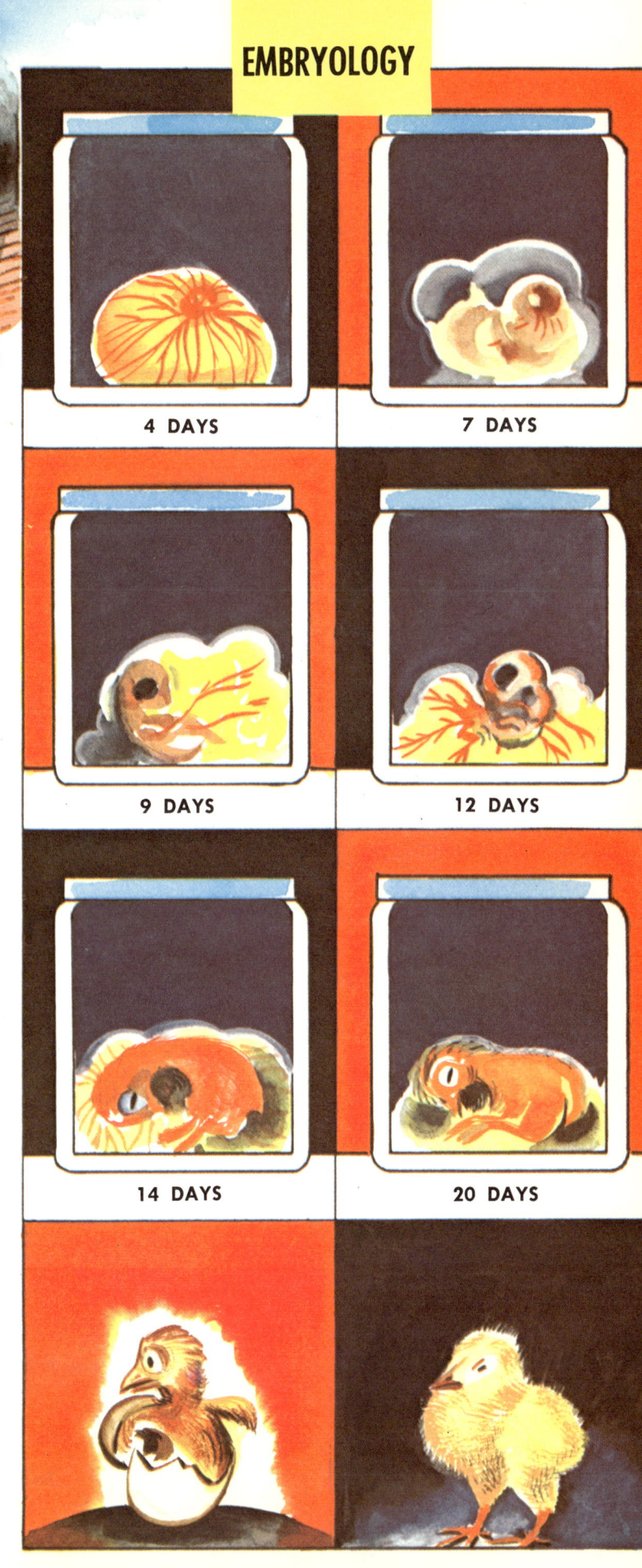

4 DAYS

7 DAYS

9 DAYS

12 DAYS

14 DAYS

20 DAYS

ENZYMES

TESTING AN ENZYME

Materials you'll need:
egg, pepsin, hydrochloric acid, milk, test tube

When you eat certain foods the chemical substances in your stomach will speed up chemical reactions in the breakdown of the food. These organic catalysts are called *enzymes*. Test their action on an egg to see how they work in your stomach.

Break an egg and separate the yellow from the white. Pour just the white part of the egg into a test tube. Hold the tube over a flame until the white is cooked. Mark the level of the egg in the test tube. Lay it in a pan of water to which one stomach enzyme, pepsin, has been added. After one day observe the results.

Now carefully add a few drops of dilute hydrochloric acid to the water and pepsin solution. Let it stand for a second day and observe the change. Pepsin is an enzyme in the stomach that breaks down proteins into simpler materials. However, it is not effective unless hydrochloric acid is present.

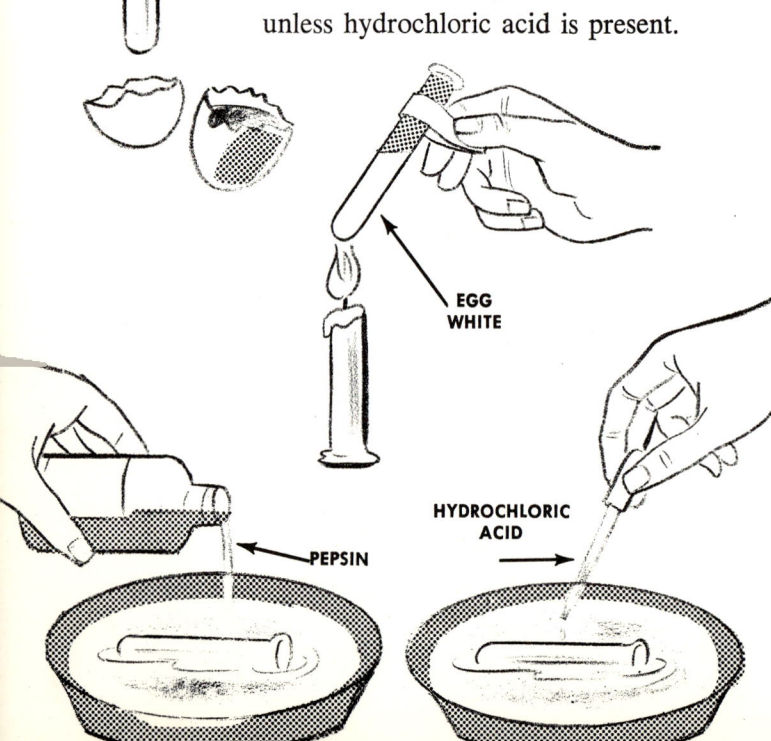

EQUILIBRIUM

ESTABLISHING PHYSICAL EQUILIBRIUM

Materials you'll need:
iodine crystals, bottle, cork

When the rates of two reactions are equal and their effects are opposite, it appears that the reaction has stopped. Actually, *equilibrium* (balance) has been established.

Place some iodine crystals in a bottle. Push a cork tightly into the neck of the bottle. After a short period, some of the iodine evaporates and the bottle fills with a purple-colored gas. Later, the color of the gas no longer changes. What has happened is that a particle of iodine, an iodine molecule, has escaped the crystal as gas, and one of the gaseous molecules has collided with the solid material and stuck. Even though there is a change, one cannot observe this change. When the number of molecules escaping the surface equals the number of molecules striking the surface and sticking, equilibrium is established.

EROSION

EVAPORATION

DISCOVERING HOW TO SAVE OUR TOPSOIL

Materials you'll need:
3 large aluminum-foil cake pans, rubber tube, clay, soil and sand mixture, topsoil, cereal grain, wood blocks, dishes

Get three large aluminum-foil cake pans and cut a hole near the top rim on one side of each pan. Tape a piece of rubber tube to each hole. Put layers of clay and soil and sand mixture in each. Add a top layer of rich topsoil. Rest one end of each pan on a block of wood to elevate it at a 30-degree angle. Direct the opposite end of each tube into a dish.

In one pan make rows across the width of the pan and plant a cereal grain—wheat, oats, or barley. In the second pan make rows the length of the pan and plant the same crop. Do not plant anything in the third field.

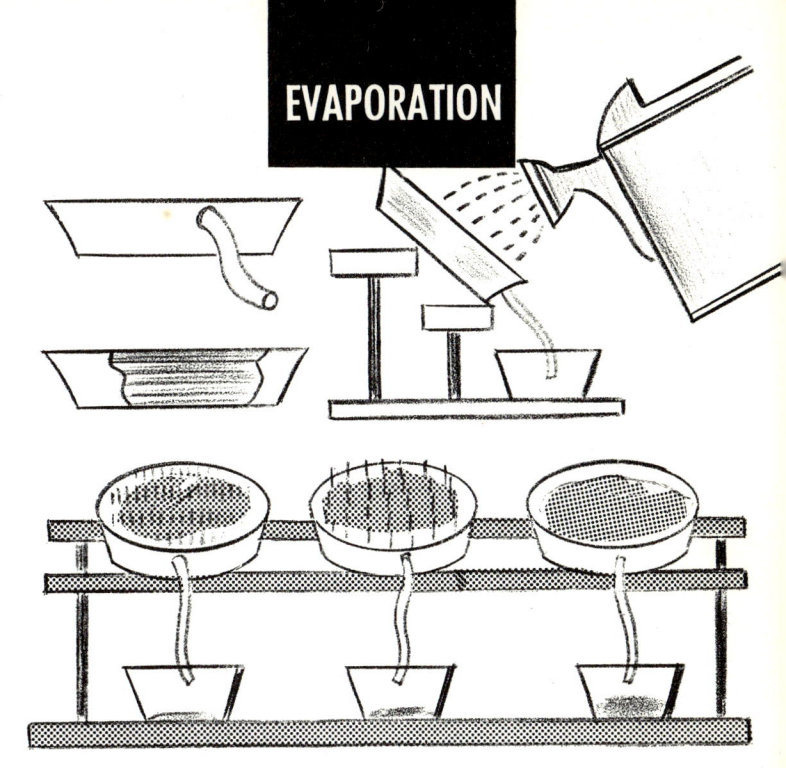

When the seedlings are about two inches tall, use a sprinkling can to pour the same amount of water (rain) over each pan. What happens to the topsoil in each case? Measure the amount of soil that collects in the dishes. Do you see how topsoil can be conserved?

TESTING THE FACTORS OF EVAPORATION

Materials you'll need:
pans, water, cup, olive jar, bowl, electric fan

Water molecules are constantly moving in all directions and at all speeds. The molecules of surface water in a lake, stream, or dish are moving so fast they escape into the air as vapor. This change from liquid to gas is called *evaporation*. Several factors affect the speed of this process.

Pour a cup of water in a pan and set it to one side. Put a cup of water in a second pan. Place this one over a source of heat for half an hour. Measure the amount of water left in both pans at the end of that time. What is the difference? Why?

Pour a cup of water in each of three different sized containers—an olive jar, a bowl, and a cake pan. Let these stand for one day. Measure the amount of water left in each container. Does the amount of surface exposed to the air affect the rate of evaporation?

Place an electric fan in front of a pan containing one cup of water. Put another pan with an equal amount of liquid on the far side of the room away from the breeze. Turn on the fan for one hour. Measure the amount of liquid left in the two containers. Which has less? Will the movement of air near water affect the rate of evaporation?

EXPANSION

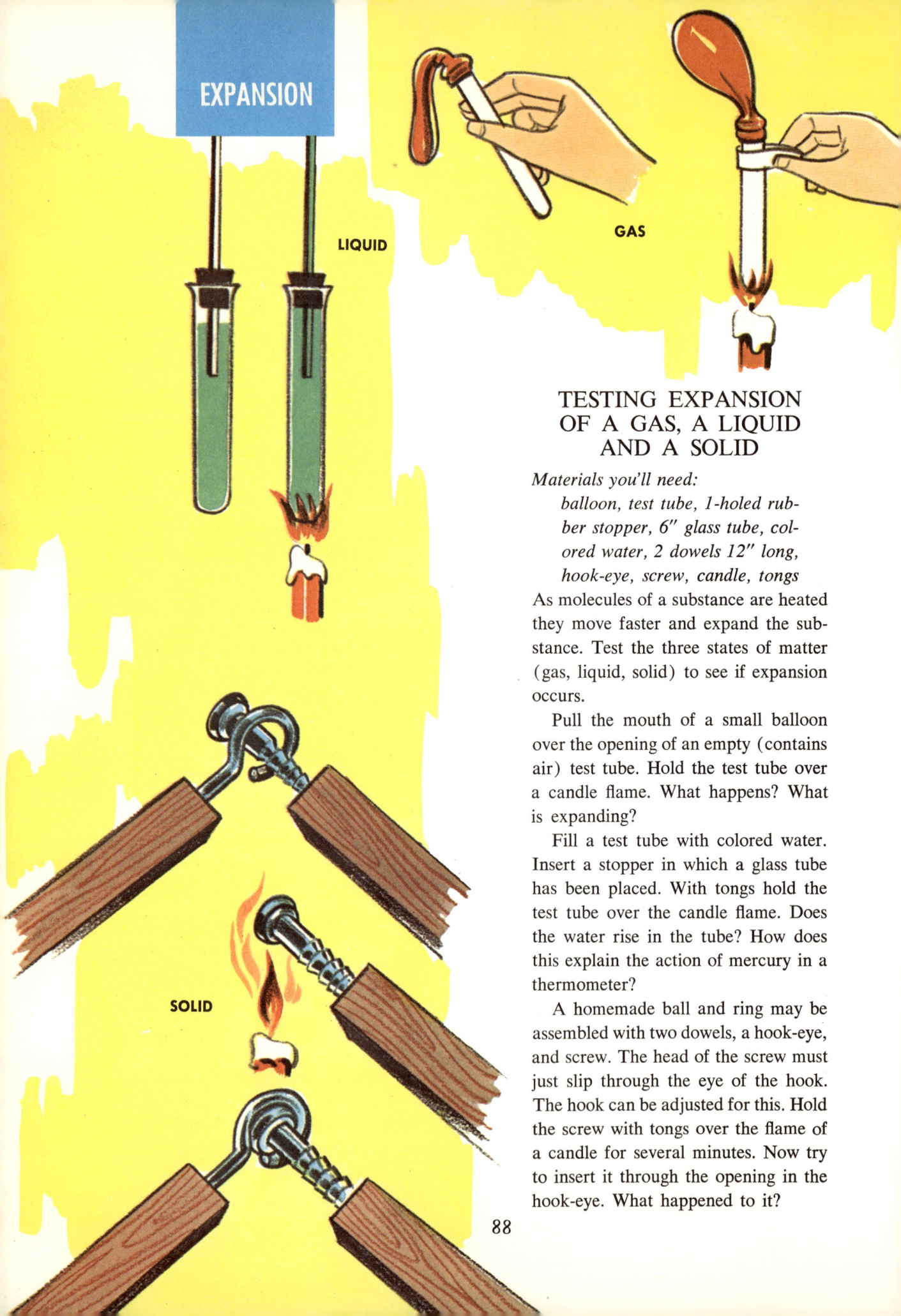

LIQUID

GAS

SOLID

TESTING EXPANSION OF A GAS, A LIQUID AND A SOLID

Materials you'll need:
balloon, test tube, 1-holed rubber stopper, 6" glass tube, colored water, 2 dowels 12" long, hook-eye, screw, candle, tongs

As molecules of a substance are heated they move faster and expand the substance. Test the three states of matter (gas, liquid, solid) to see if expansion occurs.

Pull the mouth of a small balloon over the opening of an empty (contains air) test tube. Hold the test tube over a candle flame. What happens? What is expanding?

Fill a test tube with colored water. Insert a stopper in which a glass tube has been placed. With tongs hold the test tube over the candle flame. Does the water rise in the tube? How does this explain the action of mercury in a thermometer?

A homemade ball and ring may be assembled with two dowels, a hook-eye, and screw. The head of the screw must just slip through the eye of the hook. The hook can be adjusted for this. Hold the screw with tongs over the flame of a candle for several minutes. Now try to insert it through the opening in the hook-eye. What happened to it?

EYES

DISCOVERING FUNCTIONS OF THE EYES

Materials you'll need:
colored construction paper, mirror, flashlight

Are you right-eyed or left-eyed? Hold your finger out in front of you. Line it up with some object across the room. Close your left eye. Now open your left eye and close your right eye. At which time did it appear that your finger jumped to the side? If the finger stays lined up with the object when your right eye is open, you are right-eyed.

If you have blue eyes it means the iris is blue. The iris is the covering in front of the eye. It is an extension of the choroid coat. The size of the opening in it is regulated by muscles. The amount of light entering causes the muscles to constrict or relax involuntarily. Look into a mirror. Note the size of the pupils. They are the black circles in the center. Now have someone shine a flashlight into your face. Watch the size of your pupils. Did the iris close down the opening? How does this help you to see better?

The point on the retina where the optic nerve enters is called the *blind spot* since it lacks nerve endings. When the light rays from an object hit this spot the impulse is not received. Put two small (⅛ inch) dark squares on a sheet of light-colored paper. Hold this sheet at arm's length in front of your face. Close the right eye and stare at the right square. Bring the paper slowly toward your eyes. At what point did the left square disappear?

Do your eyes get tired? Put a small piece of red construction paper on a sheet of white paper. Stare at it for a minute. Switch your gaze to another plain sheet of white paper. What color do you see now? The retina in the back of the eye gets fatigued for red. When red is removed from white all the complementary colors left make green. Experiment with different colors. What color appears on white when your eyes tire of blue? Of yellow?

The nerve endings called *rods* are located in the outer rim of the retina. They distinguish light and dark. The nerve endings situated in the center of the retina are the *cones* which are stimulated by color. Look straight ahead. Hold a sheet of colored paper at arm's length out to the side of your body. What color does the paper appear to be? Slowly swing your arm forward. At what point can you recognize the color?

FERNS

GROWING TWO GENERATIONS OF A FERN

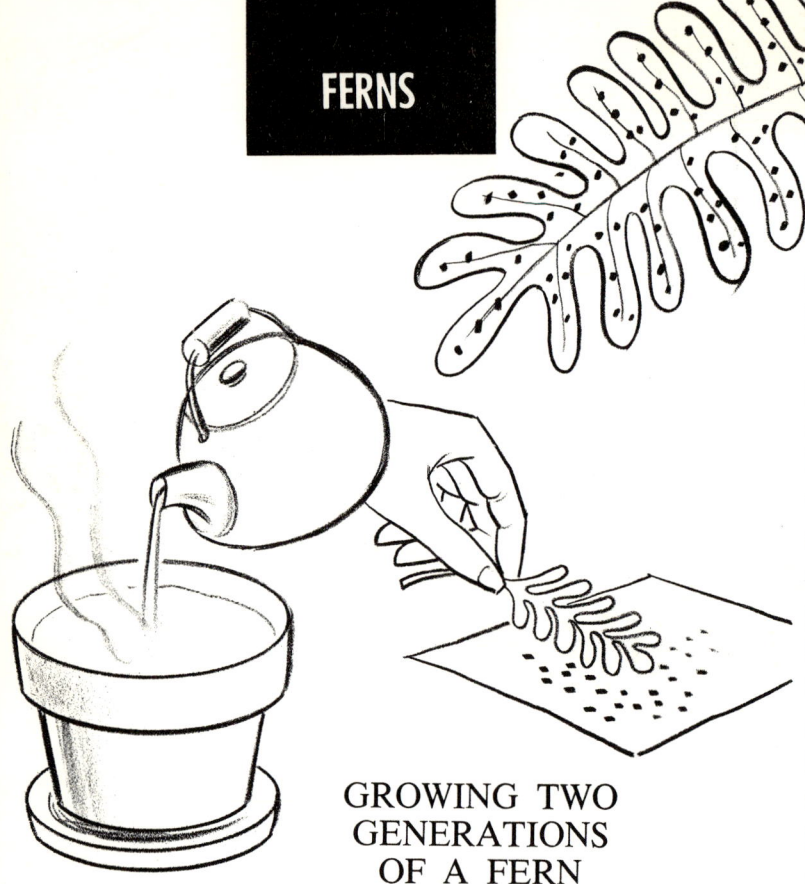

Materials you'll need:
bog terrarium, soil, peat moss, sand, boiling water, pot, saucer, piece of plastic

A fern has to go through two generations to complete its life cycle. The *asexual plant* is the familiar one you will see growing in the woods. The *sexual plant* is a tiny, heart-shaped plant seldom seen by nature lovers. You can grow both plants if you follow the directions carefully.

The *sporophyte* generation (asexual) will thrive well in a bog terrarium. Have the new home established before you go fern hunting. Ferns are found in wooded areas along the banks of streams or in a marshy environment. Dig up the plant being sure the entire underground stem is taken with it. Wrap it in wet newspaper and transfer the plant to a woodland terrarium (see page 194). Keep the terrarium in a north window and water frequently.

To grow the second generation, the *gametophyte,* wait until the spores appear on the under side of the fronds. Tap the compound leaf over a sheet of paper and the spores will fall off. Fill a pot with soil and peat moss. Put a layer of sand on the top. Pour boiling water over the whole mixture and the container to destroy any bacteria or mold spores which will attack the germinating fern spores. Let it cool. Sprinkle the spores on the sand, cover the pot with clear plastic or glass, and set the pot in a saucer in order to water from the bottom up. In several weeks the spores will develop into tiny, heart-shaped gametophyte plants. This plant produces eggs and sperms. When a sperm fertilizes an egg, a small fern sporophyte will grow out of this plant. When it is several inches tall transfer it to the bog terrarium.

90

FINGERPRINTS

MAKING PRINTS OF YOUR FINGERS

Materials you'll need:
    pencil, paper, cellophane tape

The inner layer of the skin or *dermis* has projections which fit into corresponding ridges in the outer layer of skin or *epidermis*. Sometimes these projections or knobs are arranged in rows, as on the tips of the fingers. This makes it possible to make a print of a finger. It is said that no two fingerprints are exactly alike, so fingerprints are helpful in identifying people.

With the side of a pencil lead, make a heavy dark spot on a piece of paper. Rub your finger on this spot until it is black. Press your finger carefully onto the sticky side of a piece of cellophane tape. Fasten the tape to a piece of white paper so that the print shows clearly.

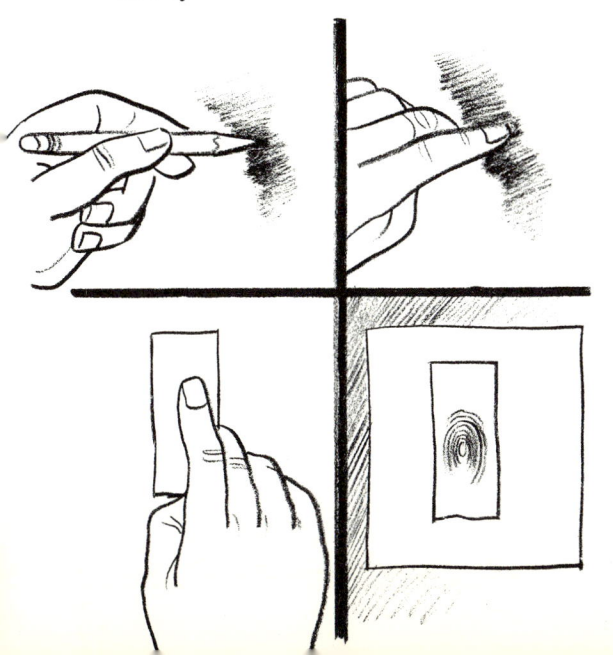

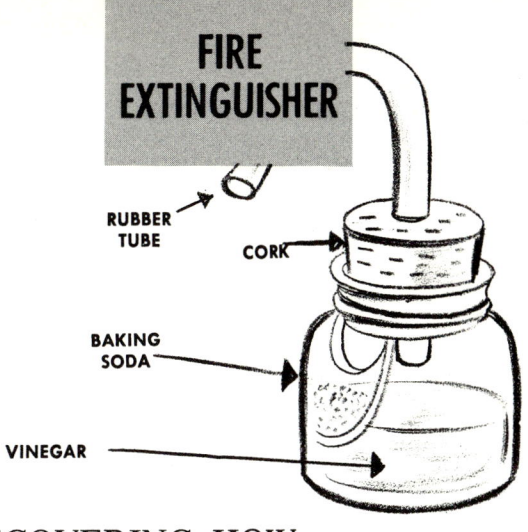

FIRE EXTINGUISHER

DISCOVERING HOW FIRES CAN BE PUT OUT

Materials you'll need:
    ink bottle with well, large cork, rubber tubing, baking soda, vinegar, cookie sheet

You can make a fire extinguisher that demonstrates the way some commercial fire extinguishers work. Your extinguisher will work only on a small fire.

Pour vinegar into the ink bottle until it is half full. Fill the small side well with baking soda. Make a hole through the cork into which the tube fits tightly. Place the cork in the bottle and turn the bottle upside down. Aim the end of the tube at a small fire you have started on a cookie sheet.

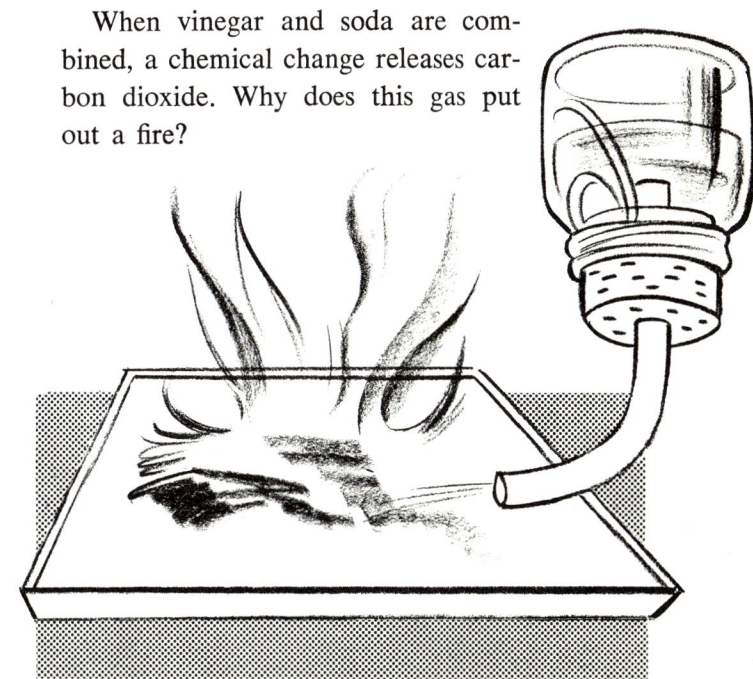

When vinegar and soda are combined, a chemical change releases carbon dioxide. Why does this gas put out a fire?

| FLOWERS | FOG | FOOTPRINTS |

MAKING FOG FORM

Materials you'll need:
   bottle, hot water, ice, alcohol

Fog is a cloud near the ground, produced by warm air coming in contact with cool air. Since cool air cannot hold as much moisture as warm, the moisture condenses in the form of droplets—fog.

Fill a bottle one-third full of very hot water. Add a few drops of alcohol. It vaporizes rapidly, letting you see the reaction more quickly. Place a piece of ice over the bottle mouth. What happens near the neck of the bottle?

DRYING FLOWERS

Materials you'll need:
   borax, large box, flower holder, specimens

Here is a wonderful idea for getting fall and winter bouquets of flowers out of season. Their colors and shapes remain practically unchanged.

The box you use must be taller than the upright flower. Stand the flower in the box using a flower holder to keep it centered and steady. Pour the borax gently around the flower until the flower is buried. Make sure the branches maintain their natural positions. It will take a week for a delicate flower to dry and several weeks to dry a thick, succulent flower. When the specimen is thoroughly dry pour off the borax. Save it to use again.

MAKING PRINTS OF YOUR FEET

Materials you'll need:
   water, baking soda, cotton, white paper, candle

Mix a teaspoon of baking soda with half cup of water. Use the cotton to wet the bottom of one foot completely with the solution. Stand carefully on the wet foot in the center of white paper. Hold the wet footprint six inches above a candle flame and warm the paper carefully.

If your arches are in good shape, the print will look something like the left picture. A "flat foot" (with a flat arch) makes a print like the right picture.

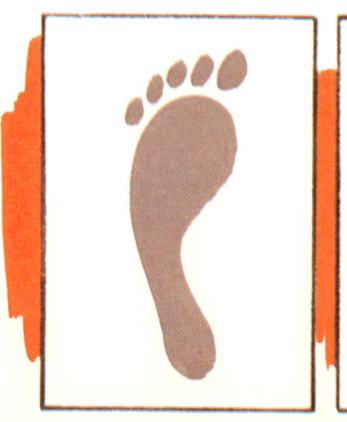

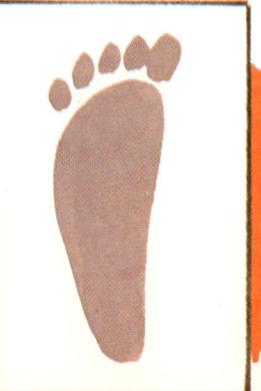

FOSSILS

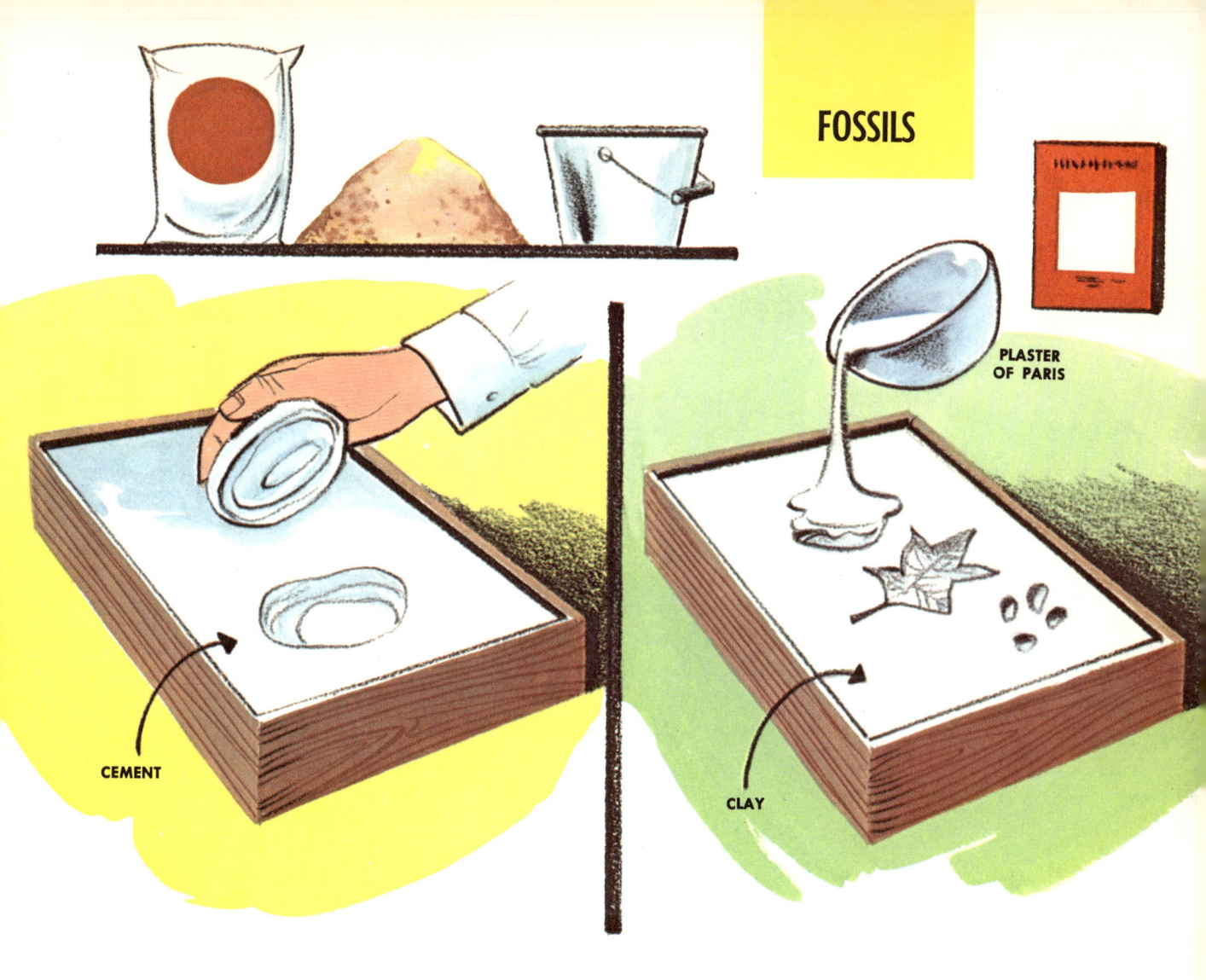

DISCOVERING HOW FOSSILS WERE MADE

Materials you'll need:
cement, sand, water, lime, box, clay, plaster of Paris

Fossils are usually found in three forms: the actual plant or animal, the petrified specimen, or an imprint. While traveling through the country you can visit the petrified forests or find an actual shell or bone of an animal in rock. You can make an imprint such as might have been made by a dinosaur.

Prepare a mixture of equal parts of cement, sand, and lime. Add water until it is about the consistency of thick pudding. This mixture is similar to sandstone—a sedimentary rock which contains many fossils. Pour this into a shallow box cover. Just before it sets press a shell, a leaf, or an animal's foot (dog's paw) into the surface of the mixture. Permit the mixture to harden without disturbing it.

Another way of making fossils is done with clay and plaster of Paris. Push modeling clay into a shallow box. Smooth the surface. Push parts of organic objects, such as leaves or shells, into the clay and remove them. Make a mixture of plaster of Paris and water to the consistency of thick soup. Pour this over the clay and let it set. Remove the cardboard box and clay from the plaster mold. A fossil impression is left on the plaster.

FRICTION

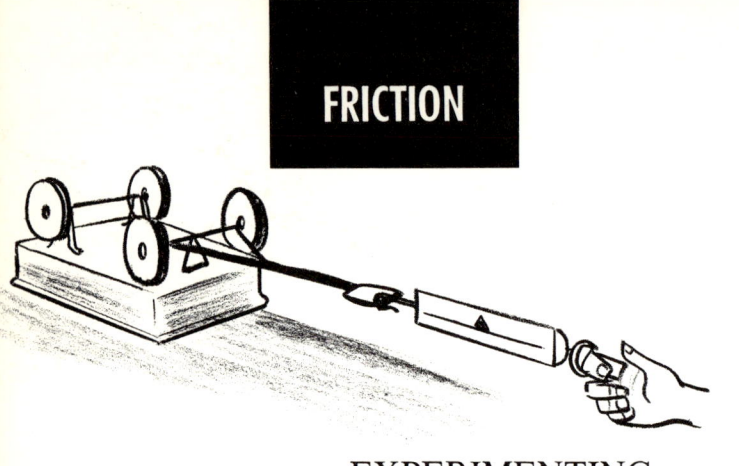

EXPERIMENTING WITH FRICTION

Materials you'll need:
small wagon, spring scale, hand cream, water

The resistance between two moving objects is called *friction*. There is more friction between sliding objects than rolling ones. Water is a form of lubrication—it makes surfaces smoother. This reduces the friction produced.

Turn a small wagon over on its top side. Hook the end of a spring scale in the handle and pull the wagon along the sidewalk. How many pounds of force is necessary to move it? Now put a layer of water on the sidewalk. Repeat the experiment. Did it take less force? What does this prove?

Rub your hands together as fast as possible. They will soon feel warm. Put hand cream on your palms. Rub them again. Does it produce as much heat now? Why?

USING BALL BEARINGS

Materials you'll need:
2 tin cans with deep grooves around tops (such as paint cans), marbles, machine oil

FRUIT FLIES

Set one can down and line the groove around the top with marbles. Now invert the other can over the first so that the marbles fit partly in its grooves, too. Turn the second can. Notice how much more easily it turns than it would if it were resting directly on the other can. You have used marbles in the same way ball bearings are used to reduce friction where one surface rubs against another. What effect does oiling the marbles have on the way the can turns?

RAISING FRUIT FLIES

Materials you'll need:
1 cup water, ¼ cup cornmeal, paper towel, glass jars, cotton, carbon tetrachloride, decayed fruit, hand lens

You may want to raise fruit flies for two reasons. You can use them as food for pet frogs and lizards or you can raise several generations and study the principles of heredity as shown in the characteristics passed on from generation to generation.

Boil the cornmeal and water together for ten minutes. Pour the mixture into a jar and partially cover it by dropping a crumpled paper towel in on top. Place a piece of very ripe fruit on top of the paper. Put a paper funnel in the mouth of the jar. This will prevent flies from coming out once they get into the jar. The fruit flies will just seem to appear from nowhere. They actually come from all over to the decaying fruit.

When several of the tiny flies enter, remove the funnel and close the top with a wad of cotton. The fruit flies will

FRUIT FLIES

lay eggs on the cornmeal. The eggs will hatch into maggots, which will feed on the meal until they are mature. When they are mature they will crawl onto the paper towel and pupate. The adult fruit flies emerge from the pupae. It takes about two weeks to complete the life cycle of the fruit fly.

The next step is to remove a female and a male adult fly. In order to get a virgin female, you may have to take some of the pupae out of the original jar and place each one in a separate jar until it hatches. It takes some practice to be able to distinguish between male and female flies with the hand lens. The male is smaller than the female and its abdomen is black-tipped. The female's abdomen is wider than the male's and it has lines across it rather than a black tip.

Put a pair of flies into a jar containing some of the cornmeal mixture. Allow the female to lay eggs for ten days, then remove both flies. The first eggs will start hatching after twelve days. Count the number of flies which hatch for the next ten days. This is the first generation. Working outdoors, drop a piece of cotton with a little carbon tetrachloride on it into the jar. Remove it after just one minute so that the flies are not killed. Pour out the flies on a white paper and examine them closely with the hand lens. Look for and record characteristics such as white eyes, red eyes, bar eyes, vestigial wings, curved wings, hairy wings, ebony bodies. Mate pairs of this first generation and observe the characteristics of their offspring. Will fruit fly parents with red eyes produce red-eyed offspring?

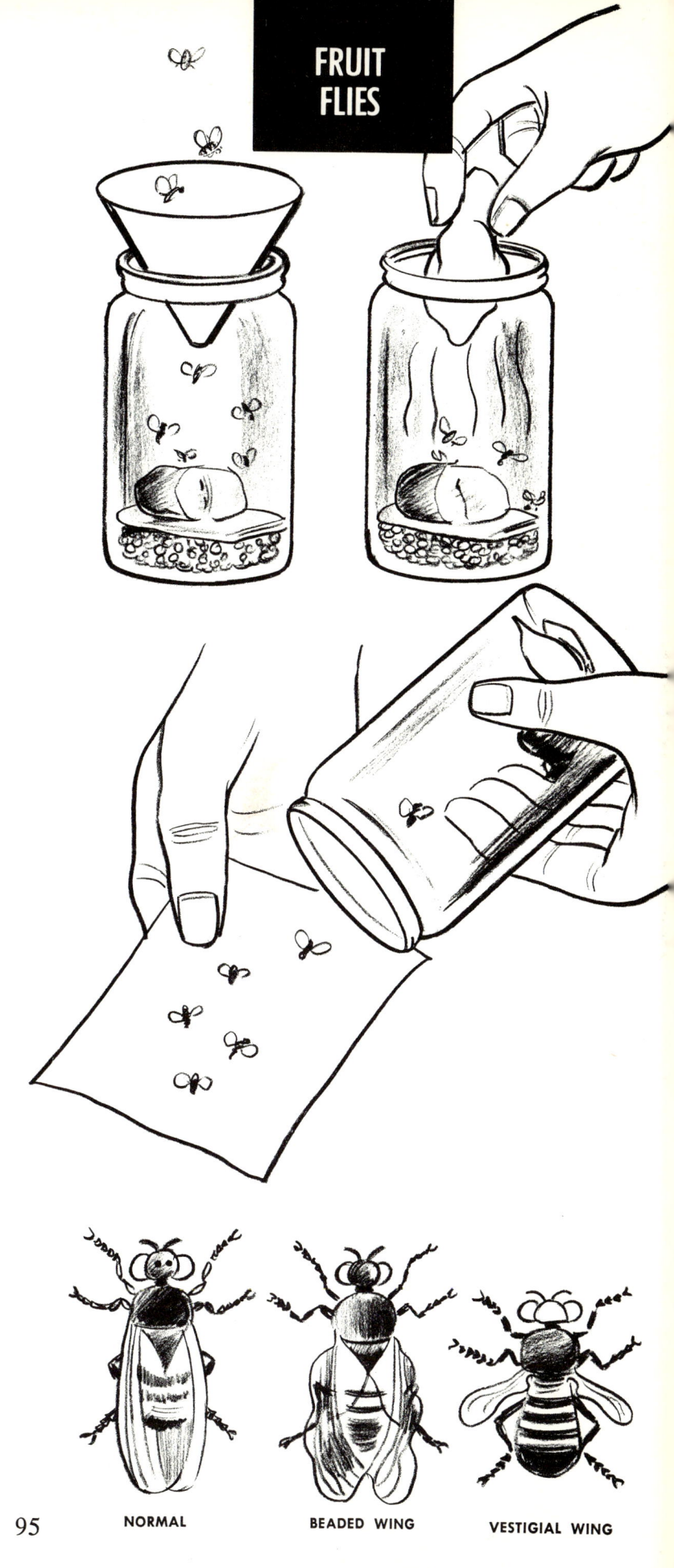

CAUTION!

NORMAL   BEADED WING   VESTIGIAL WING

FUNGUS

FUSE

COLLECTING FUNGI

Materials you'll need:
  glass jars, alcohol, terrarium

Fungi are found almost everywhere and are most successfully collected in the spring or fall months. The fungus, lacking chlorophyll, must take its nourishment from its *host,* the material to which it attaches itself. The *parasite* fungus takes life from living organisms and the *saprophyte* fungus lives on dead or decayed material.

Look for mushrooms, tree brackets, puffballs, toadstools, morels, lichen, smut, mold, rust, mildew. Some grow on trees and bushes, some on river banks, in open fields, and still others on dead logs. Dry fungi may be put in jars or boxes. Fleshy fungi should be dried or placed in alcohol.

A living fungus collection may be raised in a terrarium—half woodland and half bog environment (see page 194). The fungi grow best in warm, damp places. It is necessary to use care in digging them up from their natural habitat. Take a clump of soil and vegetation with their underground parts. Many fungi have root-like structures called *rhizoids* or *mycelium* that may break. Keep the terrarium out of direct sunlight and water it often.

TESTING THE JOB OF A FUSE

Materials you'll need:
  3 dry cells, bell wire, metal foil, 2 needles, 2 corks, light receptacle

Have you ever heard anyone say, "We just blew a fuse"? A fuse is a safety device in the electrical system of your house. If you put too many electrical appliances, such as lamps and toasters, on one circuit, the wires get hot. If people didn't use fuses or circuit breakers, fires could start.

Connect three dry cells in series with bell wire (see page 80). Cut a small strip of metal foil shaped like an hour glass. This will represent the fuse. Insert a needle through each end of the strip. Stick the needles into the top of two corks. With a piece of bell wire connect the first dry cell to one needle. Connect the wire leading from the third cell to one post on a light receptacle. Run a wire from the other post on the light socket to the second needle. What happens when the heat becomes intense, overloading the circuit?

GALVANOMETER

CONSTRUCTING A GALVANOMETER TO DETECT A CURRENT

Materials you'll need:

bell wire, water glass, wood, nail, bar magnet, string, compass, dry cell

A galvanometer is a device used to detect an electric current. There are a number of activities in this book in which so little current is involved that it will not light a small bulb. You will need this instrument to detect such a small current.

Wrap twenty-five feet of bell wire around a water glass, then slip the glass out from the wire coil. Leave about a foot of wire free on each end of the coil. Nail two small tracks of wood on to a block of wood. The coil of wire will rest on this base.

Magnetize a thin finishing nail by stroking one end in one direction only with the south end of a bar magnet. Stroke the other end of the nail in the opposite direction only with the north end of the magnet. Hang the nail by a string from the top center part of the wire coil. You could lay an ordinary compass in the coil instead of the nail. Arrange the coil so that it is parallel to the earth's poles. The compass needle will also point north and south. Connect the two ends of wire from the coil to a dry cell and use when you need to detect a very small current. The nail will swing to a position parallel to the coil of wire, indicating that current is being generated.

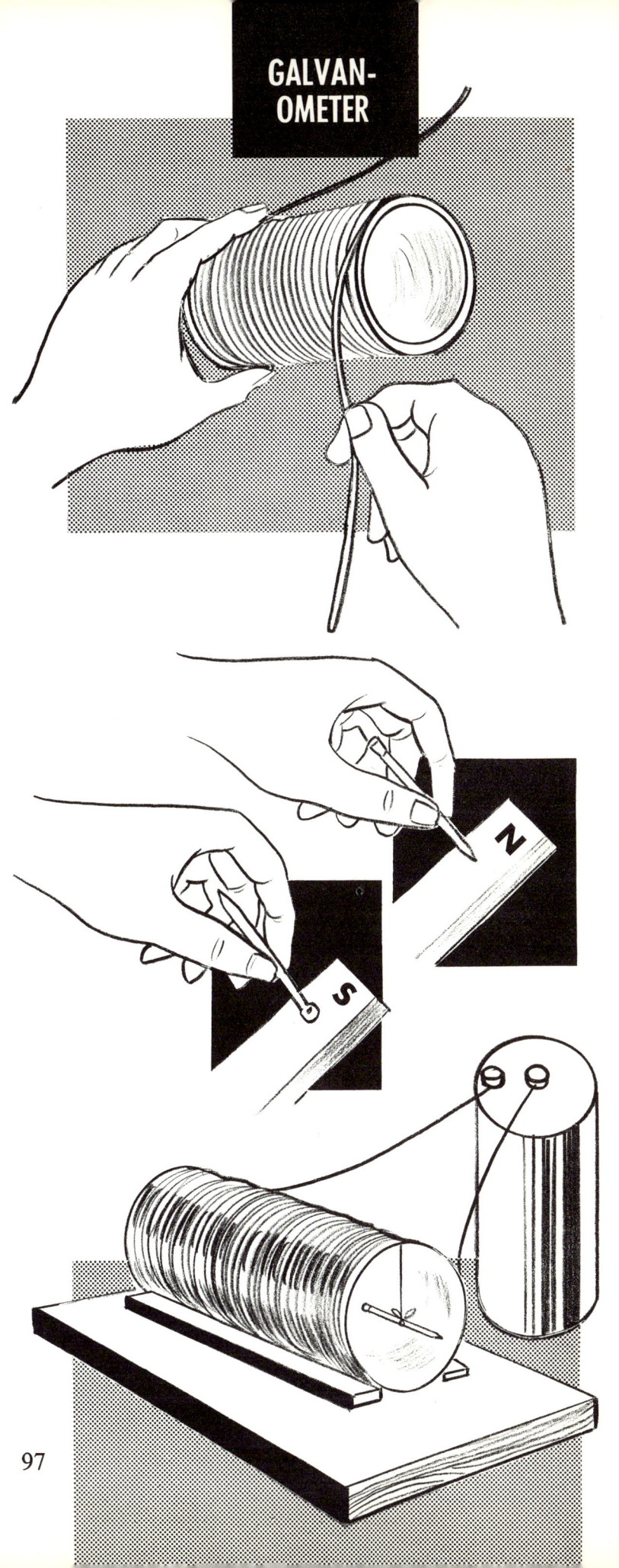

GARDENING

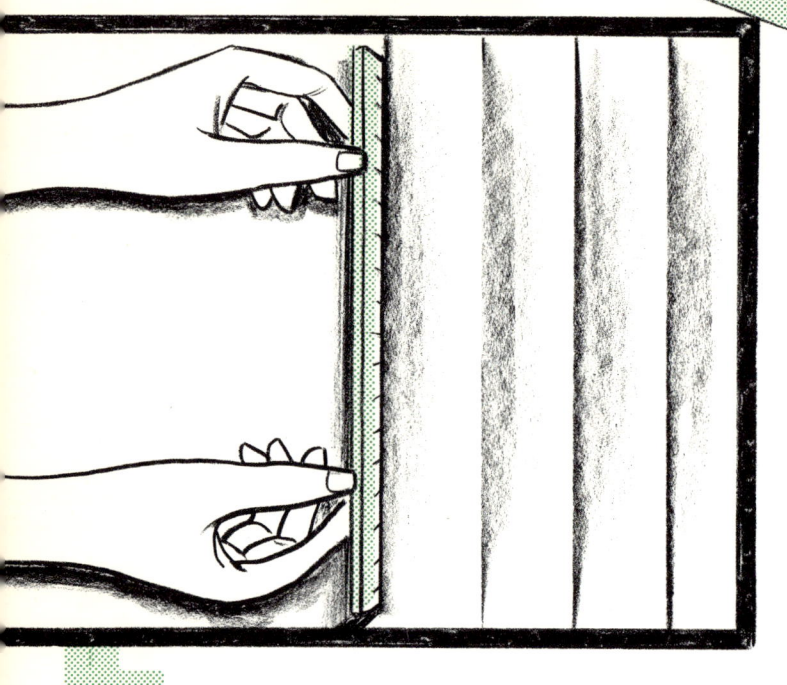

PLANTING INDOOR GARDEN FLATS

Materials you'll need:
   low wooden boxes or garden flats, newspaper, soil, sand, peat moss, ruler, gravel, sphagnum moss, seeds, soil-test kit

If you plan to have an outdoor garden, you may want to start growing plants for it indoors in early spring. You can buy garden flats at a greenhouse or use any low wooden box, preferably cedar or redwood. Do not use creosote or other preservative on wood because it causes the roots of the plants to rot. Line the box with newspaper or aluminum foil to prevent loss of soil through the cracks.

Put a layer of gravel or broken flower pot in the bottom of the flat. This will allow water to drain properly. Sprinkle sphagnum moss over this. Then add two inches or more, depending on the depth of the box, of a mixture of two parts soil, one part sand, and one part peat moss. Run a test on the soil. Just because soil is black does not mean that it is rich.

Plant seeds, such as zinnias, that are recommended for indoor planting. Make the rows two and one-half inches apart with a ruler's edge. Be careful not to plant the seeds too deep. After the seeds are in, press the soil down with a flat object. Water well but be careful not to water so heavily that the seeds are washed out of their rows. Place the flats in a dark warm room. If one isn't available, place newspaper over the flat. Water daily until the plants are up above the ground. Then bring them into the light and water less frequently. If the rows seem too crowded, thin out the plants by removing some of them. When the weather is warm, transplant the seedlings outside.

PLANTING A GARDEN OUTDOORS

Materials you'll need:
   sunny plot of ground, tools, fertilizer, seed-protectant dust, pest sprays, soil-test kit, selected seeds and seedlings

Plan to spend a good deal of time working on your outdoor flower or vegetable garden. Things necessary for a successful garden are: good seeds, adequate fertilizer, periodic cultivation, and a well-prepared seedbed.

You must find a place for it which has sun most of the day and which is close to a ready water supply. The first step is to test and condition the soil, adding whatever ingredients are needed for growth. Three primary foods needed

GARDENING

by growing plants are nitrogen, phosphate, and potash. An inexpensive soil-test kit contains the chemicals and color chart necessary to run a test on the soil. Commercial fertilizer or your own homemade compost pile (see page 66) will help rebuild the soil. Add this before cultivating to get the needed food at varying depths in the ground.

Next, plan whether you want to grow flowers or vegetables. Lay your design out on paper. If you grow flowers, you'll want to consider height of plant, time of flowering and color of bloom when you plan the arrangement.

Be sure to buy healthy seeds or plants. To protect your seedlings against disease, root rot, and rodents, use a seed-protectant dust. Put a little of this powder in a jar with the seeds and shake gently till they are coated with dust.

Spade down six to eight inches in the garden area. Break up small lumps of soil and remove big lumps, stones and sticks. Add the needed fertilizer and work it in. Finally, rake and smooth the soil level. Avoid tramping down the soil in the row areas.

Now plant the seeds or transplant the seedlings according to the directions on the package. Use string and stakes to mark off the rows. Allow thirty inches between rows for easy cultivation. As the plants grow they must be watered well at regular intervals. Never just sprinkle the garden. Keep the soil loose around the plants and pull all weeds as they appear. They will sap the food and water supply from your growing plants. Watch the plants for signs of disease and insect pests. You may need to spray with insecticide.

GARDENING

GAS

MAKING A GREENHOUSE

Materials you'll need:
 5 old storm windows, hinges, hook and eye, shelves

It is possible to grow tropical plants such as croton, orchids, caladium, sundew, Venus' flytrap, and pitcher plant indoors if you live in a cold climate. They need more moisture from the air than an ordinary room provides. It is not difficult to build a greenhouse that provides the proper atmosphere.

Plan to put it on the south side of the room where it will get morning sun. Use the storm windows for the sides of the greenhouse. Stand three of them on end and nail together to form three sides of the greenhouse. The fourth window is used as a door. Hinge it to one of the sides and secure it with a hook and eye. Half of a storm window will form the top of the structure and is nailed to the three side walls. You can build shelves on one side for the small potted plants. Tall plants can be placed on the floor. Keep the plants well watered and spray the inside of the greenhouse with water several times a week.

COMPARING GASES

Materials you'll need:
 pop bottles, vinegar, baking soda, zinc strips, hydrochloric acid, balloons

Gases, like liquids and solids, occupy space and have weight. Certain gases are heavier than air and others are lighter. Run these two tests and see if you can detect which one is heavier. *Do this test only with an adult helping.*

To fill a balloon with carbon dioxide, pour two inches of vinegar into a pop bottle. Add two tablespoons of baking soda to this and immediately pull the mouth of a balloon over the mouth of the bottle. The balloon will fill up with carbon dioxide. Tie off the balloon.

To fill a second balloon with hydrogen gas, put several strips of zinc in the bottom of a pop bottle. Pour a dilute solution of hydrochloric acid into the bottle. Do not get any acid on your hands or clothes. Pull the mouth of a balloon over the mouth of the bottle. Soon the balloon will fill up with hydrogen. Tie off the balloon.

Hold the two balloons up in the air and release them at the same time. One balloon will go up and the other will go down. Which gas is lighter than air? Which one is heavier than air?

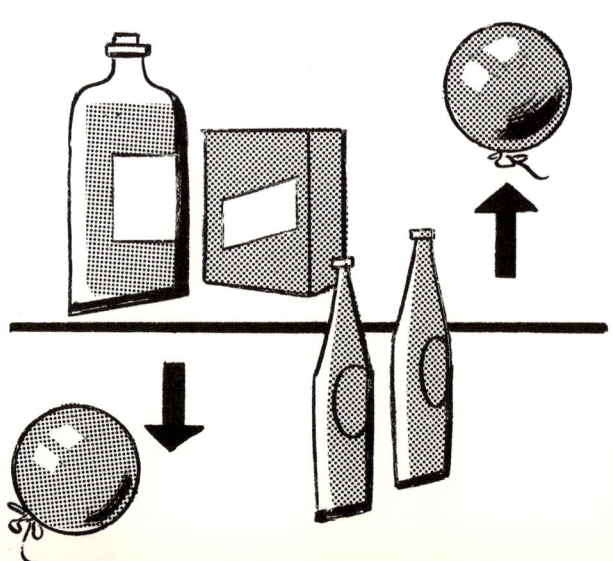

CAUTION!

GERMINATION

TESTING THE GERMINATION OF SEEDS

Materials you'll need:
  variety of seeds, 8 saucers, 2 pieces of glass, cotton, rectangular cake pan

Decide upon one kind of seed to use for all experiments. You will test the effects of four different factors on germination: temperature, amount of light, water, and oxygen. When testing one factor it is important to remember to keep the other three factors the same.

Place a blotter or layer of absorbent cotton in the bottom of each of eight dishes. Put a dozen seeds on top. Use two dishes for each of the four factors. One dish will be the experimental one while the other is the control.

Water test: Water seeds in dish number 1, but do not water dish number 2;

Temperature test: Keep seeds number 3 in a pan of ice water and seeds number 4 in a warm place;

Light test: Put seeds number 5 in a dark cupboard and seeds number 6 in a sunny window;

Air test: Leave seeds number 7 open to the air but put a sheet of glass or clear plastic over seeds number 8.

Observe the rate of germination daily. What happens to each pair? Do seeds grow better in warm or cold places, in light or dark, with or without moisture and air? Record your results.

Now that you have found out the best conditions for germination, test the rate of germination with a variety of different seeds, such as radish, corn, bean, sunflower, grass, apple, and acorn. Soak all the seeds overnight to help loosen their seed coats. Make a long glass sandwich with a cotton layer between. Place seeds in a row along one side of the cotton. Tie the sandwich together and stand it upright in a cake pan of water. Watch it daily for the first signs of germination. Which seeds sprouted first? Which ones took the longest time? Also do the activity on page 198 to see the effect of tropisms on seed germination.

GRAFTING

BUD   WHIP   SADDLE   CLEFT

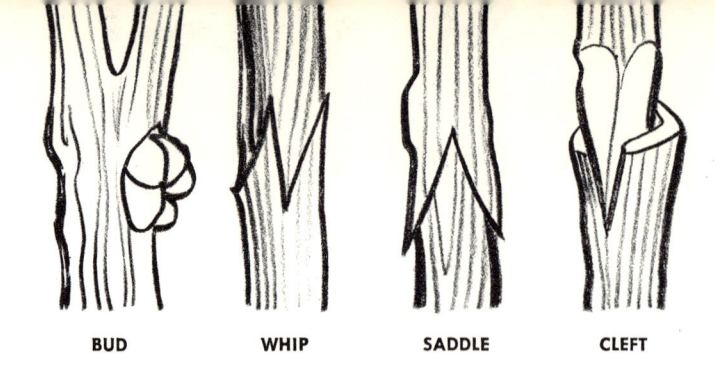

GRAFTING PLANTS

Materials you'll need:
  sharp knife, rags, resin, beeswax, tallow, linseed oil, brush, selected plants

Grafting is a technique used by gardeners to attach the growing part of one plant on to another living plant in order to develop new characteristics. It is not difficult to do if you follow certain basic rules.

   1. Graft plants only in the winter or spring when the plants are dormant.

   2. The *stock* (base plant) and the *cion* (part of another plant to be grafted) should belong to the same species. For example, a branch of a Delicious apple tree can be attached to a Winesap apple tree but not to a cherry tree.

   3. Be sure that the cambium (*meristematic* or growing layer) of the cion and stock touch each other.

   4. Select only strong, healthy plants free from apparent disease.

   5. Cover the joined parts with wax and wrap securely to prevent water loss and to keep the cion in place. A wax can be made with four parts resin, two parts beeswax, one part tallow, and one-half part linseed oil. Combine all ingredients and heat. Apply with a brush when slightly cool.

There are four basic methods of grafting: *bud, whip, saddle,* and *cleft* grafting. Follow the above illustrations while trying the four methods.

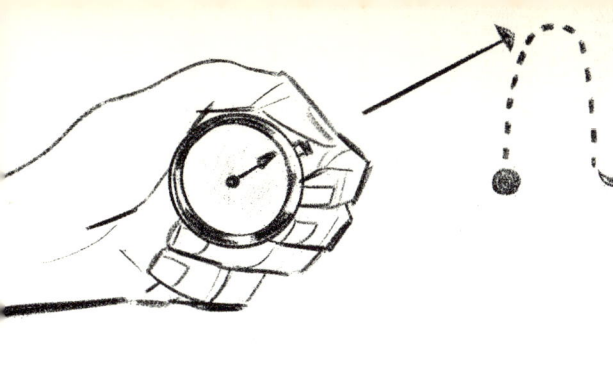

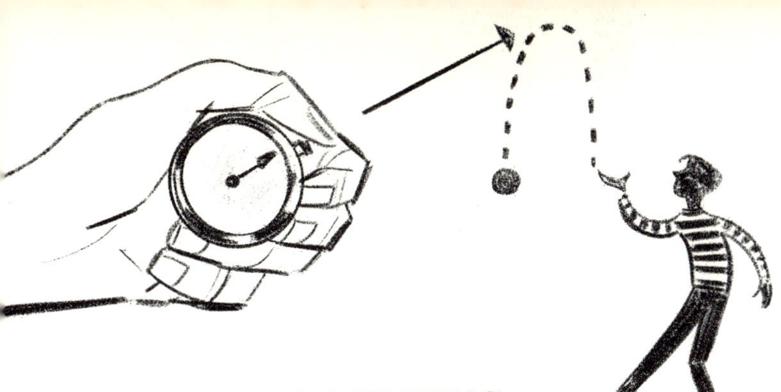

GRAVITY

EXPERIMENTING WITH GRAVITY

Materials you'll need:
stop watch, ball, mercury, glass jar, mineral oil, cork, dime, block of wood, cube of balsa

Try these tests concerning gravity, the universal force of attraction.

You will need a stop watch for this experiment and a person who is accurate in throwing certain distances. Throw a ball ten feet (about one story) straight up into the air. At the point where the ball stops and begins to descend, start the stop watch instantly. The instant the ball hits the ground, stop the watch and record the time. Repeat the experiment by throwing the ball twenty feet up and again at thirty feet. Does the rate of fall become greater the farther an object has to fall?

Now you want to find out if materials differ in specific gravity. Pour one inch of mercury into a glass jar; an olive bottle would be a good size. Put in one inch of water, followed by an inch of mineral oil. Cap the top and shake these three solutions vigorously. Allow them to settle. What happens? Which solution settled on the bottom? On the top?

Next, perform this test. Drop into the bottle a silver coin, a block of elm, maple, or similar wood, and a cube of balsa. Observe how far down each material finally goes before it settles in one place. Which one stays at which level? The position depends on the specific gravity of the object.

OBSERVING GRAVITY AT WORK

Materials you'll need:
yardstick, several coins of different weight

An Italian scientist named Galileo once did an experiment in which he dropped stones of different weights from the tower at Pisa. He found that they all reached the ground at the same time, regardless of weight.

To reconstruct this experiment, line up several different coins along the length of a yardstick. Hold the yardstick over your head and tip it so that all coins fall off at the same time. Did you guess that the heavier coins would reach the ground first? What does happen? Do you know why?

GUINEA PIGS

GUPPIES

MALE

FEMALE

RAISING GUINEA PIGS
Materials you'll need:
> *small animal cage, rabbit pellets, containers for food and water, shredded newspaper*

Guinea pigs are quite clean and odor-free and they make good pets. They will grow well on a diet of rabbit pellets and occasional nuts, grains and vegetable greens. A cage can be constructed with wire mesh and a wooden base (see page 28). Use a shallow pan such as a baking pan for the floor. It can be slid in and out for easy cleaning. Line the pan with folded newspaper and put in plenty of shredded newspaper so the guinea pig has something in which to conceal itself. Use a shallow food dish and a wide-mouthed water jar. Wire the water jar into a corner of the cage. Give the animal fresh water daily. Keep the cage at room temperature and away from drafts. See page 26 for information on breeding guinea pigs.

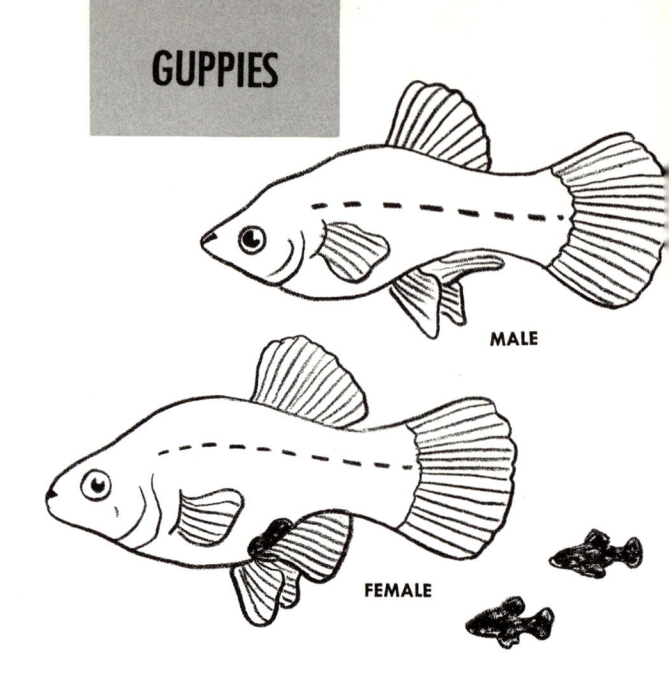

RAISING GUPPIES
Materials you'll need:
> *aquarium, aquatic plants, sand, pairs of guppies, tropical fish food*

Guppies are the easiest tropical fishes to raise. They are one of the few kinds of fishes which give birth to live young rather than laying eggs.

Prepare a fresh-water aquarium (see page 31) allowing at least one quart of water for every pair of guppies. Plant small aquatic plants in a layer of sand in the bottom. Supply ample plant life to provide hiding places for the young. The mother guppy eats many things, including her offspring.

Cover the aquarium so that water won't evaporate quickly. Do not let the temperature fall below 70 degrees Fahrenheit or exceed 100 degrees. Guppies thrive in warm waters. Feed them a small pinch of tropical fish food every other day.

When the female guppy is about to produce young, or is *gravid*, place her in another aquarium away from the male.

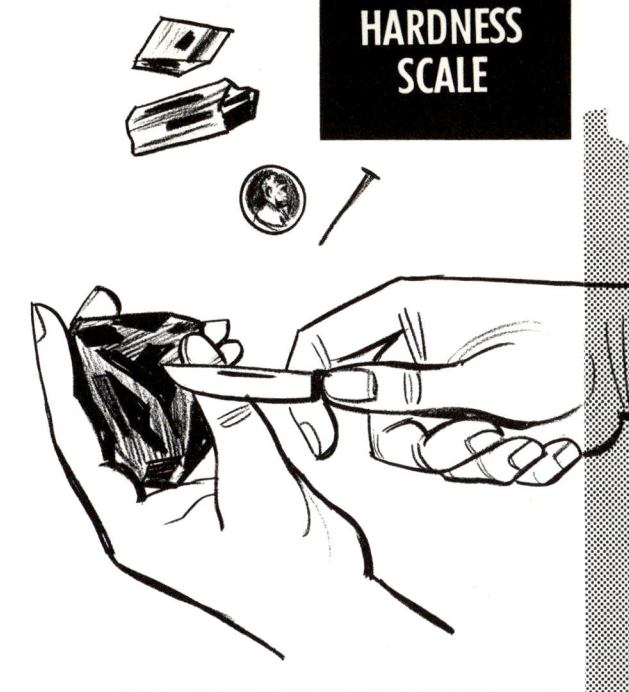

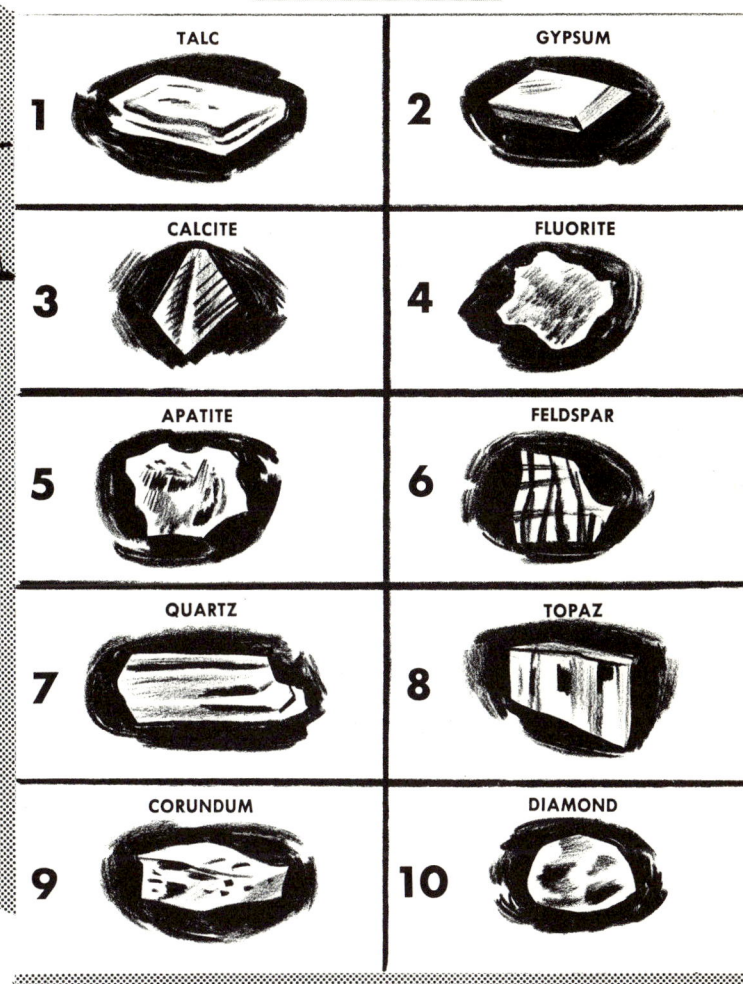

HARDNESS SCALE

HEAT

1	TALC	2	GYPSUM
3	CALCITE	4	FLUORITE
5	APATITE	6	FELDSPAR
7	QUARTZ	8	TOPAZ
9	CORUNDUM	10	DIAMOND

RATING THE HARDNESS OF A MINERAL

Materials you'll need:
piece of glass, penny, knife, quartz, topaz, and your own fingernail

Geologists use a standard table *(Mohs Hardness Scale)* to help them classify the hardness of rocks. The scale from soft to hard is this: 1—talc, 2—gypsum, 3—calcite, 4—fluorite, 5—apatite, 6—feldspar, 7—quartz, 8—topaz, 9—corundum, and number 10 is diamond.

Using the scratch test outlined below, and the tests on pages 166 and 167, will enable the young rock hound to determine which materials he has found.

Any rock which can be scratched with the fingernail has a hardness of 1 or 2 on the scale. Minerals that can be scratched with a penny are #3 on the scale. A knife scratches those with a hardness of 4 or 5. Minerals on the scale at 6 and 7 will scratch glass. Number 8 on the scale will scratch quartz and 9 will scratch topaz. The diamond, #10, such as the one in a glass cutter, will scratch all the other rocks plus itself.

CHANGING ELECTRICITY TO HEAT

Materials you'll need:
bell wire, dry cell, knife

Remove the insulation from both ends and a section in the center of a piece of bell wire. Connect the ends to the terminals of a dry cell. Place your finger on the bare wire in the center of the circle. You will not receive a shock. Does it feel warm? Leave the wire connected only a few minutes as it wears down the dry cell. Do you see why electrical wire must be coated with an insulating material?

HEAT

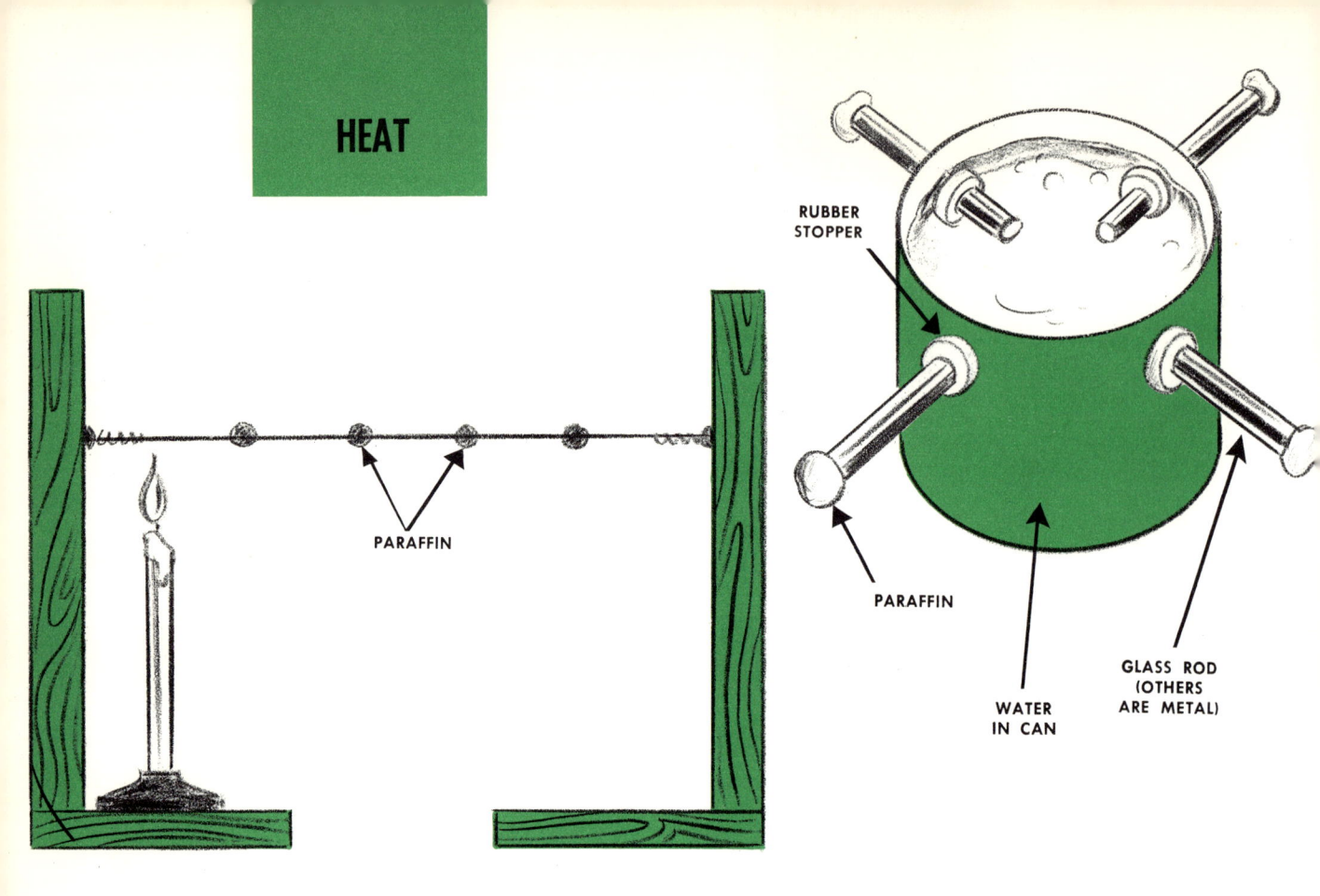

TESTING HEAT CONDUCTION RATES OF MATERIALS

Materials you'll need:
2 wooden uprights, piece of wire, source of heat, coffee can, several rods of different metals, 1 glass rod, paraffin, 1-holed rubber stoppers

You have learned by holding a metal rod in a candle flame that heat travels through solids by a method called *conduction* (page 68). You can almost see it occurring in the following way.

You will need to suspend a wire somehow so that there is room underneath it for a Bunsen burner or candle. Perhaps you would like to build wooden uprights as shown in the picture. When you have the wire in place, mold balls of soft paraffin around it at intervals. Heat one end of the wire. The paraffin balls will fall off one by one as the heat is conducted through the wire.

Solids differ in the rates at which they conduct heat. Of all solid materials, metals are the best conductors, and some are better than others. Try to acquire at least three metal rods—perhaps an iron, a brass and a copper rod—and a glass rod. Punch holes in the coffee can large enough so that the rubber stoppers fit tightly. If you have no rubber stoppers, use corks with holes through them. Insert the rods through the holes in the stoppers and fit the rods and stoppers into the can. Now put a small piece of paraffin on the end of each rod. Fill the can with very hot water. Do the pieces of paraffin fall off at different times? What does this tell you about the rates at which metals and other solids conduct heat? Which material conducts heat best? You may have to heat the water after it is in the can in order to melt all the paraffin.

106

HEREDITY

HIBERNATION

TRACING YOUR FAMILY CHARACTERISTICS

Have you ever wondered why your eyes or hair are the color they are? Did you inherit the colors from your mother, father, or a grandparent? Physical characteristics are carried from one generation to another in little cell bodies called *chromosomes*. Smaller parts of chromosomes are the *genes*, responsible for specific characteristics.

This project will take some time since you may have to write many letters to relatives and ask them to look up or recall the physical appearance of people. First, decide which characteristics you want to chart. Some traits you might follow are color of hair and eyes, height, curly or straight hair, shape of nose, baldness, color blindness, etc. Then find out what each of your relatives looked like and put all these data on a large chart. It may look something like the adjoining illustration. When you finish you may have a better understanding of why you look as you do.

TESTING A CAUSE OF HIBERNATION

Materials you'll need:

semi-aquatic aquarium, frog, ice

When the surrounding temperature becomes cold some animals hibernate. The body processes of a cold-blooded animal such as a frog are slowed down and cause the animal to become inactive. Can you make a frog hibernate?

This experiment may be performed in the winter months or it can be accomplished with ice cubes in the summer. Assemble a semi-aquatic aquarium for an amphibian. One end should be a pool of water with a mud bank tapering up to land on the other end. Place a wire screen over the top to keep the frog from jumping out.

Observe the activity of the frog in a warm room. Watch the pulsing of its throat as it breathes rapidly. Transfer the aquarium to the cold outside for several hours. It may be placed in front of an open window in winter if the rest of the space around the aquarium can be blocked off. Now observe the frog. Its breathing slows down, it becomes slow and sluggish and starts to burrow into the mud of the bank. This is hibernation. Put the frog back in a warm room and allow it to recover slowly.

HYDROMETER

MAKING A HYDROMETER

Materials you'll need:
  plastic lipstick top, 8 small screws, adhesive tape, glass

A hydrometer is an instrument used to measure *specific gravity* or the relative weight of a liquid. The density of a liquid is compared to the density of water to find its specific gravity. A real hydrometer is constructed with a hollow glass float which is weighted at the bottom so that it stands upright in the liquid. When the hydrometer is put in a liquid, the glass float sinks until it displaces its own weight of liquid. The specific gravity of the liquid can be read on a scale in the hydrometer.

Your hydrometer will not tell you the specific gravity of a liquid, but it will tell you whether the liquid is heavier (denser) or lighter (less dense) than water. It will not sink as deeply in a denser liquid as it does in water.

Put a strip of adhesive tape from top to bottom on an old plastic lipstick top. Place seven or eight small screws in the top. Test it to see whether it floats upright in a glass of water. If it sinks, take out some of the screws. If it tips, shake the screws around until it balances. Mark the water level on the tape.

Dissolve a quarter cup of sugar in the water and use the instrument without changing the number of screws to test to see whether the specific gravity of the solution is higher than that of water. If the specific gravity is higher, the liquid is denser and the tube floats higher since it has to displace less liquid to equal its weight. Test milk, alcohol, syrup and other liquids.

108

HYDROPONICS

GROWING PLANTS WITHOUT SOIL

Materials you'll need:
aquarium or similar container, wire mesh, sphagnum moss, calcium nitrate, potassium acid phosphate, Epsom salts, ammonium sulfate, distilled water, zinc sulfate, manganese sulfate, boric acid, ferrous sulfate

Hydroponics means gardening with chemicals rather than soil. Secure a large aquarium (see page 31 for making) or similar container. Take a piece of wire mesh the same width, but several inches longer than the inside dimensions of the aquarium. Bend the ends and insert it so it forms a table a few inches above the floor of the container.

You will need to make three solutions which will serve as food for your growing garden. Make solution #1 by dissolving two teaspoons of calcium nitrate, one-half teaspoon of potassium acid phosphate, one and one-quarter teaspoon of Epsom salts, and one-quarter teaspoon of ammonium sulfate in a cup of water. Pour this solution into two and one-half gallons of distilled water. Make solution #2 by dissolving one-eighth teaspoon each of zinc sulfate, manganese sulfate, and boric acid in a cup of water. Make solution #3 by dissolving one-eighth teaspoon of ferrous sulfate in a cup of water. Now add one teaspoon of solution #2 and three tablespoons of solution #3 to solution #1.

Pour this mixture into the aquarium to the level of the wire. Scatter sphagnum moss over the wire table. This serves to hold the seeds. Place a variety of seeds all over the top of the moss. Try growing corn, beans, tomatoes, cucumbers, and flowers. The seeds will germinate, roots growing down into the solution. Keep the level of the solution the same while the plants grow.

HYGROMETER

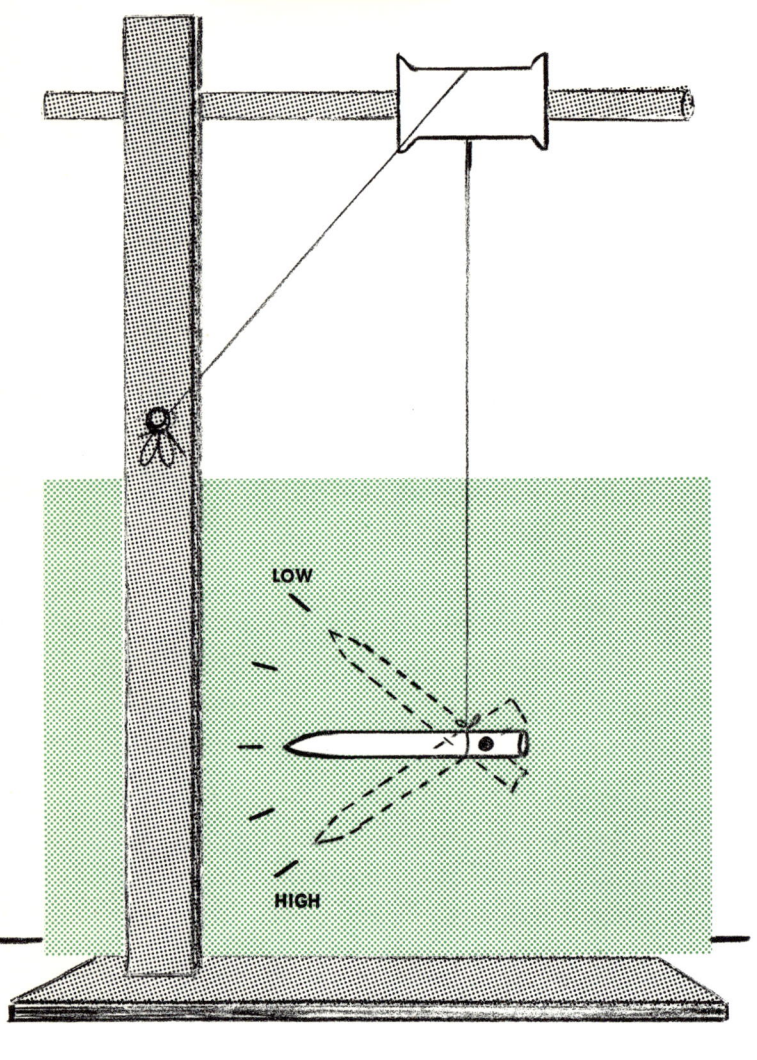

Since changes in the amount of moisture in the air affect the length of human hair, you can use hair to measure moisture or humidity by making a hair hygrometer with the materials in "A."

Use a long, straight, blond, freshly-washed hair. Construct a wooden stand similar to the one in the picture. Find a spool and dowel which fit tightly together so that the spool turns fairly easily without falling off. Fasten the hair to a tack on the side of the stand and run it over the spool.

Make a cardboard scale and attach it to the base of the stand. Cut the end of a large malted-milk straw to a point and attach it to the scale with a pintack. The straw must be free to move and the section in front of the pintack should be slightly longer and heavier than the section behind the pintack. Suspend the heavy part of the straw by tying the hair around it.

Now wet a towel with hot water and place it over the instrument. Leave it for a few minutes. Remove it and quickly mark where the straw is pointing on the scale. This will indicate high humidity. The hair should have stretched and permitted the pointer to fall. Now make the hair very, very dry by leaving the instrument near a radiator, hot air vent or furnace for several hours. Mark the spot where the straw is pointing. It should be pointing toward the top of the scale. Mark this line for low humidity.

This instrument will not give you an exact relative humidity reading, but it will indicate changes in the humidity. It is not as accurate an instrument as the wet-and-dry-bulb hygrometer.

MAKING A HYGROMETER

Materials you'll need:
  A—wooden stand, cardboard, blond hair, soda straw, pintack, thumbtack, spool, dowel;
  B—2 thermometers (preferably with bulbs exposed), narrow strip of thin cloth 5 inches long, wooden stand, small dish, nails

A hygrometer is an instrument used to measure humidity—the amount of moisture in the air.

On a humid day, hair stretches and lengthens. On a dry day, hair contracts.

HYGROMETER

The *wet-and-dry-bulb* thermometer is a hygrometer that indicates *relative humidity*—the amount of moisture present compared to the amount the air could hold at that temperature. It works on the principle that evaporation cools. If evaporation is rapid, there is a greater cooling effect. If it is slow, there is less cooling. When there is a lot of moisture in the air (high humidity), there is very little evaporation and therefore very little cooling. When the air is dry, there is much evaporation and much cooling. The wet-and-dry-bulb hygrometer is often called a *psychrometer*.

To make a wet-and-dry-bulb hygrometer use the materials in "B." Mount identical thermometers on a board. Bend nails over the edges of the cases. Wet the cloth and tie one end of it around the bulb of one thermometer. Place the other end in a glass of water.

When you are ready to read the hygrometer, fan the wet bulb. Then read both thermometers carefully and record the temperatures. Subtract the wet-bulb temperature from the dry-bulb temperature. Using the chart, find the intersection of the dry-bulb reading and the difference in degrees between the wet and dry thermometers. This tells you the *relative humidity*. If the air is dry and there is a lot of evaporation from the wet bulb, the wet-bulb temperature will be low. Therefore the difference in degrees will be large and the humidity low.

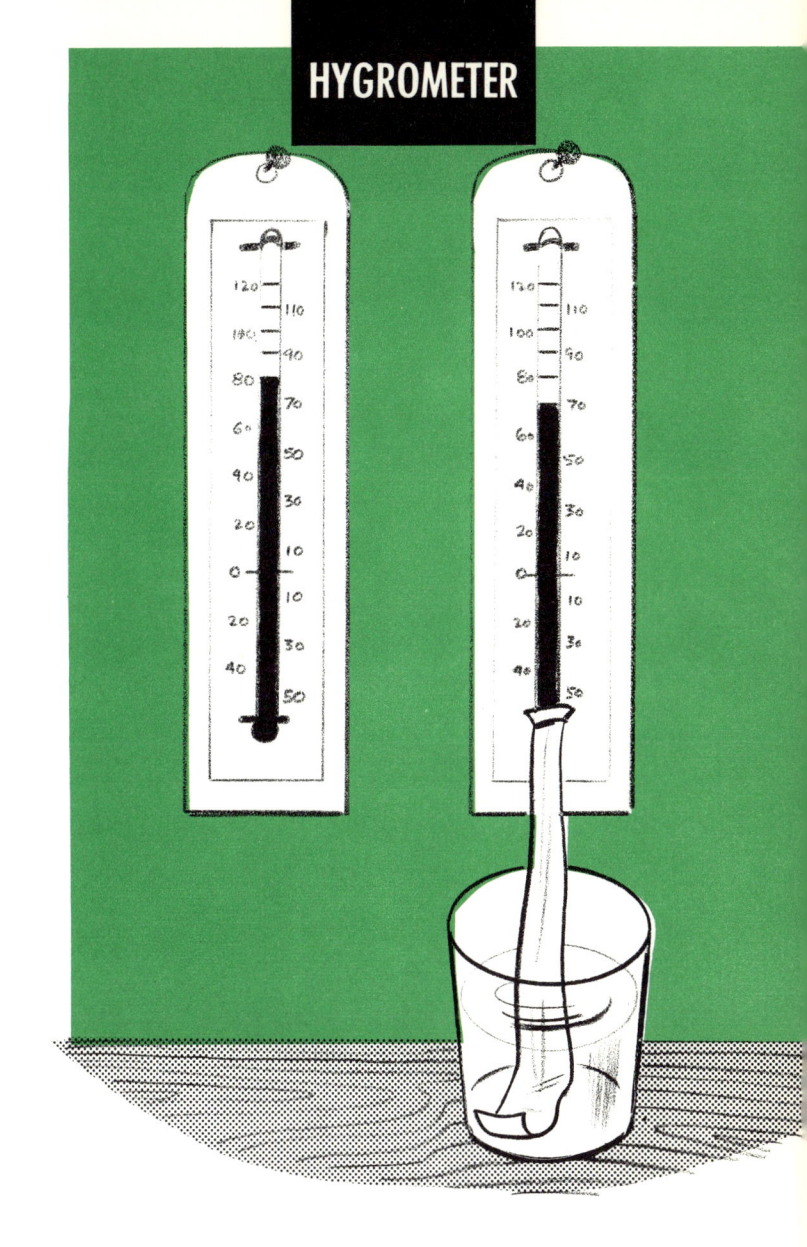

TEMPERATURE DIFFERENCES BETWEEN READINGS OF WET AND DRY BULBS

DRY BULB

	1°	2°	3°	4°	5°	6°	7°	8°	9°	10°	11°	12°	13°	14°
64°	95	90	84	79	74	70	65	60	56	51	47	43	38	34
65°	95	90	85	80	75	71	66	61	57	53	48	44	40	36
66°	95	90	85	80	75	71	66	61	57	53	48	44	40	36
67°	95	90	85	80	75	71	66	62	58	53	49	45	41	37
68°	95	90	85	80	76	71	67	62	58	54	50	46	42	38
69°	95	90	85	81	76	72	67	63	59	55	51	47	43	39
70°	95	90	86	81	77	72	68	64	59	55	51	48	44	40
71°	95	90	86	81	77	72	68	64	60	56	52	48	45	41
72°	95	91	86	82	77	73	69	65	61	57	53	49	45	42
73°	95	91	86	82	78	73	69	65	61	57	53	50	46	42
74°	95	91	86	82	78	74	69	65	61	58	54	50	47	43
75°	96	91	86	82	78	74	70	66	62	58	54	51	47	44
76°	96	91	87	82	78	74	70	66	62	59	55	51	48	44
77°	96	91	87	83	79	74	71	67	63	59	56	52	48	45
78°	96	91	87	83	79	75	71	67	63	60	56	53	49	46
79°	96	91	87	83	79	75	71	68	64	60	57	53	50	46
80°	96	91	87	83	79	75	72	68	64	61	57	54	50	47

111

ICE

TESTING THE EFFECT OF SALT ON ICE

Materials you'll need:
tin can, metal pail, chipped ice, milk, salt, aluminum foil

If you cannot obtain an ice cream freezer, make your own by putting a tin can inside a metal pail. Put a layer of chipped ice on the bottom of the pail. Rest the can—filled with milk—on this layer. Keep adding chipped ice around the inside can until it is level with the top of the can. Cover the whole surface with aluminum foil. Occasionally observe the condition of the inside can. How long does it take the milk to start to freeze?

Repeat the experiment. This time add several tablespoons of rock or table salt on every inch layer of ice chips. How long does it take the milk to start crystallizing? Why? For a solid (ice) to be changed to a solution heat is necessary. Where does the heat come from?

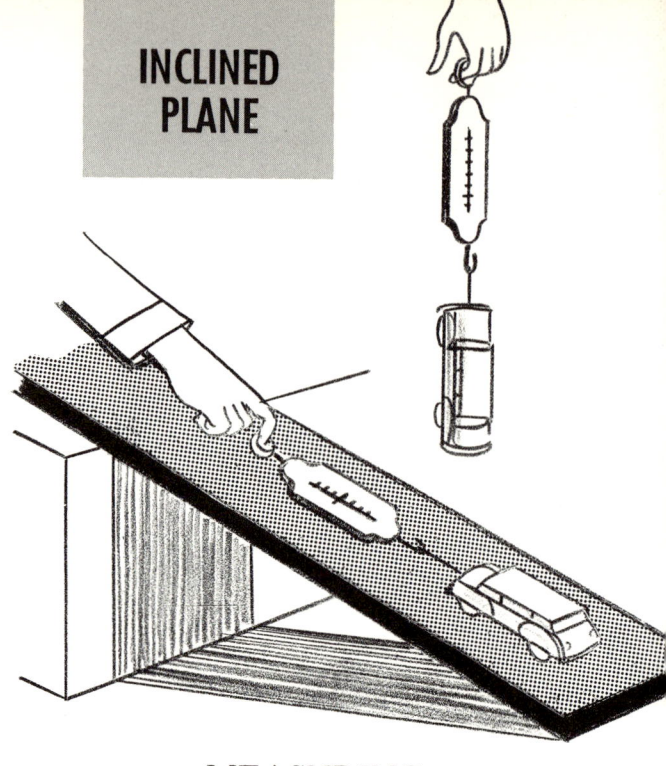

INCLINED PLANE

MEASURING THE EFFECT OF AN INCLINED PLANE

Materials you'll need:
long, smooth board at least 8 inches wide, toy car, spring scale

A machine is a device used to make work easier. An inclined plane is a simple machine. It is simply a sloping surface which makes the work of moving heavy loads easier.

You can measure how much an inclined plane can help. Attach the hook of the spring scale to the axle of the toy car and lift it straight up off the floor to the height of a desk. Read the scale. This will tell you the weight of the car and how much work you must do to lift it without the help of a machine. Now place one end of the board on the floor and the other end on the desk. Pull the same car up the sloping board and read the scale as you are pulling. You will find that you do not have to pull as hard to move the car up to the same height. You are, however, pulling it over a longer distance.

INCUBATOR

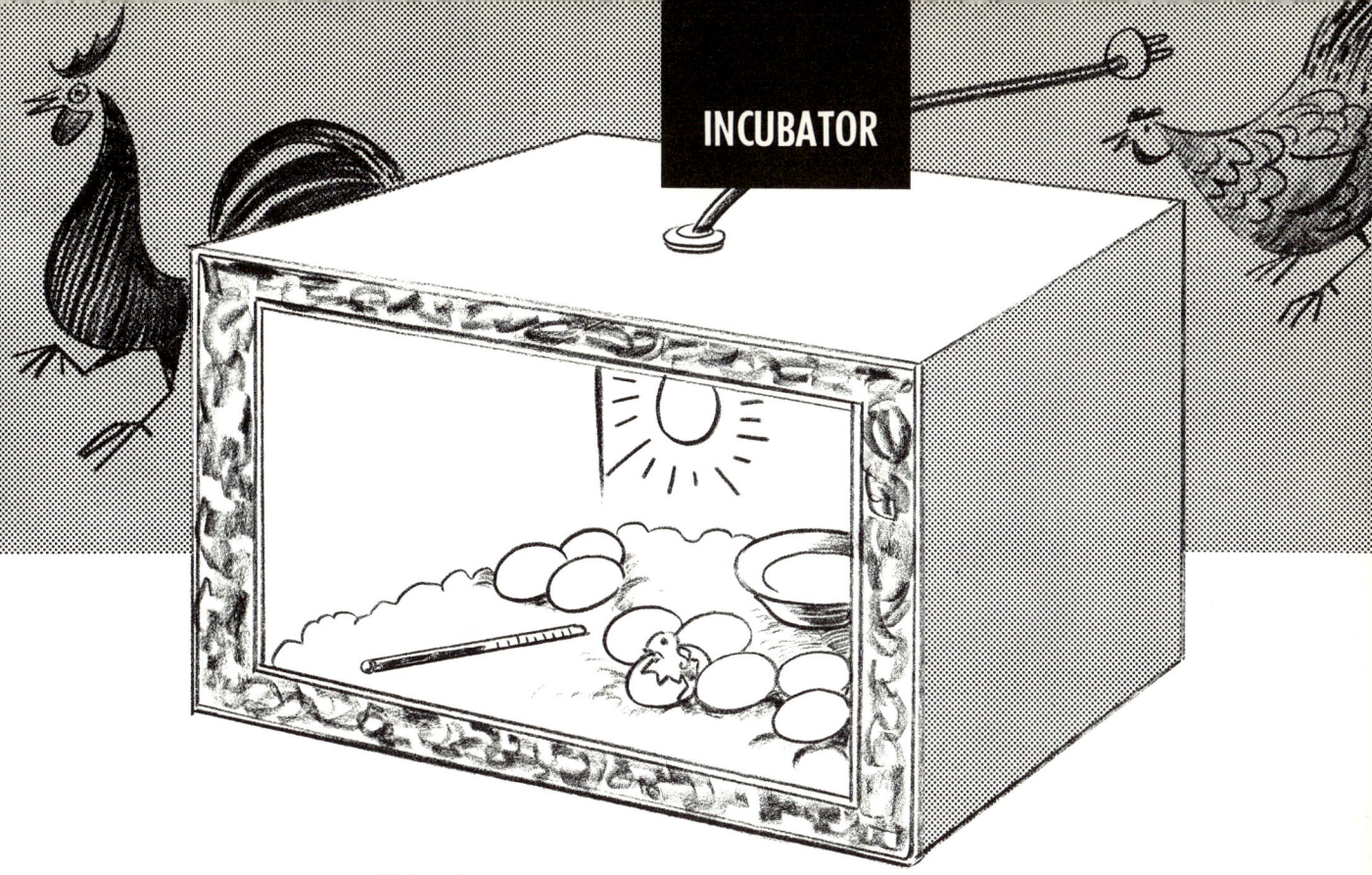

HATCHING CHICKEN EGGS

Materials you'll need:
2 cardboard boxes, insulating material, light bulb on cord, thermometer, pan, fertile eggs

It is interesting to hatch some chicken eggs in an incubator and, while you are doing it, to study the development of a chick embryo. Remember that chickens are birds so you are watching the development of a bird.

You can build an incubator for the eggs yourself. Start building it several days before you plan to buy the eggs because it may take you a few days to adjust the temperature.

The cardboard boxes should be of two different sizes. Put one inside the other and pack the space between them with insulating material, such as wool. Suspend the light bulb inside the inner box. Start with a 40-watt bulb. After it has been on for a full day, check the temperature on a thermometer which you have placed in the box, away from the light bulb and in the place where you plan to put the eggs. If the temperature is over 103 degrees Fahrenheit, replace the bulb with one of lower wattage. If the temperature is lower than 103°F., use a stronger bulb. Keep testing bulbs until you find one which keeps the temperature steady between 101° and 103°F. for a full day. The amount of insulation can also be adjusted to vary the temperature.

Secure fertile chicken eggs from a nearby farm or hatchery. Buy enough so that you can open one every day or almost every day, if you plan to study embryonic development (see page 85) or so that you have as many chicks as you want. Turn the eggs every day by hand. They need a humid environment so keep a small pan of water in the incubator. It takes twenty-one days for chicken eggs to hatch. See page 60 for making a chicken brooder to put the chicks in after hatching.

INDICATOR

MAKING A TESTER FOR ACIDS AND BASES

Materials you'll need:
red cabbage, water, 3 bottles, test tubes, solutions to be tested—vinegar, ammonia, baking soda, lemon juice

The acid-base indicator that you will use constantly when you start working with chemicals is *litmus paper*. Litmus paper indicates whether a substance is an *acid* or the opposite of an acid—a *base*. It is absorbent paper which has been soaked with a dye made from plants which are—like litmus, a lichen extract—different colors when in acids than when in bases.

Blue litmus is red in acid and red litmus turns blue in a base. You can make a similar acid-base indicator using juice from a red cabbage.

Chop a few dark leaves of red cabbage. Cover them with water in a pan and boil for about twenty minutes. The water should be purple when you are through. This is neutral cabbage juice. Put some of this in a bottle labeled "neutral." To half of the rest of the juice, add a small amount of baking soda. The juice will turn green. Label that bottle "basic." Add a small amount of vinegar to the other half and label the resulting red juice "acid."

To test how your indicator works, add a small amount of ammonia or baking soda (both are bases) to some of the basic indicator in a test tube. The color should stay the same. Add a little to some of the acid indicator. It should change from red to green. Now add a little lemon juice to some of the acid indicator. The color won't change. Add a little to some of the basic. Its color will change from green to red.

Test some of the following substances (in water) with your indicator: orange, tomato, onion, celery, rhubarb, salt, chlorine bleach, alcohol, cottage cheese, aspirin, starch, pickle juice, boric acid, and soap. Think of other substances to test. Be sure to record what you discover.

After you have experimented with making a red-cabbage indicator and have used it to test various foods, etc., try making indicators using some of these plant parts: grape juice, rhubarb stalks, red petunias, violets, cherries. Crush the plant parts, stir and boil until the water is colored.

INSECTS

COLLECTING INSECTS

An insect collector needs several field tools to help him in assembling a complete display. First, insects must be captured with an aerial insect net (see page 74 under "Dip Net"). If you are planning to keep them alive, you must construct an insect cage. Killing insects requires a certain kind of container. Some of the insects must be dried on a spreading board. If a good specimen gets too dry and brittle before you can mount it, you will need a relaxing jar. The final step in collecting is mounting and labeling your display. The following five activities will help you work with your collection.

MAKING A CAGE FOR LIVE INSECTS

Materials you'll need:
   small wire mesh, 2 cake pans, plaster of Paris, branch, wire

Roll the wire mesh into a cylinder and sew the seam with a piece of wire. Mix plaster of Paris and water to the consistency of heavy cream. Pour it into one of the cake pans and insert one end of the wire cylinder into it. Push a branch into the center of the plaster of Paris. Let this set until it has hardened. Put the other pan over the top as a movable lid. Furnish your insects with vegetation (the plants they were found on) sprinkled with water.

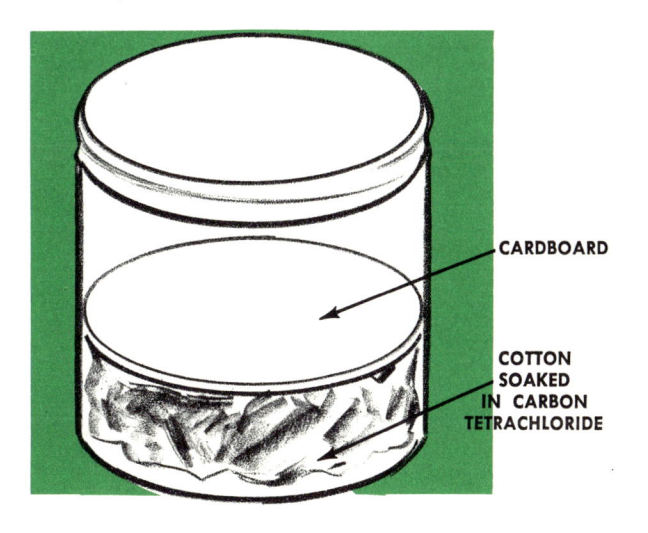

MAKING A KILLING JAR

Materials you'll need:
   peanut butter jar, cotton, cardboard, carbon tetrachloride

If you plan to mount insects, they must first be killed without damaging them. A broad-mouthed peanut butter jar makes a good container for this purpose. Soak a layer of cotton in carbon tetrachloride. Be sure to do this out-of-doors. Put it in the bottom of the jar and cover the cotton with a cardboard disk. Remember, the jar should be covered except when insects are being put in or removed. Leave the insects in the killing jar overnight.

CAUTION!

115

INSECTS

MAKING A SPREADING BOARD

Materials you'll need:
   heavy cardboard, wooden base, nails, pins

Butterflies and moths should be pinned on a spreading board in order to dry their wings in a spread formation. A spreading board can be made by nailing two stacks of several layers of heavy cardboard to a wooden base, leaving a small, even groove down the center. Lay the body of the insect in the groove and spread the wings over the cardboard. Hold the wings in place by pinning them down with little strips of paper. Follow the illustration.

MAKING A RELAXING JAR

Materials you'll need:
   peanut butter jar, cotton, cardboard disk

In order to be mounted, insects must be pliable or easily bent. If they are not, parts will break off. If an insect has been left too long in the killing jar or is found after it has been dead for some time, it will have become brittle.

Soak in water enough absorbent cotton to cover the bottom of the jar. Place it in the jar and cover it with a circle of cardboard. The insect should be placed on the cardboard rather than directly on the wet cotton. Cover the jar tightly for a few hours. The high humidity inside the sealed jar will make the insect flexible enough to mount.

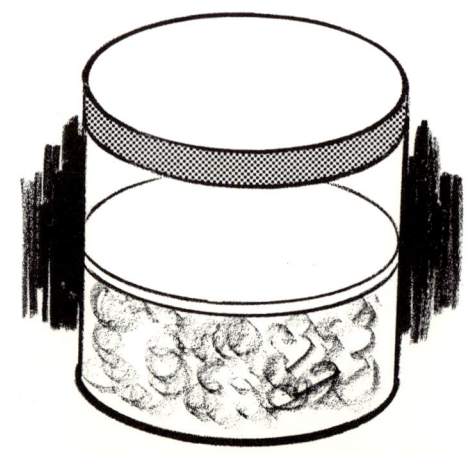

MOUNTING INSECTS

Materials you'll need:
   flat box, moth balls, cotton, sheet of glass or plastic, glue

Insects may be mounted on pins or placed directly on a layer of cotton in a flat box. Spread moth balls or crystals under the cotton to prevent other insects from destroying your collection. A spot of glue under the insect will hold it on the cotton. Make paper labels for your specimens and glue these beside the insects. Tape a sheet of glass or clear plastic on the top of the box. This will keep it relatively airtight and the display will last for years.

116

JET PROPULSION

MAKING A JET PLANE

Materials you'll need:
> carbon dioxide cylinder, balsa wood, wire, sharp nail, 4 screw eyes, pillow

Fashion your own model of a jet plane from a block of balsa wood. If you want to add wings, cut them from a thin piece of balsa and insert them in slots cut to hold them. Use lightweight wire to hold the cylinder of carbon dioxide (available in any hobby shop) securely to the bottom of the plane. The plane is to be suspended from a wire strung across a room. There should be a pillow or something soft at the point of impact at the end of the wire.

Fasten two of the screw eyes in the top of the plane. Attach short wires ending in screw eyes to the two in the wood. Thread the long wire through the top screw eyes, fasten it in two corners of the room.

Puncture the back end of the carbon dioxide cylinder with a sharp nail. The plane will zoom across the room. It works on the same principle as jet propulsion—for every action there is an equal and opposite reaction. The action is the carbon dioxide escaping from the cylinder and the reaction is the forward motion of the plane. In a real jet plane the action force is provided by the escaping exhaust of burning fuel.

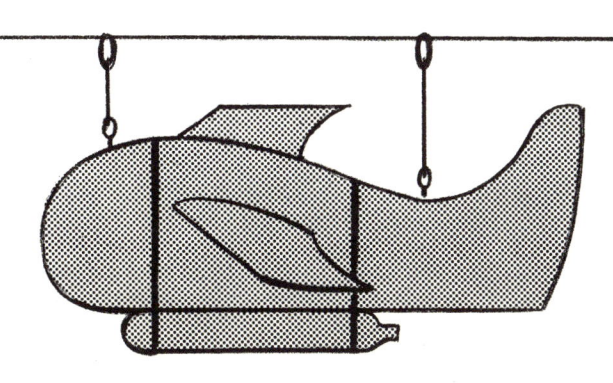

DEMONSTRATING JET PROPULSION

Materials you'll need:
> a wagon, several bricks

Sir Isaac Newton described jet propulsion in his *Third Law of Motion*. It states that for every action there is an equal and opposite reaction.

Stand in a wagon which holds a number of bricks. Hold the handle up. Throw one brick out behind you. This starts the wagon rolling in the opposite direction. As you throw each brick out, motion is added to the wagon. Note that the last brick thrown out adds more motion than the earlier bricks. Why does this happen?

A heavy fuel-laden rocket barely moves. But as the pushing force acts on a rocket which is losing weight, the rocket accelerates until the fuel is exhausted or turned off.

KALEIDOSCOPE

MAKING A KALEIDOSCOPE

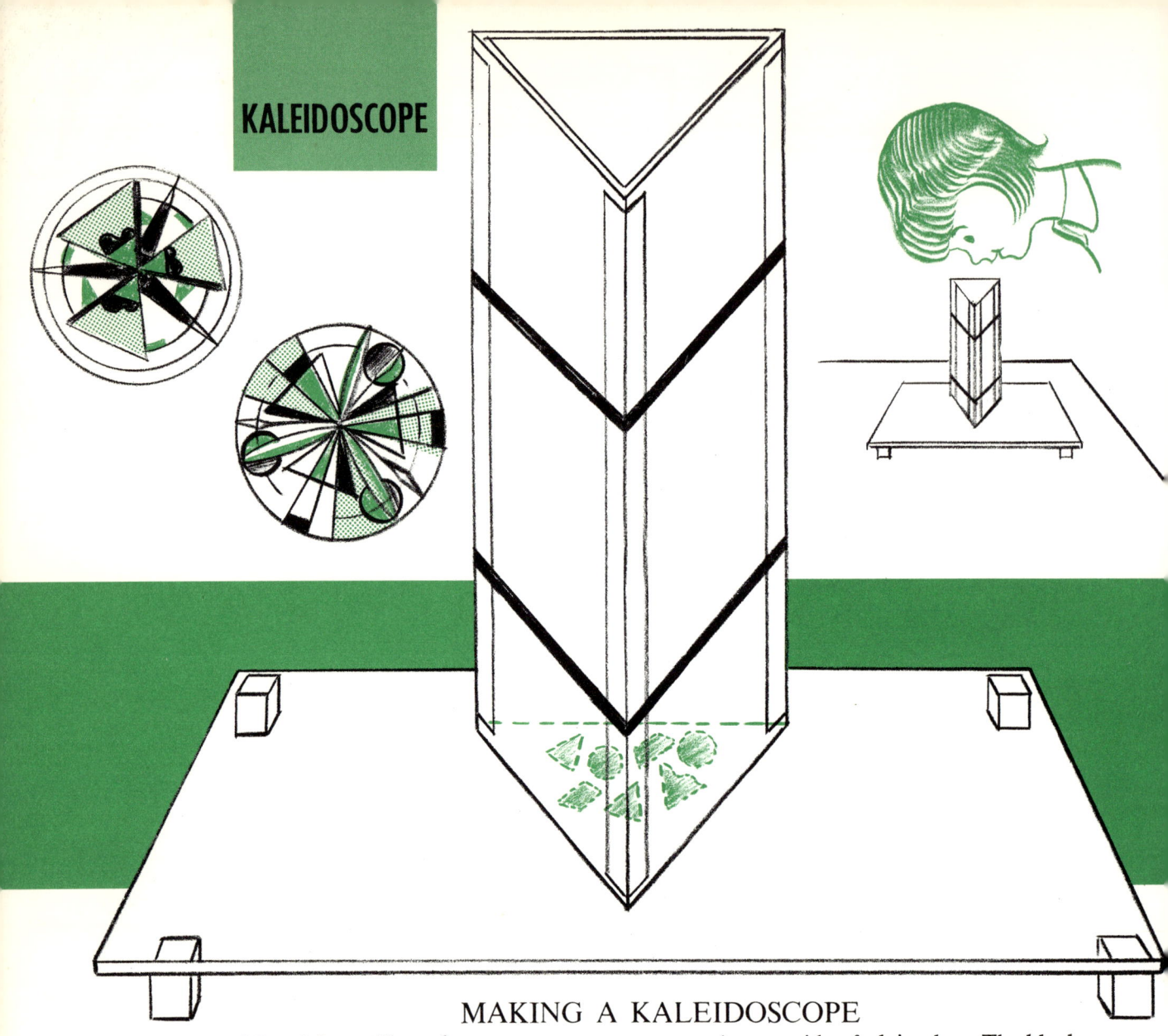

Materials you'll need:
2 pieces of mirror about 1½" x 4½", 1 piece of cardboard 1½" x 4½", tape, 2 rubber bands, pieces of colored glass or marbles, sheet of glass

The important parts of a kaleidoscope are the two mirrors, each set at an angle of sixty degrees, which run the length of the tube. The mirrors reflect in symmetrical patterns whatever transparent objects are looked at through the kaleidoscope.

You can make your own kaleidoscope, using two pieces of mirror. If you have no mirror, use black paint to paint one side of plain glass. The black side should be outside. Cut a piece of cardboard the same size. Fasten the two pieces of mirror and the cardboard together in a triangular prism using tape on the edges and rubber bands. Whatever you look at through your kaleidoscope should form a regular symmetrical pattern. Set your pieces of colored glass on a sheet of glass that is raised above the base surface. Light must be able to get under the colored glass. Put your kaleidoscope down over it. Look down through the opening on the top. Move the glass bits and watch the pattern change.

COLLECTING AND PRESERVING LEAVES

Materials you'll need:
identification book, newspaper, weights, cardboard, shellac, glue, adhesive paper

When you collect leaves, be sure to get a variety of kinds, including simple and compound leaves; alternate, opposite and whorled arrangements of leaves; leaves showing both palmate and pinnate venation; and leaves with different margins. Keep leaves from bushes separate from tree leaves so that they are easier to identify. Use a tree identification book both while you are collecting leaves and while you are sorting them to help you find what kinds of leaves you have. Take a magazine and some loose pieces of newspaper with you on your collecting hike so that you can slip the leaves between the pieces of newspaper into the magazine or carry a botanical press (see page 50). Then place weights on the magazines and let the leaves dry for several days. Never dry leaves in a book. The moisture from the leaves will ruin the pages.

There are several different ways in which you might like to display the leaves you have collected. For example, you can make a display which shows how leaves change color as the weather becomes cold. For this you would collect leaves early in the fall while they are still green, then collect leaves from the same trees after they have changed color, and mount them together.

You should have a good way to mount the leaves so they can be handled and easily stored without damage. Try cutting pieces of cardboard which are large enough for one or two leaves. Cover each piece with wood-patterned adhesive paper. Glue the leaf to it and shellac the whole surface including the leaf. This hard surface will protect the leaf from damage when the cards are handled and stacked.

The next four activities suggest other ways of preserving leaves for studying or your collection.

LEAVES

MAKING SPATTER PRINTS OF LEAVES

Materials you'll need:
white paper, fine mesh screen, toothbrush, water colors, wooden form

For spatter prints, place the leaf on a sheet of paper. Hold a piece of fine mesh screen, nailed to a wooden form, over the leaf. Push a toothbrush, dipped in paint, back and forth over the screen. Be careful that drops do not form on the bottom of the screen. Different colored paints can be used for different leaves.

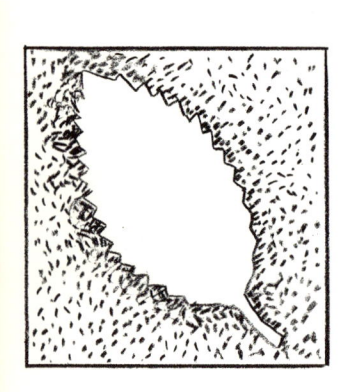

MAKING SMOKE PRINTS

Materials you'll need:
grease, glass jars, candle, paper

Grease the outside of a glass jar. Hold this jar over a candle flame until the whole outside becomes dark gray with carbon. Place a leaf, underside up, on a stack of papers which will act as a cushion. Roll the smokey area of the jar over the leaf. Then put a white sheet of paper over the leaf. Roll again with a clean jar. The details of the leaf will appear on the paper. These are called *smoke* or *carbon prints*.

WAXING LEAVES

Materials you'll need:
pan, paraffin wax, heat source

Heat the wax until it melts. Dip a leaf into this solution by holding on to the petiole. Tie a string to the petiole and hang the leaf to dry.

MAKING SKELETON LEAVES

Materials you'll need:
pressed and dried leaves, paper, hammer, plastic envelopes

To make it easy to study the arrangement of the veins in a leaf, first press and dry the leaf thoroughly. When the leaf is so dry it is brittle, place it between two sheets of paper. Pound it carefully so that all the plant cells except the veins crumble away and just the leaf skeleton remains. These may be sealed in plastic envelopes.

LEVER

USING A LEVER

Materials you'll need:
triangular block of wood, wooden plank, books

A lever is a simple machine consisting of a plank or bar used to move heavy loads. It operates around a fixed point called a *fulcrum*. The distance from the weight to be moved to the fulcrum is called the *weight arm* and the distance from where the force is applied to the fulcrum is called the *force arm*. Usually, in using a lever, a small force is applied through a large distance to move a weight a small distance.

Place the plank on the triangular block of wood (fulcrum) so that the fulcrum is exactly in the center (Figure 1). You will find that three books on one end of the plank will balance three books of the same size on the other end. Now move the plank so the fulcrum is close to where the force will be applied at the end of the plank (Figure 2). Put three books at the end of the long arm (the weight arm). Try and lift them by placing three books on the force arm (short arm). Find out how many books (how much force) it takes to raise the weight of three books. Now move the fulcrum so that it is close to the weight (Figure 3). You will find that now it takes very little effort—perhaps only one book—to raise the weight of three books.

CLASSIFYING LEVER ACTION

The fulcrum of a *Class I* lever is between the weight and the force. In a *Class II* lever the weight is between the fulcrum and force, while *Class III* operates with the force between the weight and the fulcrum. Do as many of these activities as you can and classify each lever into Class I, II or III.

1. Pull a nail out of a board by using the claws on a hammer.
2. Throw a ball as far as you can.
3. Sweep the floor with a broom.
4. Move a load from one place to another in a wheelbarrow.
5. Punch a hole in a tin can with a can opener.
6. Break a nut with a nutcracker.
7. Move a stone with a crowbar.
8. Write your name with a pencil.
9. Remove a thumbtack from the floor with a screwdriver.
10. Row a rowboat around the lake.

All of the devices you used in these activities are levers and made your work easier. Did you have trouble putting them into classes? Let us help you with the last one—rowing a rowboat. The weight or resistance you want to move is, of course, the boat. You are applying force on the handles of the oars. No, the fulcrum or fixed point is not the oarlock, but the water at the blade of the oar. The water seems to stand still while you push against it to make you and the boat go forward. So it is a Class II lever.

LIFT PUMP

PISTON VALVE

FOOT VALVE

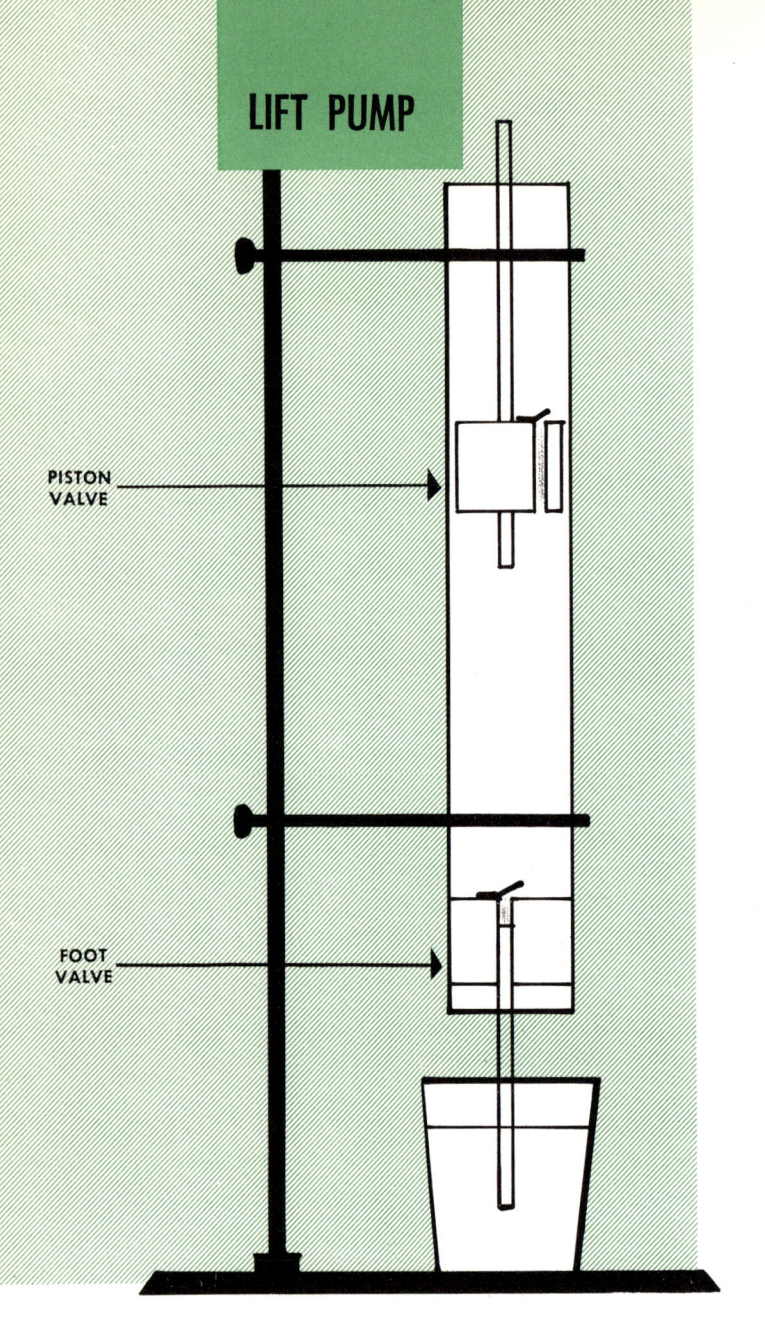

BUILDING A LIFT PUMP

Materials you'll need:
  lamp chimney with straight sides, 2-holed stopper, 1-holed stopper, pieces of thin rubber from rubber glove, thumbtacks, metal rod, pan of water, stand and clamps

A lift pump depends on air pressure for its operation. The pressure of the air supports a column of water and pushes it upward into a container from which air has been forced.

You may either support the pump with a stand and clamps or hold it in your hand as you operate it. Fit the lamp chimney with a two-holed stopper which fits tightly yet can move up and down. Start with a rubber stopper which is too large to go inside the chimney altogether and shave it with a razor blade and sandpaper to make it smaller. Put a metal rod through one of the holes so that you can move the stopper up and down with it—this is the *piston*. Cut a flap of thin rubber big enough to cover the other hole and tack it to the stopper. It is the *piston valve*.

Carefully put glass tubing through the one-holed stopper. The glass tubing should not extend into the lamp chimney when the stopper is put into the bottom of the chimney. Cover the hole in the stopper with another flap of rubber so that it acts like a valve as above. This is called the *foot valve*.

Place water in a pan below the chimney so that the glass tubing extends down into it. Prime the pump by pouring a little water in the top of the chimney. Operate it by moving the piston up and down. Watch the valves operate. The first downstroke of the piston empties some of the air from the lamp chimney. On the upstroke, the pressure of the air on the container of water below pushes the water from the container, through the tube and up into the lamp chimney where the air pressure is less than it is outside.

From that point on, moving the piston up and down brings water from the pan under the pump up through the pump and out its top.

CAUTION!

122

LIGHT

TURNING ELECTRICAL ENERGY INTO LIGHT

Materials you'll need:
  bell wire, cork, ink bottle, dry cells, fine wire

Scrape the insulation off two ends of bell wire and push them through a cork. Wrap fine wire around the end of one wire, then put it across and around the second wire. This will be the filament in a homemade lightbulb. Insert the cork into the mouth of an ink bottle. Connect the other ends of the wires to a series of dry cells. When the circuit is complete the filament will glow. Eventually the filament burns up since there is oxygen in the bottle. Most of the oxygen has been removed in commercial bulbs.

MAKING A LIGHT BRIGHTER

Materials you'll need:
  bell wire, dry cells, light receptacle, small bulb

Connect one end of a piece of bell wire to one terminal of a dry cell and the other end to the screw on a small light receptacle. Do the same with a second piece of wire to the remaining posts. The very fine filament in the bulb becomes so hot it glows and produces a light. Now connect a second dry cell to the first one. Does the light burn brighter? Try a third cell in the electric circuit. Is there a limit to how bright the light from the bulb will get?

EXPERIMENTING WITH REFLECTION OF LIGHT

Materials you'll need:
  glass jar, milk, water, flashlight

Shine a flashlight into the top of a jar of clear water. Notice how bright it is in the water, yet the sides look dark from the outside. Add a few drops of milk to the water and stir. Shine the light into the jar again. This time does the jar appear brighter on the inside and lighter on the outside?

In the clear water the light hits the jar at such a small angle that total reflection occurs. When other particles are added to the water the light hits the particles and is reflected out through the glass.

LIGHT

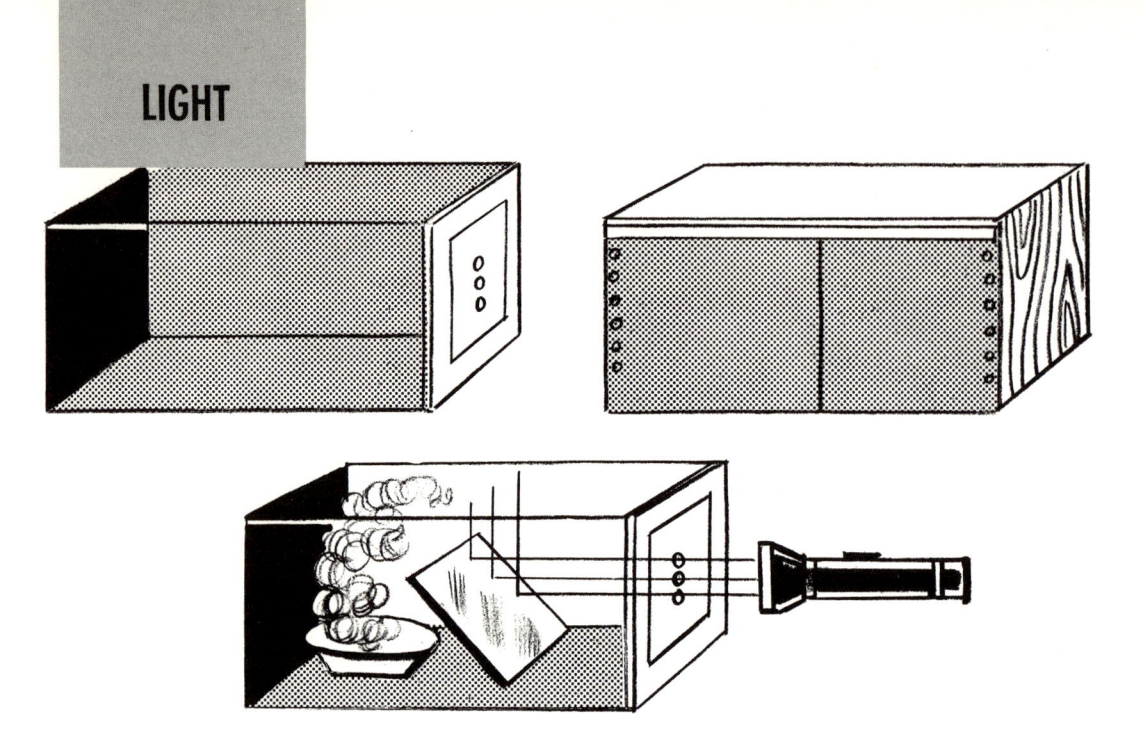

USING A SMOKE BOX TO STUDY REFLECTION

Materials you'll need:
wooden box about 1' wide, 1' deep and 2' long, black cloth, black poster paint, glass cut to fit top and front of box, tape, 5" x 8" index cards, flashlight, mirror, incense or punk

A smoke box is the best way to study light. You can build a smoke box that will allow you to see plainly how light is reflected or refracted and how lenses work.

You can make a wooden box the right size if you do not already have one. Panes of glass cut to fit should be put in the front and top and taped in place. Remove the back wall of the box and cover it with black cloth, hung like a curtain. Make the curtain in two sections which overlap so you can easily put your hand in the box. Tack the cloth to the sides and tape it to the glass top. Cut a window in one end of the box, about three inches from the glass front. The window should be about three and one-half inches long and two and one-half inches wide. It will be covered with an index card with various shaped holes in it, depending on the experiment you are doing.

For this experiment with reflection, cut three holes in a card, the same distance from each other and one-fourth inch in diameter. Fill the smoke box with smoke. The easiest way to do this is to place a saucer containing burning incense or punk in one corner of the box. The smoke will make the light rays visible.

Focus the flashlight on the three-hole card by moving it back and forth until the light rays are well-defined in the smoke. Hold a mirror in the box at a forty-five degree angle from the floor of the box. You will see the rays reflected with almost no scattering of light.

To see the contrast with reflection from a rough surface, rough a piece of cellophane with steel wool and fasten it to a piece of glass. The light will be scattered rather than reflected in well-defined rays. Hold a piece of wood in the path of the light rays. Are they reflected? Try other surfaces.

LIGHT

EXPERIMENTING WITH REFRACTION OF LIGHT

Materials you'll need:

   coin, coffee can, water, partner

This is a very simple test which shows you something about refraction of light. Light waves bend and change direction (refract) when they go from one material, such as air, to another kind of material, such as water. The speeds at which the light waves travel through air and water are different.

   Put a coin in the bottom of a coffee can. Stand so that you can see the coin. Now move slowly back so the coin just barely disappears from sight. Stop. Now have a partner pour water slowly and carefully into the can so that the coin is not moved. The coin will suddenly come into your sight again. The coin has not moved but the light rays coming from the coin to your eyes are bent or refracted at an angle different from before.

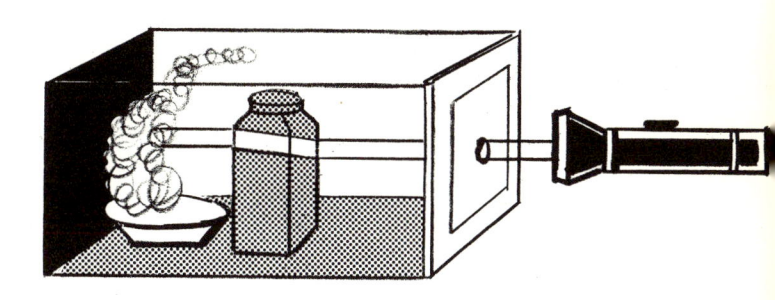

USING A SMOKE BOX TO STUDY REFRACTION

Materials you'll need:

   smoke box, index card, flashlight, rectangular bottle, milk

Fasten an index card with one single hole in it over the small window in the end of the smoke box (see page 124). Focus the flashlight so that a beam of light goes through the hole into the box.

   Fill the bottle with water, put a few drops of milk in it to make the water cloudy and put the top on it. Fill the box with smoke. Hold the bottle in the box so that the beam of light hits it. What happens to the light ray when it passes through the water? Now tip the bottle and observe what happens to the ray of light. The light will be bent or refracted as it goes from the air of the box through the water in the bottle.

LIGHTNING

MACHINES

DISCOVERING SPEEDS OF LIGHT AND SOUND

Materials you'll need:
   thunderstorm with lots of lightning

Remembering that sound travels about one-fifth mile per second and light travels 186,000 miles per second, try to figure the distance of the next thunderstorm you see and hear.

The instant you see the lightning start counting off the seconds—by saying "one thousand and one, one thousand and two," until you hear the clap of thunder. If you have counted up to five seconds ("1000 and 5"), the center of the storm is about one mile away. By counting periodically you will be able to tell whether the storm is coming toward you or going in the opposite direction.

KNOWING SIMPLE AND COMPLEX MACHINES

Simple machines have been classified into six categories: *lever* (page 121), *pulley* (page 159), *wheel and axle* (page 211), *inclined plane* (page 112), *wedge* (a double inclined plane), and *screw* (page 170). When two or more simple machines are put together in the same device or instrument, it is called a *complex machine*.

After you have done activities with the simple machines, study the illustrations on this page. There are six examples of simple machines among the complex machines. Can you find them?

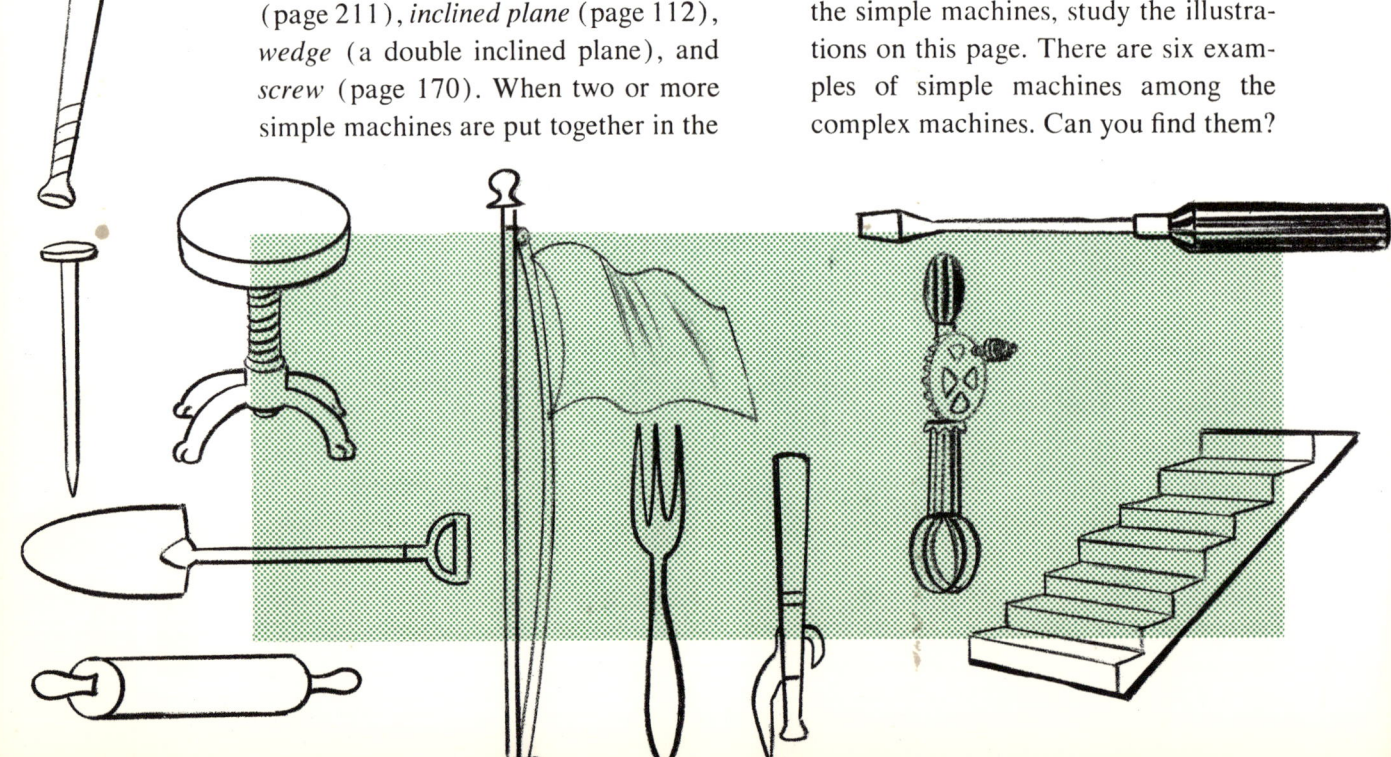

MAGNETIC DIP CIRCLE

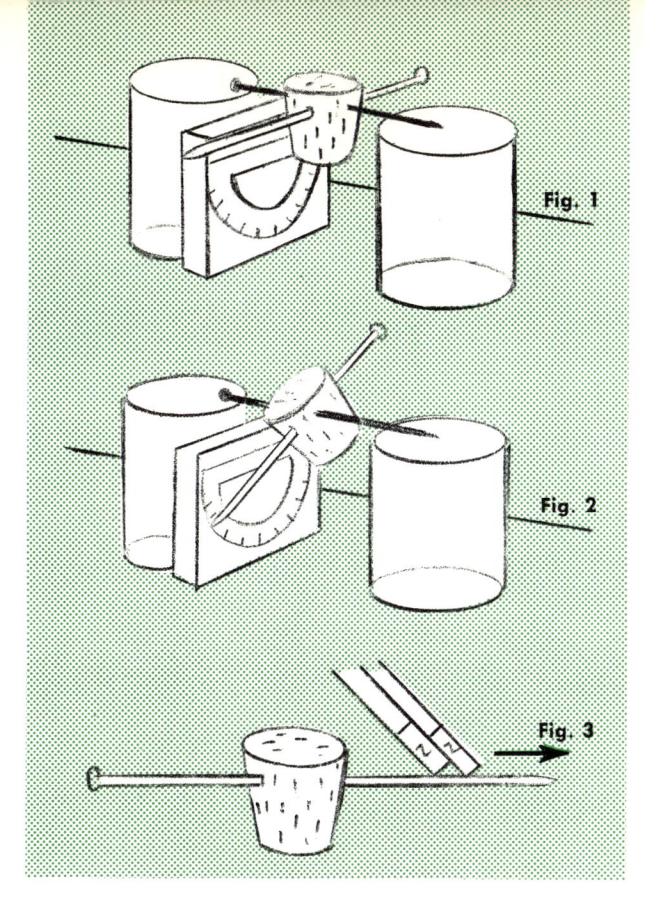

MEASURING EARTH'S MAGNETIC FIELD

Materials you'll need:
large cork, steel knitting needle, 2 sewing needles, piece of wood, compass, protractor, 2 bar magnets, 2 water glasses

You may know already that the earth itself is a magnet. Around every magnet is a magnetic field in which the lines of force operate. Everything within this magnetic field can be influenced by the magnet. The earth has a magnetic field around it in which we live all the time. It never stops working.

You can build an instrument which will show the influence of the earth's magnetic field. It is magnetism that causes the needle of the instrument to dip. The needle would be horizontal to the earth at the equator and would point straight down toward the earth at either of the magnetic poles.

Push a steel knitting needle all the way through a large cork so that the protruding ends are equal in length. It should be through the large end of the cork—as close to the top as possible. Push a sewing needle in each side of the cork so the two are opposite each other. Balance the sewing needles on two water glasses so the knitting needle balances horizontally (Fig. 1). Fasten a protractor to a block of wood so the top of it is level with the knitting needle. Put it between the glasses. If the knitting needle is turned downward, its point falls on the protractor scale (Fig. 2).

Remove the cork and needles from the glasses. Find north with the compass. Point the sharp end of the knitting needle toward the earth's magnetic north pole. Hold two magnets with the north poles together so they form one strong magnet. Stroke one end of the knitting needle in one direction along the north pole of the double magnet (Fig. 3). Hang the cork back on the glasses, so the needle points east and west. If the needle swings at all, both ends should dip equally. Immediately turn it so that the end of the needle which you have stroked with the north pole of the magnet points north (use the compass to make sure of this). If the needle is swinging, the north end should dip more sharply. The needle may stop swinging and hold its dip. The amount it dips depends on the strength of the magnets used and the length of time you stroked it. It does not indicate latitude. The purpose of the protractor is just to help you determine whether or not the needle is dipping at all. If you have trouble seeing this, a toothpick stuck in the bottom of the cork might help you to see the dip.

MAGNETISM

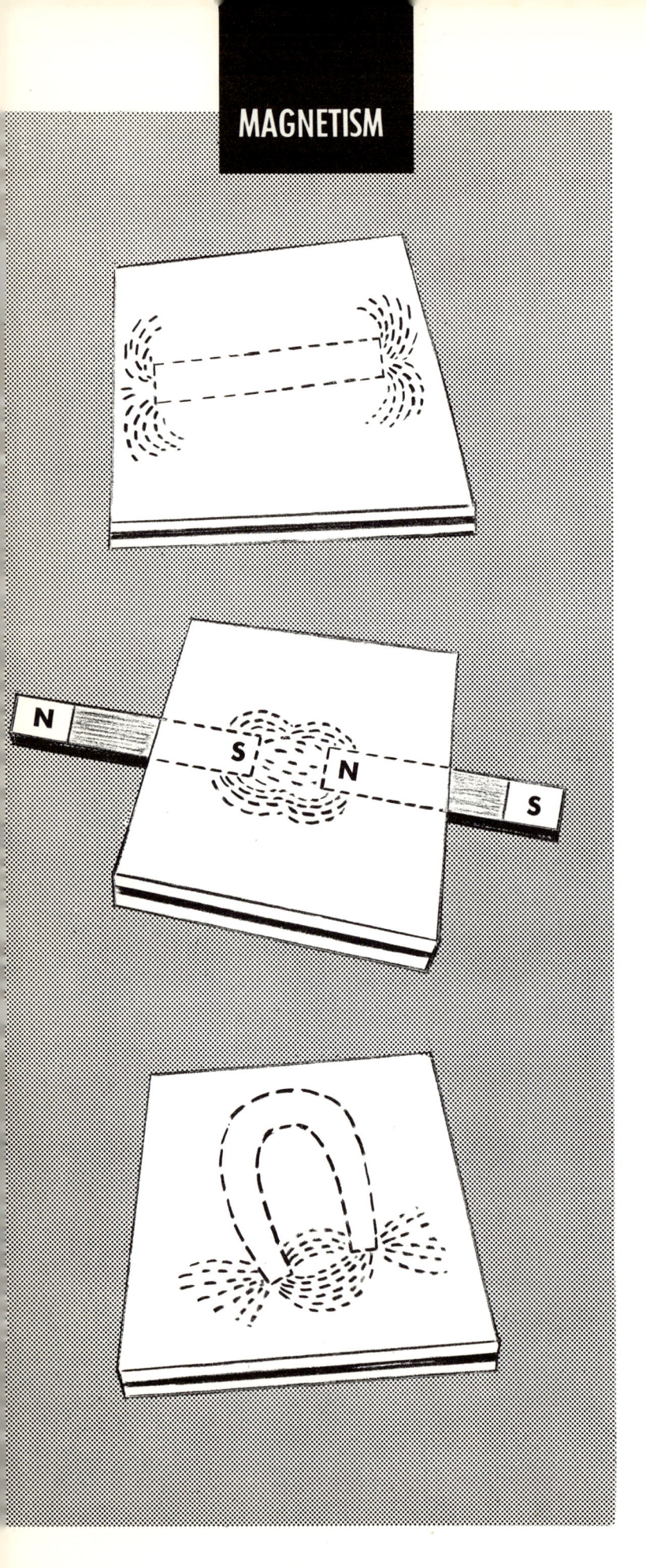

BLUEPRINTING A MAGNETIC FIELD

Materials you'll need:
blueprint paper, 2 pieces of glass, 2 bar magnets, horseshoe magnet, iron filings

The magnetic field of a magnet is actually invisible. However, iron filings will arrange themselves so that they follow the invisible lines of force which form a magnetic field.

Wait until a calm, sunny day for this activity. While you are still indoors, place a sheet of blueprint paper between two pieces of glass. You can buy the paper or make it according to directions found on page 47.

Place the glass sandwich over a bar magnet and sprinkle iron filings over it. The filings will arrange themselves in a pattern. Without disturbing the pattern, carry the glass and paper out into direct sunlight. Expose it to the light for several minutes or long enough for the paper to fade. Carry it carefully indoors, pour off the iron filings, remove the paper from the glass and rinse the paper in water. The pattern of the filings will become white against the darkened paper. You have made a picture of the lines of force of a magnet.

Do the same thing using two bar magnets with like poles together or with unlike poles together. Make a picture of the lines of force of a horseshoe magnet. Are they any different from the lines of force of a bar magnet?

MAGNETISM

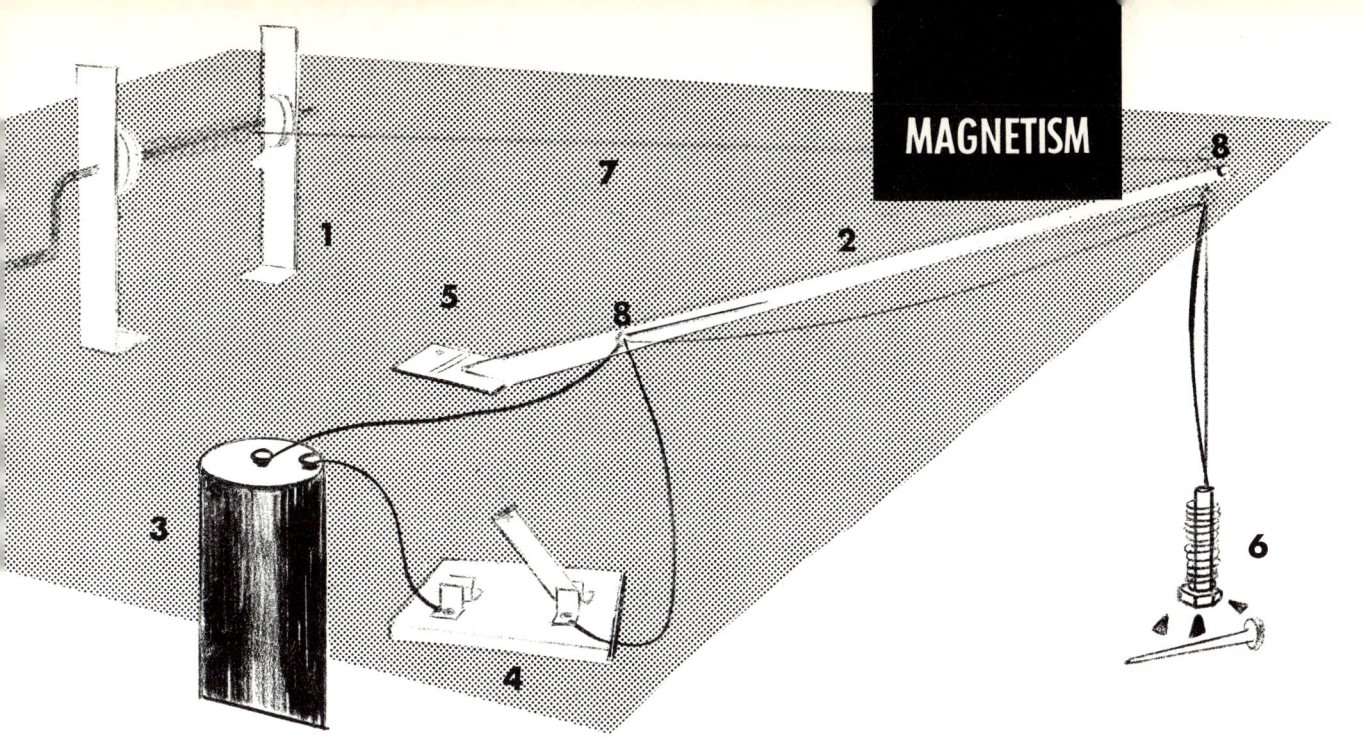

MAKING A MAGNETIC CRANE

Materials you'll need:
plywood, knife switch, bell wire, dry cell, iron bolt, eye hooks, string, dowel rod, elbow hinge, windlass

Construct a cab for the crane out of plywood. Make it similar to ones used on most road or house construction jobs. Fasten a miniature windlass (axle and two wheels off a toy car) (1), a dry cell (3), and a knife switch (4) on the floor of the cab. A projecting arm (dowel rod or 1" by 1" stick) (2) with the lower end sawed at a 45-degree angle should be fastened by an elbow hinge (5) toward the front of the cab floor. Fasten one eye hook (8) into the top forward end of the projecting arm and another at the lower end. Take several feet of heavy string (7), anchor one end to the axle of the windlass and the other end to the eye hook at the top of the projecting arm. By turning the handle of the windlass you can raise and lower the projecting arm.

Fasten one end of a piece of bell wire to the outside terminal of the dry cell and the other end to one terminal on the knife switch. (See page 188 for directions on making a switch.) Now take several feet of bell wire, fasten one end to the other terminal of the knife switch, continue through the eye hook at the lower end of the projecting arm, up its length to the forward end, through the second eye hook. Let several inches hang free. Then wrap the wire as a coil around an iron bolt which will be the electromagnet (6). Lead the wire back to the top of the projecting arm, through the eye hook, down the arm, through the lower eye hook. Fasten this remaining end of the bell wire to the middle terminal on the dry cell.

When you turn the windlass arm it will lower the electromagnet to the ground level. Close the knife switch and the magnet will attract any object made of iron or steel. This type of machine is used in industry to lift heavy objects, such as cars in junk yards, from place to place, pile driving, and loading or unloading cargo from ships.

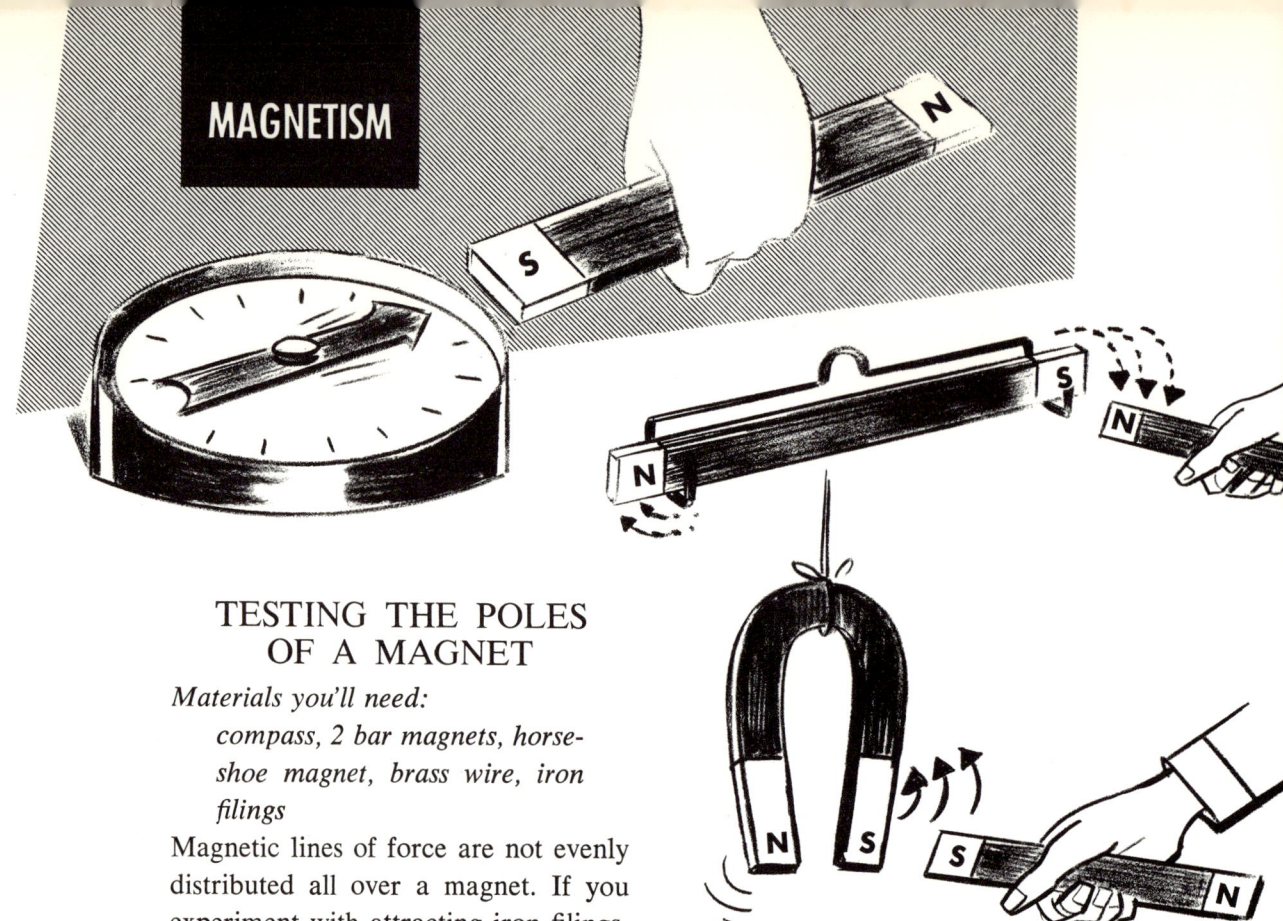

MAGNETISM

TESTING THE POLES OF A MAGNET

Materials you'll need:
compass, 2 bar magnets, horseshoe magnet, brass wire, iron filings

Magnetic lines of force are not evenly distributed all over a magnet. If you experiment with attracting iron filings, you will find that the filings will be attracted in large clusters to the ends of a magnet where the magnetism is strongest. These ends are called *poles*. Like the earth, every magnet has a north pole and a south pole. This experiment will help you find which pole is north and which is south on a magnet and will also help you make up rules about poles.

You probably already know that a compass needle is a magnet. The end with the arrow point always points toward the north magnetic pole of the earth. On a magnet, it is also called the *north pole*. (More accurately, this pole of the compass needle should be called the *north-seeking pole*.) The other end of the compass needle is the *south pole*.

Bring one end of the bar magnet near the compass. If the north pole of the compass needle is attracted to it (moves toward it), mark that end with an "S" for "south." If the north pole of the needle is repelled by it (moves away from it), mark it "N." Do this with both ends of the bar magnets and with the horseshoe magnet.

You have seen two north poles repel each other and you have seen a north pole and a south pole attract each other. Is this always true?

Bend a brass wire so that it forms a cradle for a bar magnet. Suspend it from a solid surface with string. Lay one marked magnet in the cradle. Bring the pole marked "N" on a bar magnet in your hand close to the one marked "N" on the suspended one. What happens? Now bring two south poles together. Next, bring a north pole and a south together. Tie a string around the center of the horseshoe magnet and hold it suspended. Test its poles in the same way, using a marked bar magnet. What rule about magnets have you discovered?

130

MAGNETISM

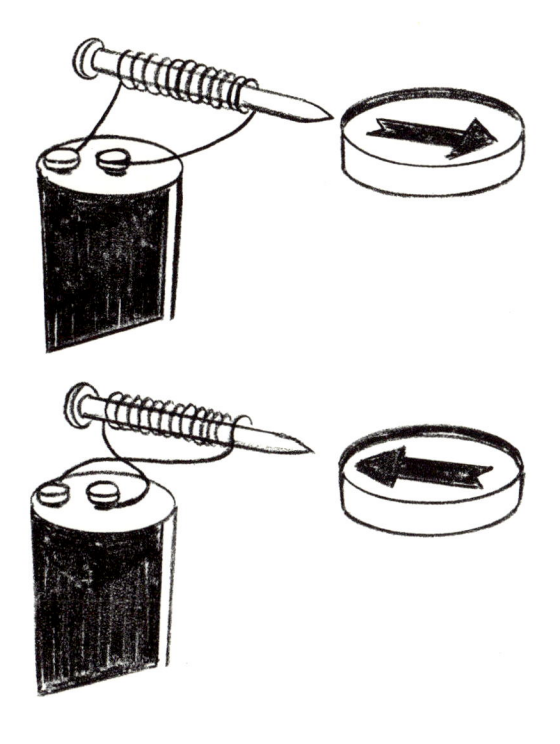

TESTING THE POLES OF AN ELECTROMAGNET

Materials you'll need:
long spike or nail, 25 feet of bell wire, dry cell, iron filings, compass

First, make an electromagnet the way you learned on page 84. Now, find the north pole of the compass needle. Using what you learned on the last page of the rules about poles of magnets, locate the north pole on your homemade electromagnet. Next, disconnect the wire ends from the dry cell and connect them just the reverse of the way they were before. The current is now going through the wire of the electromagnet in the opposite direction. What does this do to the poles of the electromagnet?

The rule you have just learned about the poles of an electromagnet changing when the flow of current is reversed is important to remember when you start learning about motors (page 142).

FINDING THAT MAGNETISM ACTS THROUGH MATTER

Materials you'll need:
pane of glass, piece of plywood, cardboard, cloth, aluminum foil, iron filings, magnet, books

Use a horseshoe magnet or a bar magnet for these experiments. Any kind of magnet will attract iron filings. When the magnetic lines of force pass through a substance to the iron filings on the other side of it, the filings will stand upright and follow the magnet as it is moved about. They look almost as if they were dancing.

If you are unable to buy iron filings at a hobby shop or machine shop, make them yourself by filing a large iron nail with a very coarse file.

Build a stand with two piles of three books each. Place the sheet of glass on the piles of books. Sprinkle iron filings on top of the glass and move the magnet around underneath it. Does the magnetism act through glass? Try the same experiment using cardboard, a wooden board and aluminum foil. Do the magnetic lines of force pass through all these substances?

MATCHES

MEALWORMS

RAISING MEALWORMS FOR PET FOOD

Materials you'll need:
  glass jar, oatmeal, raw apple or potato, mealworms

Mealworms are the favorite food for many amphibian and reptilian pets. While raising them for this purpose, you can also study the complete metamorphosis of beetles. These "worms" are the larvae of a little black beetle.

Place several layers of uncooked oatmeal in a large glass jar. Sprinkle this with water but do not make the mixture soggy. This is the food for mealworms. Put in several pieces of raw apple or potato. This is the food for the adult beetle. Drop in several mealworms from a pet shop. Cover the mouth of the jar with a very fine mesh screen. Occasionally sprinkle in a little more water. In several weeks the mealworms develop into beetles, the beetles lay eggs, and the eggs develop into mealworms. The cycle continues indefinitely as long as the environment is satisfactory, so you always have a supply of pet food.

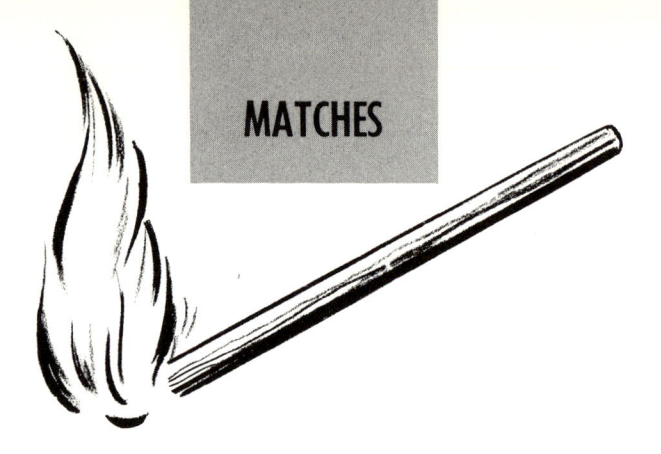

MAKING MATCHES

Materials you'll need:
  wood, knife, potassium chlorate, antimony trisulfide, glue, wax, sand, phosphorus, box

Do this activity only with the help of an adult. Whittle little pieces of wood to resemble match sticks. Combine one-half teaspoon of potassium chlorate with one-fourth teaspoon of antimony trisulfide. Add a little glue to this mixture. Dip one end of each stick into melted wax. Then dip these ends into the mixture previously prepared. Let the matches dry overnight.

To prepare a scratching surface that will ignite the matches, combine one-half teaspoon each of fine sand, phosphorus and glue. Spread this on the side of a small box and let it dry. Now you are ready to strike the homemade matches to produce a fire.

CAUTION!

METAL

OBSERVING REPLACEMENT OF METALS

Materials you'll need:
copper sulfate, glass of water, spoon or table knife, sand paper, iron screws

Some metals react with water and replace some of the hydrogen. *Hydroxides* are formed as hydrogen is given off.

Dissolve a few copper sulfate crystals in a glass half full of water. Place a spoon or table knife into this solution. What happens to the surface of the knife? The iron on it will go into solution. Then the copper accumulates on the surface of the utensil. Silver polish will remove the copper.

Place four iron screws in a solution of copper sulfate. The copper in the solution will collect on the iron.

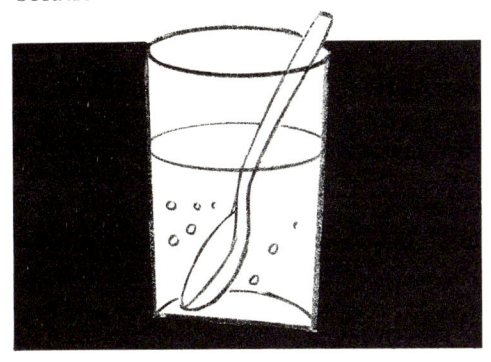

MICE

RAISING WHITE MICE

Materials you'll need:
small animal cage, pair of mice, food and water dishes

White mice make interesting pets. You must be sure that the cage you keep them in has no exposed wood on the inside that the mice can gnaw. See page 28 for making a cage. Cover the wooden frame inside with wire mesh. Make the floor of wire mesh, too, and keep a shallow pan beneath to catch waste material. This will make the cage easy to clean. The mice should be kept at normal room temperature and out of drafts and direct sunlight. The food and water containers must be fastened to the sides of the cage so that they can't be overturned. Feed your mice leafy vegetables, bird seed and potatoes. They must have fresh water daily.

A female may be bred when three months old. When she is pregnant, give her milk. She'll also need shredded newspaper with which to build a nest. You must be careful not to disturb the mother after the babies are born. Try not to handle her. If she becomes frightened she might eat her babies. She shouldn't be bred again until the young mice are three to four weeks old and can be weaned.

MICRO-PHOTOGRAPHY

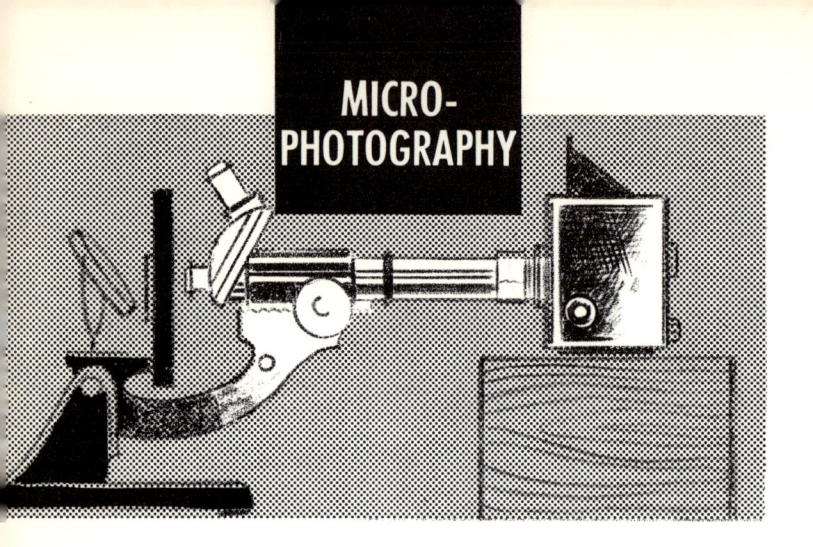

PHOTOGRAPHING MICROSCOPIC SPECIMENS

Materials you'll need:
microscope slide, standard microscope, 35mm. camera and film, masking tape

Select the microscope slide you wish to photograph. (See page 137 for preparing slides.) Place it on the microscope stage and adjust the mirror under the stage so that there is the maximum amount of light on the slide. Adjust the focus until the object to be photographed is seen very clearly.

If you can set your camera, set the shutter speed at one twenty-fifth of a second. The lens opening should be set at eight and the range finder at infinity. Now you are ready to mount the camera on the microscope. Either turn the microscope to a horizontal position and rest the camera on a block of wood so that the lens opening of the camera is directly next to the eyepiece of the microscope or invert the camera over the vertical microscope. In either case have another person wind tape around the contact point to prevent any light from filtering in. Snap the picture.

If your first pictures are not successful, you will have to experiment with changing shutter speed or exposure time. If you are a "camera bug" you will soon be able to make fine pictures.

MICROSCOPE

USING A MICROSCOPE

Materials you'll need:
compound microscope, glass slides, cover glasses, lens paper, forceps, medicine dropper, scalpel, scissors, balsam, xylol or acetone

If you are a beginning microscopist you may want to buy a microscope for under $20. As you become skilled in the use of the instrument and your interests expand, you will turn to a larger compound microscope with finer lenses and greater magnification and adaptability.

It is necessary to learn the parts and functions of your microscope. Follow the illustration as each part is described. The *eyepiece* is a lens, usually with a magnifying power of 5X or 10X. This means it will make something look five times or ten times larger than it actually is. The eyepiece is in a large *tube* leading down to the nosepiece which turns to bring each *objective* (lens or group of lenses) in line with the tube. Microscopes usually have one, two or three objectives. The shorter one is the *low power* and has the magnifying power marked on the side. To illustrate total magnification, assume that your eyepiece is 10X and your low-power objective is 43X. A specimen seen would appear to be 10 times 43 or 430 times larger than its actual size. Would this figure increase with your high-power objective (the longer one)? Multiply the powers and see.

The *coarse adjustment* (large knob) moves the tube up and down quickly.
(cont. on page 136)

134

MICROSCOPE

PARTS OF A COMPOUND MICROSCOPE

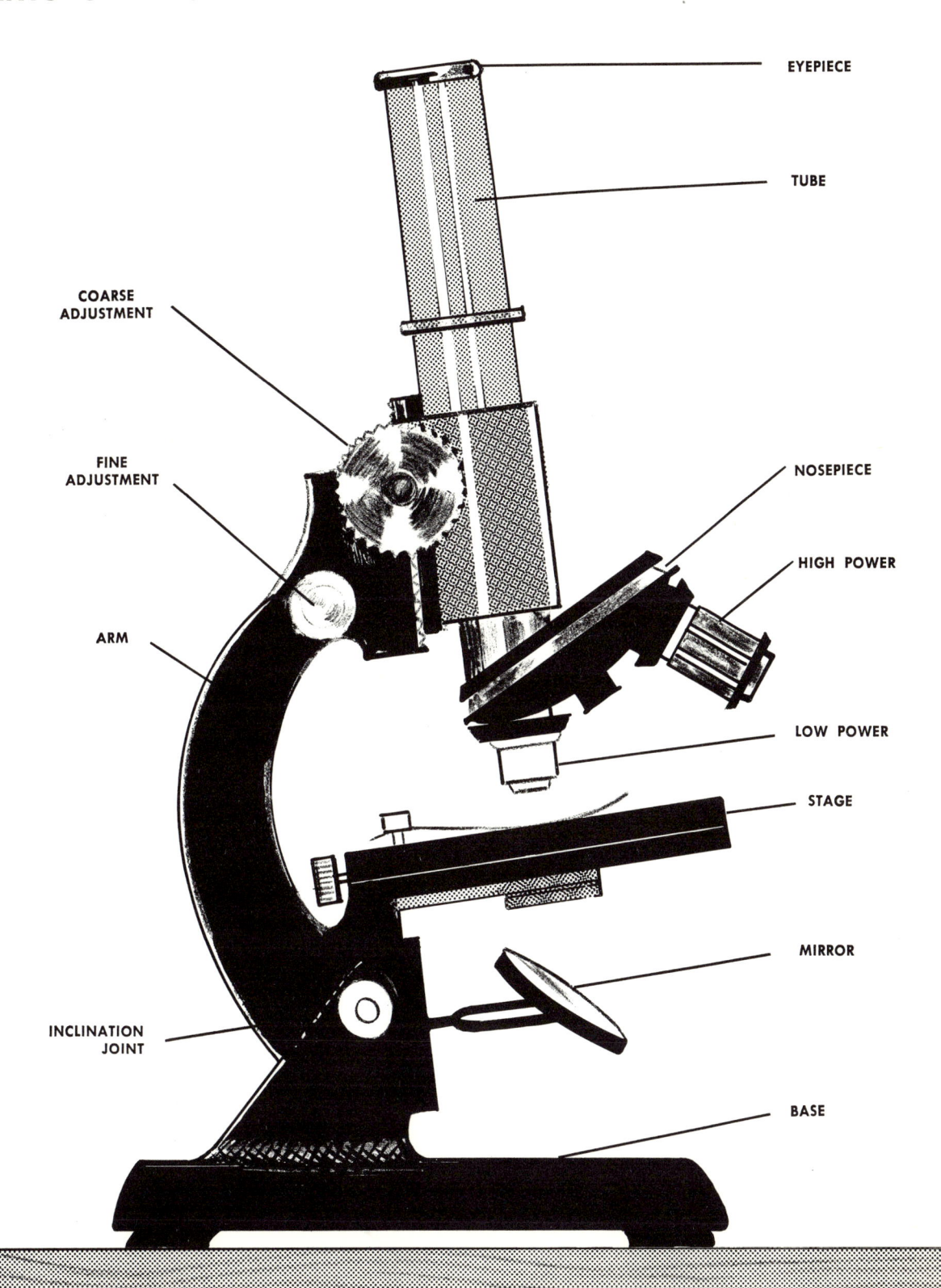

- EYEPIECE
- TUBE
- COARSE ADJUSTMENT
- FINE ADJUSTMENT
- NOSEPIECE
- HIGH POWER
- ARM
- LOW POWER
- STAGE
- MIRROR
- INCLINATION JOINT
- BASE

MICROSCOPE

Use it first in order to locate the object. Then use the *fine adjustment* to sharpen the picture. The *stage,* with clamps, holds the slide and permits light to enter through the hole. The *mirror* below the stage directs the correct amount of light through the hole onto the specimen.

When moving your microscope from place to place hold firmly to the *arm* and put your other hand under the *base* for support. Never swing the instrument or turn it upside down since the eyepiece is loose and will fly out. Some microscopes have an *inclination joint* which is used to tilt the top of the microscope backward on its base. This is to make it easier to sit and observe rather than having to stand over the instrument. Do not tip it back too far since a slight bump will cause it to fall over.

Now that you are familiar with all the parts of the microscope, begin by looking at a homemade slide. Peel off the outer membrane of an onion and place a piece in a drop of water in the center of a microscopic glass slide. The water will keep it flat. Carefully place a cover glass over this. Set the slide on the stage of the microscope with the specimen directly over the hole. Swing the nosepiece until the low power clicks in place under the tube and over the slide. Looking in the eyepiece, adjust the mirror under the stage until you have a bright light. While you are watching the low-power objective, turn the coarse adjustment away from you until the lens is very close to the slide. Do not look in the eyepiece while you are doing this. Can you see how easily you could ram the objective into the slide, breaking it and scratching the fine lens on the microscope? Remember, never focus downward while looking in the instrument. Now look in the eyepiece and very slowly turn the coarse adjustment toward you (counter-clockwise) until the specimen comes into view. If it is fuzzy, use the fine adjustment to clear it up. When you are ready to swing the nosepiece to bring the high-power objective into line with the tube, be sure the specimen is in the exact center of your circle of vision. Since the high power has greater magnification it will enlarge the center, while specimens to the edge of the circle of light will be out of range.

Periodically your lenses will become dusty and fingerprinted. With lens paper and xylol clean the objectives, eyepiece, and mirror. Slides and cover glasses should be wiped clean of lint and prints before using them. The supplies listed at the start will help you discover the many objects in nature you will want to observe. Clean these materials after using them each time and store them in a covered box. Remember, anything that can be put on a slide will give you fascinating observations through your microscope.

MAKING MICROSCOPIC SPECIMEN SLIDES

Materials you'll need:
microscopic slides, cover glasses, balsam, biological specimens, knife or razor blade, eosin solution

The owner of a microscope has many exciting hours in store for him. He can look at plants and animals too tiny to see without magnification.

Purchase a box of plain microscopic slides and cover glasses. Put a drop of stagnant pond water on a slide and place a cover glass over it. If your microscope has two lenses, look for specimens under low power first, then turn to high power when the specific object is centered in the first view. You can watch one-celled animals eat if you add a tiny drop of eosin solution at the edge of the cover glass. This seeps under and soon *Paramecia, Euglena,* and *Amebae* will be filled with little red dots.

Numerous temporary slides can be made by adding a specimen to a drop of water on the slide. You can study epithelial tissue by lightly scraping the inside of your cheek with a toothpick. Take a piece of fresh meat, spread out the fibers, and observe muscular tissue. With a sharp knife or razor blade cut very thin slices of raw liver, skin, beef heart, intestine, stem, leaf, root, onionskin, and other living tissue. How are animal and plant cells different and similar?

If you wish to make permanent slides you will need a bottle of balsam. Set it in a pan of hot water. As the balsam warms it will become thinner and easier to work with. Place your specimen in the center of a slide. Put a small droplet of balsam on top of it. Lower the cover glass until it touches the balsam before you release it. Dropping it on will cause bubbles to form. Tap gently until the balsam spreads to the edge of the cover glass. If you put too much balsam on the slide it will make the cover glass too high or it will ooze out around the edges. Set the slide aside for a couple of days until it dries. Secure a slide box in which to file the labeled slides. Record all you notice about each slide.

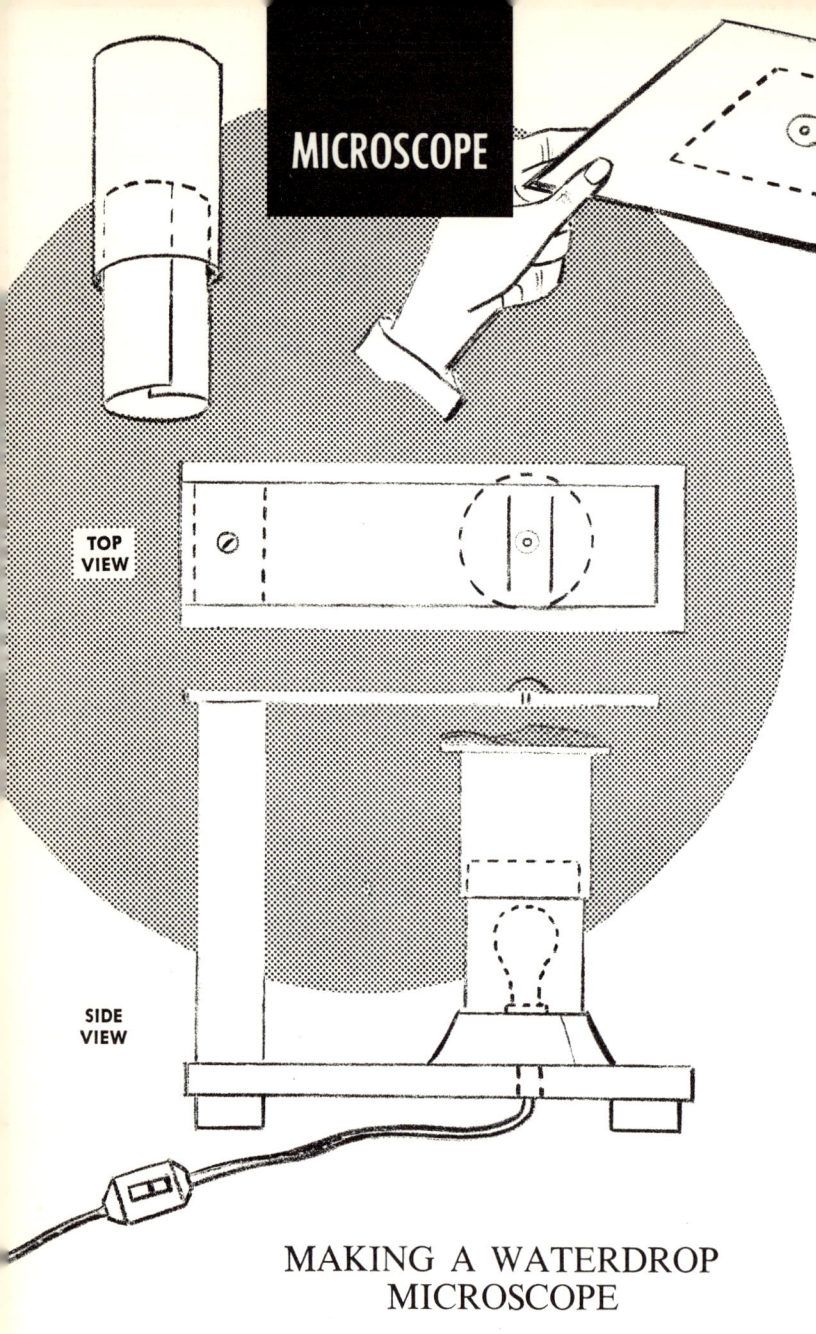

MICROSCOPE

WATERDROP OVER CELLOPHANE TAPE-COVERED HOLE

CLEAR TAPE

CARDBOARD

TOP VIEW

SIDE VIEW

You have experimented with refraction—the bending of light which occurs when light rays move from one material to another (page 126). The lens found in a magnifying glass or microscope is curved so that it bends light in such a way that objects seen through the lens look much larger. A drop of water can serve as a lens, bending light rays and magnifying objects.

Cut a small hole in a piece of cardboard. Tape a piece of cellophane tape over the hole and put a drop of water on the little window you have made. Look at printing through the drop and you will see that it is greatly enlarged.

Making a good microscope with a glass lens is both complicated and expensive, but you can make a good waterdrop microscope using the principle just seen, with ease and little expense.

Assemble your microscope stand by following the illustration. Remove the tops and bottoms from two round oatmeal boxes. Cut one of the cardboard cylinders from top to bottom so that it may be fitted into the other one. Be careful that the inner cylinder fits tightly. Tape only the bottom of this inner cylinder.

Fix the light socket, cord and plug in the base of the stand according to the illustration. If you haven't had experience with wiring, get help with it.

Tape the telescoping cardboard cylinders to the base directly over the bulb. The cut cylinder which fits inside the uncut one is the lower one in the diagram and is fastened to the stand.

The metal sheet which will support the "lens" should be made of as thick a piece of metal as can be supported by

MAKING A WATERDROP MICROSCOPE

Materials you'll need:

cardboard, cellophane, oatmeal boxes, piece of wood ½" thick and 8½" by 4", piece of wood ½" thick by 5¼" by 4", four pieces of wood ½" thick and 1" square, clear cellophane tape, 7½-watt frosted lightbulb, lamp cord, switchless light socket, square piece of glass, thin sheet of metal 4" by 5½", medicine dropper, distilled water, miscellaneous screws and nails the frame and easily drilled with the tools you have available. The 1/16-inch hole must be placed as nearly as possible over the center of the cardboard cylinders. The screw holding the metal to the top of the frame should not be tightened all the way down. The lens support should be movable so that focusing on specimens and changing lightbulbs can be done easily. File the hole drilled to remove all roughness. Put a small piece of cellophane tape over the hole.

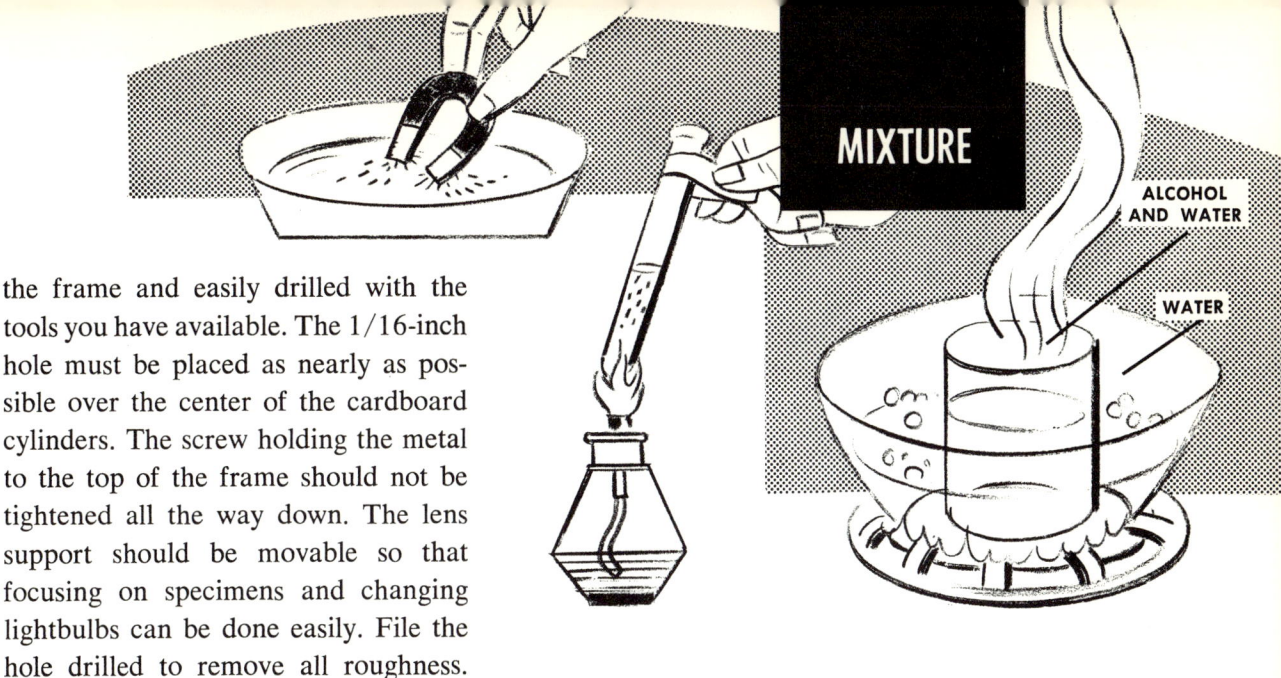

Place the square of glass over the cardboard cylinder. This glass is the platform on which the specimen to be examined will be placed.

With the medicine dropper, place a drop of distilled water over the hole on the tape on the metal sheet. You can obtain distilled water by removing some of the frost which has accumulated on a freezing unit and melting it. It contains none of the minerals found in tap water and will be a cleaner lens.

Place a feather on the glass plate and, with the light on, move it directly under the "lens." With your eye as near the waterdrop as possible, focus by carefully moving the outer cardboard cylinder up and down over the inner one. If you are unable to get a sharp image, try a different lens. Wipe away the drop and try a new one. When you have determined proper drop size and lens-to-specimen distance, you will find your waterdrop microscope a satisfactory instrument.

Use it to look at a fly's wing, a magazine picture or any other items that you might be investigating. The magnification is not great so use large objects.

TESTING A MIXTURE

Materials you'll need:
iron filings, sulfur powder, magnet, carbon disulfide, alcohol, water, 2 beakers, source of heat

A mixture is made up of two or more elements or compounds stirred together. It is different from a *compound* in that the parts of the mixture are not chemically united. They can be separated by physical means.

Mix together iron filings and sulfur powder. They can be separated rather easily. Simply pull the iron out with a magnet or dissolve the sulfur in carbon disulfide. They haven't been chemically changed by being mixed.

Mix them again and heat them this time. The heat causes a chemical change to take place. Iron sulfide is formed. The iron and the sulfur cannot be easily separated. A chemical process would have to be used.

Try mixing alcohol and water. Heat it cautiously by placing the beaker of alcohol and water in a larger beaker or pan of water. Heat the water in the larger beaker. The alcohol will be boiled off at a much lower temperature than the water. They are a mixture and so can be separated by physical means.

CAUTION!

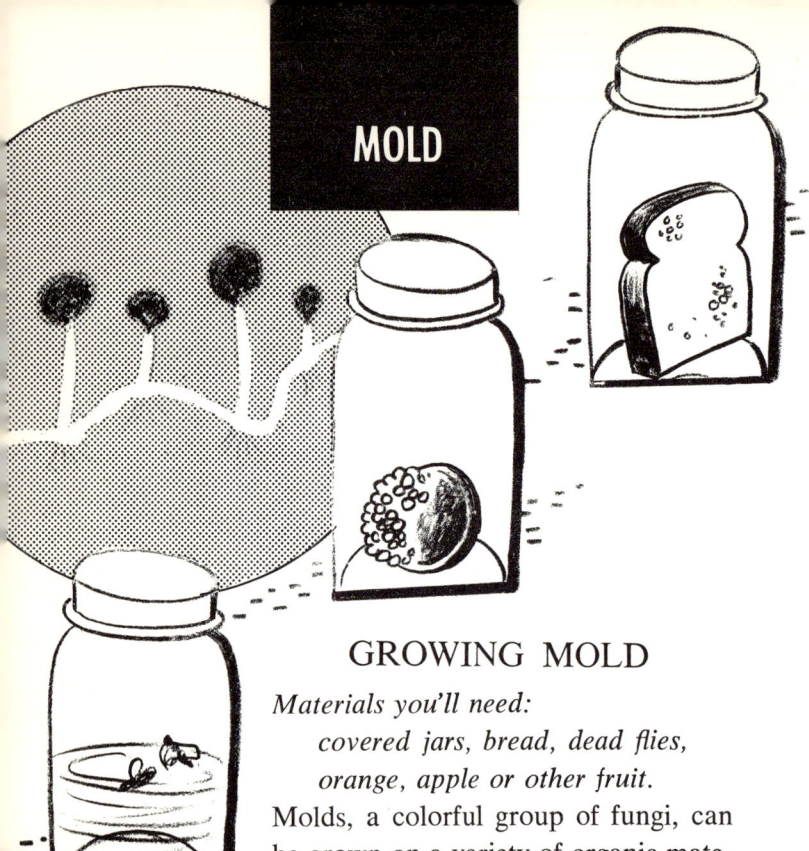

MOLD

GROWING MOLD

Materials you'll need:
covered jars, bread, dead flies, orange, apple or other fruit.

Molds, a colorful group of fungi, can be grown on a variety of organic materials. They must be grown in covered jars since the host begins to smell bad as the mold feeds upon it.

Expose a slice of bread to the air for an hour. Mold spores will fall upon it from the air. A quicker method is to wipe up a dusty floor with the slice of bread. Sprinkle it lightly with water and place it in a covered glass jar. Put the jar in a warm, dark cupboard for a week. Bread mold has white stalks with little black balls on the ends. These are the *spore cases*.

Water mold can be made by placing dead flies in a jar of water. In a few days the insects are covered with a white fuzz. This is mold.

An orange, apple, or other fruit which has been bruised can be bottled. The mold and bacteria working on the fruit gradually cause the cells to disintegrate.

Take four slices of the same kind of bread and leave them in the open air for one hour. Sprinkle each slice with the same amount of water. Place in separate covered jars. Put one jar in a warm, dark cupboard. Keep a second jar in the refrigerator, a third jar in the cupboard but without a cover, and the fourth jar in the sunlight. Leave all the containers in these places for the same length of time. Compare the growth of mold after several days. Does mold grow faster in a warm or cold temperature, in light or dark, and under wet or dry conditions?

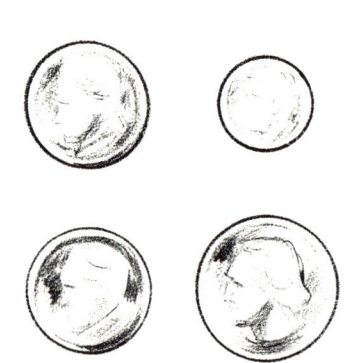

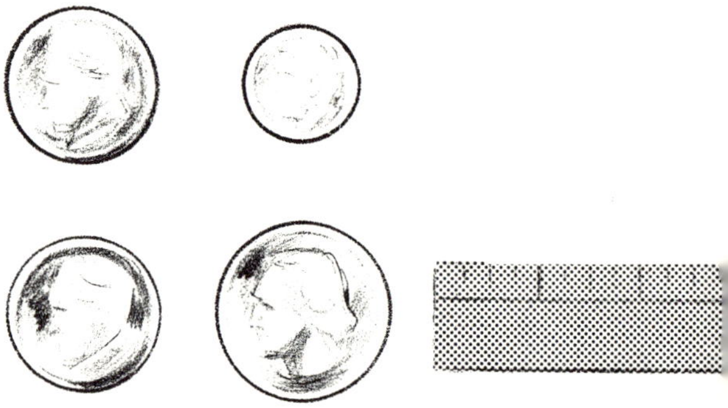

MOMENTUM

DEMONSTRATING MOMENTUM

Materials you'll need:
2 nickels, dime, quarter, ruler

Place the coins equal distances apart on a smooth table top. With a ruler give the quarter a push so that it slides into one nickel. Push the dime with the same speed into the other nickel. The first nickel moved farther than the other. Why?

Mark the resting positions of two nickels. Slide one into the other. Note that the nickel that was hit did not move as far as the one that hit it. They have the same mass but some energy was lost by the hit coin. What caused this? Does the weight of each coin have any effect on momentum?

MOON

MOSS

SHOWING THE PHASES OF THE MOON

Materials you'll need:
   lamp without a shade, ball, dark room

During the course of a month, the moon is seen to go through phases according to how much reflected light we receive from it. These changes are caused by its position in relation to the earth as the moon revolves around us. Try this demonstration.

Set the lamp without a shade on a table in a dark room. Stand several feet away from the source of light. Hold the ball out in front of you so it is in line with your eyes and the bulb in the lamp. The light is the sun, the ball is the moon, and you are on the earth. Now move the moon (ball) slightly to the left of the bulb. How much of the moon is lighted at this point? Turn on your heels so that the ball moves in a circle. At which point is there a full moon? A new moon?

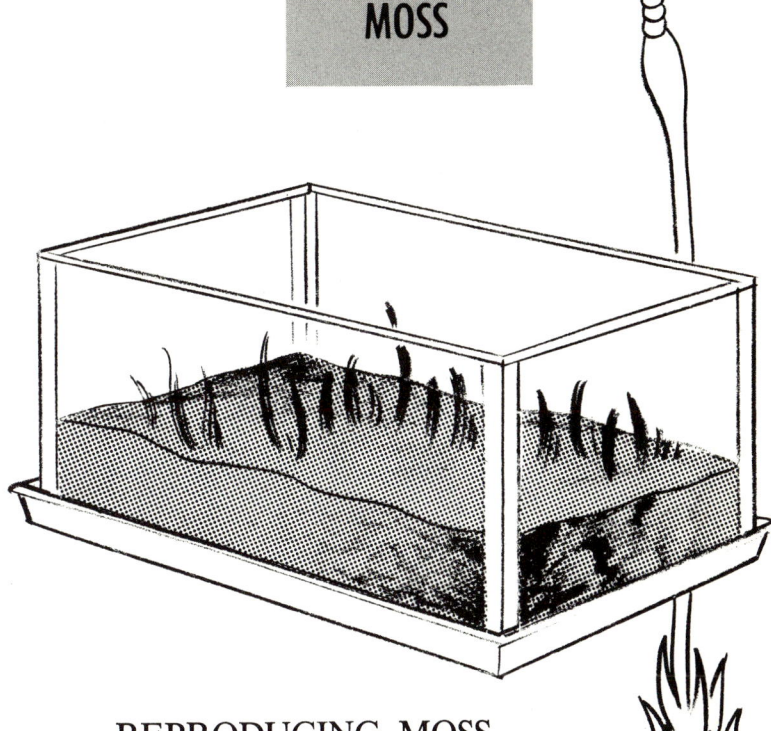

REPRODUCING MOSS

Materials you'll need:
   woodland terrarium, sulfur, moss, hand lens

Take a hike into the woods to gather moss. It will usually be found in moist, shady places. Transfer the plants and soil to a woodland terrarium (see page 194 for instructions on building). Water well and do not keep your moss house in direct sunlight. A little sulfur sprinkled in the soil will prevent growth of mold.

Examine the tops of the little upright shoots with a hand lens. One kind will produce the sperm and another will form the eggs. After the egg is fertilized by the sperm a little stalk grows up out of the female head. At the top of the stalk will be the capsule containing the spores. When the capsule breaks open the spores fall to the soil and germinate into new plants.

MOTOR

MAKING AN ELECTRIC MOTOR

Materials you'll need:

3 iron spikes, rectangular piece of wood, iron nail, large cork, medicine dropper, metal foil, tape, small nails, spool of bell wire, 3 dry cells

The main parts of an electric motor are the *field magnets* (F), the *armature* (A), the *commutator* (C), and the *brushes* (B). (Look for the letters in the picture.) The field magnets and the armature are electromagnets.

Remember that every magnet has a north and a south pole. Remember, too, that like poles repel each other and unlike poles attract each other. Also, the direction of the current in the coils of the model armature changes each time it goes through half a turn. The change of current direction determines which armature pole is north and which is south. (See the activity on electromagnets on page 131.)

The wiring for the field magnets of the motor that you are going to make is arranged so that their poles remain unchanged. Instead, it is the commutator that reverses the current in the armature just when the north pole of the armature comes next to—and swings past—the south pole of the field magnet. This movement reverses the brush contacts with the commutator, so that the north pole becomes the south pole, and the armature is pulled onward, attracted by the other field magnet. In this way, the current coming in from the brush wires is being reversed every half turn at their sliding contact on the commutator. The change is timed so that opposite poles are always attracting and the armature is always turning.

You can build a working electric motor by following the diagram carefully. The motor will not work if the wires are not wound in the right direction or are not fastened securely.

Drive three iron spikes (1, 2, 3 in the diagram) through the back of a large board, spacing them as shown. To start the armature, insert a long iron nail (6) crosswise through a large cork (5). Slip the medicine dropper (4) over the center spike (2), on which the cork and nail should rotate freely. Be sure that the nail-in-the-cork (6 and 5) rotates very close to the upper ends of the spikes (1 and 3).

To make the commutator, cut two strips of metal foil (7a and 7b) and fasten them temporarily with tape. Fasten them as half cylinders around the lower end of the medicine-dropper tube, leaving a little space of uncovered glass between the pieces of foil.

To support the brush wires against the commutator, drive two small nails (8, 9) into the wood about one inch on either side of the center nail (2).

Now you are ready to use the spool of bell wire. Be sure to remove the insulation at all contact points, but nowhere else. To wind the first field magnet, fasten the end of one wire (10) to one terminal of three dry cells connected in series (see page 80). Make 100 turns of insulated wire around the field magnet (spike 1), looping the end around the nail (8). The end of this wire should be stretched straight and insulation removed, so it can slide (as

142

MOTOR

DETAIL OF BRUSHES AND COMMUTATOR

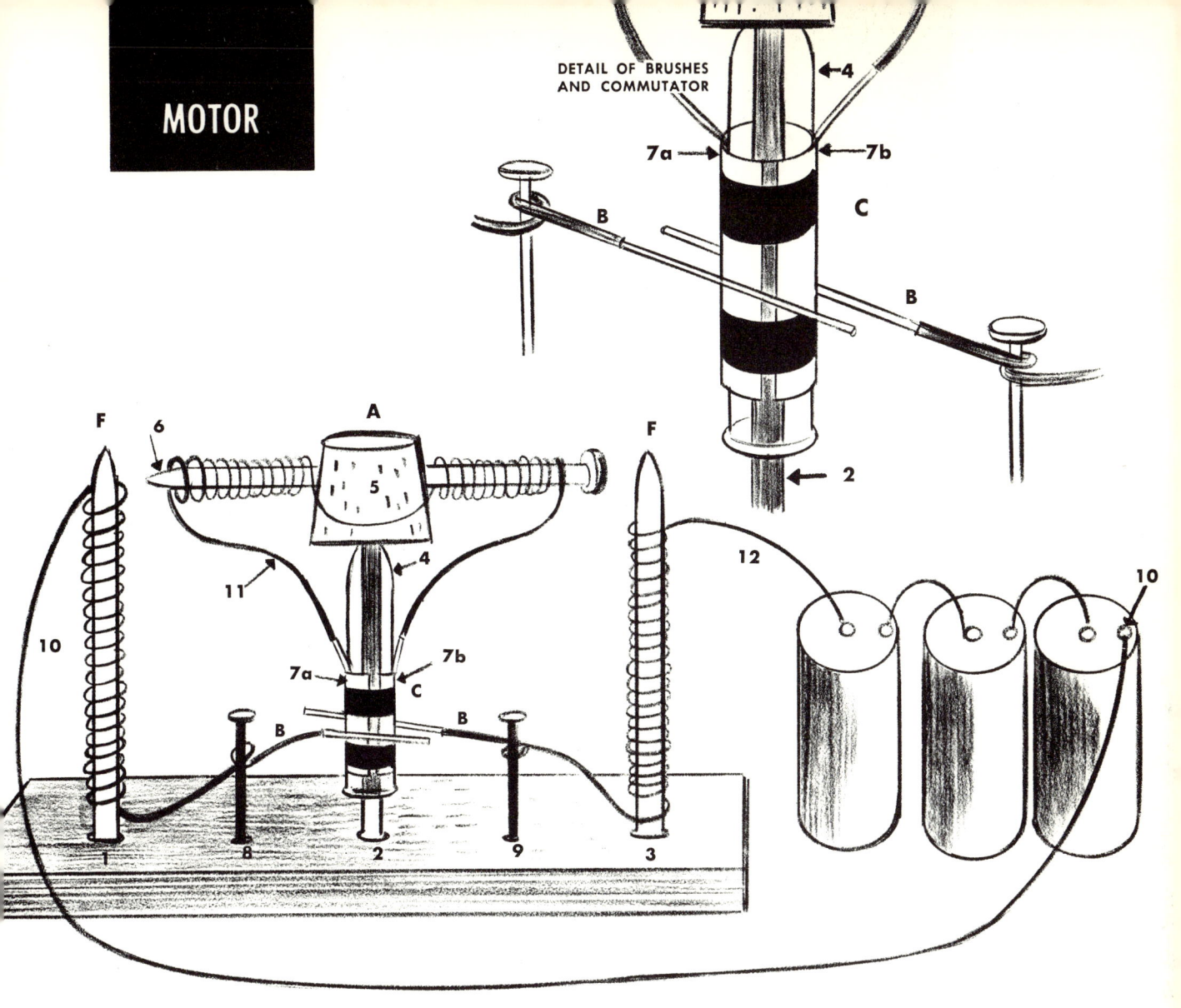

a brush) in contact with first one, then the other of the two half-strips of foil as they rotate.

Take the second wire (11) and, leaving about two inches of bared wire free, start at an outer end of the nail-in-cork (6), and wrap 40 turns around that end of the armature. Then extend the wire across the cork and continue to wrap 40 more turns—in the same direction—on the other half of the armature nail. Leave about two inches of bared wire at this end, too. Now gather the two bare ends and insert them, each under one of the half-strips of foil and retape the two halves securely around the medicine dropper.

To wind the second field magnet, fasten one end of the third wire (12) to the remaining terminal of the dry cell series. Wind 100 turns around the spike (3)—in the same direction as that of the first spike. Loop the end over the nail (9), stretching its bared end so that it can slide as a second brush in contact with first one, then the other of the two half-strips of foil (7a, 7b). But it should touch the commutator on the opposite side from that of the first field-magnet wire.

Your motor should now start turning. It may be necessary to give the armature (6) a slight push to start it rotating.

143

MUSICAL INSTRUMENTS

MAKING MUSICAL INSTRUMENTS

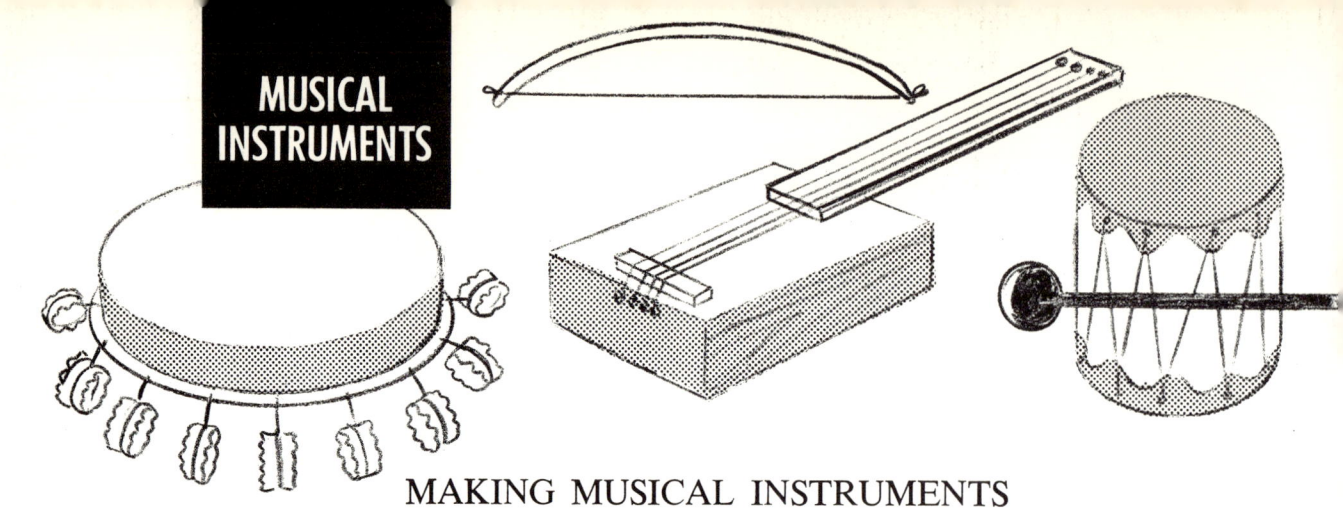

Materials you'll need:

8 pop bottles, cigar box, wood, picture wire, 8 eye screws, stick, long hairs, coffee cans, tire inner tube, cord, 1' dowel rod, solid rubber ball, aluminum pie pan, 24 bottle caps, sandpaper, wooden blocks

If you and your neighborhood friends each make a musical instrument, you can form a rhythm band.

Musical bottles: Find eight bottles that are the same weight and dimension. Leave one bottle empty. Put varying amounts of water in the other seven so that the column of air left in each bottle can be tuned to a note of the musical scale. The stick may be used to tap each bottle or you may blow across the mouth of each bottle. Which bottle makes the highest note? The lowest note? What material (glass, water, or air) is vibrating to cause the sounds?

Violin: Cut a large hole in the taped-down cover of a cigar box. Screw down a strip of wood on one end. Fasten four small eye screws on the top end of this board and on the side of the other end of the box. Attach four pieces of picture wire across the violin to these screws. They may be turned in order to loosen or tighten the wires while tuning your violin to a piano or tuning fork. A small piece of wood should be inserted under the wires near one end of the box. A bow may be made from a curved stick and several strands of hair from a friend's ponytail or real pony.

Drums: Remove both ends from a one-pound and a two-pound coffee can, and a large potato-chip can. Cut circles of tire tubing about two inches larger than the open ends of the drums. With heavy cord or leather thongs lace the circles over the ends of the cans as shown in the illustration. The drums may be hit with the hand or a beater made with a dowel rod inserted into a solid rubber ball.

Tamborines: Wire two bottle caps back to back. Fasten pairs of these to the rim of an aluminum pie pan. They will add "music" to your rhythm band.

Sand blocks: Tack strips of sandpaper to wooden blocks. Fashion a handle for the top. Use different coarsenesses of paper for each set to vary the sounds. Rub them across each other in rhythm.

NATURE TRAIL

NERVOUS SYSTEM

SETTING UP A NATURE TRAIL

Materials you'll need:
identification books, cardboard labels, plastic envelopes, sticks

If your school is near a park or woods, you can do the school a service and have fun at the same time by marking out a nature trail for students to follow.

In order to mark various plants along the trail, you will need identification books showing trees, flowers, mosses, ferns, fungi, and shrubs. Write your labels as you move along the trail you've chosen and insert them in plastic holders to protect them from the weather. The labels can be nailed directly onto trees. But in the case of flowers or moss and the like, attach the labels to sticks and insert them in the ground as close to the plant as possible. Some plants will die over the winter while others will appear in the same place every spring.

TESTING YOUR REACTIONS TO STIMULI

You are always responding to stimuli in your environment—things around you that cause you to react in some way. Most of the time you can decide what to do about the stimuli. But there are some responses called *reflexes* which are controlled by your *autonomic nervous system*. You cannot stop these reactions from happening. They are done automatically by the nervous system and are usually out of your control. Can you see the advantage this has for the proper functioning of our bodies? Try these tests.

1. Have a partner make a quick motion in front of your eyes. Try not to blink.

2. Have him tickle the back of your neck with a feather. Can you stop from having "goose bumps" on your skin?

3. When you are embarrassed keep yourself from blushing. Try not to let the blood vessels dilate in your face. This causes the flushed appearance.

4. Sit relaxed on a chair and cross your legs. Have someone tap with the side of his hand just below your knee when you aren't watching. Can you keep your foot from kicking out?

5. When you get a strong impulse to sneeze, try to stop it. Do not touch your nose with your hand.

NERVOUS SYSTEM

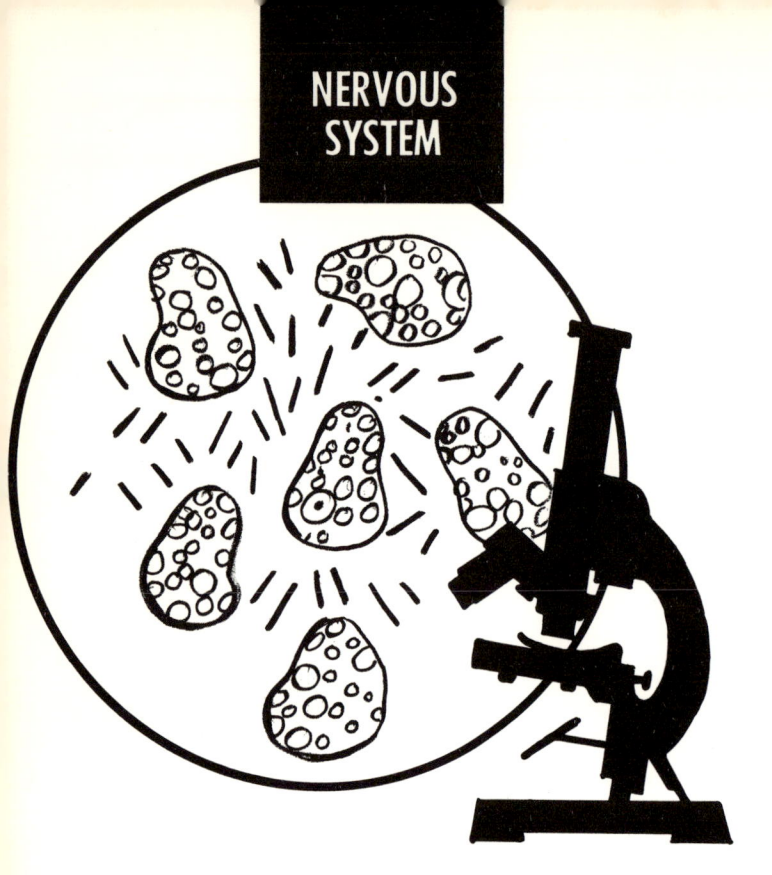

SEEING IF ONE-CELLED ANIMALS REACT

Materials you'll need:
　microscope, glass slide, cover glass, Protozoa, steel wool, eye dropper

One-celled animals, *Protozoa,* have no nervous system, eyes, ears, or other sense organs that react to the environment. Is it possible then for them to react to outside stimuli?

Cut up several strands of steel wool into tiny bits and put them in the center of a glass slide. Place a drop of *Protozoa* culture (see page 158) on top of this and cover with a cover glass. Quickly bring the specimens into focus under the low-power objective of the microscope. If the animals appear too small to observe well, swing the high power into place. You will notice the tiny animals bumping into pieces of steel wool. Continue to watch for several minutes. What changes occur? Did the *Protozoa* "learn" to go around the solid particles?

OPTICAL ILLUSIONS

TESTING YOUR EYES

Materials you'll need:
　cardboard, felt pen or crayon

Here are a couple of experiments with which you can fool your friends. They show that you can't always trust your eyes.

Cut out two pieces of cardboard exactly the same size. Cut them the same shape as in the illustration in Figure 1, making sure that they are exactly the same width. Lay them down, one above the other, on a dark surface. Does one look longer than the other? Are they the same size? Switch them around. Which one looks longer?

The second illusion (Figure 2) depends on *perspective* to make it work. When we use perspective in a drawing, we draw objects in the background smaller than those close-up in order to get the appearance of distance.

In the second drawing, the distant part of the fence is smaller than the front. Which boy looks tallest? Is he actually taller when you measure him?

Fig. 1

Fig. 2

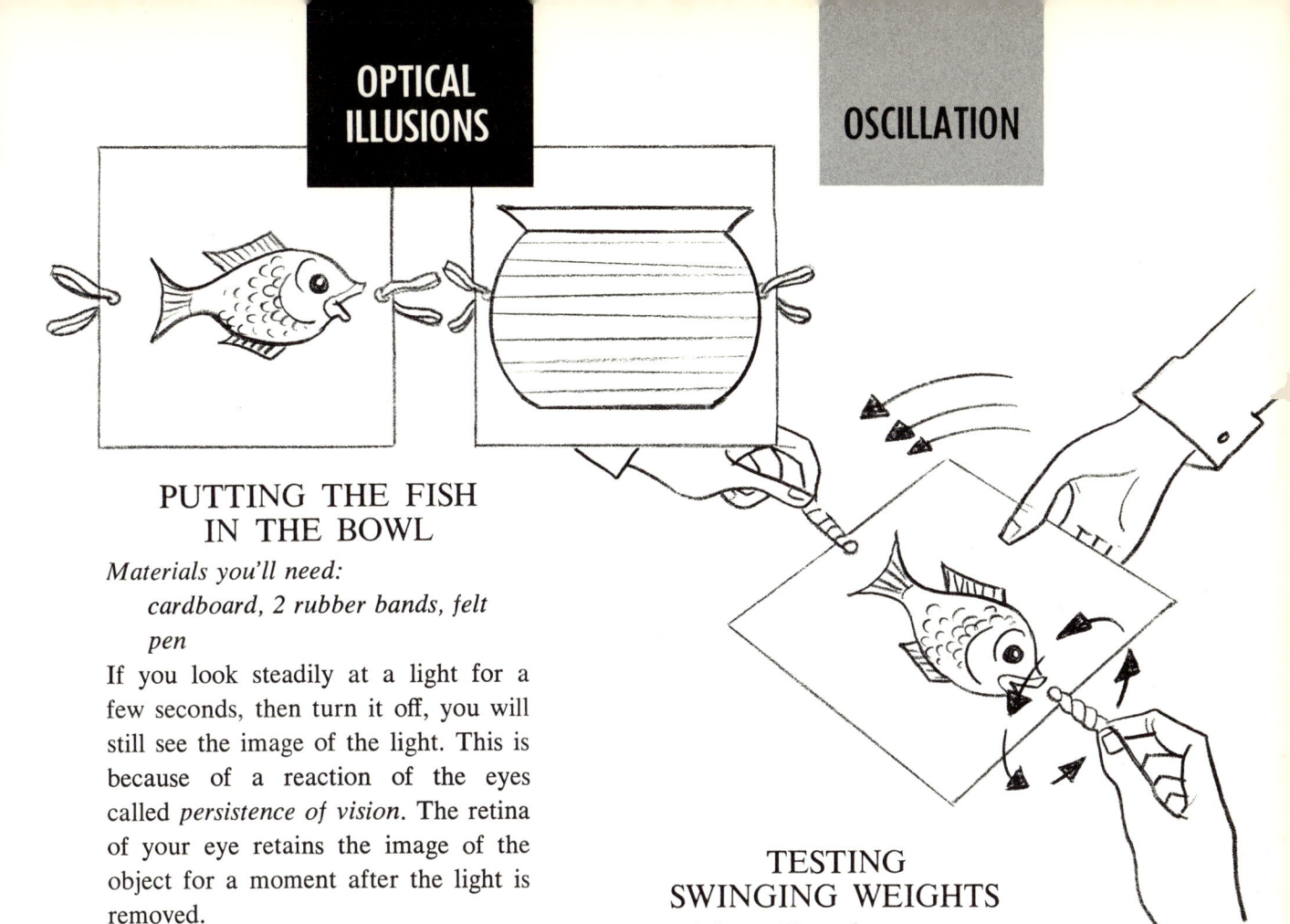

OPTICAL ILLUSIONS

PUTTING THE FISH IN THE BOWL

Materials you'll need:
   cardboard, 2 rubber bands, felt pen

If you look steadily at a light for a few seconds, then turn it off, you will still see the image of the light. This is because of a reaction of the eyes called *persistence of vision*. The retina of your eye retains the image of the object for a moment after the light is removed.

Before motion pictures were invented, people tried many ways of getting action in pictures using what they knew about persistence of vision. This is one method they used.

Cut a square of cardboard about four by four inches. Draw a picture of a fish on one side of it, pick up the bottom and turn it over, bottom to top. Draw a picture of a fish bowl on the other side.

Punch a hole in each side of the card, exactly in the middle between top and bottom. Thread one rubber band through each hole and double it back. While you hold on to the ends of the rubber bands, have a partner "wind up" the card as shown in the illustration. When he lets go, it will spin so fast that you will seem to be seeing the fish and bowl at the same time—with the fish swimming in the bowl.

OSCILLATION

TESTING SWINGING WEIGHTS

Materials you'll need:
   2 stones, rope, eye screw

This experiment will help you determine whether the weight of a swinging object determines the speed with which it swings.

Insert an eye screw in a door frame. Tie one rope around a large rock and another around a small rock. Tie the ends of both of the ropes to the screw eye. Make sure both ropes are the same length.

Swing the rocks at exactly the same time from the same point. Does the heavier rock swing faster than the lighter one?

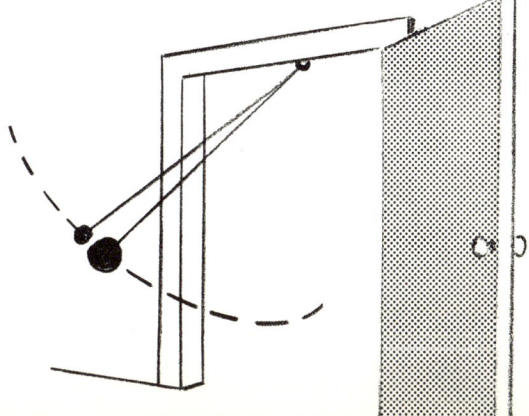

147

OSMOSIS

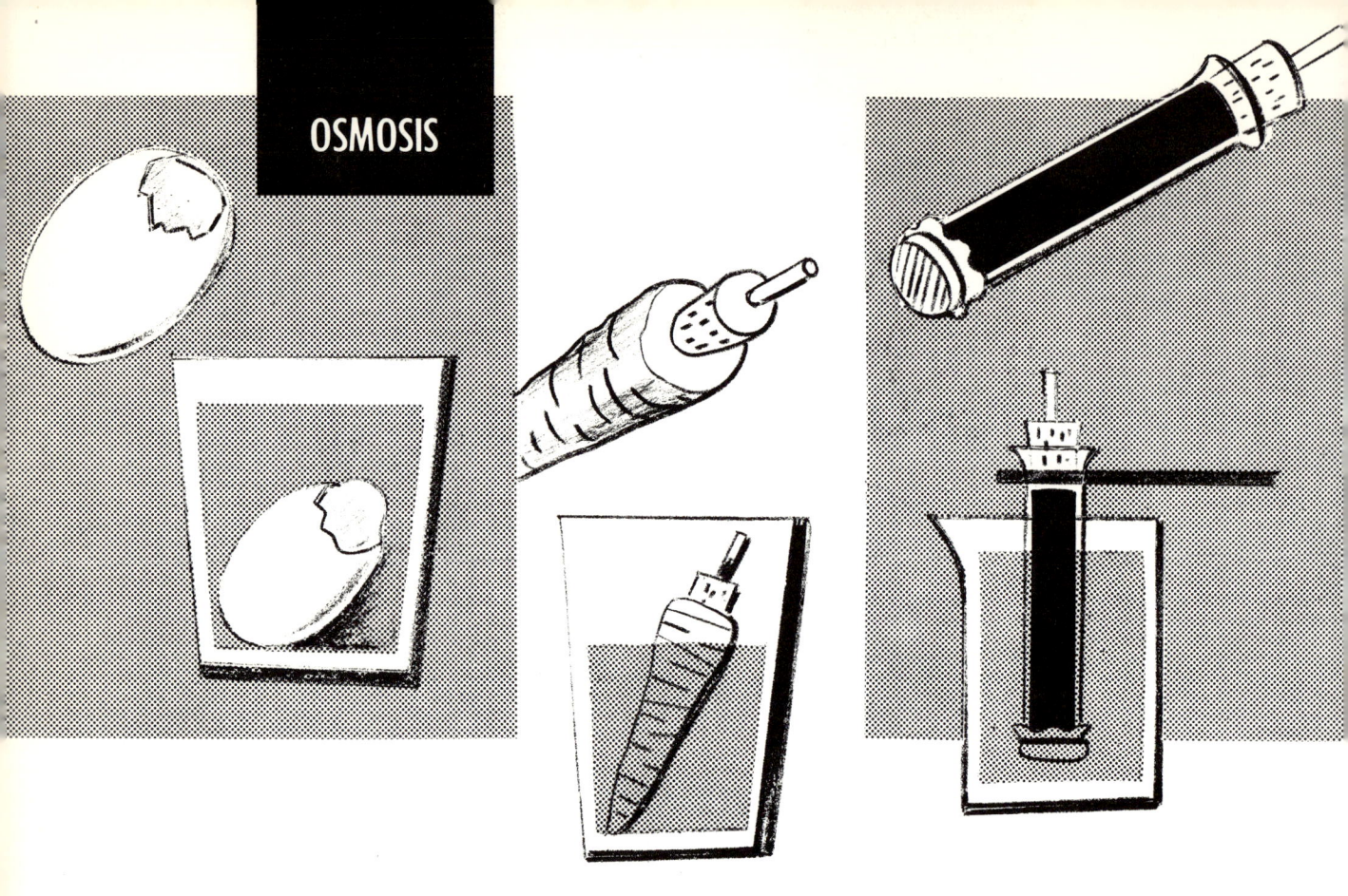

OBSERVING OSMOSIS

Materials you'll need:
egg, glass of water, carrot, 2 1-holed corks, 2 glass tubes, wax, ink, test tube, wire, sausage casing, rubber band, molasses, beaker, ring stand, vegetable dye

When two solutions are separated by a thin membrane, the more dilute solution will pass through it and move into the more concentrated solution if the membrane is permeable to it (if the particles can pass through). (See page 73 for the activity on diffusion.) Set up several *osmometers*, following directions below, to determine which solutions go in which direction.

Carefully remove part of the shell at the large end of an egg. Do not break the membrane under the shell. Immerse the egg in a glass of water. What happens to the water?

Hollow out the top end of a carrot or beet. Insert a one-holed cork into the hollow and put melted wax around it to seal it closely to the root. Carefully put a glass tube in the cork. Now place the carrot in colored water. What comes up the tube, clear water or colored water?

Remove the bottom of a test tube by winding a wire around it and then holding this end over a flame. When the wire becomes hot it will break the end off the tube. Be sure to file the broken end so it is smooth. Cover this open end with a cleaned piece of sausage casing. Fasten the membrane on tightly with a rubber band. Fill the tube with a solution of molasses and water. Cap the tube with a cork and glass tube. Suspend the tube in a beaker of water from a ring stand. Which way does the molasses solution move?

CAUTION!

OXIDATION

TESTING OXIDATION

Materials you'll need:
   ice cubes, pan, source of heat, match, glass jar, steel wool

When a substance unites with oxygen to form an oxide, the process is called *oxidation*. Try these tests to help you learn more about it.

1. Place a pan of ice cubes over a flame for several seconds. Now feel the bottom of the pan. Is it damp? Many of the materials used for fuel consist of hydrogen and carbon compounds. Carbon and oxygen form the gas carbon dioxide, while the hydrogen and oxygen combine to make water. The carbon dioxide gas escapes and the water collects under the pan. This shows that oxidation is a chemical change.

2. Light a match and insert it into an "empty" glass jar. What element is in the jar that causes it to keep burning? Sprinkle a ball of steel wool with water and put it in a jar. Cover it tightly. Observe the change occurring to the steel strands. The steel wool is chemically combining with something in the jar to cause it to rust. After 24 hours, remove the cover of the jar and immediately insert a lighted match. What happens to the flame? Steel wool cannot oxidize without oxygen nor can a fire burn without oxygen.

PARAKEETS

CARING FOR PARAKEETS

Materials you'll need:
   oblong cage (1½' long by 1' wide), canary and millet seed, leafy vegetables, cuttlebone, gravel

Parakeets, members of the parrot family, are also sometimes known as *budgies*. They are a popular home bird. The shell parakeet comes in a variety of colors. Be sure to select your pet from a reliable breeder and have the new home ready before buying it.

The cage should have a removable tray of gravel which should be cleaned daily. Set or hang the cage in a corner of a room which is free from drafts and has plenty of reflected light. The seed dish and water cup should be filled with fresh supplies every day. A cuttlebone wired to the inside of the cage will give the bird the calcium it needs. The perches should be scraped clean occasionally but never washed. Wet wood can make the bird sick.

With patience and kindness you can teach your parakeet to mimic words you speak. After you train the bird to sit on your finger, hold it in front of you and repeat a single word for fifteen minutes. Do this twice a day until it learns to repeat the word. They are easiest to train when they are around three months old. Have patience.

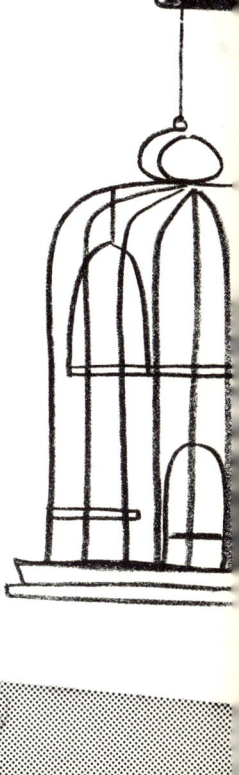

PARAMECIA

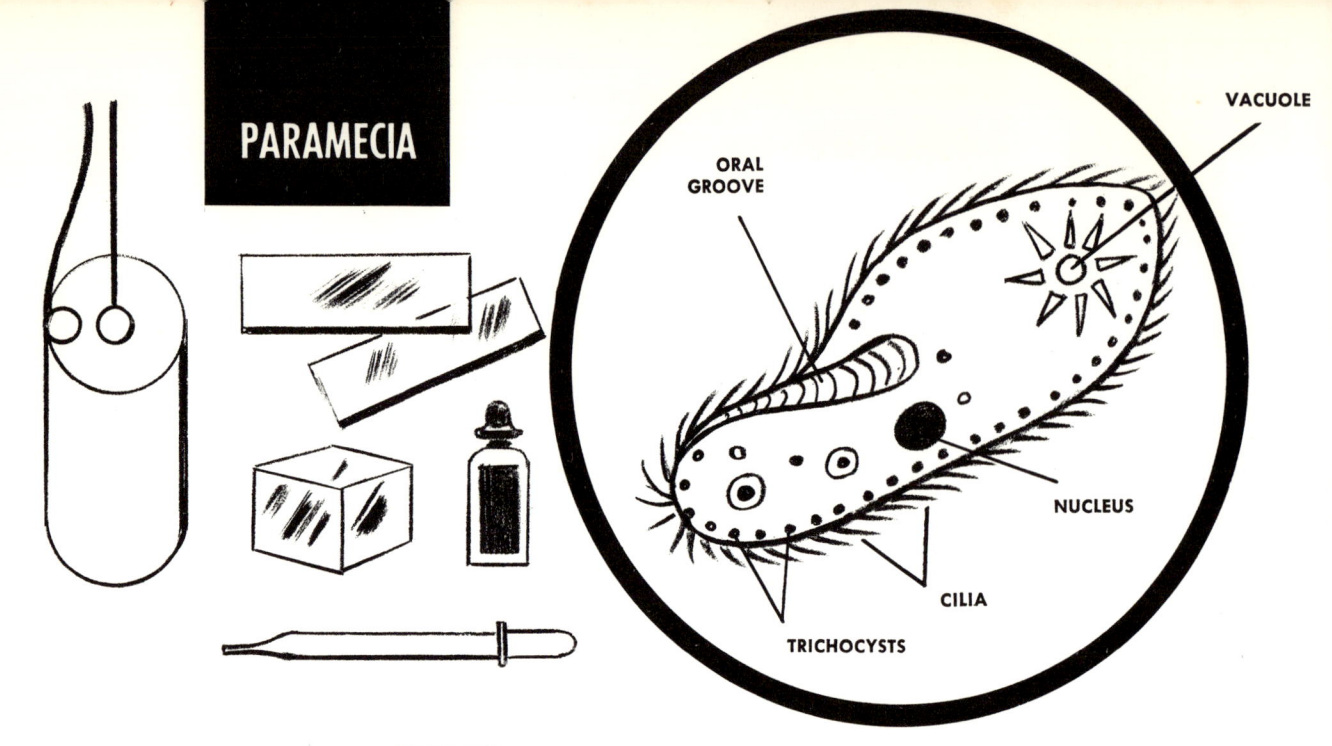

EXPERIMENTING WITH PARAMECIA

Materials you'll need:
  Protozoa culture, carmine, glass slide, cover glass, microscope, ice, wire, dry cell, steel wool, eye dropper, iodine

First, grow a *Protozoa* culture (see page 158 for directions). Isolate some paramecia (the slipper-shaped animals) by putting a drop of the culture on a glass slide that has some steel wool strands on it. Pick up with an eye dropper just the paramecia caught in the strands. Put them in water on another slide.

Put a few tiny crystals of carmine in the edge of the drop of water. Cover with a cover glass. Place the slide on a microscope and bring the paramecia into focus. A powerful hand lens will work almost as well if a microscope is not available. Observe the paramecia as they approach the crystals. The movement of the cilia causes them to roll, go forward and back up.

Continue to experiment with different materials, starting each time with a fresh culture on the slide. Place a small chip of ice in one place in the drop of water. Which way will the paramecia turn? Cover one-half of the slide to keep light out. Do they move to the darkness? Connect a wire to each terminal of a dry cell. Touch the exposed ends of the wires together in part of the solution. A very slight current will be discharged. Can these little one-celled animals respond to an electrical charge?

The little one-celled paramecia possess weapons of defense, as do most animals. Just inside the cell membrane are tiny sacs, each holding a coiled thread. When the animal is attacked by another animal or foreign material, these weapons, called *trichocysts,* will explode, discharging the threads. When this happens over a large area the many threads entangle the victim.

Study the animals so you can recognize the cilia, hair-like structures for locomotion. Do not confuse these with exploded trichocysts. Next, place a drop of iodine at the edge of the cover slide. It will seep under and reach the paramecium. Watch closely. Did this cause your paramecium to defend itself by shooting out its tiny weapons?

150

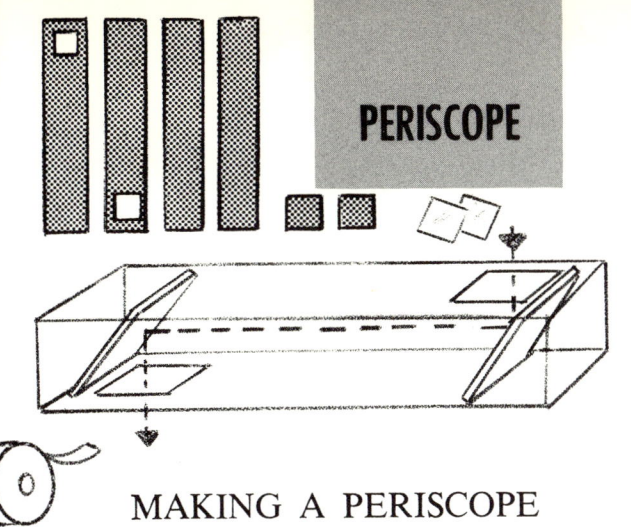

PERISCOPE

MAKING A PERISCOPE

Materials you'll need:
   balsa wood, 2 pocket mirrors,
   tape

If you are too short to see over people's heads in a crowd, a periscope will help you. It will also let you peek around corners without being noticed.

Cut four strips of balsa wood measuring three inches by one foot. These will form the sides of the tube. Cut two more pieces three inches square for the top and bottom of the long box. Cut out a two-inch square near one end of each of two side strips. Tape two mirrors at 45-degree angles to the two sides with the holes. Follow the illustration carefully. Tape the remaining sides and the top and bottom pieces to form a completely closed box. It is now ready for use. Hold the tube upright and look through the bottom opening. Since light travels in straight lines the mirrors will reflect the objects down to your eyes.

MAKING A PHOTOMETER

Materials you'll need:
   florist's clay, board, 3 candles,
   miniature lamp and socket,
   white cardboard, pencils

A photometer is an instrument which measures the intensity or brightness of light. It compares an unknown source of light with a known one.

PHOTOMETER

Make a groove in a block of wood that will hold a piece of white cardboard upright. The cardboard must be white on both sides. Put florist's clay in the groove to help hold it firmly. Drill holes, one on each side of the cardboard and an inch and a half from it, to hold the pencils, lead up. If you haven't the tools for drilling holes, a mound of florist's clay will hold the pencils. This is the photometer itself.

Mounds of clay on separate pieces of wood will hold the candles. The two candles should be very close together so they shine as one. The candles should all be about the same height.

Place the double candle and the single candle about two feet apart with the photometer an equal distance between them. One shadow will be darker than the other. Move the photometer back and forth until the shadows are equally dark. Notice that the photometer is about half as far from the single candle as it is from the two candles. When the photometer is an equal distance from the light sources and the shadows are equally dark, the sources are equally bright. Test a miniature lamp in a socket. Place it exactly as far from the photometer as the candles are placed on the other side. Add candles until the shadows are equally dark. You have found the candlepower of the lamp.

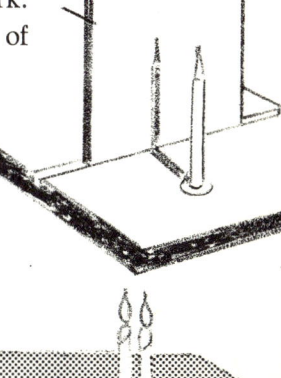

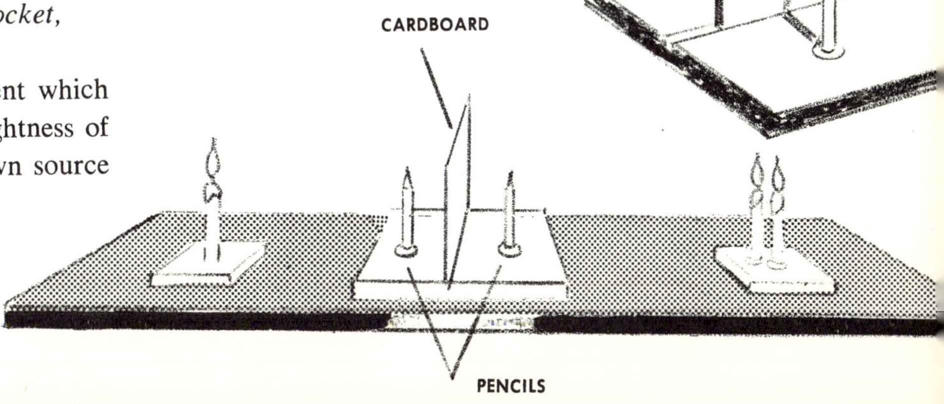

CARDBOARD

PENCILS

PHOTO-SYNTHESIS

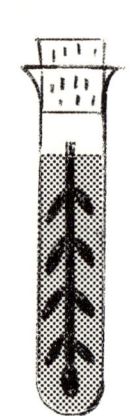

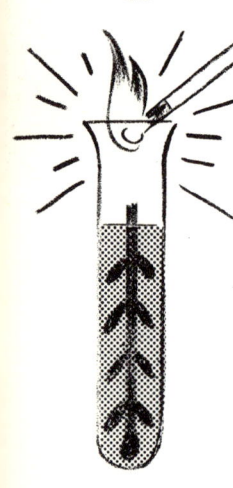

FINDING A PRODUCT OF PHOTOSYNTHESIS

Materials you'll need:
  Elodea, test tube, boiled water, cork, matches

Place a sprig of *Elodea*, a water plant, cut end up, in a test tube which is three-quarters full of boiled water which has first been permitted to cool. Cork the test tube and set it in a dark closet or drawer for an hour. Remove the cork and quickly hold a lighted match in the top of the tube. How brightly does the flame burn? Now repeat the process but place the test tube in the bright sunshine. Remove the cork and hold a lighted match in the tube after the plant has been in light for an hour. Does the flame burn brighter? What did the plant give off to cause this?

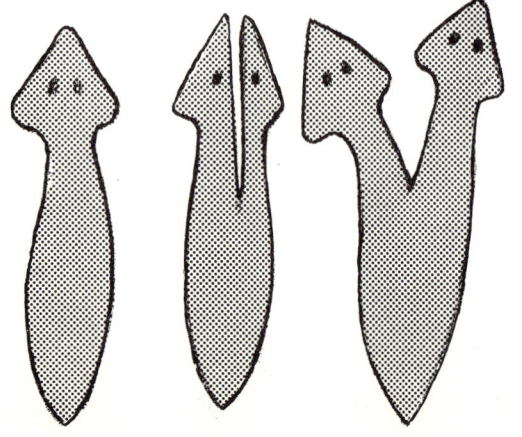

PLANARIA

WATCHING REGENERATION OF PLANARIA

Materials you'll need:
  large olive bottle, wire screen with tiny mesh, raw liver, sharp razor blade, shallow dish

Planaria are common fresh-water flatworms that are found in streams, on sticks and under stones. They look like small leeches and are shaped like spearheads. They are one of the kinds of animals which can regenerate or grow new parts after old parts are destroyed. You can either purchase planaria from a biological supply house or collect them yourself in a small stream.

To collect them, put a piece of raw liver in a tall olive bottle. Cover the bottle's mouth with fine wire screen to keep larger animals from getting the food. Tie a cord around the bottle and lower it into the water. The other end may be fastened to a stake driven in the ground on the edge of the bank. It could take several hours before planaria find the liver. They are very small so you must look closely.

Transfer the planaria to a shallow dish of fresh water for their future home. To demonstrate the remarkable powers of regeneration, place a planarian on a hard surface. With a sharp razor blade or knife, make a cut half way down its anterior end. Place the planarian back in the dish of water. It will take about two weeks for each half to become complete again. As soon as there are two complete heads, feed the animal raw liver again. Leave the food in the water for an hour only, then remove it to prevent contamination.

PLANETS

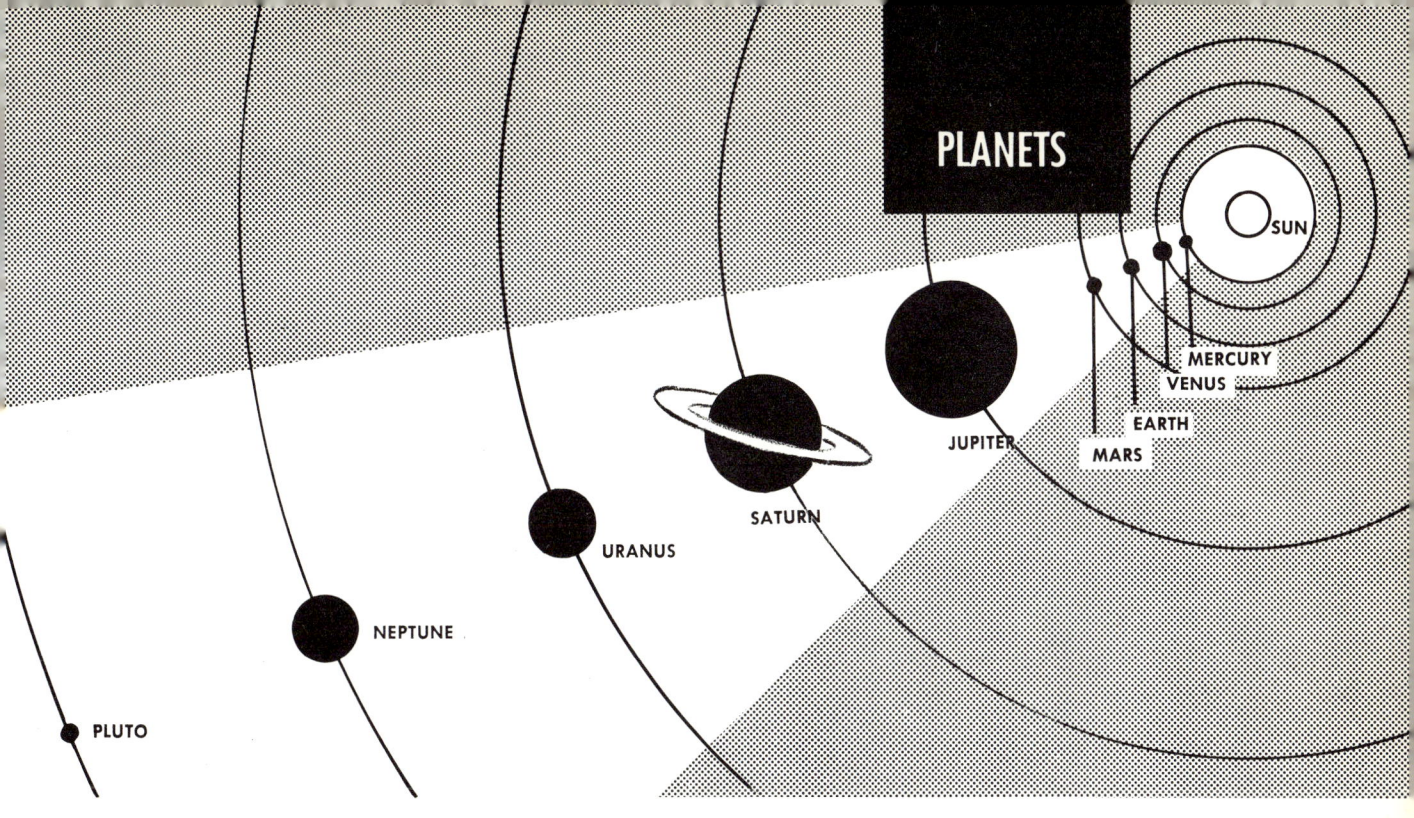

BUILDING PLANET MODELS

Materials you'll need:

papier-maché, balloons, string

In order to see the relationship in the size of planets and their relative distance from the sun you can construct models to scale. The accompanying chart provides the diameter of the planets and the number of inches each model should be made when one inch equals approximately 4000 miles. Models made of papier-maché (flour, water and newspaper strips) can be used. Shape planet the size desired and bake it in an oven for one-half hour. For the larger planets blow up a balloon to one inch less than desired size. Mold a half-inch of papier-maché over the balloon and let it dry for several days.

The planets may be suspended by strings from the ceiling of your room. Arrange them in order from the sun by following the chart. The scale for distance is based upon one inch equaling forty million miles. Moons and other bodies may be added to make your solar system more complete.

PLANET	MILES FROM SUN (Ave. distance)	SCALE #1	DIAMETER IN MILES (size)	SCALE #2
MERCURY	36,000,000	.90"	3,100	.78"
VENUS	67,200,000	1.68	7,700	1.93
EARTH	92,900,000	2.32	7,920	1.98
MARS	141,500,000	3.55	4,215	1.05
JUPITER	483,300,000	12.08	88,000	22.00
SATURN	886,100,000	22.15	71,500	17.80
URANUS	1,783,000,000	44.57	32,000	8.00
NEPTUNE	2,793,000,000	69.82	28,000	7.00
PLUTO	3,670,000,000	91.75	3,700	.93

Scale #1, one inch = 40 million miles   Scale #2, one inch = 4000 miles

PLANTS

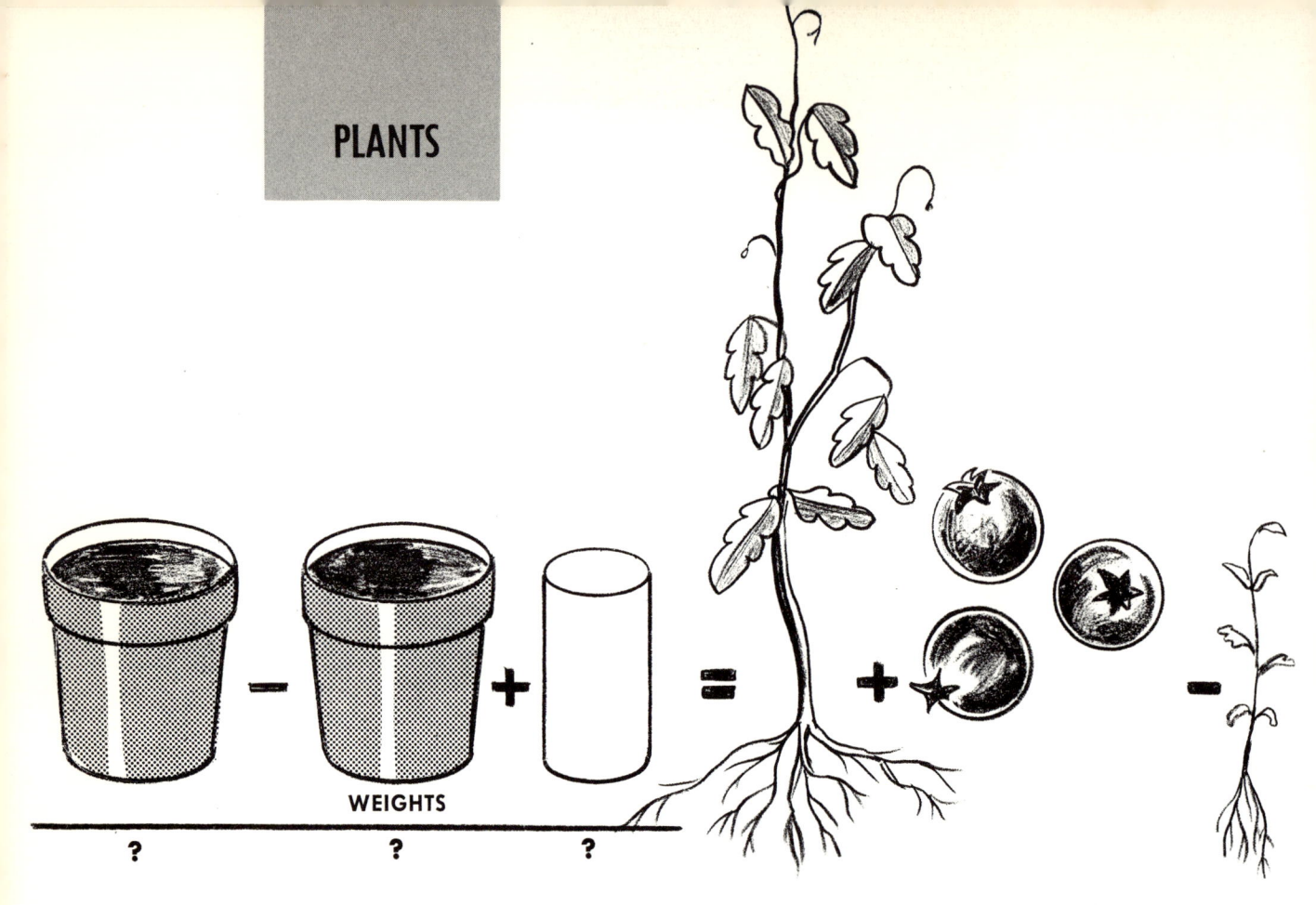

DETERMINING HOW MUCH SOIL A PLANT USES

Materials you'll need:
large clay pot, tomato plant,
scale, pint jar

How much material does a growing plant take out of the soil before it matures and bears fruit? A scientist named Van Helmont was the first one to figure this problem out. See if you can, too. It will take careful measurements so be exact in your figures.

Put two inches of coarse gravel in the bottom of a large flower pot. Fill it almost full with good soil. Place the pot on a scale and weigh it. Record this amount in your science notebook. Take a small tomato plant and carefully remove all the soil from around its roots. Weigh the plant and record this number.

Now plant the tomato plant in the pot of soil. Pour exactly one pint of water over it. Continue to water it whenever it is dry. Each time you do, measure and record the amount of water given. When the plant is mature and produces tomatoes you may harvest your crop, recording the weight of each fruit picked. When the plant stops bearing tomatoes, dig it up and carefully shake all soil from the roots back into the pot. Weigh the pot and the soil again. What is the difference between the weight of it now and before you grew tomatoes?

Add up the weights of all fruit picked plus the weight of the plant at the end. Subtract from this number the weight of the plant before you began to experiment. How many ounces of plant were produced? How many pints of water did you give the plant? Using the figures you have, what is your conclusion about the source of the raw materials a plant uses in growth?

PLANTS

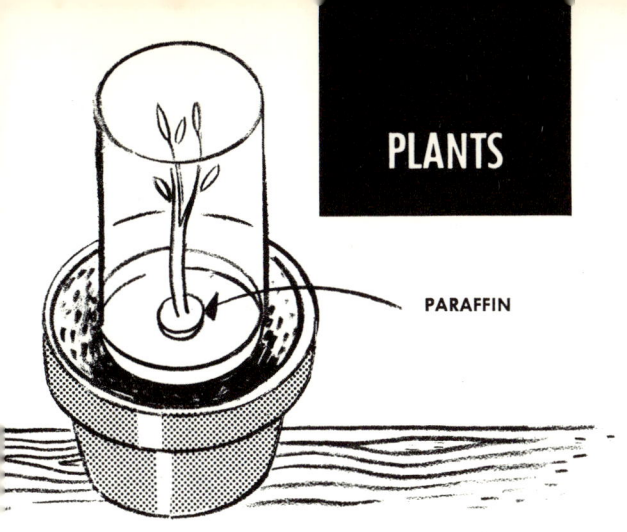

FINDING OUT THAT PLANTS BREATHE

Materials you'll need:
  plant in flower pot, quart jar with screw top, paraffin

You probably have learned that plants take carbon dioxide from the air to use in making food. This is part of the process of *photosynthesis*. But did you realize that plants breathe and require oxygen just as animals do?

Grow a plant from seed in a large flower pot. A bean seed is a good one to use since the plant grows rapidly. When it is five or six inches tall and looks healthy, dig it up carefully so that you don't break its roots. Punch a hole in the lid of a jar large enough to pass the roots through. The roots should go through from the inside to the outside of the lid. Replant the roots in the flower pot so that the jar lid is upside down. Water the plant after replanting. Seal the hole around the stem with soft paraffin so that it is airtight. Screw the jar down into the lid.

Keep the plant in a dark place overnight. Unscrew the jar and very quickly drop a lighted match into the jar. It will go out immediately, indicating that oxygen has been used up and carbon dioxide produced inside the jar. The carbon dioxide was given off in the process of respiration. Why must the plant be kept in a dark place?

PLASMOLYSIS

CAUSING CELLS TO LOSE WATER

Materials you'll need:
  onion, microscope, glass slide, cover glass, iodine, salt, eye dropper

Have you ever wondered why people use salt, vinegar, and brine solutions on cucumbers (pickles) to preserve them? What happens to bacteria and mold spores when they fall upon this solution? A fresh cucumber soon decays but a pickle is not affected. One reason for this is the process called *plasmolysis* in which water from a cell is pulled out because of osmosis (see page 148 for activities on osmosis).

Place a small section cut from an onion skin membrane on a glass slide. Add a drop of iodine to this. The iodine is permitted to go through the cell wall and stains the protoplasm. Staining helps you to observe what happens.

Place the slide under the low power of the microscope. With an eye dropper put a drop of salt solution at the edge of the cover glass. Gradually the solution will seep in and come in contact with the onion cells. Watch closely to see what happens. The cell walls will not permit the salt to enter but instead water is pulled from the protoplasm by osmosis. What does this do to the cells? When bacteria fall upon an open pickle jar they are killed by this process—*plasmolysis*. Can you see why people should not drink salt water?

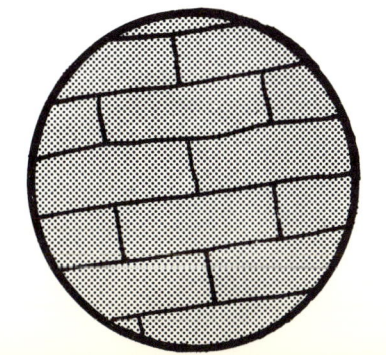

POLLEN

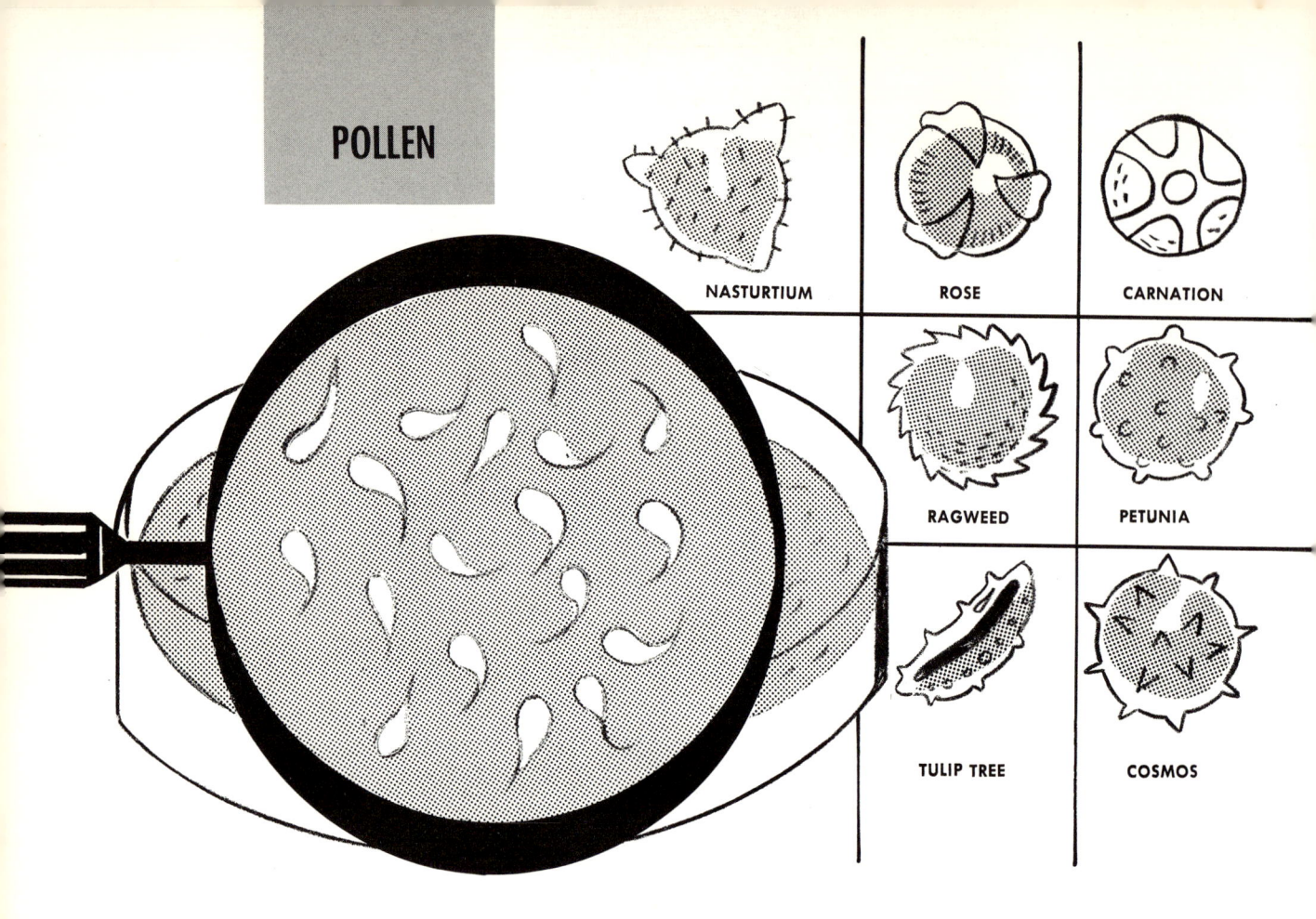

NASTURTIUM **ROSE** **CARNATION**

RAGWEED **PETUNIA**

TULIP TREE **COSMOS**

EXPERIMENTING WITH POLLEN

Materials you'll need:
flowers, glass slides, glue, cover glasses, microscope, sugar solution, shallow dish with cover, hand lens

Collect flowers from as many plants as you can find. Spread a thin film of glue in the center of several glass microscope slides. Shake a different flower over each slide. The pollen will stick to the glue. Carefully place a cover glass over each sample. Observe them under a microscope. How many shapes and sizes do you find? Pollen identification is helpful to doctors in determining allergies, and to honey farmers in knowing what pollen their bees are collecting. The illustration shows a few shapes to look for.

Pollen forms on the male part of a flower called the *stamen*. Some of the pollen grains are dusted onto the head of the female part of the flower, or *pistil*. The pollen must grow an extension that will go down through the pistil into the ovary of the flower in order to reach the egg to fertilize it. Only when this happens do the new seeds develop.

Make a thin sugar solution. This will serve as a medium in which the pollen grains can grow. Locate a freshly-opened flower. Shake the stamen (the stalk usually with yellow knobs) over the solution. Cover the dish and let it stand for an hour. Using a hand lens, observe the long extension which has sprouted from each grain. This is the pollen tube which grows down the pistil so that the pollen nucleus can join the nucleus of the egg.

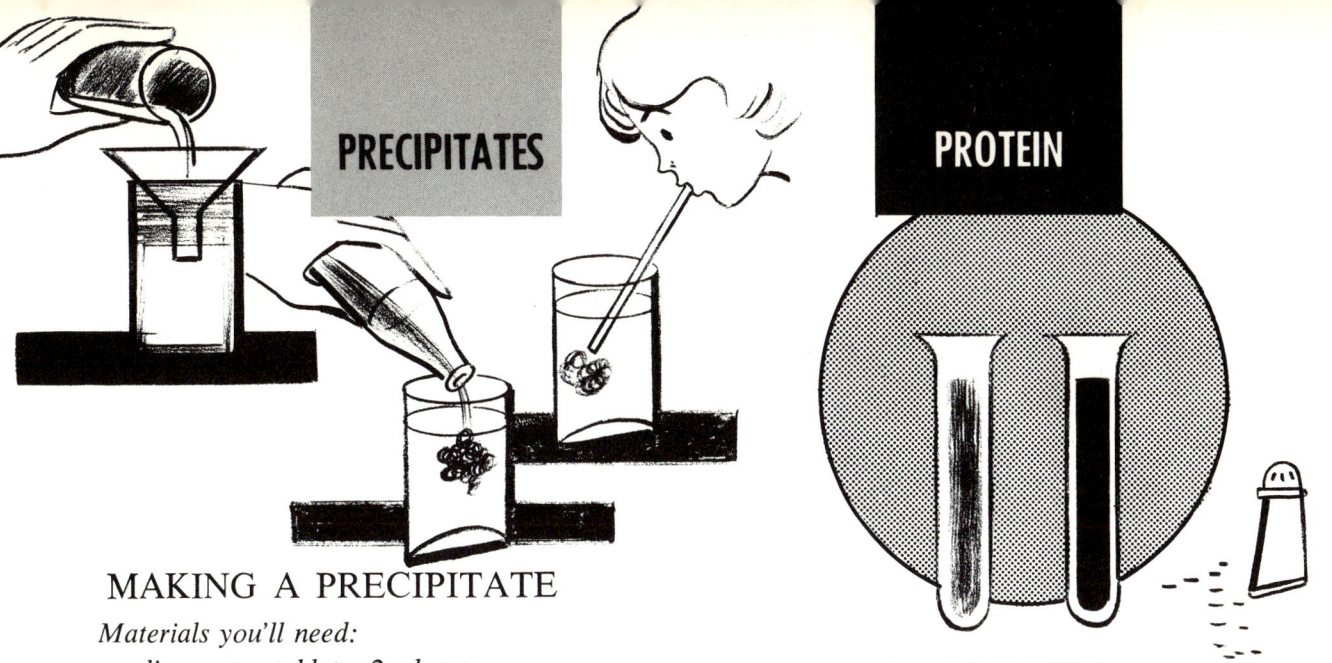

PRECIPITATES

MAKING A PRECIPITATE

Materials you'll need:
  limewater tablets, 2 glasses or test tubes, funnel, filter paper, soda water, straw

Sometimes when a new chemical is added to a solution, a solid mass of material is formed. This solid mass results from the reaction of the chemicals in the solution with the new one which was added. This solid, insoluble material is called a *precipitate*.

Dissolve one or two small limewater tablets in a glass of cold water. Do not let this solution touch your skin. (If it does, rinse it off immediately with cold water.) Line a funnel with filter paper and filter the limewater solution. Immediately divide the clear limewater into two parts. Add a little fresh soda or carbonated water to one part. The white precipitate that forms is *calcium carbonate*.

You can make the same precipitate (calcium carbonate) by blowing into the second portion of clear limewater through a straw. Since your breath contains carbon dioxide, calcium carbonate will be formed in the limewater. It will look like a white cloudy mass in the clear solution.

You can redissolve the calcium carbonate by continuing to blow. Soluble calcium bicarbonate will be formed.

PROTEIN

TESTING FOR PROTEIN

Materials you'll need:
  lime powder, copper sulfate, water

Proteins are part of the materials which make up the protoplasm of body cells. Our bodies cannot manufacture their own proteins. We are dependent on the plants and animals we eat to supply them.

Since proteins are so important to us, it is a good idea for us to know which foods supply us with the most protein. If a food containing protein is mixed with lime and copper sulfate, the mixture will become violet colored. Make two solutions and keep them separate until you add a little of each to the foods to be tested. Make solution #1 by stirring in as much copper sulfate as a small amount of water can hold. Make solution #2 by dissolving lime powder in water. Add equal parts of these two solutions to the food. Is there protein (as seen by the violet color) in the following foods: hamburger, flour, butter, eggs, sugar, salt, cheese, and bread? Do some of these appear to have more protein than others?

157

PROTOPLASM

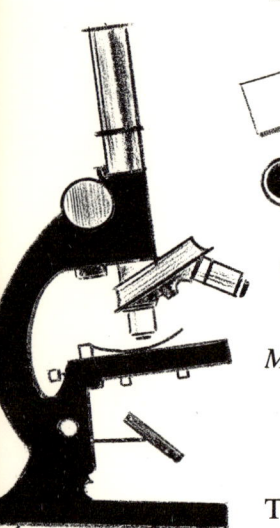

WATCHING MOVEMENT IN LIVING CELLS

Materials you'll need:
microscope, glass slide, cover glass, eye dropper, Elodea, warm water

The living material in cells is called *protoplasm*. When green plant cells are exposed to light the living material streams around within the cell wall in the process of manufacturing food (*photosynthesis*). *Elodea* (a water plant) should be used in this activity because the plant leaf is only two cell layers thick.

Place a sprig of *Elodea* in a glass of warm water under a strong light for fifteen minutes before you begin. Then remove a small leaf near the tip of the plant, place it in a drop of warm water on a microscopic glass slide. Put a cover glass over this before setting the slide on the stage of the microscope. Using low power, focus the objective until the plant cells are clearly in view. The tiny green bodies moving about are *chloroplasts*. They tend to stream around the cell just inside the wall. The large clear area nearer the center is a *vacuole*. The darker circle along one side is the nucleus.

PROTOZOA

GROWING A PROTOZOA CULTURE

Materials you'll need:
quart jar, hay or dry grass, cooked rice, water from pond or stream, narrow glass tube

Some of the wonders of life are so small that they cannot be seen by the naked eye. You must use a microscope to see the smallest form of animal life—*Protozoa*, one-celled animals.

To raise your own *Protozoa* culture, collect a quart jar of water from a pond or stream. Make sure you include some water plants and mud in the jar. *Protozoa* must be fed. They will grow and reproduce rapidly on the proper diet. Just add a little hay or dried grass and a few grains of cooked rice to the culture. Place the jar, uncovered, in a warm, dark place for several days.

Remove a drop of the culture from close to a rice grain on the bottom of the jar; by sucking it up in the tube. Place the drop on a clean microscope slide. Cover it with a cover glass. You should be able to see several kinds of *Protozoa* as well as algae, bacteria, flatworms and roundworms. How many can you identify? Keep the culture to have protozoans for other activities.

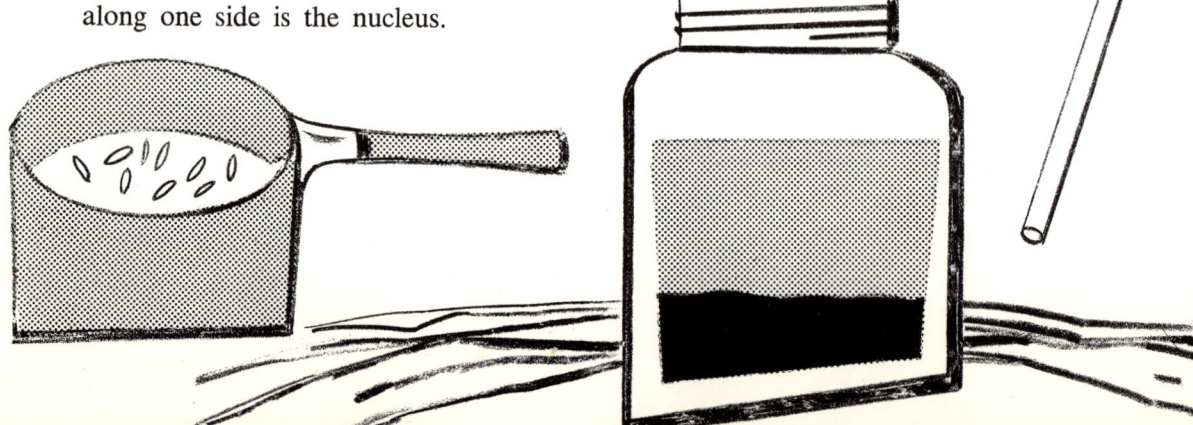

PULLEY

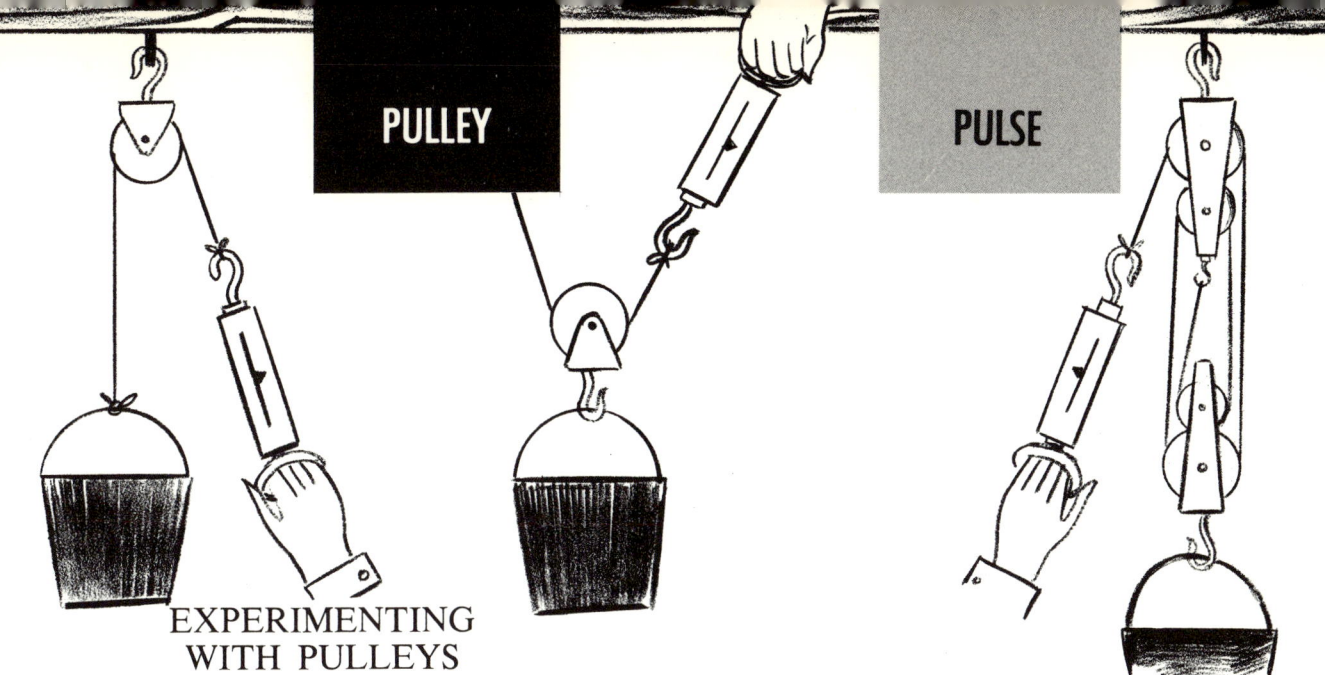

EXPERIMENTING WITH PULLEYS

Materials you'll need:
support containing screw eyes, spring scale, 2 single pulleys, 2 double pulleys, pail of water

A pulley consists of a grooved wheel over which a rope runs. Construct a support on which to fasten a *stationary* or *fixed* pulley. Thread a heavy cord through the pulley. Weigh a pail of water and record the weight. Tie one end of the cord to the handle of the pail and the other end to a spring scale. Raise the pail by pulling on the spring scale. Record the force needed to raise it. This pulley simply gives you the advantage of direction. The effort used and weight of the pail should be about equal.

By following the diagrams set up a movable pulley on the support. You will see why it is called *movable pulley* when you pull on the spring scale. Repeat the experiment. Did it take much less effort than with a fixed pulley? It should cut your work about in half if the pulleys are well lubricated.

Now try combining a fixed single pulley and a movable single pulley. The effort you use should be about equal to one-half the weight of the pail if the pulleys are well oiled.

Combining a fixed double pulley and a movable double pulley will show you something more about how much effort is saved by using pulleys. The effort you use should be equal to about one-fourth the weight of the pail. The fixed pulley gives you no effort advantage but here you have two movable pulleys. Each movable pulley, then, reduces your effort by how much?

PULSE

SEEING YOUR PULSE

Materials you'll need:
thumbtack, toothpick

The pulse is a rhythmic beat felt in an artery close to the skin. It is due to sudden expansion of the artery. This expansion is ordinarily easier to feel than to see but there is a way to see it.

Stick the end of a thumbtack through a toothpick so that the toothpick balances when the thumbtack stands on its head. Find the pulse in your wrist between the wrist bone and a tendon. It is easily felt with the fingertips of your other hand. Don't use your thumb because it has a pulse of its own. Stand the tack with the toothpick on it on its head on the pulse in your wrist. The toothpick should move in time with your pulse.

QUIZ BOARD

MAKING AN ELECTRICAL QUIZ BOARD

Materials you'll need:
plywood 18" by 24", 20 L-hooks, bell wire, dry cells, buzzer, cardboard, copper strip, clamps, screws

Making an electrical quiz board will test what you know about complete and incomplete electrical circuits while you are building it and give you a fascinating game as a finished product. You can use it to review a science lesson, to learn arithmetic combinations or as a question-and-answer game.

Leave the top two inches of the plywood board to hold a title on the front and the buzzer on the back. In the remaining twenty-two inches, space and screw in twenty L-hooks in two even rows. The ends of the hooks should stick out on the back side of the board.

Fasten the dry cell to the top of the back of the board, using a bent copper strip for it to rest on. Fasten it with two strips of bell wire which are attached to screws at the sides. Next fasten the buzzer to the dry cell. Run a wire from one screw of the buzzer to one terminal of the dry cell, and from the other terminal of the dry cell around to the front of the board. Run another piece of wire from the other screw of the buzzer around to the front of the board on the other side. Put alligator clamps on the free ends of the two wires on the front of the board.

Run wires from one row of L-hooks to the other, making sure that no wire goes directly across to the hook next to it.

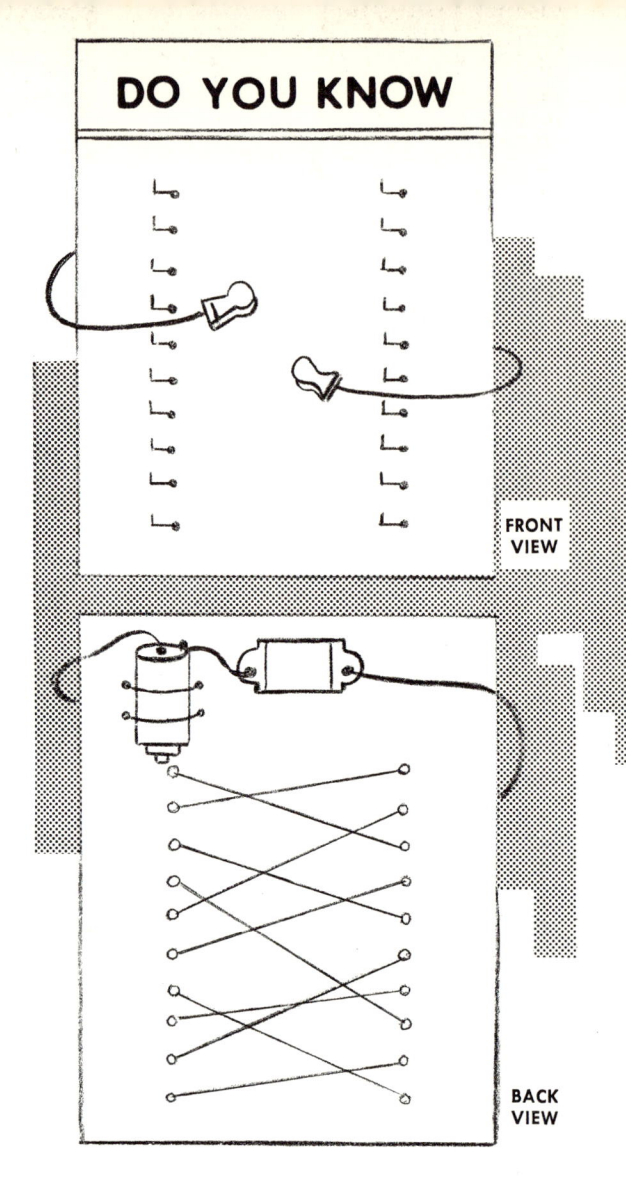

Make cards for the game you have chosen—questions for one row of hooks and corresponding answers for the other row. Perhaps you want to practice bird identification. You'd then paste pictures of ten birds on ten pieces of cardboard and print the names of the same ten birds on the other ten cards. Hang cards on the front of the board, making sure you put a question and its correct answer on two hooks which are wired together.

If the wiring is done correctly, when you clamp a correct question and a correct answer at the same time, the buzzer will sound. Can you trace the circuit and show why this happens?

RABBITS

EASTERN COTTONTAIL

BRUSH RABBIT

WHITE RABBIT (ALBINO)

BELGIAN HARE

RAISING RABBITS

Materials you'll need:
   cage, straw or shredded newspaper, food, water

Rabbits are gentle animals and make good pets. You must provide a large cage with enough clean straw or shredded newspaper to cover the floor. This floor covering must be changed frequently.

Feed your rabbits cereals, clover, carrots, lettuce or commercial rabbit pellets (sold in most pet stores). It will help keep the cage clean if there is a wire mesh rack to hold the vegetables. Rabbits must be fed regularly and they need fresh water daily.

Cut the nails of your pets' paws so that you are not scratched when you handle them. Never lift them by their ears. Instead, grasp the fold of skin on the neck with one hand and support the rump with the other.

When they are about seven to eight months of age, a pair of rabbits will breed. You can expect a litter of five to eight babies after a gestation period of thirty-one days. Wean the babies when they are two months old.

RADIOACTIVITY

CONSTRUCTING A CLOUD CHAMBER

Materials you'll need:
black velvet cloth, alcohol, jar, sheet of glass, radioactive paint (from luminous clock or watch dial), dry ice, flashlight

Radium and uranium are two radioactive materials found in the natural state. Radium is used in the paint on the dials of watches or clocks that can be seen in the dark. The *luminescence* —natural light—is caused when particles from the radium strike other special materials.

Radium disintegrates, giving off particles which cannot be seen by the naked eye. However, the trails the particles make can be seen with the help of a cloud chamber.

Saturate a small strip of black velvet cloth with alcohol and place it at the bottom of a jar. Scrape a little of the luminous paint from the face of an old clock or watch and place it on the inside of the jar. Cover the jar with a sheet of glass.

Set the jar on a cake of dry ice. The extreme cold will cause the vaporizing alcohol to condense. It will condense along the trails of the disintegrating particles. Shine the flashlight into the jar and the vapor trails will be visible.

RAIN

CREATING A LITTLE RAINSTORM

Materials you'll need:
flat of grass, teakettle, pan of ice cubes, source of heat

Man makes rain by scattering dry ice or silver iodide crystals over an area in which water vapor is present. Since you are too young to fly a plane you will have to resort to this experiment to make a rainstorm—actually more like a drizzle.

Place a wooden flat of grass on a table near a kettle of boiling water. Hold the pan of ice cubes or crushed ice over the kettle spout. As steam hits the cold bottom of the pan, droplets of water will form. As the drops increase in size they will fall on the grass as rain.

The warm air coming from the teakettle is heavy with water vapor. As it hits the cold surface it must lose some. Cool air cannot hold as much moisture as warm air can.

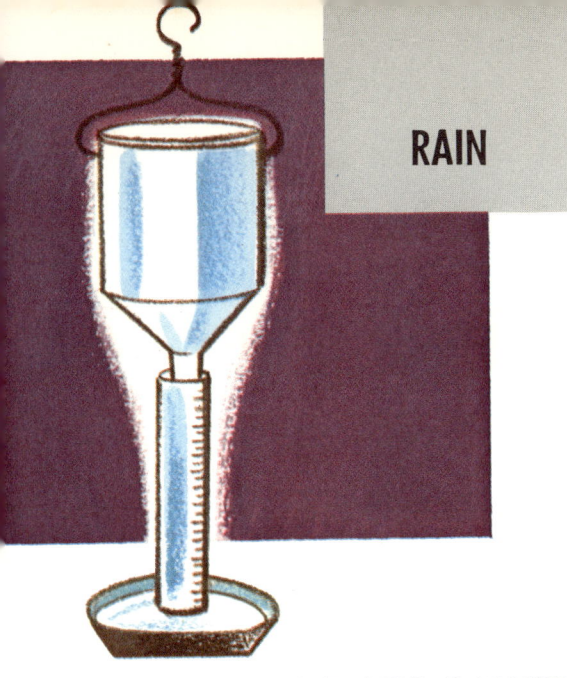

RAIN

MAKING A RAIN GAUGE

Materials you'll need:
> sheet metal, aluminum or copper sheeting, funnel, coat hanger, plaster of Paris

If you want to be absolutely accurate in measuring the rainfall, make yourself a rain gauge the same size as the weatherman's. He uses an eight-inch gauge.

Construct a receiver with a diameter of eight inches out of sheet metal. Bend the ends of the metal together and hammer them flat. Cut a section from the long side of a coat hanger. Bend the rest of the coat hanger so that the cut ends can be inserted in holes in the sides of the receiver. Put a funnel at the bottom of the receiver leading into the measuring tube. This tube is twenty inches long and two and one-half inches in diameter. You can fashion the tube out of metal and make a base to hold it by setting it in a small pie tin of plaster of Paris and water. Mark the tube off in inches from the bottom. Ten inches of water in the measuring tube equals one inch of rainfall (precipitation). One inch in the measuring tube equals one-tenth inch of rainfall, and so on.

REACTIONS

TESTING YOUR REACTION TIME

Materials you'll need:
> dollar bill, paper, partner

Many things outside your body stimulate your senses. When you see something or feel something, a message travels quickly to your brain and another message goes from your brain back to your muscles, causing them to react appropriately. It seems as though your muscle reaction takes place at the same time as the stimulus, but this isn't so. There is a short period of time between the stimulus and the reaction called *reaction time*.

Your reaction time depends on your age, state of health, state of fatigue, state of nerves and many other factors.

Cut a piece of paper about the size of a dollar bill. Ask a friend to hold out his hand with his thumb and forefinger about an inch apart. Suspend the paper between them with your hand above his. Ask him to catch the paper as you drop it. Chances are he won't be able to close his fingers fast enough after he sees you let go.

If you feel wealthy and confident, try the same trick with a dollar bill, offering to give your partner the dollar if he can catch it.

Experiment to find out whether your friend comes closer to catching the paper before or after eating, early in the morning or late at night, before or after strenuous physical exercise. Is a young person or an old person better at catching the falling paper?

163

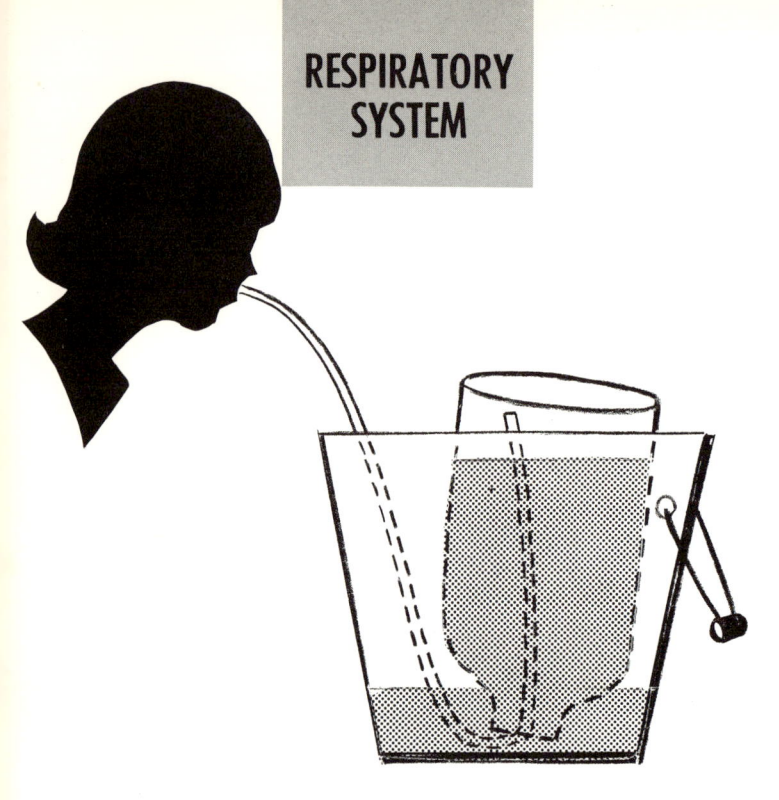

RESPIRATORY SYSTEM

TESTING YOUR LUNG CAPACITY

Materials you'll need:
   bucket, gallon jar, rubber tubing

You can increase the capacity (the amount of air you can inhale in one breath) of your lungs by regular exercise accompanied by deep breathing. This is an important part of keeping fit and healthy. Here is a simple way to measure your lung capacity before and after your physical fitness campaign to see if it changes.

Put about two inches of water in a large bucket. Fill a jar with water and invert it quickly in the bucket so that the water stays in the jar. Tilt the jar slightly so that one end of the rubber tubing can be inserted into the mouth of the jar.

Inhale as deeply as you can and then blow on the outside end of the tube. You will force water out of the jar into the bucket. The closer you can come to emptying the jar, the larger your lung capacity.

CONSTRUCTING A RESPIRATORY MODEL

Materials you'll need:
   gallon jar, piece of inner tube, Y-shaped glass tube, 2 balloons, 1-holed cork

Locate a large glass jar and remove the bottom. This may be done with a glass cutter. If you do not have a glass cutter have an adult help you soak a string with lighter fluid. Tie it tightly around the jar where you wish to cut it. Set fire to the string and the minute it burns out, plunge the jar into ice water. It should break where the string was tied. Tape the cut edge to avoid injury while working with it. If you don't have a one-holed stopper, drill a hole in a cork and insert the Y-tube. On the end of each fork of the glass tube place a balloon. The balloons serve as the "lungs." A piece of inner tube should be fastened with large rubber bands over the bottom of the jar—this is the "diaphragm."

Push the diaphragm up into the jar with your clenched fist. The muscle is in this position (dome-shaped) when it is relaxed. What happened to the lungs (balloons)? Release the pressure on the diaphragm. As the diaphragm in our body contracts it becomes shorter and flat. What happens to the lungs now? We inspire (breathe in) when the muscle contracts and expire (breathe out) when it is relaxed.

CAUTION!

164

RHEOSTAT

ROCKS

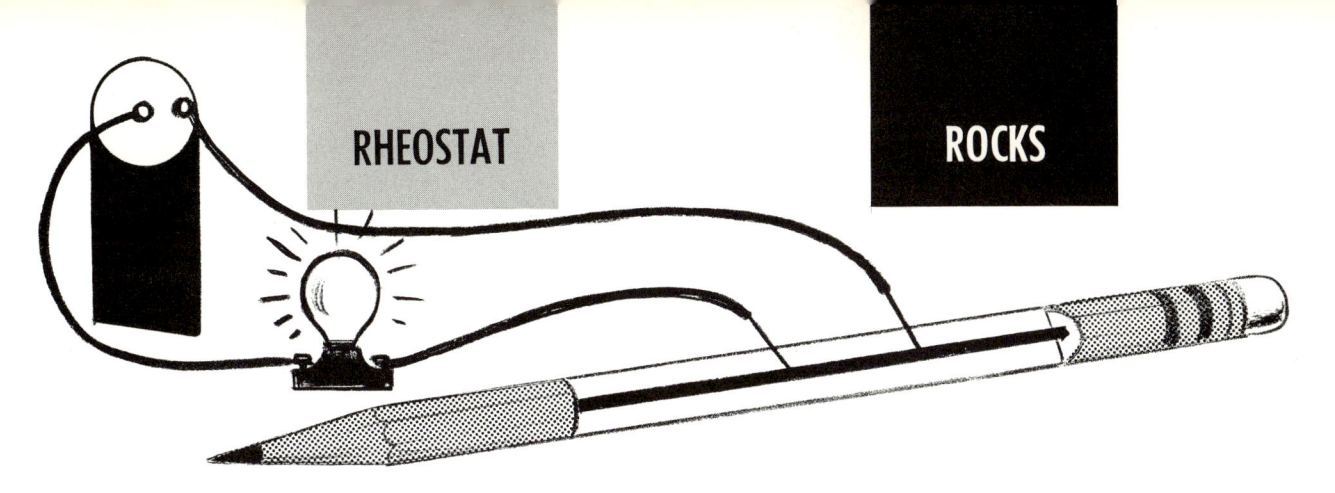

CONSTRUCTING A RHEOSTAT

Materials you'll need:
pencil, bell wire, small lamp, dry cell

A rheostat is a device used to vary or change the amount of current flowing through an electric circuit. For example, when the lights in a theater dim slowly, it is because a rheostat is being used. Rather than using an ordinary switch which breaks the circuit completely, some sort of *resistance*, such as a poor conductor of electricity, is wired into the circuit so that the strength of the current can be changed gradually.

The simplest kind of rheostat can be made using an ordinary lead pencil. Cut away a strip of wood three inches long and half the diameter of the pencil. Since a pencil is usually made of two pieces of wood, the split can be made simply by making two cuts down to the lead. This should expose three inches of pencil lead. Graphite (pencil lead) is a poor conductor of electricity.

Cut three pieces of bell wire and scrape the insulation off the ends. Wire the lamp to two of the pieces. Connect the wires to the terminals of a dry cell as shown in the illustration. Hold the free ends of the wire together to make sure the circuit is closed. The lamp should light. Now hold them both on the pencil lead, an eighth of an inch apart. The lamp will light. As you gradually move one wire farther from the other keeping both pressed tightly to the lead, the lamp will shine less and less brightly. By increasing the length of lead in the circuit, you are increasing the resistance.

COLLECTING ROCKS

Materials you'll need:
strong canvas bag, hammer, chisel, newspaper, notebook and pencil, adhesive tape, gloves

You can look for rocks in several places. Quarries, of course, are a good place to hunt. Other kinds of excavations, such as river beds, ravines, and even school playgrounds may yield specimens to a collector with curiosity. In some places it will be necessary to get permission to collect.

Try to pick fairly large rock specimens. Use the size of a closed fist as a guide. If you are working in an excavation, collect samples from all layers.

When you find a rock you want to keep, stick a small piece of adhesive tape on it. Number the rock and make an entry in your notebook, next to the corresponding number, describing where the rock was found. Wrap the marked rock in newspaper and drop it into your bag. Use the sample as a guide to decide how certain land formations came into being. See the next three pages for help in identification.

ROCKS

IDENTIFYING ROCKS

Materials you'll need:
vinegar, hammer and chisel, unglazed white tile, egg carton or muffin tin

Now that you have collected a number of rock samples and have made notes about where the samples were found, it is time to identify or grade them. There are several techniques you can use to help with this identification: the acid test, the cleavage test, the streak test, and the hardness scale (see page 105 for using the hardness scale).

The acid test is very simple. Rocks containing calcite or lime will bubble or fizz when an acid is poured on them. Use vinegar as your acid. If you hold the rock close to your ear and listen carefully, you'll be able to hear the fizzing.

When you break rocks, they will either cleave (an easy, flat break) or fracture, depending on the minerals present in them. Some cleavages are good clues to identifying minerals in rock. The way a rock fractures is also a clue to its identity. Hit the rock with a hammer to break it. Place a cloth over the rock before you hit it so that chips won't fly. Use the cleavage chart for help with identification.

When you scratch a piece of unglazed white porcelain (the back of a bathroom tile will do) with certain rocks, they make characteristic streaks. For example, although pyrite in rock form looks yellow, it always leaves a black streak on the tile. Many rocks can be identified by noting the streak it makes (see page 168).

If you want to group your rocks according to whether they are igneous, sedimentary, or metamorphic, use the following general description of the three kinds of rocks and compare your samples with the classification pictures. Sedimentary rocks have a layered appearance but usually break easily and feel gritty. Igneous rocks have a crystalline appearance, with the crystals mixed and never in layers. Metamorphic rocks are very hard and more crystalline than igneous rocks, but the crystals of each mineral are lined up in bands or layers.

Remember that the outside surfaces of a rock are weathered, and you must expose a fresh surface if you wish to study the characteristics of the rock. Use the hammer to break the rock open so that you can see a clean interior surface.

CLEAVAGE TEST

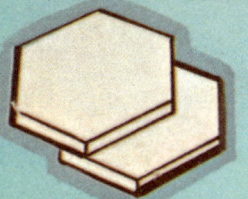

SINGLE
2 flat cleavage surfaces parallel to each other; mica

CUBIC
6 flat cleavage surfaces; each cleavage face square or rectangular; each cleavage surface at right angles to the others; galena, halite

RHOMBOHEDRAL
6 cleavage surfaces; surfaces not at right angles to others; each face is diamond shaped; calcite; surfaces slightly curved on dolomite and siderite

OCTAHEDRAL
8 cleavage surfaces; each cleavage face is triangle shaped; fluorite

DODECAHEDRAL
12 cleavage surfaces; each cleavage face is diamond shaped; sphalerite

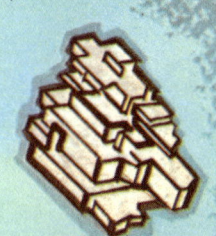

RIGHT ANGLE
cleaves in 2 directions at right angles to each other; other surfaces are uneven fractures; feldspar

ROCKS

FRACTURE TEST

EVEN
magnesite
novaculite
break with smooth surface not as flat as a cleavage surface

UNEVEN
serpentine   apatite
olivine   garnet
break with rough surface

CONCHOIDAL 
beryl
quartz
obsidian
tourmaline
broken surface looks like a conch shell

SUBCONCHOIDAL
rose quartz
smoky quartz
milky quartz
surfaces made of many little curved surfaces

SPLINTERY
tremolite   hornblende
surfaces look like splinters of wood

HACKLY
native silver
native copper
rough jagged surfaces which feel as if they were full of broken wires

SCIENTIFIC CLASSIFICATION

SEDIMENTARY
CONGLOMERATE    SANDSTONE    LIMESTONE    SHALE

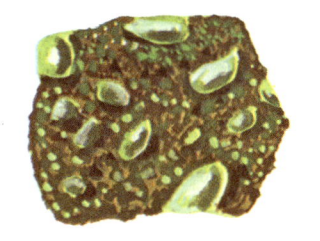

IGNEOUS
GRANITE    BASALT    PORPHYRY 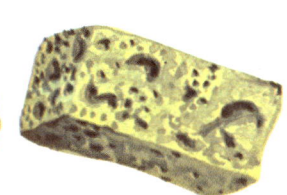   PUMICE    OBSIDIAN

METAMORPHIC
SLATE 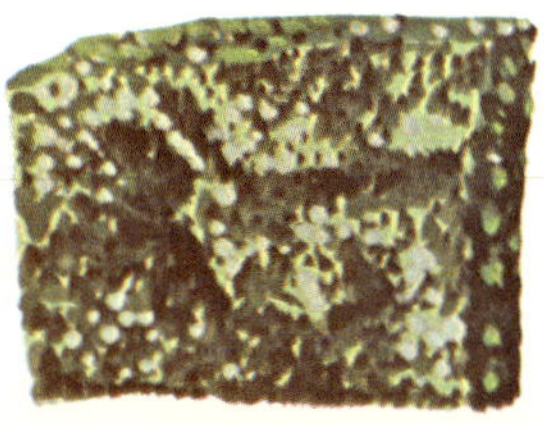   GNEISS    SCHIST 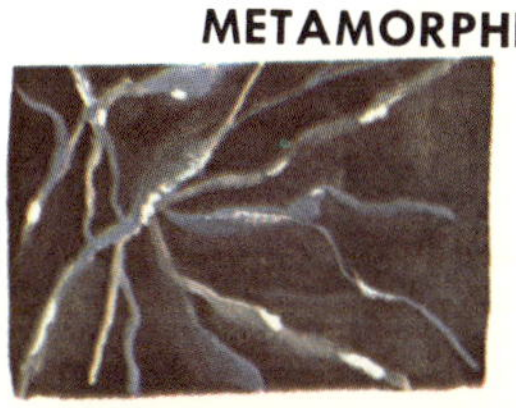   MARBLE

ROCKS

STREAK AND HARDNESS CHART
FOR IDENTIFYING ROCKS AND MINERALS

MINERAL	COLOR	STREAK	HARDNESS
Albite (feldspar)	white, bluish, grayish	uncolored	6-6½
Almandite (garnet)	red, purplish-red	white	6½-7½
Analcite	colorless, white	white	5-5½
Apatite	sea-green, bluish-green, yellow, purple, white	white	5
Arsenopyrite	silver-white to steel gray	grayish black	5½-6
Azurite	azure blue	lighter blue	3½-4
Barite	white, gray, red, blue	white	2½-3½
Beryl	emerald green, light blue, rose-red, blue-green	white	7½-8
Biotite	green to black	uncolored	2½-3
Calcite	white, gray, red, green, blue, violet	white or grayish	3
Celestite	white, pale blue, reddish	white	3-3½
Chalcopyrite	brass yellow	greenish-black	3½-4
Cinnabar	cochineal red, dark red	scarlet	2-2½
Copper	copper-red	copper-red	2½-3
Corundum	blue, red, yellow, brown	uncolored	9
Cuprite	red, various shades	brownish-red	3½-4
Diamond	colorless, blue, pink	uncolored	10
Diopside	green, various, dull	white to gray	5-6
Dolomite	white, reddish, brown	white	3½-4
Fluorite	white, green, yellow, blue, violet, red	white	4
Galena	lead-gray	lead-gray	2½
Gold	gold yellow to pale yellow	yellow	2½-3
Graphite	iron-black to dark steel-gray	steel-gray	1-2
Gypsum	usually white	white	1½-2
Halite	colorless or white	white	5½-6½
Hematite	steel gray, red, brown	reddish-brown	5½-6½
Hornblende	dark green to black	uncolored very pale	5-6
Kyanite	blue, white, green	uncolored	5-7¼
Limonite	brown	yellowish-brown	5-5½
Magnetite	iron-black	black	5½-6½
Malachite	bright green	paler green	3½-4
Molybdenite	pure-lead gray	greenish-gray	1-1½
Muscovite	colorless, brown, pale green	uncolored	2-2¼
Natrolite	white, colorless	uncolored	5-5½
Opal	white, yellow, red, brown, green, sometimes rich play of colors	white	5½-6½
Pectolite	whitish or grayish	white	5
Pyrite	pale brass-yellow	greenish-black	6-6½
Quartz			
Rock crystal	colorless	uncolored	7
Amethyst	purple	uncolored	7
Smoky	smoky, black	uncolored	7
Rose	pink	uncolored	7
Agate	several colors, banded	uncolored	7
Jasper	red, brown, green	uncolored	7
Chalcedony	tan, white, blue	uncolored	7
Flint	gray, brown, black	uncolored	7
Rhodonite	brownish-red, flesh red, rose-pink	white	5½-6½
Serpentine	leek-green, brownish yellow	white	2½-4
Siderite	ash-gray, brown, brownish-red	white	3½-4
Silver	silver-white	silver-white	2½-3
Sphalerite	yellow, brown, black	brownish to light yellow	3½-4
Spinel	red, blue, green, black	white	8
Staurolite	dark reddish-brown	uncolored	7-7½
Stilbite	white, brown	uncolored	3½-4
Sulfur	sulfur-yellow, honey-yellow	white	1½-2½
Talc	apple-green to white	usually white	1-1½
Topaz	straw-yellow, blue, white, colorless	uncolored	8
Tourmaline	black, blue, green, red, yellow, often several zones of color	uncolored	7-7½
Tremolite	white, gray, green	uncolored	5-6
Uraninite	velvet-black, greenish	brownish-black	5½
Zircon	brown, green, blue, colorless	uncolored	7½

ROOTS

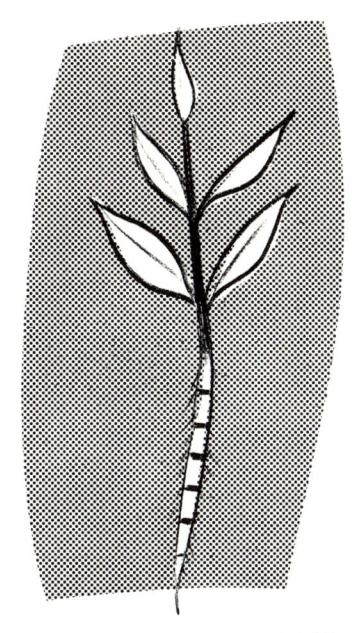

DISCOVERING THE GROWING AREA OF ROOTS

Materials you'll need:
  young seedlings, ruler, needle, ink

Does the entire root of a plant grow down into the ground? To find out, germinate some seeds on a layer of wet cotton in a covered glass dish for a week or so (see page 101 for studies of germination). When the young seedlings have developed a one-inch root you are ready to experiment.

With a ruler measure one-eighth of an inch from the root tip and make a tiny line using a needle dipped in ink. Now make a mark one-quarter inch from the tip. Continue until the entire root is measured and marked into one-eighth-inch sections. Cover the dish and let the seedling continue its growth. Each day observe and measure the distance between marks. Did all sections of the root grow the same amount? Which part is the growing and elongation area of a root?

Repeat the test by marking the stem of a seedling. Compare stem and root growth.

TESTING THE ACIDITY OF GROWING ROOTS

Materials you'll need:
  seeds, litmus paper, glass-covered dish, cotton, distilled water

Germinate several seeds on moist cotton in a glass-covered dish. When the seedlings have grown good root systems you are ready to run the acidity test. Moisten several pieces of blue litmus paper with distilled water. Place the strips of paper beneath and on top of the rootlets. If the cotton in the germinator is too wet the test will not work. In two days observe the color of the litmus paper. Is it still blue? Knowing what acid does to rocks, does this explain how growing plants help break up the earth's surface?

169

SCALE

MAKING A SCALE

Materials you'll need:
3 pieces of wood 1" by ½" by 18", rectangular block of wood, screws, heavy wire, 2 metal pie pans, long bolt and nut

You can make a scale called a *balance*. It compares the weight of the object being weighed with a known weight. If they are the same weight, the pans will balance. If one is heavier than the other, the beam is thrown off balance.

Drill holes up through the rectangular base and into the ends of the two supports, the long pieces. Use flat-headed screws to fasten the uprights to the base.

Make your scale according to the illustration. The holes through the tops of the uprights should be exactly the same size as the bolt, so that the bolt fits tightly into them. The hole in the balancing beam (a lever) should be made with a bit slightly larger than the diameter of the bolt, so that the beam moves freely on the bolt. Make sure the hole is in the exact center of the beam.

Finish the scale with the pie pans and wire as shown in the illustration. For the weights, use a variety of objects such as curtain weights, plumber's bobs, nuts, and other pieces of metal. Weigh each article on an accurate scale and paint its weight on it. Be sure the pans are always clean.

SCREW

DEMONSTRATING THE PRINCIPLE OF A SCREW

Materials you'll need:
cardboard disk, ruler, 36" tape measure, yardstick, spring scale, toy car

A road winding around and around a mountain in a spiral resembles the threads which wind around a screw. Both are examples of an inclined plane. Of course, an inclined plane is a simple machine; therefore, it must make work easier for us. Here is a way to see for yourself that a screw or spiral road makes work easier.

Cut a large circle of cardboard. You can make a cone-shaped mountain out of it by cutting to the center of the circle and overlapping and fastening the edges. In the illustration the cone was made large enough so that a 12-inch ruler leaned against it reached exactly from top to bottom. This ruler

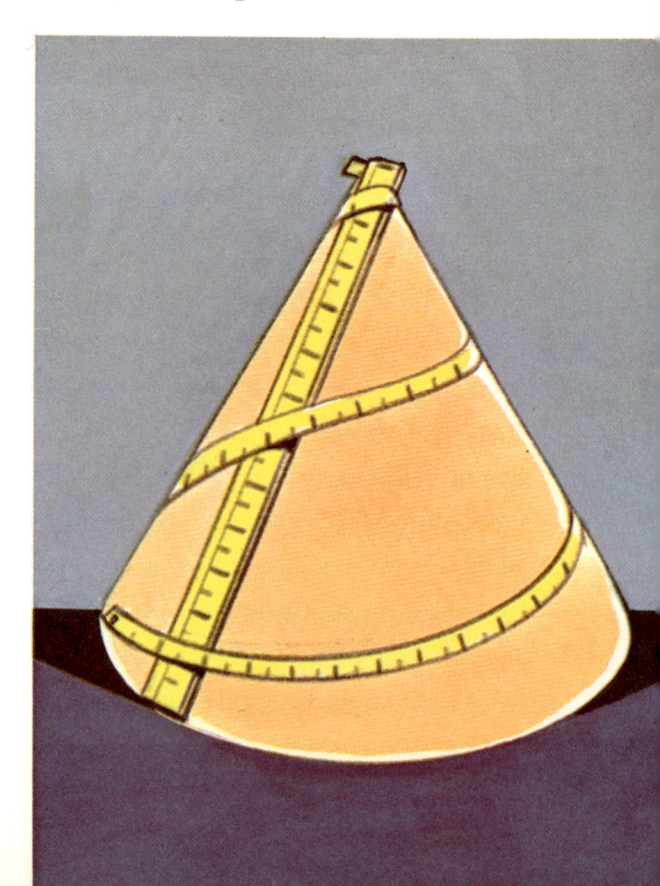

SCREW

SEEDS

represents the road which runs straight up the mountain without winding around it. Now wind a 36" tape measure around the mountain fastening it at top and bottom. This is the longer but less steep road.

Remove the ruler and tape measure. Substitute a 36" yardstick for the tape measure. Put one end of the ruler and one end of the yardstick at the same height against a solid object so that they form inclines. The incline or slope which the yardstick forms is not as steep as the incline formed by the ruler. Fasten a spring scale to the front of a small toy car. Pull the car up the slanted ruler and record how much force was necessary. Do the same thing using the yardstick. Notice that it takes more force, or is more work, for the car to ascend the steep slope but that the force is exerted over a shorter distance than on the more gradual slope.

FIGURING THE PLANTING DEPTH FOR SEEDS

Materials you'll need:
  corn or bean seeds, soil, jar

Select a glass jar which is at least eight inches high with a mouth large enough so you can put your hand in and out with ease. Put a one-inch layer of good soil on the bottom. Plant several seeds around the edge so you are able to see them from the outside of the jar. Sprinkle this layer slightly with water. Spread another inch of soil and plant a Put another inch of soil and plant a second circle of seeds. Continue with the layers, watering each, until the soil and seeds reach the opening. Set the jar in a warm place and continue to water when it appears to be drying up.

After two weeks observe the germination rate of each level of planting. Which seeds germinated? Which ones grew into healthy plants? Be sure to remember the correct depth in case you want to plant a garden later.

SEEDS

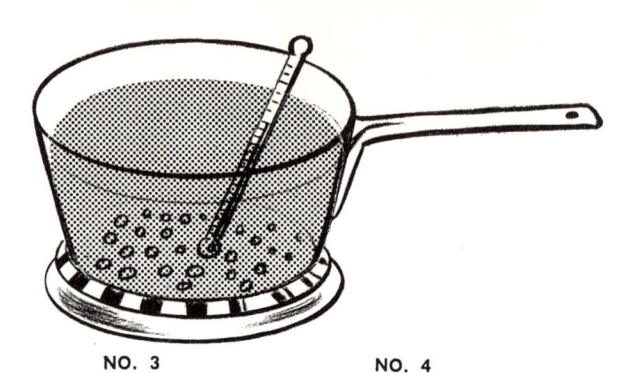

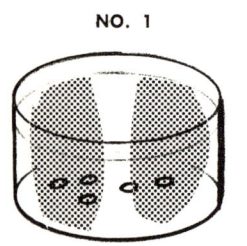

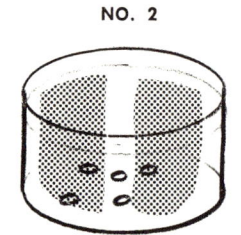

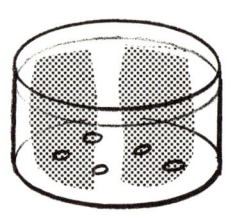

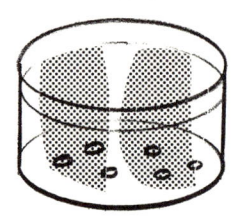

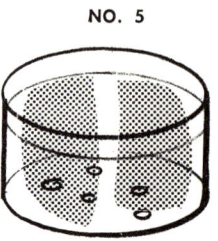

NO. 1   NO. 2   NO. 3   NO. 4   NO. 5

TESTING HEAT ON GERMINATION

Materials you'll need:
   pan, thermometer, 5 covered bowls, blotter, seeds

Cut disks of blotting paper to fit into the bottoms of five bowls. Moisten the blotters and keep them covered until ready for use. These are the germinators. Number labels on the dishes from #1 to #5.

Put twenty-five corn or bean seeds in a pan of water. Using a water thermometer check the temperature of the water. Turn on the heat and as soon as the thermometer reads 50 degrees Fahrenheit (10 degrees Centigrade) adjust the heat so that the temperature is maintained for five minutes. Remove five seeds and place them in germinator #1. Continue to heat and hold the temperature at 68 degrees F. (20 degrees C.) for another five minutes. Remove five more seeds and place them in germinator #2. Repeat this process at 130, 185, and 212 degrees Fahrenheit for five minutes until the last five seeds are in the last germinator. Observe the growth of all five germinators for a week. What amount of heat is best for germination? At what temperature were the seeds killed?

SHOWING THE STRENGTH OF GROWING SEEDS

Materials you'll need:
   many seeds, covered plastic container, tape

The number of seeds needed for this experiment depends upon the size of the plastic container. It must be full to the brim. Pour water over the seeds and let them soak for twenty-four hours. Pour off the water, put on the cover, and tape it securely in several places. Keep the container in a warm place for several days. What happens? Does this help explain how rocks and sidewalks are often broken by growing plants?

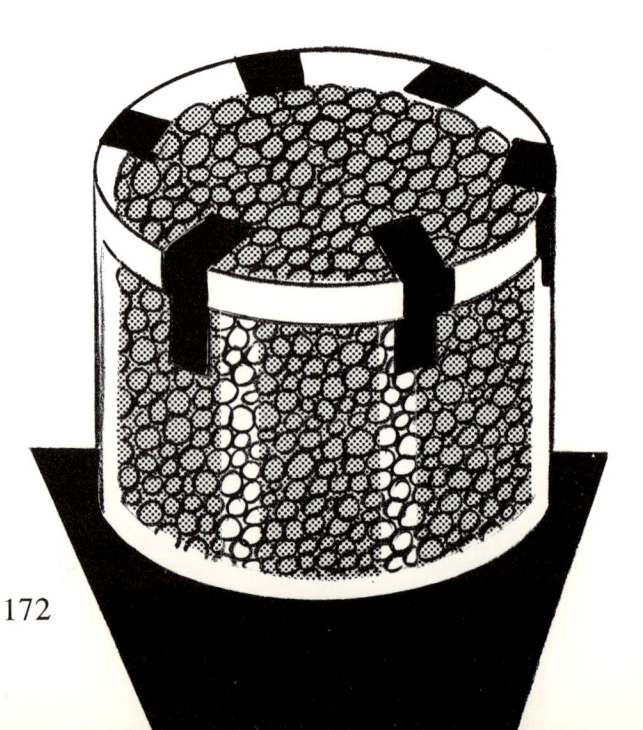

SHORT CIRCUIT

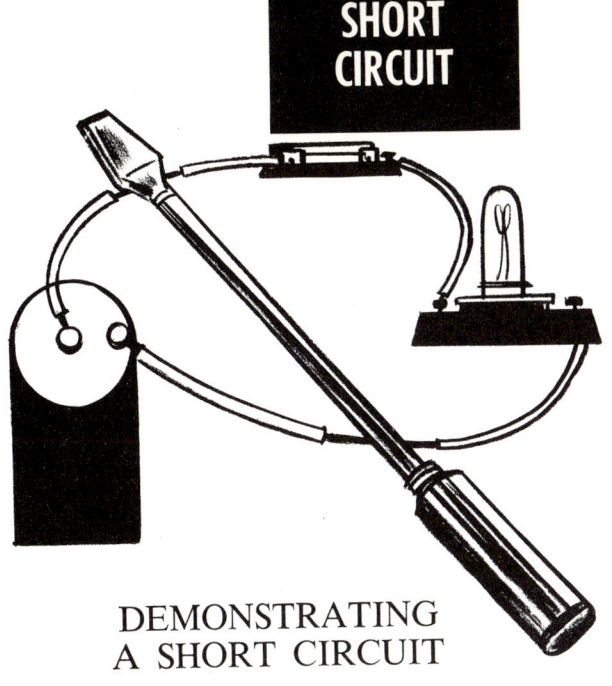

DEMONSTRATING A SHORT CIRCUIT

Materials you'll need:
  dry cell, lamp, switch, bell wire, screwdriver

An electric current follows a path called a *circuit*. In the ordinary house, the current flows from a source through a *resistance*, such as an appliance. When the current finds a path without resistance, it takes this path. Large amounts of current flow and the wires become hot. Sometimes fires are started by such short circuits.

In a simple circuit containing a switch, a dry cell and a lamp, the resistance is the lamp. (See page 188 for making a switch.) The filament is made to glow by the current flowing through it. If the current can avoid the lamp (resistance) and take an easier path, a short circuit occurs.

Disconnect the circuit and remove the insulation from places on two of the wires. Lay the metal part of the screwdriver across the two bare places and reconnect the circuit. In this case the current flows over the screwdriver rather than going through the lamp. The bulb will be very dim. Feel the screwdriver after a few minutes.

SILKWORMS

RAISING SILKWORMS

Materials you'll need:
  silkworm eggs from a biological supply house, shoe box, supply of mulberry or osage-orange leaves

Purchase the eggs of the silkworm moth from a supply house. Place them in a shoe box and cover with a piece of glass. They will hatch in a few days at room temperature. When the worm-like larvae appear, put in fresh mulberry or osage-orange leaves each day. Do not serve them wet leaves. Remove the old food each time you put in fresh. The larvae feed for a month and then stop eating and growing. During this time a silkworm larva grows so rapidly that it molts (splits its skin) four times. Place a twig in the box. The larvae will fasten their cocoons to this.

To obtain the raw silk fiber, place the cocoons that have formed in boiling water for a few minutes. This will kill the pupae and, as the water cools, the silk fiber can be unraveled carefully and slowly. Astonishingly enough, one cocoon can contain as much as two miles of unbroken fiber.

The cocoon or pupal stage lasts for two weeks. At the end of this time the adult silkworm emerges, lays its eggs and dies. It has undergone a complete metamorphosis.

SKELETON

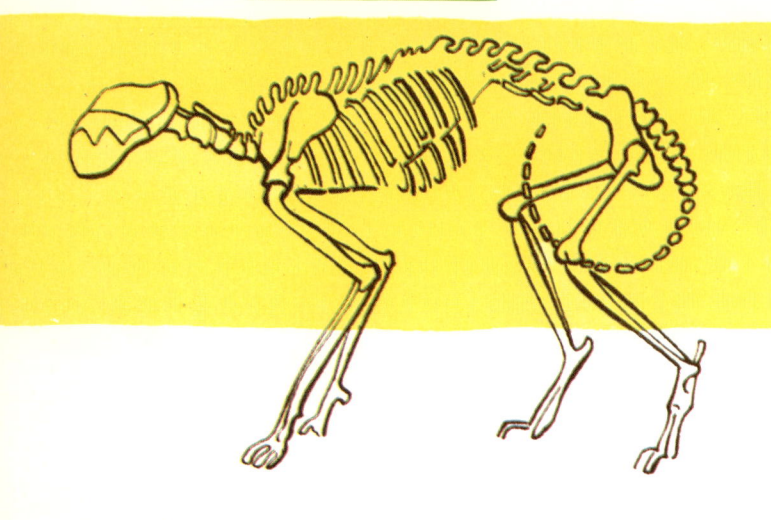

CLEANING AND ASSEMBLING SKELETONS

Materials you'll need:
 knife, scissors, forceps, caustic soda, carbon tetrachloride, household bleach, wire, screws

A skeleton gives an animal support and shape. The skeleton of a vertebrate is called an *endoskeleton* because it is on the inside of the body. Scientists group vertebrates into *classes* depending on how alike they are in structure. The way their skeletons are constructed is one clue used in their classification. It is interesting to study the skeleton structure of one member of each class of vertebrates to see likenesses and differences. The best way to study a skeleton is to clean and assemble it yourself.

Use for your class representatives a fish (*Pisces*), a frog (*Amphibia*), a turtle (*Reptilia*), a chicken (*Aves*), and a mouse (*Mammalia*).

The first step is to remove the skin from the animal. You will need dissecting instruments for this—the knife, scissors, and forceps. After removing the skin, boil the carcass for half an hour. Cut and pick away all the muscles and internal organs. Be careful not to remove the ligaments which hold the bones together.

If the tissue is not all off the bones, carefully soak them in a caustic soda solution. If the solution dissolves the ligaments, it is too strong and you must start over, using a weaker solution.

There will still be traces of grease on the skeleton which must be removed. Soak it in carbon tetrachloride and water for at least one day. This must be done outdoors, since the fumes of carbon tetrachloride are dangerous.

You'll want to bleach the bones next, because they will have a grayish look. Any bleach will make them white.

The last step is to reassemble the skeleton into the original animal shape. Use a stiff wire bent into a curve for a vertebral column. Vertebrae and appendages can be attached to this. Use wire and screws to attach bones which have separated from the skeleton. You may have to use glue to reconstruct the skeleton of a fish.

See which bones you can identify as similar in the different classes of vertebrates.

CAUTION!

SNAKES

BANDED (OR COMMON) WATER SNAKE

COMMON VIPER

GREEN SNAKE

GARTER SNAKE

PRAIRIE RATTLER

KEEPING SNAKES AS PETS

Materials you'll need:
terrarium with wire top, pan of water, cloth bag, forked stick

The best place to keep a pet snake is in an old aquarium which you have fixed up as a terrarium (see page 194). If you must build a snake cage, be sure the sides and floor are of smooth, painted or varnished wood or glass. A snake might be injured in a wire cage. The top should be fine wire mesh to allow ventilation. A wooden frame around the sides will make a tight fit.

The kind of terrarium you fix will depend on what kind of snake you have. In general, there should be a layer of dirt or sand on the floor, a branch or piece of wood, and an anchored pan of water. Sink the pan in dirt or sand. Keep the terrarium out of direct sunlight and have the temperature between 65° and 80° Fahrenheit.

Before you even go hunting for snakes, be sure to find out what poisonous snakes live in your region. Be able to identify them on sight.

To capture your snake you will need a cloth bag or cardboard box and a forked stick. During the spring and summer you should be able to catch a snake in a grassy meadow, under a log, in a garden, or near a pond. Pin the snake down with the forked stick (not too hard) and grab it behind the head. Support the rest of the body and slip it into your bag.

A snake needs fresh water daily and food once a week. It will eat earthworms, frogs and mice, depending on its size. You may be able to press hamburger on a string and dangle it, inducing the snake to strike at it. If the snake refuses to eat after two weeks in captivity, return it to its natural environment.

Snakes shed their skins periodically, as they grow. When your snake's coloring becomes dull and its eyes filmed, it is getting ready to shed. Put a large pan of water in the cage and leave the animal alone. Its disposition is bad while it is shedding.

CAUTION!

175

SNOW GAUGE

MEASURING SNOWFALL

Materials you'll need:
  2-pound coffee can

A snow gauge measures the amount of snow that has fallen. The easiest way to do it is to mark off inches on a large coffee can. Put the can outside, away from the house in a calm, protected area but not under a tree.

Read the depth of snowfall directly off the collecting can. About ten inches of snow is equal to one inch of rain so if you wish to know the amount of precipitation, divide the depth of the snow by ten.

As a check on this measurement, allow the snow to melt at room temperature. This will keep evaporation at a minimum.

SOIL

STUDYING ONE SQUARE YARD OF SOIL

Materials you'll need:
  1 square yard of soil, tape measure, magnifying glass

Use a tape measure to mark off one square yard of soil. It might be in the woods, in a meadow, or in your own backyard.

Examine first the animals, trees and other vegetation, and climate of the area. You can make some good guesses about what to expect when you look at your "yard" more closely.

Now come down to the surface of the soil. Look at what is above the soil: insects, decaying organic material such as leaves, flowers, etc.

Next dig into the soil, observing as you dig the layers of humus and clay and the rocks. You will probably find earthworms and burrowing insects if you look closely. What do you see through the magnifying glass?

Even a piece of soil as small as a square yard will furnish you many surprises. Try picking many different places for your "square yard" and comparing them. You will be studying *ecology* when you do this.

SOIL

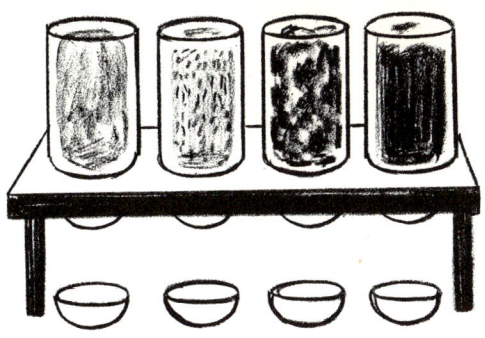

OBSERVING THE WAY SOIL HOLDS WATER

Materials you'll need:

4 bottles, tape, plywood stand, gravel, sand, topsoil, clay, water, gauze

Soil is the name given to the material found above the solid rock of the earth. It consists of particles worn from rock mixed with decaying animal and vegetable matter. There are some easily recognizable common types of soil—clay, gravel, sand—which differ in texture. Some are made up of finer particles than others and in some the particles are more closely packed than in others. For these reasons, different types of soil differ in the degree to which they hold water.

To find out how they differ, you must first remove the bottoms of four bottles. This can be done by following the directions on page 70.

Build a small plywood stand to hold the bottles upside down. Tape a piece of gauze over the mouth of each bottle. Fill one with gravel and sand, a second with sand and topsoil, the third with topsoil and clay, and the fourth with clay. Place dishes under each to catch the drippings. With a partner, pour one cup of water into the top of each bottle at exactly the same time. Observe the length of time it takes water to pass through each type of soil. Do you think the farmer needs to know which type of soil holds water best and which loses it fastest?

COLLECTING SOILS

Materials you'll need:

various kinds of soils, containers, labels

To learn more about the earth's surface, try collecting different kinds of soils in your own community. Fill clear plastic containers or glass jars with samples of sand, silt, clay and loam. It would be interesting to add to your collection samples of soil from various parts of the country, gathered during a vacation trip. Make labels for the containers, noting all the classification and location information about each sample. *(Cont. on next page)*

177

SOIL

Soils are made up of three kinds of particle groups or *separates,* as they are called. These separates are sand, silt and clay. But no soil found in nature consists completely of one of these separates. It is always a combination of separates. These combinations are called *classes.*

You will want to try to identify the soil class to which each of your samples belongs. In a laboratory, a scientist would add a large amount of water to the sample, the grains would separate out and the proportions of sand, silt and clay could be figured. You will have to depend on cruder classification methods. The best way to do it is by texture. To determine texture, you must moisten the sample and rub it between your fingers. You can identify the sample by comparing the way it feels with the list of classes below.

1. *Sand*—a mixture but largely sand; coarse and gritty to the touch; separate particles are easily seen; doesn't hold together when moist but falls apart in your hands as separate grains.
2. *Loamy sand*—holds together a little when slightly moist.
3. *Sandy loam*—holds together when moist but hardly makes any smear on your fingers.
4. *Loam*—makes a rough smear and feels sandy.
5. *Silt loam*—makes some smear when moist but doesn't rub out thin like clay before becoming rough and broken.
6. *Clay loam*—
7. *Silty clay loam*—
8. *Silty clay*— } make smears midway between silt loam and clay when moist; are easily crushed fine between fingers when dry; particles are difficult to distinguish.
9. *Clay*—a mixture but largely clay; sticky and plastic when wet, and hard and difficult to crush when dry; when moist and rubbed between fingers, makes a smooth, thin, continuous smear; separate particles can be seen only under microscope.

You will also notice differences in the colors of your samples. They may range from black through brown, red, yellow and light gray to white. Colors do not necessarily have any connection with soil classes but you certainly should add color to the class name so that samples are described as "red sandy loam" or "white clay," etc.

Finally, add the name of the town or city near which the soil was found. Scientists use these place names to describe soils, so you might read about "Miami sandy loam" or "Barnes clay loam."

SOUND

FINDING OUT ABOUT SOUND

Materials you'll need:
  pail, rocks, wooden table, metal fence at least 75 feet long

Sound is a form of energy. Vibrations moving through materials makes waves. We hear sound when our ears can pick up these waves and the brain receives the impulses. There are many interesting laws you can learn about sound.

1. Will sound travel through liquids? Fill a large pail, or other container with water. Hold two rocks down in the water and strike them together hard. Did you hear a sound?

2. Will sound pass through solids? Put your ear close to the end of a wooden table. Ask another person to scratch the wood at the opposite end of the table with a fingernail or other sharp object. Can you hear a sound?

3. Does the density of a material affect the speed of sound? This experiment requires a length of metal at least seventy-five feet long. An iron fence will have continuous rods running through it or a roll of wire may be stretched the length of your backyard or school ground. Stand at one end with a partner at the opposite end holding two rocks. Place your ear very close to the wire or rod while your friend strikes the rocks together with the wire trapped between. Listen closely for two sounds—one following immediately after the other. The sound is coming through the air as well as through the metal. Do sound waves move faster in a gas (air) or a solid?

EXPERIMENTING WITH RESONANCE

Materials you'll need:
  piano, your own voice

A vibrating object may cause another object nearby to move back and forth. The vibrations of this second object are called *resonant* or *sympathetic* vibrations. Can you cause a piano to make a noise without touching the keys?

Lift the covering lid of a piano while at the same time you press down on the right-hand or sustaining pedal. Hum or sing a loud, clear note into the open piano, with pedal held down. Suddenly stop singing the note and listen. What note comes from the piano? Which string was in resonance with your voice? Can you see why resonance is important in music?

SOUND

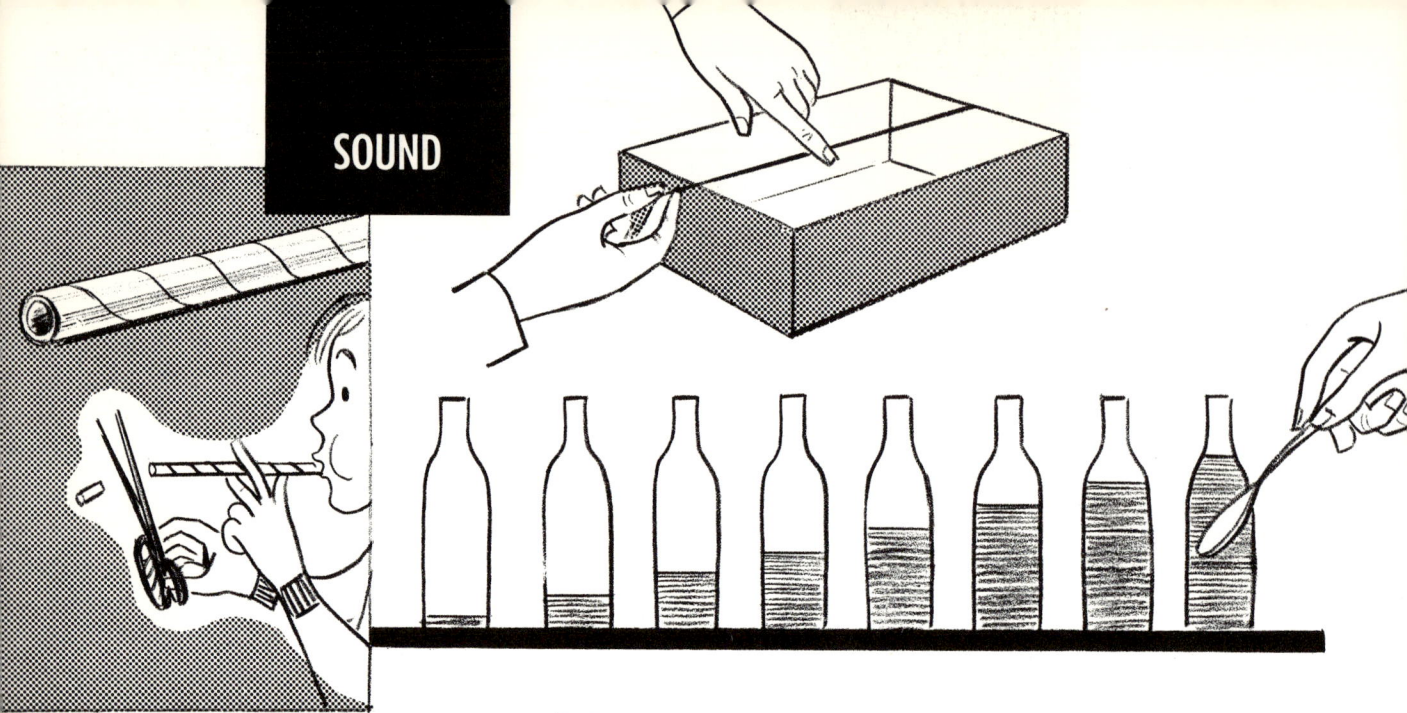

DEMONSTRATING PITCH

Materials you'll need:
  cigar box, rubber band, 6 water glasses, spoon, drinking straws, scissors

Sounds are made by vibrating objects. Pitch is one of the characteristics of sound. Any vibrating object makes a certain definite number of vibrations every second. The more vibrations it makes, the higher the pitch of the sound is. A very high key on the musical scale is caused by many vibrations and a low one is caused by a few. This is hard to understand unless you can see it happen.

Stretch a rubber band across an empty cigar box. The purpose of the cigar box is to make the sound louder. Anchor the rubber band on one side with a pin or tack and hold it tight to the other side. Pluck it. Listen for the sound it makes and watch it vibrating. Pull it tighter across the box and pluck it again. The sound should be higher. The tighter the band is stretched, the faster it vibrates.

Sounds are also made by vibrating columns of air. This is how sounds are made by many musical instruments. Fill eight identical water glasses or bottles with varying amounts of water. You will find if you tap them with a spoon that each makes a sound with a different pitch. Add or take away water until you can play the notes of the scale on the bottles. The vibrating glass is causing the column of air inside to vibrate. The shortest column of air vibrates the fastest.

Another experiment with a vibrating column of air requires only a large drinking straw (of the milk shake variety) and a pair of scissors. Cut diagonally across the corners of one of the straws. Hold this end rather loosely between your lips and blow into the straw. You may have to experiment quite a bit with cutting straws before you produce a good straw. When you are able to make a sound, either cut finger holes in the length of the straw in the manner of a clarinet or chop pieces off the end of the straw with the scissors as you blow. You will discover that as you shorten the straw or make the column of air in it shorter by closing holes with your fingers, the pitch of the sound changes.

SOUND

BUILDING SOUND PIPES

Materials you'll need:
8' of ¾" aluminum tubing, saw, wooden frame, hard rubber ball, dowel, string

When a length of pipe is struck a sharp blow, a sound is heard. That is because the air inside the tube has been made to vibrate. The pitch of the sound can be controlled by cutting the pipe to a certain length, so that the column of air inside vibrates the correct number of times per second.

For example, a piece of pipe exactly 12⅞ inches long will vibrate at the same frequency or pitch as Middle C on the piano. You can put together a series of sound pipes on which you can play accurate scales and tunes.

First build a wooden V-shaped frame to hold the pipes. Put a length of pipe over the top from which the sound pipes will be suspended. Make each of the next pieces longer or shorter to make a scale. You may have to file the tubes a little to get the right pitch. Test the pitch by striking the corresponding note on the piano. Drill holes in the ends of the tubes and hang them with string from the horizontal bar. You can make a mallet for striking the sound pipes by inserting a dowel into a small, hard rubber ball.

APPROXIMATE SCALE	
Middle C — 12⅞"	G — 10-21/32"
D — 12¼	A — 9-31/32
E — 11½	B — 9⅜
F — 11⅛	C — 9

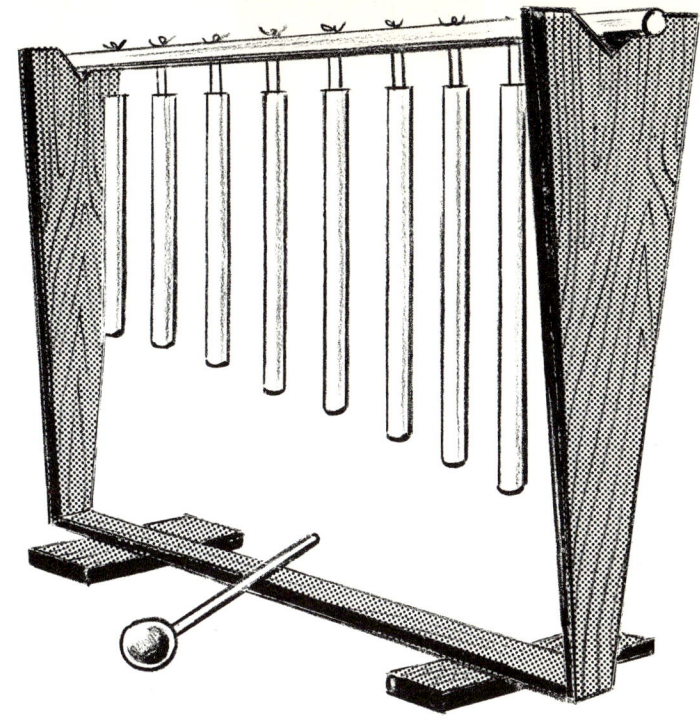

MAKING A TIN-CAN TELEPHONE

Materials you'll need:
2 tin cans, a long piece of string, 2 buttons

A tin-can telephone shows the way in which sound travels. A real telephone sends sound over wires by changing sound vibrations into electrical impulses inside the telephone mouthpiece or transmitter. The telephone receiver changes the electrical impulses which it receives back into sound vibrations.

Punch a small hole in the bottom of two tin cans. Thread the string through each hole and tie it to a button on the inside of the can bottom. The button will anchor the string so that it can't pull out when the string is pulled tight. Give one can to a friend while you hold the other. The string should be long enough so that you can get far apart—too far apart to talk to each other in normal voices. Stretch the string tight and, while you talk into one can, have your friend hold the other to his ear. Does it become harder to hear each other when the string is allowed to hang loose? Why?

SOUND

ONIONSKIN PAPER
SALT CARTON
MIRROR

SEEING THE SOUND OF YOUR OWN VOICE

Materials you'll need:
salt carton, piece of mirror, onionskin paper, glue, white cardboard, flashlight

When you speak or sing, your vocal cords vibrate. This causes the air around to vibrate and sound waves are formed. When you speak into something like a cardboard carton, the air vibrations cause the carton to vibrate at the same rate. Here is a way to "see" these vibrations.

Obtain an old pocket mirror which is no longer needed and wanted. Wrap the mirror in cloth so that you can safely hit it with something to make it break. You need a piece about one-quarter inch square.

Cut one end off a round salt box. Then cut out a disk in the other end, leaving about an inch all the way around. Paste a circle of onionskin paper onto the rim left so that it covers the opening.

Glue the small piece of mirror on the outside of the thin paper in an off-center position. Have a friend hold a flashlight so that it shines on the mirror. Hold a piece of white cardboard so that the reflected spot of light from the mirror shines on it.

Talk into the carton. The reflected ray of light will make a pattern on the cardboard as the mirror vibrates. Experiment with singing, making vowel sounds, shouting. What is the difference in pattern between a high-pitched sound and a low-pitched sound? A loud and a soft one?

This instrument is similar to an *oscilloscope* except that an oscilloscope shows a picture of an electrical signal made by the vibrations rather than of the sound itself.

SPECTRUM

MAKING A SPECTRUM FROM WHITE LIGHT

Materials you'll need:
   glass prism, pocket mirror, container of water, hose

Sunlight is seen as almost white light but white light is really made up of many colors, each color with a different wave length. The way to see these colors lined up one after another as in a rainbow is to bend the white light. The shorter waves bend more than the longer ones and the colors fall next to each other instead of all together. This line-up of color is called the *spectrum*.

Sunlight shining through a glass prism is the easiest way to produce the spectrum. Simply hold the prism in a narrow beam of sunlight and focus the resulting spectrum on a white ceiling or wall. You can make a narrow beam by directing the sunlight through a small hole in a piece of cardboard.

You can make your own prism from a mirror and glass of water. Put the mirror in the glass so that it leans backward. Sunlight striking the mirror and reflected back through the water will separate into a spectrum on the wall.

A spectrum or rainbow can also be made by letting sunlight pass through a spray of water from the garden hose. In the early morning or late afternoon, with the sun behind you, aim the water spray at a dark building or clump of trees. The rainbow should be visible as the light is bent by the drops.

SPIDER WEBS

PRESERVING SPIDER WEBS

Materials you'll need:
   black and white construction paper, spray cans of white and black enamel, spray can of clear plastic

You can find spiders' webs in many places—corners of buildings, between two shrubs, between rows in a cornfield. They are very beautiful and well-worth collecting.

First, spray the web on both sides with either white or black enamel. Don't get too close or it might break. Next, carefully mount it on the contrasting construction paper, trying to touch all parts of the web to the paper at the same moment. Cut the web guy lines with scissors to free it. Lay it flat to dry and spray it with plastic in order to preserve it.

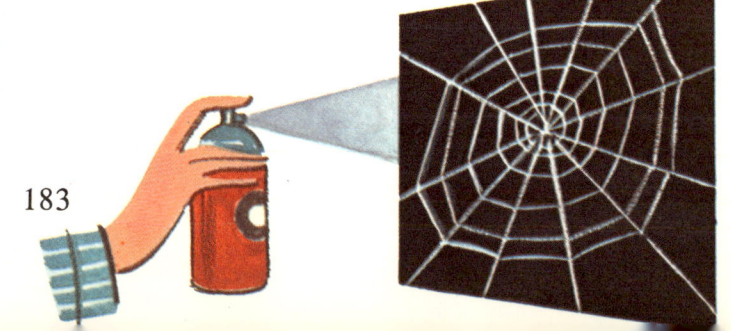

SPORES

MAKING SPORE PRINTS

Materials you'll need:
   pencils, colored cardboard, clear plastic or glass dish, glue, mushrooms

Mushrooms reproduce by spores. The spores are tiny cells, found on the underside of the mushroom cap. They grow into new mushrooms. One of the methods used to identify plants is to make spore prints. A variety of mushrooms may be collected from damp wooded areas or marshy regions. Remove the *stipe* or stalk from each one. Spread a film of glue over a piece of cardboard. Rest the *pileus* or *cap* of the mushroom on two pencils over the cardboard. Put a plastic dish over this. The spores will fall and stick to the glue. Use contrasting colors of cardboard depending upon the spore color. Can you tell the difference between spores under a microscope? Tap spores onto glass slides and see.

STALACTITES

MAKING STALACTITES AND STALAGMITES

Materials you'll need:
   cardboard box, 2 tall jars, heavy string, Epsom salts, 2 nails

Stalactites and stalagmites are cone-shaped formations which look a little like huge icicles. They are found in caves. They are calcium deposits made by calcium-laden water dripping through the ceiling and onto the floor of the cave. The water evaporates, leaving the calcium. These are formed in two ways: a *stalactite* forms like an icicle hanging from the cave roof. When the calcium water drips to the floor and the deposit builds upward, a *stalagmite* is formed.

Place a tall jar on either side of an open-topped box. Tie four pieces of heavy string to two nails. The strings must be long enough so that they reach from one jar, over the box, to the bottom of the jar on the other side.

Make a solution of Epsom salts and water. You may add food coloring if you wish. Fill the jars with the salt solution. Place a nail in each jar with the strings leading over the cavern. Water and salt will move up the cord. As the water evaporates, the salt will accumulate. Leave it alone for a week. Soon, piles of salt will build up.

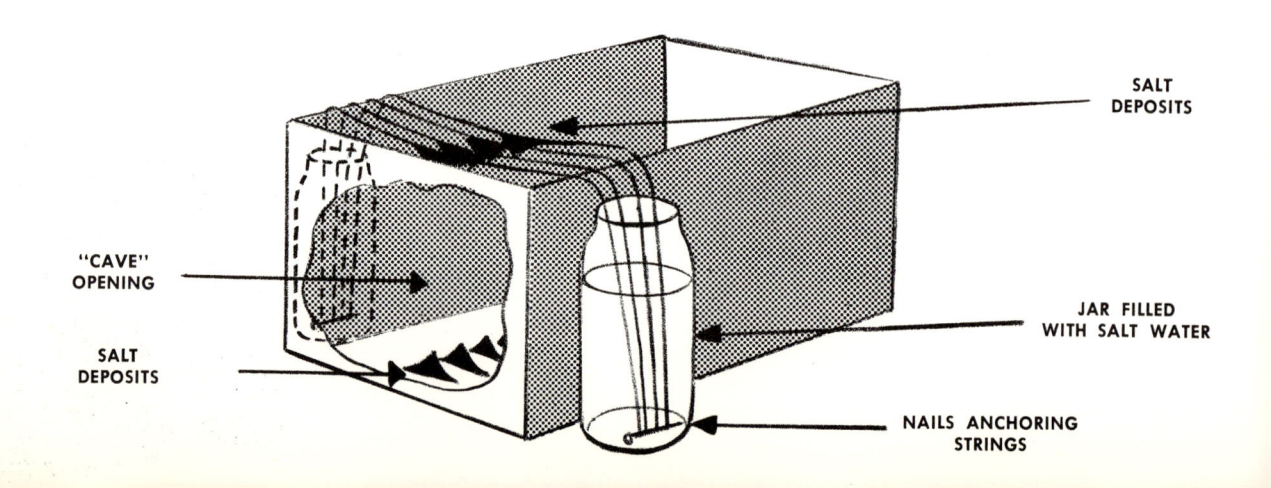

STATIC ELECTRICITY

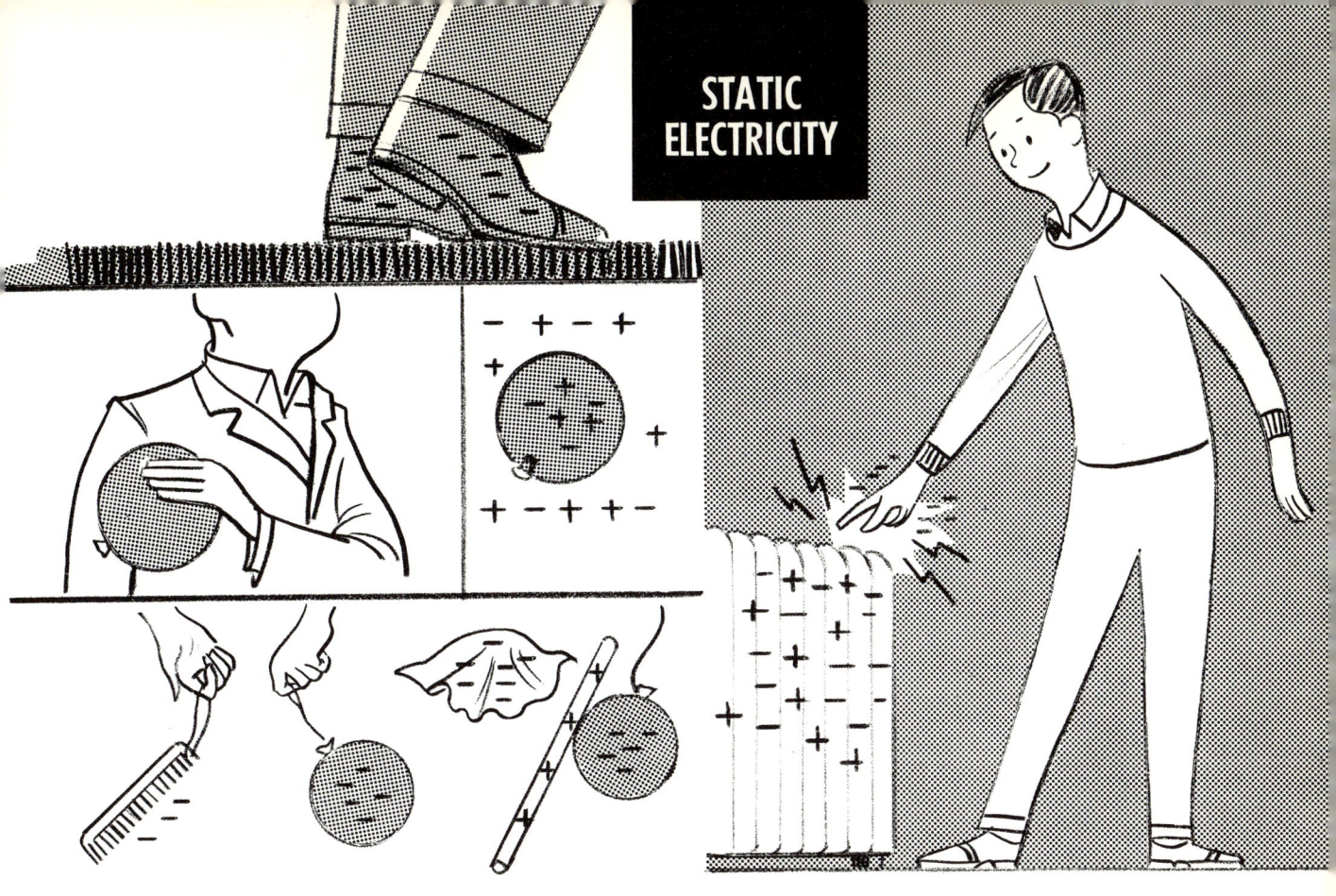

EXPERIMENTING WITH STATIC ELECTRICITY

Materials you'll need:
rubber comb, balloon, glass rod, silk scarf

On a cold, dry day shuffle your rubber-soled shoes back and forth on a wool rug. Step over to a metal pipe or radiator and quickly tap it with your finger. The spark that you see fly between the two objects is static electricity.

Comb your hair rapidly with a rubber comb. What happens to your hair?

Blow up a balloon and tie it. Rub it on the sleeve of a wool sweater. Touch the wall with the balloon. Does it cling to the wall?

Bring the charged comb (charged by combing your hair) close to the charged balloon. Do they attract or repel each other? Why?

Rub a glass rod with a silk scarf thirty times. Hold the rod close to a small stream of water coming from a faucet. What happens to the water?

Charge the glass rod again by rubbing it with silk. Bring it near the balloon which has been rubbed with wool. What happens?

Rubbing two objects together causes the electrons in the atoms of one material to jump to the other object. This upsets the neutrality of the objects and they become charged. The object that loses electrons is positively charged. The object which has picked up excess electrons—the balloon or comb—is negatively charged. Objects with like charges repel each other, therefore the comb and balloon repelled each other.

The glass rod with its positive charge attracted the balloon with its negative charge. The spark in the first test was produced by the excess of electrons you had accumulated on your body by rubbing the rug. They jumped over to the metal pipe, producing a spark when they collided with the atoms in the air.

STEAM

MAKING TURBINES

Materials you'll need:
A—baking powder can with lid, wooden stand, source of heat, string, ice pick; B—wooden stand, large can top, large nail, small nail, Pyrex flask, bent glass tube, 1-holed stopper, stand, nut and bolt, washer

A steam turbine is a machine which changes the energy of moving steam to mechanical energy so that work can be done. It is made of a series of wheels, each larger than the next. The wheels rotate, turning a rotating shaft by means of which work is done. You can make two types of turbines.

For the simpler turbine, collect the materials listed in "A" above. The lid of the baking powder can must fit tightly. With an ice pick punch three holes approximately one-half inch from the bottom on different sides of the can. Tie a string lightly around the top of the can and fasten three strings from it to the washer and nut and bolt in the top of a stand. The can must be able to swing freely.

Put a small amount of water in the can—not enough to reach the holes—and put on the lid. As you heat the water, steam will escape from the holes and cause the can to turn.

A more complex turbine can be made with the materials listed in "B." The first thing to do is to cut the top from a large tin can. The disk should be at least four inches in diameter. Using the large nail and a hammer, make a dent, or "dimple," in the center. Next make a series of half-inch cuts in from the edge of the tin wheel. They should be about one-fourth of an inch apart. With gloves on, or with cloth over your hands, bend the sections of tin between the cuts so they form blades. Hammer the small nail up through the wooden stand and place the wheel on it, with the point of the nail in the "dimple."

Put the straight end of a bent glass tube through a one-holed stopper. (Be sure to soap the tube so that it goes through easily without breaking.) Fill a flask about half full of water and put the stopper and tube in the top. Adjust the stand so that the end of the tube is at the same level as the turbine wheel. When the water in the flask boils, the steam coming out of the tube will hit the blades and cause the wheel to turn.

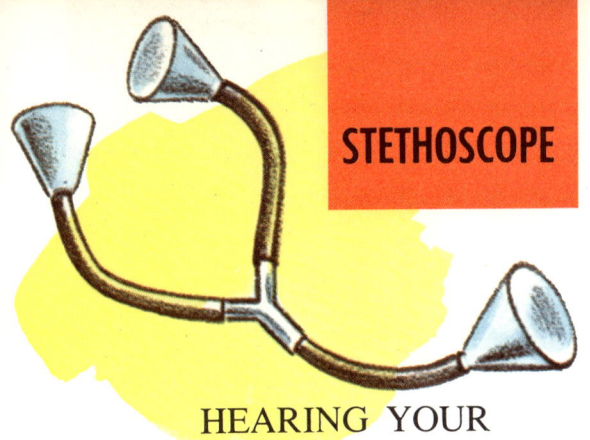

STETHOSCOPE

HEARING YOUR HEART BEAT

Materials you'll need:
3 small metal funnels, glass Y-tube, rubber tubing

Would you like to hear your own heart beat? You can make an instrument almost like a doctor's stethoscope which will magnify the noise your heart makes and help you hear it.

Join the ends of three two-foot pieces of rubber tubing to the three arms of a glass Y-tube. Put small metal funnels on the free ends of the tubing. This will serve as a stethoscope. Have your partner hold two funnels tightly to his ears while you place the third funnel over your heart. Have him count the heartbeats he hears for one minute. Now run around the room for several laps. Count your heartbeat again. What happens when you exercise strenuously? How long is it before your heart returns to its regular beat?

MAKING A SUNDIAL

Materials you'll need:
plywood, paint, nails

Long ago men noticed that as the sun seemed to move across the sky, the shadows it cast moved also. They devised an instrument to tell time using the sun and shadows. This instrument was called a *sundial*.

Cut a round dial face out of a ten-inch square piece of plywood. The shadow-caster is called a *gnomon*. It is a triangular piece of plywood with a base equal to the radius of the dial

SUNDIAL

face (five inches). Draw a line dividing the dial face in half and make a groove along the line wide enough so the gnomon can slide into it. Nail the gnomon in place from underneath. Be sure the high point of the triangle is at the outside edge of the dial.

Painting the sundial will make it weatherproof. When it is dry, fasten it to a post outside where the sun will shine on it all day. If you live in the Northern Hemisphere, point the outside edge of the gnomon toward the North Pole. In the Southern Hemisphere, it should point toward the South Pole.

When the sun's rays are directly over the gnomon and no shadow is cast, it is twelve o'clock. So paint a "12" beneath the gnomon on the dial. An hour later draw a line from the center along the edge of the shadow cast. Number this one o'clock. Continue drawing and marking all the hours around the dial. If you wish, you can also mark half and quarter hours. The shadow at six a.m. and six p.m. should fall at right angles to the low point of the gnomon and directly east and west (by compass). Remember that this is sun time and the hour must be adjusted if you live in an area of daylight-saving time.

SURFACE TENSION

INVESTIGATING FLOATING OBJECTS

Materials you'll need:
½" lengths of heavy string, sawdust, feather, tin can lid, screw, fork, detergent, water

Molecules on the surface of a bowl of water are attracted downward toward the other water molecules in the bowl. This causes a strain or tension at the surface of the water which acts almost like an elastic skin. Light objects can float on the surface of water and water is sometimes unable to penetrate fabrics.

First try floating the lightest objects such as the sawdust, the feather, the lengths of string. They will float until a little detergent is added to the water. The detergent decreases surface tension, permitting the objects to get wet, get heavy and sink. Does soap have the same effect as detergent?

Next take the lid of a tin can, place it on a fork. Slowly and carefully lower it onto the surface of the water. Remove the fork. The weight of the lid is spread over such a large area that the surface tension of the water is enough to support it. If you touch the prongs of the fork to the water next to the lid, the surface tension will be broken and the lid will sink. Add a little detergent to the water while the lid is floating. What happens?

Try lowering a screw onto the surface of the water using the fork. Does the screw float? Why? Try other objects.

SWITCH

MAKING A SWITCH

Materials you'll need:
insulated wire, dry cell, miniature lamp socket, knife switch, block of wood, 2 large screws, large coffee can

It would be helpful before making your own switch to wire a commercial knife switch into an electric circuit.

Cut a three-foot piece of bell wire into three pieces. Scrape one-half inch of insulation off both ends of each piece. Connect one pole of the dry cell to one side of the lamp. Run a wire from the other pole of the cell to one end of the switch. Wire the other end of the switch to the other side of the lamp. When the knife switch is pushed down, the circuit is closed.

Now try making your own switch. First, cut a metal strip one inch by five inches from a coffee can. Cut a block of wood three inches by five inches by one inch. Any scrap of wood about this size will do. Hammer a nail into one end of the metal strip to make a hole in it. Bend the strip in the shape shown in the illustration. Fasten it to the wooden base with a screw, leaving one-eighth inch of screw sticking up. Put a screw in the other end of the wood beneath the end of the switch and protruding enough so that it is one-fourth inch below the switch. Wire your switch as the knife switch was wired. When the switch contacts the screw, the circuit is closed.

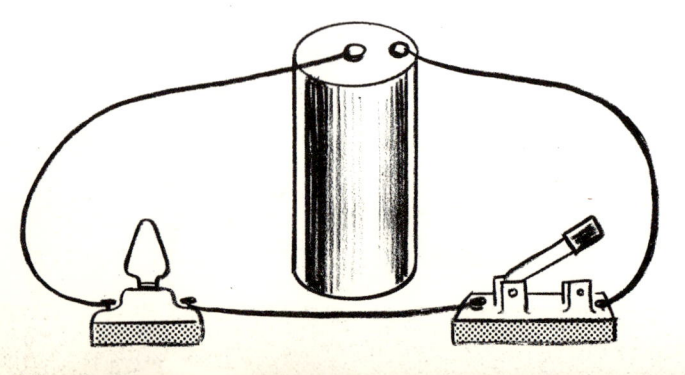

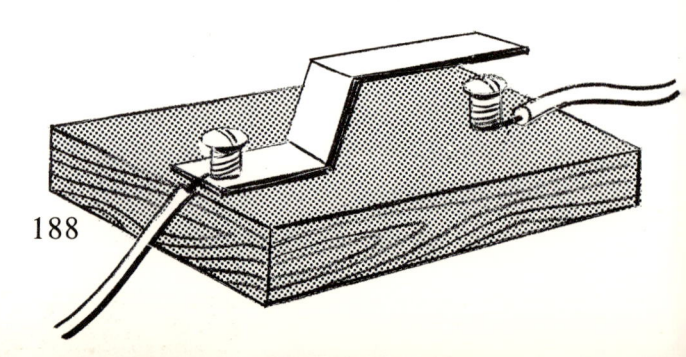

TADPOLE

TASTE

STUDYING TADPOLE GROWTH

Materials you'll need:
  6 tadpoles, thyroid powder, aquariums

The thyroid is a gland found in many animals including man, some fish and all amphibians. It helps regulate growth and development of the body.

Since frogs have thyroid glands, you can use tadpoles and frogs for an experiment with thyroid powder. Use three tadpoles for the experiment and three for the control group. Put the groups in separate tanks. Feed the control group a balanced diet (see page 22). Feed the experimental group the same balanced diet but, in addition, sprinkle the water with thyroid powder daily. Change the water after the powder has been in it for a couple of hours.

The tadpoles in the control group will take the usual length of time to undergo metamorphosis while those receiving the thyroid powder will, within a week, start to change into frogs. They will grow legs and lose their tails and very shortly mature into frogs. They grow faster but they will be miniature in size and sexually immature. Move them to a terrarium.

TESTING YOUR TASTE BUDS

Materials you'll need:
  salt, sugar, lemon juice, aspirin, toothpicks

Embedded in your tongue are taste buds which pick up certain sensations of sweet, salt, bitter, and sour. These areas are in specific places instead of being scattered generally over the whole tongue. Try to find the centers for each of the four taste sensations.

Dip a wet toothpick into salt and place it on a certain spot on your tongue. If it did not taste salty, continue moving it until you find the section which picks up this taste. Repeat the procedure with sugar, lemon juice or vinegar, and finally with a concentrated aspirin solution. When all experimenting is finished you should be able to diagram the tongue and label the taste centers.

TAXIDERMY

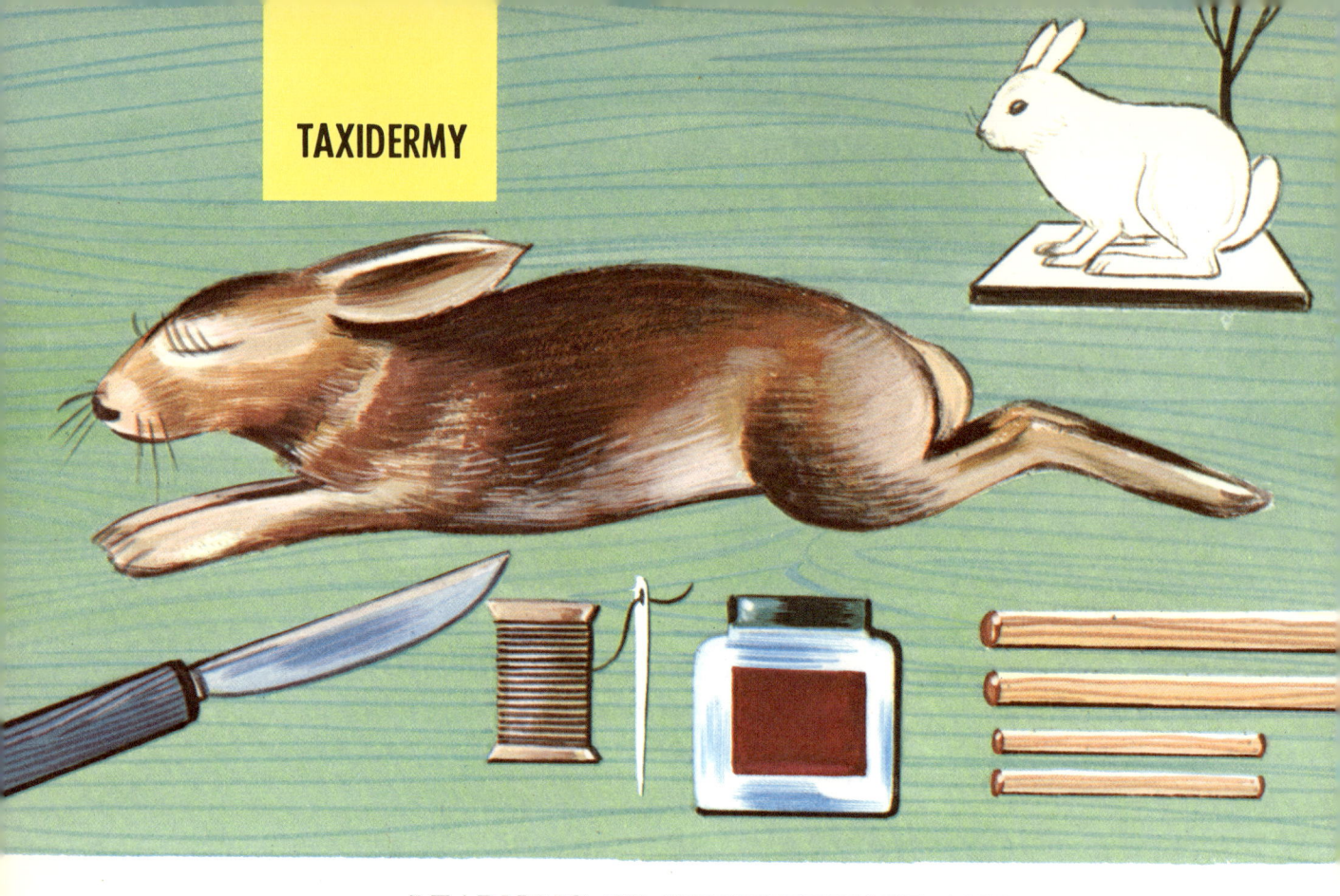

LEARNING TO RECONSTRUCT ANIMALS

CAUTION!

Materials you'll need:
freshly-killed animal, corn meal, sharp knife, borax powder, cotton stuffing, dowels, buttons

Taxidermy is a process by which animals are preserved for study and display. The methods vary for different animals but usually the animals are skinned and the skins sewn around models. You can skin an animal and stuff it carefully so that it looks like the live animal.

You must begin with a freshly-killed animal, such as a rabbit. An animal that has been dead for a long time may be diseased and should not be handled. An adult should supervise you if you do the killing. Chloroform is one of the easiest things to use.

Use a sharp knife to open the skin on the ventral or under surface. Separate the fur or feathers so that they are not damaged. They will cover the incision when the animal is sewn up. Sprinkle corn meal around the incision to soak up the blood.

Skin the animal as carefully as possible, pulling the muscle away from the hide. Rub borax powder into the hide on both sides and let it stand for several hours before removing it. Then scrape off the powder along with the remaining muscle tissue so that the skin is as clean as possible.

It will be necessary to cut off the appendages and skull. Be sure the skin stays partly attached to the appendages. Soak the skin and appendages in a borax and water solution overnight and dry them. The skin is now protected against decay and insects.

Insert dowel rods into the appendages and skull. Stuff the body with cotton and sew up the incision. Small buttons can be painted to look like eyes and glued into the eye sockets.

TELEGRAPH

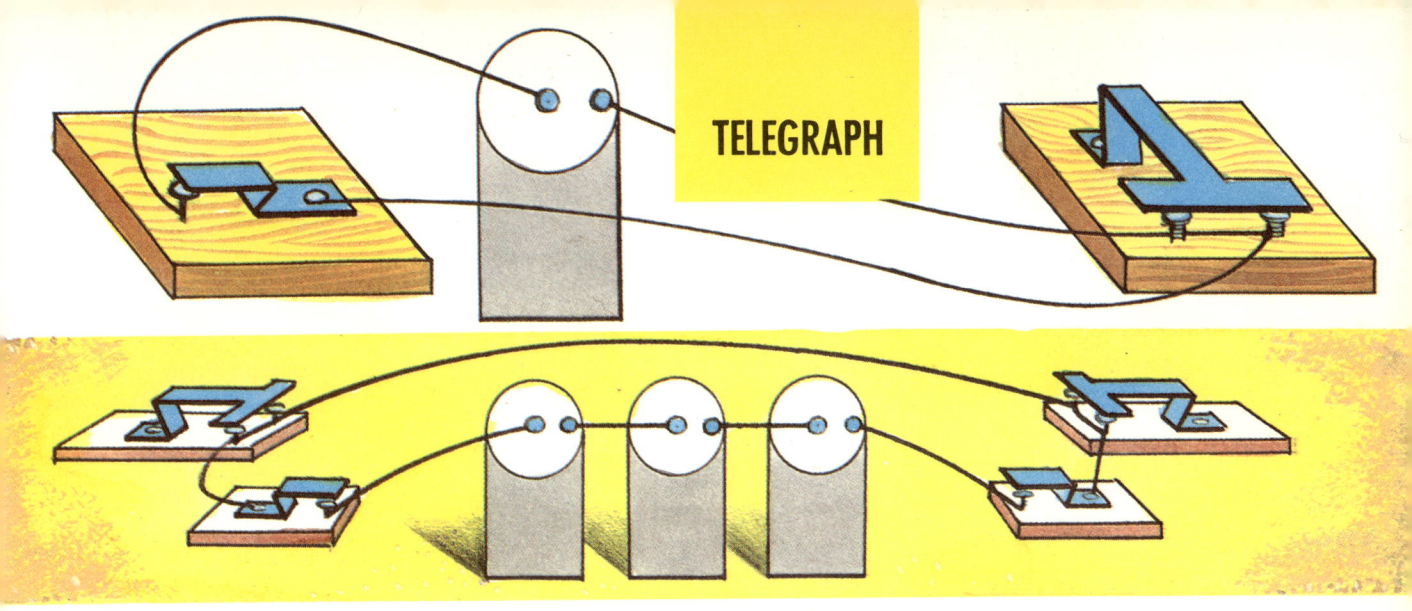

MAKING A TELEGRAPH SET

Materials you'll need:
2 long nails, 2 blocks of wood, small nail or tack, 4 feet of bell wire, dry cells, tin cans

A telegraph set consists of a *sounder* and a *sending key*. The electricity in your set will be supplied by a dry cell. When the circuit is closed by pressing the key, the metal of the sounder is attracted to the electromagnet and produces a click. When the sending key is released, the metal strip springs away. The clicks of the sounder are varied according to the Morse Code.

Construct the sounder by driving two long nails into one of the blocks of wood. Start in the center of the length of bell wire and wrap it around one nail clockwise for at least twenty turns, then around the other nail counterclockwise for twenty turns. This is the electromagnet. Cut a T-shaped piece of metal from a tin can, bend it as shown and nail it to the block so that it is just a fraction of an inch above the nail heads. You may have to do some further bending so that it is not so close that it won't spring back when the circuit is broken, yet is close enough to be attracted.

Assemble the sending key by driving the tack into the other block. Nail another strip of metal onto it as shown.

Connect two free ends of bell wire leading from the telegraph sounder to the nail holding down the sending key and to one terminal of the dry cell. A third piece of wire connects the other terminal of the dry cell to the tack on the sending block. Learn the Morse Code from the table and practice sending messages with your set. Use a short pause for the dash and a longer one between words. If you want to send messages from one set to another, construct two identical sets wired as in the second picture. Add more dry cells if more power is needed.

INTERNATIONAL MORSE CODE

A	._	J	.___	S	...	2	..___	Period	._._._
B	_...	K	_._	T	_	3	...__	Comma	__..__
C	_._.	L	._..	U	.._	4	...._	SOS	...___...
D	_..	M	__	V	..._	5	.....	Start message	_._
E	.	N	_.	W	.__	6	_....	End message	._._.
F	.._.	O	___	X	_.._	7	__...	Error	....
G	__.	P	.__.	Y	_.__	8	___..		
H	....	Q	__._	Z	__..	9	____.		
I	..	R	._.	1	.____	0	_____		

TELEPHONE

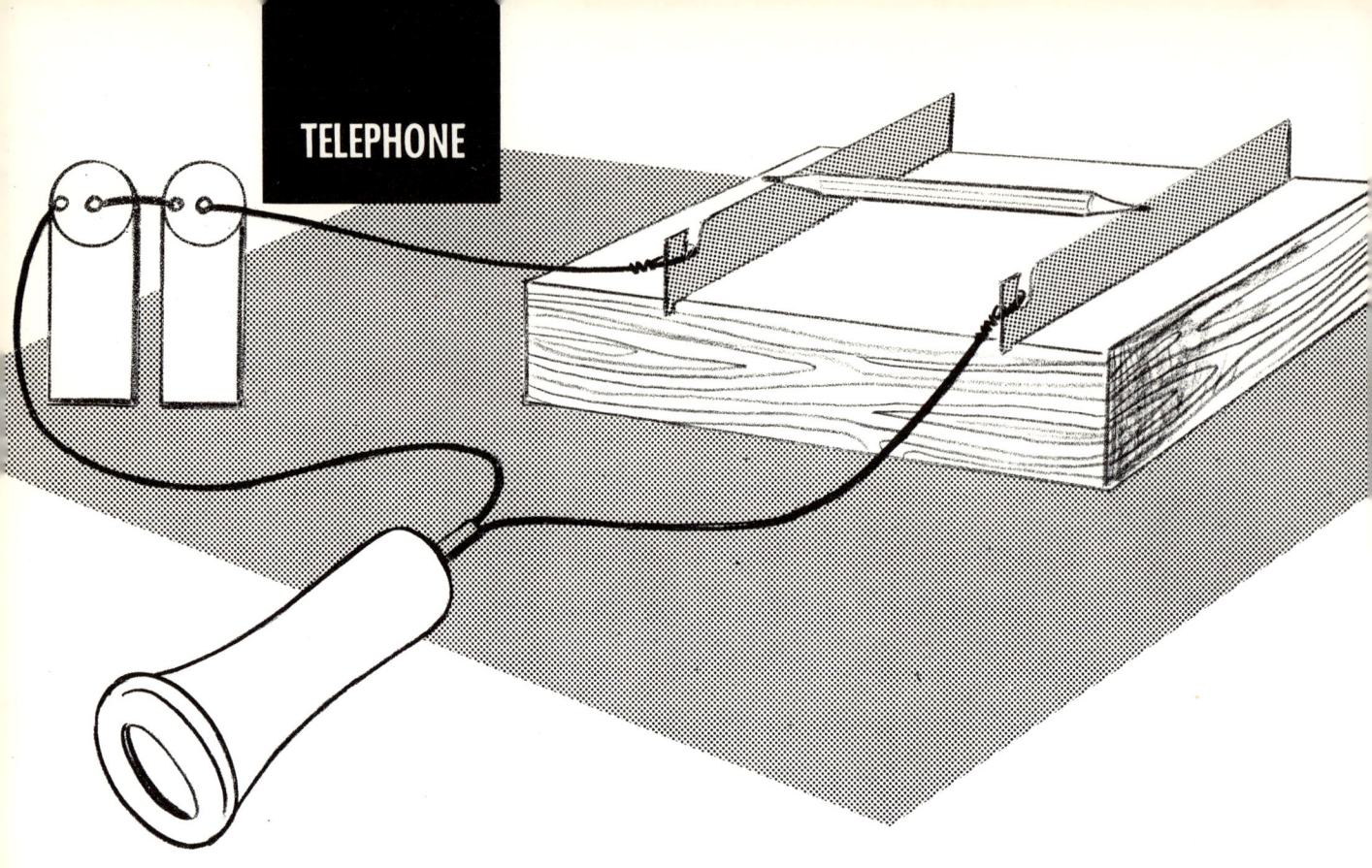

SETTING UP A TELEPHONE TRANSMITTER

Materials you'll need:
cigar box, 2 strips of metal from can, pencil sharpened at both ends, 2 dry cells, an old telephone receiver, bell wire

When you speak into a telephone transmitter, the vibrations caused by your speaking are changed into electrical impulses. The impulses are carried over the wire and changed back into vibrations and sound waves in the receiver. In this simple telephone transmitter, the vibrations caused in the wooden box by your voice make the pencil jump. The current flowing through the circuit (which includes the pencil lead) is interrupted by the jumping of the pencil. This causes a pattern of electrical impulses to flow through the wire. This pattern of electrical impulses is changed back into vibrations and sound waves in the receiver.

Your local telephone company will probably have an old receiver of the type shown and will be glad to let you have it. Rural communities, particularly, are likely to have just removed the old-style telephone a few years ago. Strip the insulation from the cord and locate two wires.

Cut strips from metal cans. Cut hooks on the ends of them for easy wiring. Groove the cigar box in two places as widely separated as from one end of a double-sharpened pencil to the other. Use florist's clay or melted wax to stand the metal strips upright in the grooves. Lay the pencil over the strips, making sure the lead ends rather than the wood center part touch the metal strips.

Wire the instrument as shown. Adjust the pencil and speak close to the box while a friend holds the receiver to his ear. Keep moving the pencil and talking into the box until your friend can hear your voice distinctly through the receiver instead of through the air.

TELESCOPE

MAKING A TELESCOPE

Materials you'll need:
2 double convex lenses or plano-convex or plano-concave lens,
2 cardboard mailing tubes—7" and 4" long, tape

A telescope causes distant objects to appear closer to the person using it. A refracting telescope is the easiest kind of telescope to make. In order to make this telescope you must place two lenses in line with each other so that the light rays collected from the object by one lens are focused a little in front of the second lens.

You can construct a telescope using two double convex or plano-convex lenses which will give you an upside-down view of the object you look at. (To understand why see Figure 1.) This is fine for looking at the moon, planets and stars but confusing for viewing objects on the earth. If you want an exact image (right-side-up) use a concave lens for the eyepiece (either double concave or plano-concave, Figure 2). You'll need to order your lenses from a supply house, giving the diameters and focal lengths you want. A suggested focal length for the eyepiece is 1" and for the objective, 8". To order, you'll have to translate from inches to millimeters. Keep in mind that one inch = .025 meters and 1000 millimeters = one meter. Using lenses of these focal lengths will yield a magnification of eight times.

One cardboard mailing tube should be slightly smaller than the other tube so that it slides smoothly in and out. For the size lenses recommended, the larger (outside) tube should be approximately seven inches long and the smaller one four inches long. The diameters are determined by the lens' diameter.

Tape or fasten with florist's clay the objective lens in one end of the larger tube and the eyepiece in one end of the smaller tube. Place the small tube inside the larger one and move it in and out until the object at which you are looking is in clear view.

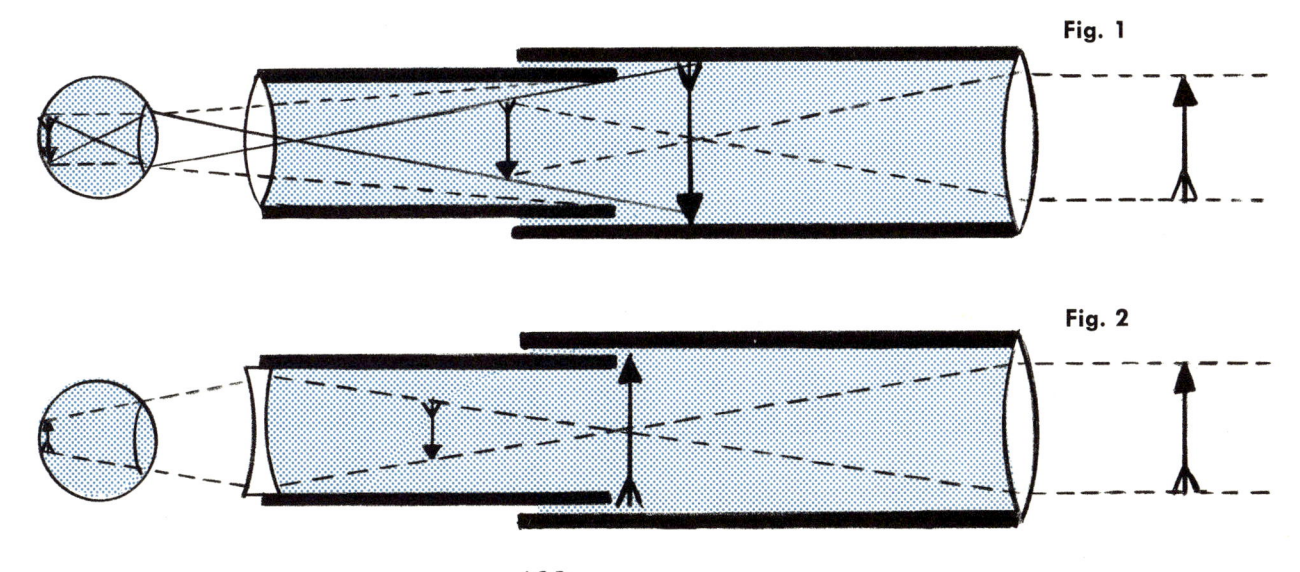

Fig. 1

Fig. 2

TERRARIUM

BUILDING A TERRARIUM

Materials you'll need:
  baking pan, 4 glass sides, adhesive tape, plaster of Paris

A terrarium contains a miniature world of plants and animals. It imitates a community of living things on land in the same way that an aquarium imitates a water community. If you have an old aquarium, it will serve nicely as a terrarium. If you have no available aquarium and you have woodworking tools and an adult to help, you can make the following simple terrarium.

Get a large square cake pan the size you want your finished terrarium to be. If the metal is not aluminum, paint it with aluminum paint. You will have to have glass especially cut for the sides and ends. Order the pieces just large enough to meet in the corners of the pan. They should be about eleven inches high.

Lay the four pieces of glass out flat on the floor according to the illustration. Tape the joints with strong tape. The taped side will be on the outside of the glass. Tape the top edges also to protect you from being cut.

Mix plaster of Paris to the consistency of pudding and half fill the pan. Let it start to harden, then fold the glass pieces into a rectangle and stand it in the pan. Tape the fourth corner. When the plaster is dry your terrarium is ready to use.

STOCKING A TERRARIUM

A terrarium is always a miniature scene of outdoor life. It can be used just for plants or you can use it as a home for small animals. Large animals trample and kill the plants. Decide what kind of scene you want to build and then gather the appropriate plants and animals. The soil will be different in each kind of terrarium.

A glass jar, an old aquarium, or a terrarium you constructed yourself may be used to hold these different earth scenes.

A *woodland terrarium* needs a layer of gravel and bits of charcoal on the bottom, covered with several inches of rich garden soil. Small woodland plants, such as wild strawberry, fern, and moss, may be transplanted into it. Water the plants right after transplanting. Salamanders, toads, and tree frogs enjoy this kind of world. Do not put the woodland terrarium in direct sunlight

TERRARIUM

WOODLAND TERRARIUM

DESERT TERRARIUM

BOG TERRARIUM

SEMI-AQUATIC TERRARIUM

because these plants and animals thrive in shady places. If you have no animal life, try sealing the terrarium. This means that the moisture inside will continually evaporate and condense. Put a sheet of glass over the top and watch conditions inside for a week. If no mold has formed (indicating too much moisture) or the earth is not dry and cracked, seal the top to the sides with melted paraffin.

A *desert terrarium* needs sandy soil in which cacti and succulent plants are grown. Small snakes and horned toads thrive in this environment. This kind of a terrarium can use more sunlight than the others.

The *bog terrarium* should contain a mixture of one part sand, one part peat moss, and one part gravel. Bog life needs more moisture than the others. This environment is ideal for insectivorous plants, such as the pitcher plant, sundew, and Venus' flytrap.

The scene in a *semi-aquatic terrarium* imitates the environment along a river bank. It is a good kind of home for amphibians. A pan at one end of the container holds the water, and the remaining section should be built up with rich soil. Small plants found on the edge of a stream may be transplanted. Aquatic bladderwort, for example, thrives in this world. Tadpoles and water insects may be kept in the water habitat.

THERMOMETER

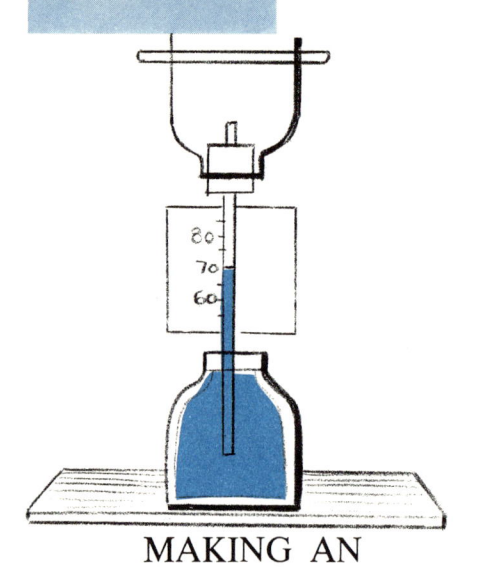

MAKING AN AIR THERMOMETER

Materials you'll need:
  2 ink bottles, 1-holed stopper, glass tubing, paraffin, food coloring, candle, wooden support

A thermometer measures temperature. This air thermometer will measure room temperature. If you know what effect heat has on a gas, you will be able to figure out how it works.

Locate two empty ink bottles or similar containers. Use a one-holed stopper for one of the bottles or you can make one by drilling a hole in the center of a cork. Carefully insert a piece of glass tubing and put wax around it. This will make it airtight.

Fill the second bottle with colored water. Turn the bottle with the stopper upside down over the second bottle so that the glass tube reaches into the solution. Fasten this apparatus to a wooden support. Use a candle to warm the upside-down bottle for a few seconds. After two or three bubbles of air have escaped into the colored water, remove the heat. The colored solution will rise in the tube. If it goes further than halfway up the tube, start

TRANSPIRATION

over again and do not warm the inverted bottle as long.

Make a scale by observing the temperature readings daily on a regular commercial thermometer and marking off the corresponding levels of the water column. When the temperature drops, does the fluid go up or come down in the tube? Does air expand or contract when it gets colder?

OBSERVING TRANSPIRATION IN PLANTS

Materials you'll need:
  clear plastic bag, string, potted plant

Plants give off water through tiny openings on the undersides of their leaves, much as man gives off water through his skin. A large tree may lose gallons of water each day.

To observe this process of transpiration, tie a clear plastic bag over the leaves and stem of a plant. Be sure none of the plant touches the plastic except where the bag is tied securely around the stem just above soil level. Set the plant in the sun for several hours. Observe what happens on the inside of the bag.

196

TRAP

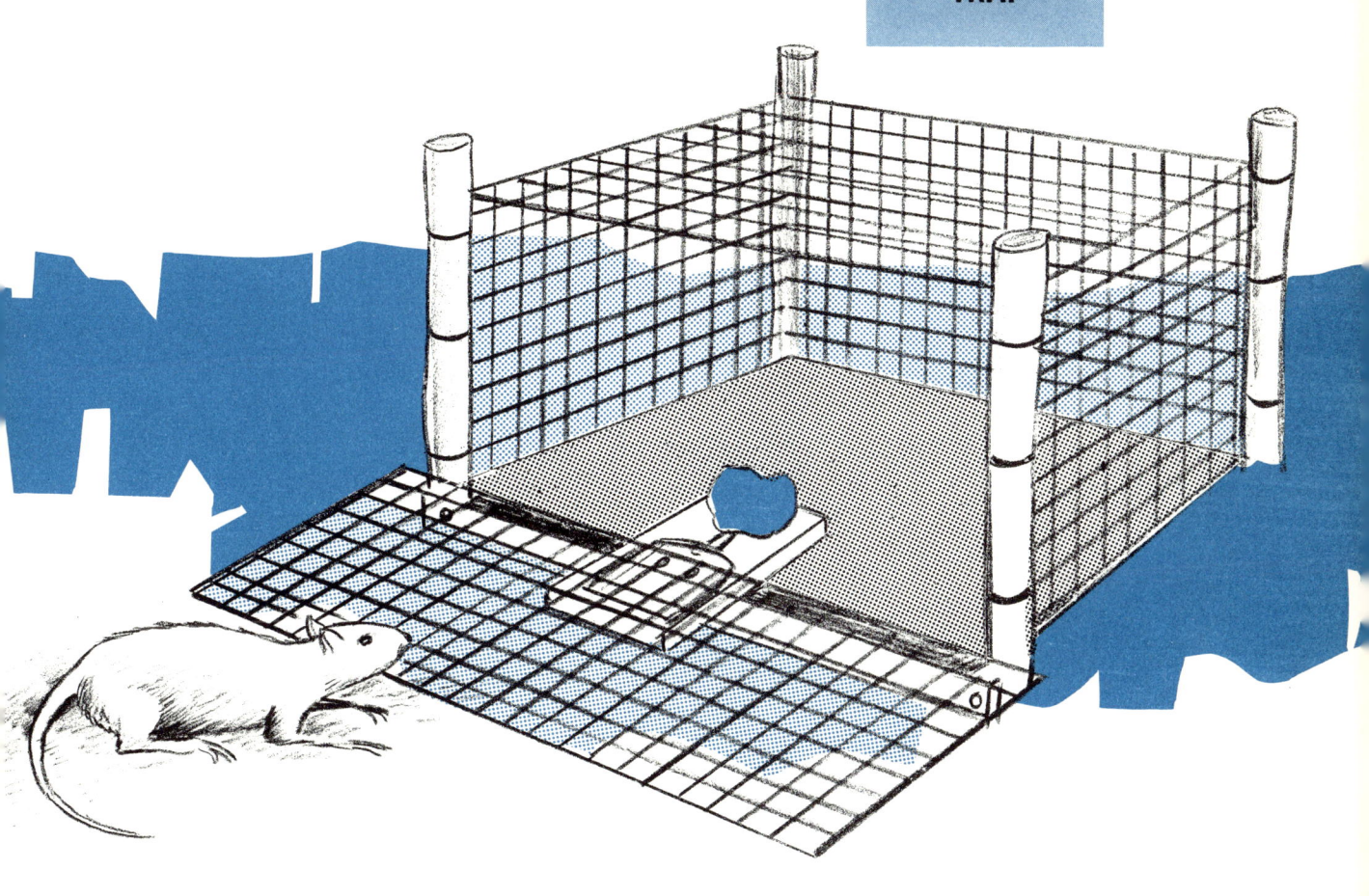

MAKING A TRAP FOR SMALL MAMMALS

Materials you'll need:
  piece of plywood, wire mesh,
  large rat trap, 4 wooden stakes,
  wire

Raccoons, opossums, field mice, rabbits and moles will make interesting pets if they are caught and handled with care. A trap can be made from a wire cage, large rat trap and stakes. Be sure that the finished cage is large enough for the animals you want.

To make the cage, cut the wire mesh cloth in the corners, bend the sides over and fasten them with wire. Cut one side from the cage to make the opening. Use the mesh from the side cut out to form the door of the cage. Nail the cage to the plywood base. The cage, with its wooden floor, should be staked firmly to the ground. Nail the trap to the floor wood which is firmly fastened to the stakes. Set the trap. Fasten the wire mesh door to the side of the trap spring when it is set.

Check the trap daily. If you find you have caught an animal, wire the piece of wire mesh over the opening and use it as a door. You can fashion hinges for the bottom of the door out of circles of wire. Unhook the cage from the stakes.

Furnish the animal with food and water immediately. After a week, if the animal is unhappy and does not adjust to captivity, return it to its natural environment.

TREES

TROPISMS

MEASURING A TREE

Materials you'll need:
7′ of 1″ by 2″ board, paper or protractor, 2 nails, string, weight, tape measure

You can make an instrument to measure the height of a tree without having to climb it. First, cut the board and nail the two pieces together as shown.

Five feet from the bottom of the upright board draw a diagonal line at a 45-degree angle. Use a protractor or a folded piece of paper to draw the line at the proper angle. Fold the paper as shown and lay it on the board so that the edge is even with the edge of the board. Drive two nails in along the line formed by the paper. Hang a string with a weight on the end of it from the lower nail.

To use the instrument, first guess at the height of the tree. Stand as far from the tree as you think the tree is high. Sight from the lower nail up along the upper nail until you see just the top of the tree. The weighted string must be hanging straight down along the side of the upright when the sighting is made. You'll probably have to move back and forth until you are in the correct position to sight the tree. Measure the distance from where you are standing to the tree trunk and add five feet.

DISCOVERING HOW PLANTS REACT

Materials you'll need:
2 pieces of glass, cotton, glass planter, soil, variety of seeds, clay pot, wooden stakes, shoe box, copper wire

Unlike most animals, plants have only limited movement. They react toward their environment when different parts of the plants turn toward or away from a stimulus. This stimulus can be light, water, gravity, touch, or chemicals. Try these experiments on plants to test their ability to move. Have patience—don't expect a reaction in minutes. Some tropisms take hours to be noticeable.

Thigmotropism: Plant some seeds of sweet pea, clematis, or garden peas in a clay pot or directly in the garden soil if it is spring. As the plant matures, drive thin wooden stakes in the ground next to the stem of each plant. Observe the action of the stem or tendrils as they reach for the stake. This is called *thigmotropism* and is caused by a touch stimulus (*thigmo* means "touch").

198

TROPISMS

Phototropism: Line a shoe box with metal foil to make it waterproof. Cut the top one inch off one end of the box. Fill the bottom with a layer of gravel and cover this with good soil until the box is half full. Plant a variety of seeds: corn, bean, radish, and grass. Water the seeds well. Place the cover of the shoe box on and remove it only to water the young seedlings as they grow. After two weeks remove the cover and note the position of the tiny plants. Which direction are they leaning? What are they reaching for? This reaction is called *phototropism*.

Hydrotropism: Find an old aquarium or similar container for this experiment. Partly fill it with good soil. Plant seeds along the glass side at one end of the planter. At the opposite end bury a clay pot to within an inch of its top rim. Always water the plants by pouring the water into the flower pot and not on the soil at the end where the seeds are planted. Cover the sides of the planter with dark paper for several weeks. Then periodically observe the root growth of the seedlings. What are they turning for? This reaction is called *hydrotropism*.

Chemotropism: Fill a jar half full of soil. Now place a ring of copper wire around the inside of the jar so that it touches the glass. Finish filling with soil. Plant several seeds next to the glass. Cover the outside of the jar so that light cannot get in. Water the seeds well. Every week observe the roots growing straight down because of the geotropism. What happens, though, when the tips of the roots are near the copper wire? This reaction is called *chemotropism*.

Geotropism: Put a layer of cotton on a piece of glass. Place several seeds in a row across the center of the cotton. Corn, bean, and radish seeds will germinate quickly. Put a second piece of glass over the seeds and cotton, thus making a sandwich. Tie the glass together and set it on end in a pan of water. In two or three days the small seedlings will appear. In which direction are the roots growing? After the

TROPISMS

TURTLES

first week turn the glass sandwich around so the top edge is immersed in the water. Notice the roots are pointing up and the little shoot downward. After a week in this position, which part of the plant is growing down toward the center of the earth?

Make another glass sandwich as described above. Select one kind of seed, such as sunflower seeds. Place three seeds with the pointed end up, three with the rounded end up, and three of them on their sides. Observe the direction of growth of each tiny plant as it germinates. Can you see a pattern? Why does this occur? These reactions are called *geotropisms*.

CARING FOR TURTLES
Materials you'll need:
    old aquarium, soil, moss, fern, pan

A turtle will thrive well in an unused aquarium partly filled with soil. A pan of water at one end will serve as the pond for the turtle. It prefers to return to water to eat. The land area can be landscaped with moss, fern, and other woodland plants. Place a rock or two in the water for the turtle to climb on. Change the water frequently as it becomes stagnant from leftover food.

Keep the temperature of a turtle's home around seventy-two degrees Fahrenheit, not lower than 68 degrees, since sudden chills are harmful.

Supplement its diet of commercial turtle food with raw meat, leafy vegetables and pieces of fruit.

Turtle shells should never be painted. This warps the growing tissue of the shell. If the shell has been painted, the paint should be scraped off carefully with a knife.

All turtles must return to the water's edge to lay their eggs in the sand. The eggs hatch from the heat of the sun and the offspring receive no care from the parents while young.

UNDERSHOT WATER WHEEL

MAKING AN UNDERSHOT WATER WHEEL

Materials you'll need:

> 6" by 12" piece of plywood, 2 pieces of plywood 2" by 10", 2 large wooden spools, a wooden dowel, 2 circles of ¼" plywood 6" in diameter, 2" by 24" piece of plywood

If you enjoy working with wood, you can follow this plan for a water wheel. This type is called *undershot* because the water goes under instead of over it.

Put together the six by twelve-inch plywood with the two by ten-inch pieces to form a stand which will hold the wheel. Drill holes through the centers of the two circular pieces of plywood as large as the holes through the wooden spools. Purchase a dowel just the right size to fit snugly through the spools and circles. The blades are made by cutting the two by twenty-four-inch plywood into six equal lengths.

The dowel should be glued to the spools and plywood circles, but should be free to turn in the supports. Glue the blades in place. They should extend beyond the circles. When water from a hose is aimed at the lower blades of the wheel, its force, striking the blades, will turn the wheel. This kind of wheel will turn and do work if placed in a fast-flowing stream of water.

GROWING FLOWERS FROM VEGETABLES

Materials you'll need:

> pots of wet sand or vermiculite, variety of vegetables

Purchase from the market or select from your family garden a variety of vegetables which store food in their roots or stems. Be sure that all parts of the plant are intact. Many of these plants are *biennials*. A biennial needs two growing seasons to complete its life cycle. The first year it produces roots, a stem and leaves. The roots live through the winter and the new plant, which bears the flower, fruit, and seeds, springs up from the roots the following spring. People don't often see this second year of the vegetable's growth.

Cut the bottom half from a root such as a carrot, beet, turnip, radish, and sweet potato. Push the cut ends into a pot of wet sand or vermiculite.

An underground stem, such as the white potato, will root if half of it is submerged in a glass of water. Onion bulbs may be planted directly into a pot of rich garden soil.

All of these vegetables will take root, send up new shoots, and soon a flower head will appear.

VEGETABLES

Volcano

EARTH SURFACE
SEDIMENTARY
METAMORPHIC
IGNEOUS

DEMONSTRATING HOW A VOLCANO ERUPTS

Materials you'll need:
modeling clay, metal can, ammonium dichromate, match heads, piece of plywood for base

A volcano appears at the earth's surface and erupts where the melted rock (*magma*) beneath the earth's crust finds an opening in the crust. The magma is under tremendous pressure inside the earth and comes out with such force that it sometimes causes great damage.

Use the plywood as a base on which to build the volcano. There should be at least six inches of board extending beyond the clay so that the erupting "magma" doesn't run onto the floor.

Using a variety of colors of modeling clay, let each color represent a kind of rock. The lower layer will be igneous; the second layer will be metamorphic; the third layer will be sedimentary and the last, the earth's surface. You may want to use a fifth color to line the opening through which the magma comes. Build up a volcanic cone on top leaving a small hole. Insert a small metal can in the hole.

Buy ammonium dichromate crystals from a drug store or hobby shop which sells chemicals. Mix a few match heads with a little of the chemical in the metal can. Drop in a burning match.

When the dichromate burns, it forms a dark green ash which tumbles over the cone in the same way as lava (released magma) flows in a real volcano.

202

WATER PURIFICATION

MAKING A MODEL WATER FILTER

Materials you'll need:
  plywood stand, glass chimney, fine wire mesh, clear plastic or glass dish, coarse gravel or pebbles, coarse sand, fine sand

The filtering beds are an important part of a water purification system. Not only are dirt and other large impurities filtered out of the water, but also a good many bacteria and other microbes are caught by a filter. The filter you are about to construct, because of its small size, will not remove the bacteria or even all of the mud from the dirty water you put into it, but it will show the principle on which a filter bed is made.

Make a simple plywood stand with a hole in the top large enough to support the glass chimney. Tie the wire mesh over the bottom opening of the chimney. Rest the chimney in the stand and fill it with two inches of coarse gravel, two inches of coarse sand, and two inches of fine sand, in that order. A good place to get the gravel and sand is the water purification plant in your community. Filter beds are frequently rebuilt and there are materials left over. Wash all the materials.

Place the dish underneath the chimney and pour dirty water into the top of your filter. The water should be noticeably cleaner when it comes out the bottom into the dish. You might try inoculating sterile dishes of agar-agar (see page 36) with a drop of the dirty water and a drop of filtered water. Compare the growth of microbe colonies a few days later and see how effective the filtering was.

SETTING UP A WATER PURIFICATION PLANT

Materials you'll need:
  3 plastic dishes, 3 1-holed stoppers, 3 pieces of glass tubing, 3 one-foot lengths of rubber tubing, 1 glass chimney, fine wire mesh, plywood stand, sand, gravel, alum, chlorine bleach, carbon, 3 pinch clamps, water glass, paraffin

Lake or river water must be treated before it is safe to drink. The water is treated in water purification plants. Usually the setup of the plant follows the pattern pictured on the next page. Chemicals are added to a mixing tank. Alum is particularly important because it causes foreign particles to clump together and settle faster. The water then goes to a settling basin where much of the dirt sinks to the bottom. Water is

203

WATER PURIFICATION

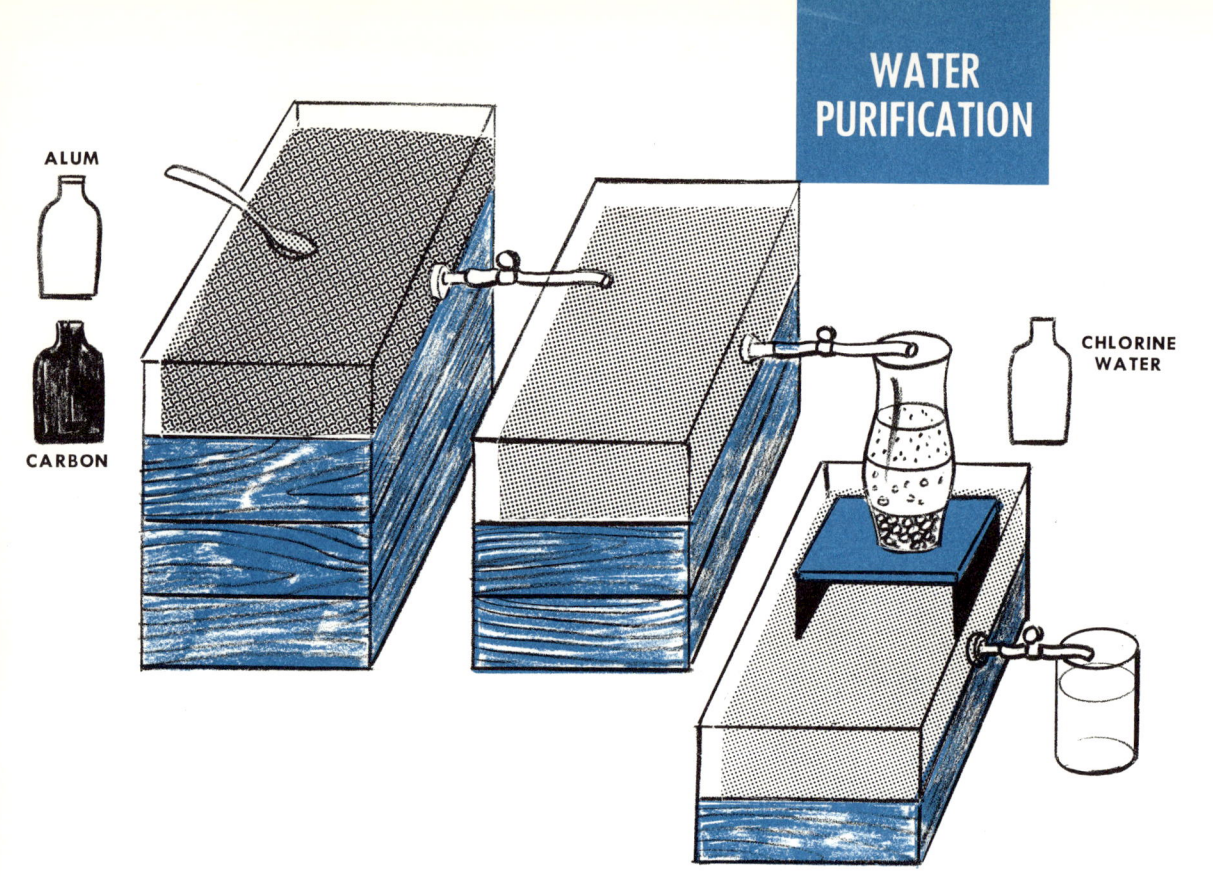

taken from the top of the settling basin to filter beds and allowed to run through them slowly. This removes most of the impurities. Chlorine is added to kill bacteria.

Your model plant will depend on gravity to cause the water to move from one container to the next, so the containers must be at different levels. Pay careful attention to where the holes are made in the containers. In the settling basin, for example, water is taken from the top. The pans must be kept almost full of water for the process work best.

Drill holes in the plastic containers large enough to admit one-holed stoppers. Seal the stoppers into the holes with paraffin. Put a glass tube through each stopper and run rubber tubing from it to the next pan. Follow the directions in the previous activity to construct the filter bed. Set the plywood platform in the last plastic dish. Put pinch clamps on all rubber tubing to stop the flow when desired.

Fill the mixing basin with dirty water. Mix about a teaspoonful of dirt with tap water for best results. Add a teaspoonful of alum and a few particles of carbon to the basin. You can get the carbon by scraping off the residue made by a candle flame on a glass dish. You will see the dirt become trapped in the clumps of alum. Stir it and release the clamp so water can flow into the settling basin. Allow the dirt to settle out; release the next clamp; and let the water flow into the filter. Add bleach (chlorine in solution) to the plastic dish underneath the filter. The water then flows into the water glass. *Do not* drink the water. The proportion of chlorine is probably too high and your model, because of its small size, probably did not do an efficient job of purification. Run tests for bacteria count using sterile agar-agar plants or gelatin mixture (see page 36) and one drop each of the dirty water and the final product.

CAUTION!

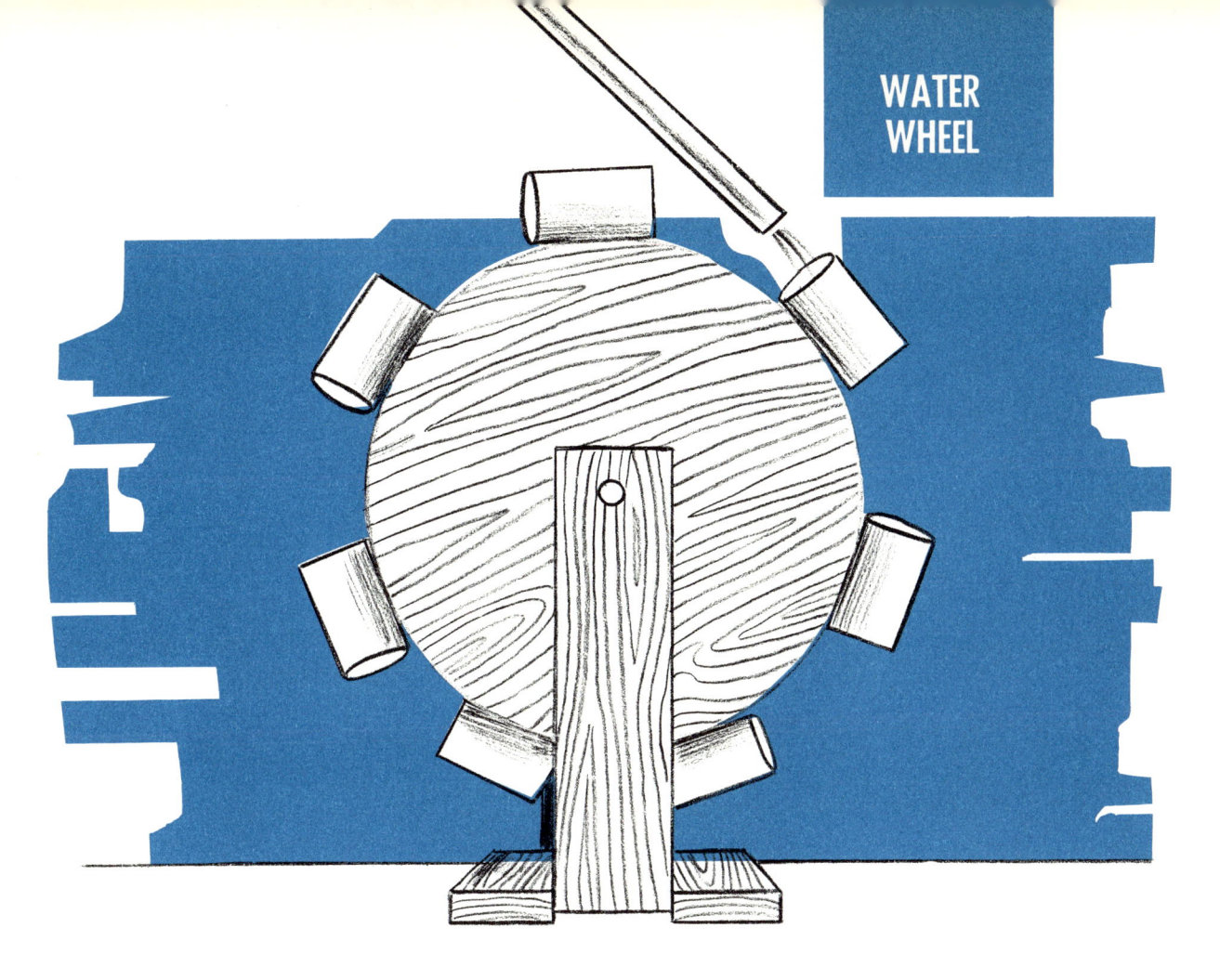

CONSTRUCTING AN OVERSHOT WATER WHEEL

Materials you'll need:
a piece of plywood 6" by 12",
2 pieces of plywood 2" by 14",
circular piece of plywood with
a 12" diameter, 7 small juice
cans, wooden dowel, hose

This overshot water wheel is the type which provided power before man learned to use steam power. There are still water wheels to be seen in some rural areas. The weight of the water falling onto the blades of the wheel caused the wheel to turn. The turning of the wheel ran machinery.

Drill a hole the exact size of the dowel through the center of the circular piece of plywood. Nail the cans, evenly spaced, to the wheel, making sure the openings all face in the same direction. The wooden stand is made of a base of six inch by twelve inch plywood and the two supports of the longer pieces of plywood. Force the dowel through the center of the wheel. It should be very tight so that when the wheel turns, the dowel axle will also. The turning shaft or axle is what would carry the power to the machinery of the mill. Make holes in the supports through which the dowel goes large enough so that the dowel can turn in them. Nail a small piece of wood on each end of the dowel to keep it from slipping out of the supports. Paint all of the wooden pieces so that they will not be warped by the water.

Use a garden hose as the source of water. Fill the cans on one side with water and the difference in weight will make the wheel start to turn.

WEATHER

KEEPING A DAILY CHART OF WEATHER

Materials you'll need:
14" by 24" piece of plywood, L-hooks, 60 2" by 2" pieces of tagboard, colored construction paper

This weather calendar would be an interesting project for you to make for your schoolroom. All of the students could help with recording weather changes on the calendar.

Use the large piece of plywood as the background. Heavy cardboard will do if you can't get plywood, but it wouldn't be as sturdy or last as long.

Divide the bottom ten inches of the plywood into 35 two-inch squares. Screw an L-hook into the top of each square. On the space left above the squares put a row of L-hooks to hold the name of the month and the year. The top of the plywood holds an illustration suitable for the month of the year. The hooks on either side of it hold extra cards.

Make many cardboard two-inch by two-inch squares, each with a hole in the top. You'll need enough letters so that you can spell all the months; you'll need cards with numbers from 1 to 31; you'll need a card for every day of the week; and you'll need extra numbers for indicating the year.

At the beginning of each month, arrange the dates properly under the days of the week. Each day, make a symbol out of colored construction paper to indicate the kind of weather on that day. You might have an umbrella for rain, yellow sun for a clear day, etc. Use your imagination! You want your calendar to be as colorful and clear as possible. Hang the paper weather symbols on the hooks over the cards that show the date.

206

WEATHER

RECORDING AND PREDICTING WEATHER FROM YOUR OWN STATION

Materials you'll need:

    weather instruments, tagboard,
    L-*hooks, notebook*

In order to forecast the weather, meteorologists (weathermen) use a number of instruments to determine temperature, wind velocity, wind direction, precipitation, air pressure, relative humidity, and cloud formation. To set up a weather station in your own backyard or outside the school, you will need to construct instruments. Information about and directions for making instruments are found throughout this book. See:

    "Anemometer"—page 24
    "Barometer"—page 39
    "Hygrometer"—page 110
    "Rain gauge"—page 163
    "Snow gauge"—page 176
    "Thermometer"—page 196
    "Wind scale"—page 208
    "Wind sock"—page 209
    "Wind vane"—page 209
    "Wind vane-anemometer"—page 210

The anemometer, rain gauge and snow gauge should be placed in an open area away from buildings and trees. Other instruments such as the barometer, hygrometer, thermometer, and Beaufort wind scale should be housed in a wooden shelter so that they are open to the outside but can't be damaged by wind and rain. Take daily readings of all instruments and record on a weather chart. Remember that these recordings are only approximate readings. Check the daily newspaper for comparisons.

Make the weather chart out of tagboard. Divide the tagboard lengthwise into seven vertical columns and eight horizontal columns. Put **L**-hooks in all of the squares created so that the chart can be used over and over.

Across the top, the headings are:

WEATHER

WIND

Date, Temperature, Relative Humidity, Air Pressure, Wind Direction, Wind Speed, Precipitation. Along the side are the days of the week. Under the heading *Date,* hang a piece of cardboard telling the weekly date.

Write the daily readings on light cardboard and hang the cardboard squares on the L-hooks in the proper places. Your weather station will be principally a means of recording daily weather changes. With practice, you may be able to forecast weather using information about changes in air pressure, cloud direction and relative humidity. If you keep a written record in a notebook, you can also compare one year with the next. Such records make predicting easier.

USING THE BEAUFORT WIND SCALE

Materials you'll need:
  poster board, felt pen

The Beaufort scale describes wind speed in chart form. It uses the effect of wind on objects around it to describe its speed. It is not as precise a measure as the anemometer, but it is still used occasionally by the weather stations. The scale was originally devised by Sir Francis Beaufort.

Copy the Beaufort scale on a large poster board that you can hang in your weather station and use for quick reference. Illustrations on your chart will help make it clearer and more interesting. By watching the effects of wind you can estimate the speed.

BEAUFORT WIND SCALE

NO.	TITLE	EFFECT OF WIND		MPH
0	Calm	Smoke rises vertically		Less Than 1
1	Light air	Smoke drifts		1-3
2	Light breeze	Leaves rustle		4-7
3	Gentle breeze	Flags fly		8-12
4	Moderate breeze	Dust, loose paper raised		13-18
5	Fresh breeze	Small trees sway		19-24
6	Strong breeze	Difficult to use umbrellas		25-31
7	Moderate gale	Difficult to walk		32-38
8	Fresh gale	Twigs break off trees		39-46
9	Strong gale	Slight damage to roofs		47-54
10	Whole gale	Trees uprooted		55-63
11	Storm	Widespread damage		64-75
12	Hurricane	Devastation		Above 75

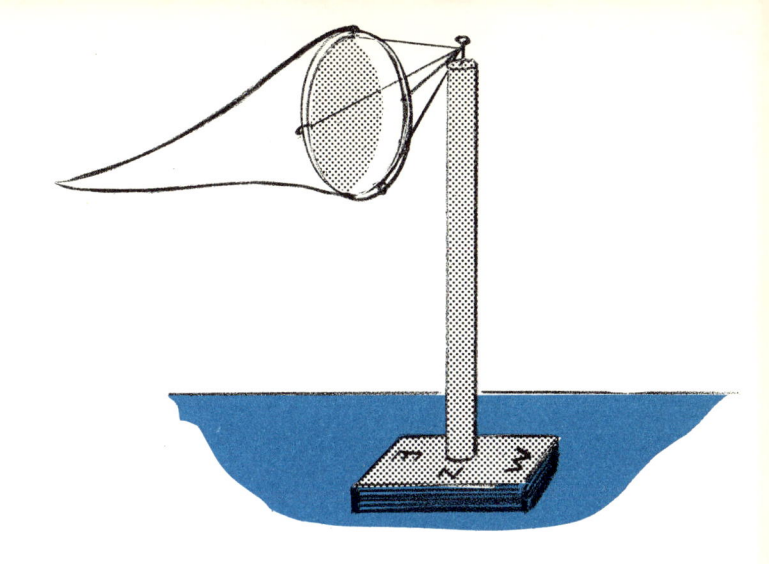

WIND

MAKING A WIND SOCK

Materials you'll need:

wire coat hanger, nylon stocking or other thin net-like material, string, ½ to ¾-inch dowel or broomstick, nail, heavy wooden block at least 6" square

Many small airports still use wind socks to indicate to pilots the direction from which the wind is blowing. This helps the pilot to know which direction to land. Such a wind-direction indicator is very important at airports that don't have radio equipment for landing and takeoff instructions.

To make a small yet workable wind sock, bend a wire hanger into a circle. Sew the open end of a nylon stocking to it. You can also use a cone about two to four feet long made from another light netted material such as cheesecloth. Attach the wind sock to a nail in the top of a dowel which may be set in a wood block or sharpened and driven into the ground.

MAKING A WIND VANE

Materials you'll need:

½-inch wood or stiff cardboard, nails, ¾-inch dowel or broomstick, paint

To make a simple wind vane, cut an arrow from a piece of wood not thicker than one-half inch. You can use a heavy piece of cardboard or balsa wood, but neither will last long in wet weather. Determine where the center of gravity in your arrow is by balancing it on your finger. Put a nail through that point, making certain it will come through the bottom of the arrow by at least an inch or two. If you use cardboard or balsa wood you will have to use tape or some other means of attaching the nail. Now either fix a suitable base or stand for your arrow or sharpen the dowel so it can be driven into the ground easily.

Drill a hole in the top of the dowel. If the nail in the arrow protrudes one inch, be sure that the hole made in the dowel is not deeper than three-fourths of an inch. Wax or grease the hole and insert the nail. If the fit is proper the first breeze will activate your vane and all you need is a compass to tell you exactly where that breeze is coming from. For example, when the arrow turns to the south, the wind is from the south and is called a *south wind*. If your vane is on a wooden stand, you may want to paint the main compass points on the base.

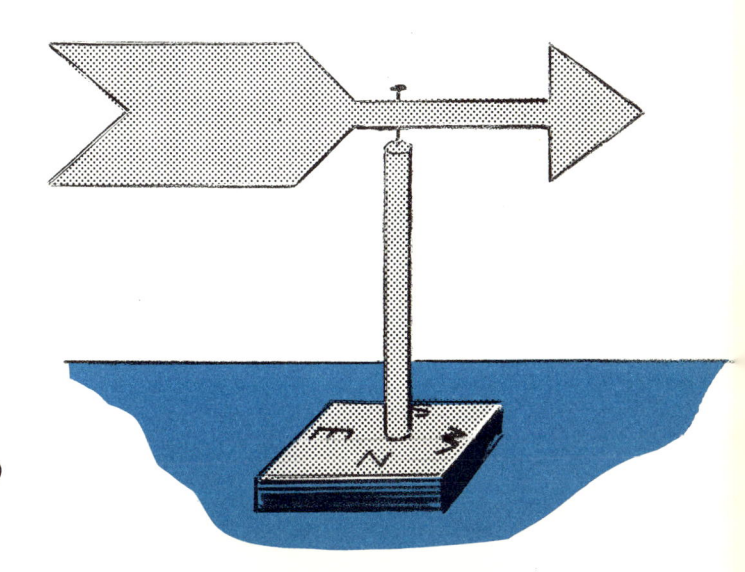

209

WIND

WIND TUNNEL

MAKING A COMBINATION WIND VANE AND ANEMOMETER

Materials you'll need:
thin metal wire, wooden wind vane, sheet of tin, heavy cardboard or 1/8" plywood, nails

Weather stations usually have mounted on a tall mast a *rotating-cup* anemometer and wind vane. You can modify the wind vane described in the preceding activity and make a simple combination.

To the stem of the arrow on your wind vane nail a wooden arm which will support a swinging, gate-like, wind-speed indicator. Follow the illustration in constructing. Use either cardboard or a very thin piece of wood for the wind scale. It can be tacked or nailed to the side of the arrow stem. Use a piece of flattened tin can or heavy cardboard for the "gate" and wire to make rings for attaching the "gate" to the bracket. A fairly accurate means of calibrating the anemometer is to hold it out a car window on a calm day while someone drives first five, then ten and fifteen miles per hour, etc. Mark the wind scale with a pencil and later the complete scale can be lined and numbered with India ink or paint.

CONSTRUCTING A WIND TUNNEL

Materials you'll need:
12 milk cartons, heavy tape, electric fan

A wind tunnel may be a necessary tool for you to use in your experiments with airplane controls. With it you can direct a definite stream of air against a model. It is very simple to construct.

Cut the ends off twelve milk cartons of equal size. Stack them on each other as shown and tape them together. Direct the stream of air from an electric fan through your wind tunnel and you are ready to test airfoils (see page 20) and other airplane surfaces.

WINDLASS

MAKING A WINDLASS

Materials you'll need:
scraps of wood for supports, broom handle, stone, rope, spring scale, salt box, spike, tacks

A wheel fastened to a rod so that when the wheel is turned, the rod turns also, is called a *wheel and axle*. A small amount of force applied to turning the wheel will cause a large turning force to be applied to the axle. The wheel and axle is a simple machine.

The windlass, used for lifting heavy objects, is a wheel and axle. Follow the illustration and build a windlass with which you can prove that the wheel and axle makes work easier.

Use scraps of lumber to build a support for the windlass. Drill holes in the supports for the ends of the broom handle. Drive two small tacks side by side into the broom handle (axle).

Lift a heavy object, such as a stone with strings around it, about two inches off the ground with a spring scale. How much force was required? Tie a rope to the stone and fasten the other end of the rope to the tack on the axle. Hook the spring scale onto the other tack and turn the axle enough revolutions to lift the weight two inches. Did it require as much force to lift the stone this way?

Now fasten an empty salt box to the broom handle by driving a long spike all the way through the box and handle. This is now the wheel. Attach the spring scale to this as shown. How much force is required now to lift the weight two inches? If the wheel had a diameter twice that of the axle, only half the force would be needed to lift the object. You are trading distance for force in doing work.

WOOD

XYLOPHONE

COLLECTING AND MOUNTING DIFFERENT KINDS OF WOODS

Materials you'll need:
  various wood scraps, clear varnish, India ink, colored pencils, poster cardboard

An interesting and attractive display of varieties of woods may be put together with these simple materials. The people at the lumber yard will be helpful in furnishing scraps of various hard and soft woods. Be certain you have proper identifications before you begin. Cut the scraps to a uniform size—approximately one and one-half to two inches wide, three to five inches long and one-half inch thick. Sand one large surface carefully. Use green or black pencil to outline the tree's shape and its leaf shape on the sample; then brush the sample with clear varnish. Mount your finished samples on white poster board and label with India ink.

MAKING A XYLOPHONE

Materials you'll need:
  clear and soft pine wood, saw, drill, felt strips, nails, dowel pins, glue, sandpaper

The xylophone seen in use today is descended from ancient oriental instruments and is related to one or more instruments common among the people of middle Europe. It is a percussion instrument on which tones are produced by striking wooden sounding bars with hard rubber or wooden mallets. The sounding bars today are frequently made of rosewood, although pinewood and glass have been used.

Most xylophones have three or more octaves but a simple eight-note model can be easily built. Using clear pine about one-half to three-quarter inches thick, cut a bar about one and a quarter inches wide and five inches long. Be certain to cut sounding bars so the grain runs parallel to the length of the

XYLOPHONE

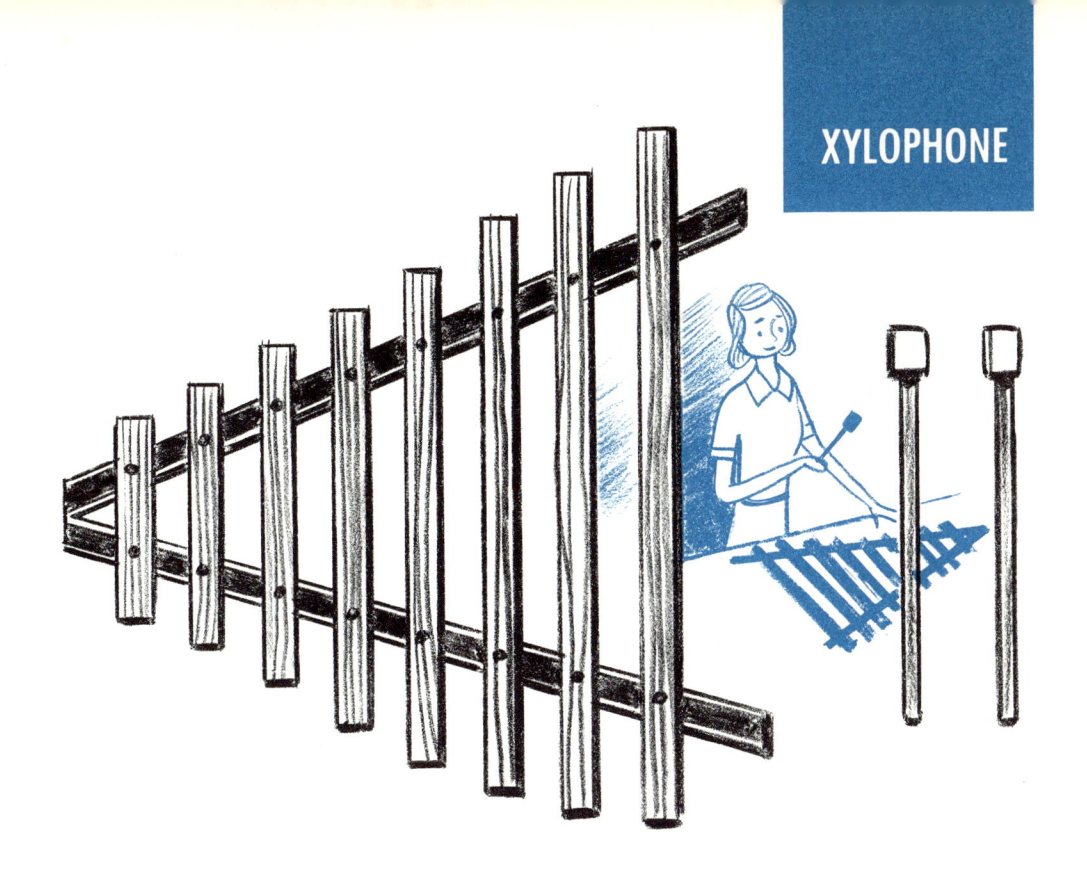

bar. Hold this first bar lightly between two fingers and tap it with another piece of wood to determine on a piano what key you have produced. Cut another piece about four and one-half inches long and by tapping both and checking with a piano, see if they are consecutive or nearly consecutive notes. Remember, the shorter the sounding bar, the higher the tone.

If your second bar is too much like the first, saw off what you think may produce the desired tone. Thus, by trial and error, cut eight sounding bars, four longer and three shorter than the first, and sand each so it will be smooth and free of splinters.

Now cut two narrow pieces of wood about fourteen inches long and one-half inch square. Next, cut felt strips as long and about as wide as these mounting pieces for the sounding bars. Glue the felt strips to the mounting pieces. Now, following the illustration, set the mounting pieces in a wide "V" and place the sounding bars along the felted side with a space of about one-quarter inch between each bar.

Make a final check to see that you are satisfied with your scale. If you are, drill holes in the bars where they meet the mounting pieces. The holes should be just slightly larger than the nails you intend to use. Be certain the nails have heads large enough to prevent the bars from falling off the mounting pieces when the instrument is being carried. Also be careful that the nails are not so heavy that they split the mounting pieces.

Now all you need is a mallet or two. To make them, drill a hole just large enough to accommodate the dowel pin handle (which should be about seven to ten inches long) in the center of a block of wood about one inch long and three-quarters of an inch wide. Glue the handles in place and when they have dried, see if you can play a tune on your own xylophone.

YEAST

OBSERVING YEAST WORK

Materials you'll need:
   molasses, 2 cereal bowls, 2 water glasses, commercial yeast cake, coasters

Yeast is a tiny plant which can ferment sugar, producing alcohol and carbon dioxide gas. Molasses is a good food for the yeast to work on since there is so much sugar in it.

Mix one-half cup of molasses and one quart of water. Fill each cereal bowl about half full with the mixture. Fill both glasses with the diluted molasses and drop one-fourth of a yeast cake into one of the glasses. Hold a coaster over the top of each tumbler and turn it upside down in the bowl.

As the yeast starts to ferment the molasses, carbon dioxide gas (CO_2) will be formed. The gas will push the molasses out of the glass into the bowl. In three or four hours all the molasses will have been pushed out of the glass. What has happened in the other glass?

SEEING THE EFFECT OF YEAST ON DOUGH

Materials you'll need:
   flour, sugar, commercial yeast, water, large screw-top jar, candle wax, 2 feet of rubber tubing, limewater

Puncture an opening in a metal cover of a glass jar. Insert one end of a length of rubber tubing through the hole. Place melted wax around the hole to be sure the connection is airtight. Submerge the other end of the tube in a glass of limewater.

Combine one cup of flour, one tablespoon of sugar, one-fourth package of commercial yeast, and one-half cup of water. This is a crude form of bread dough. Place this mixture in the glass jar. Screw on the top immediately.

Set this jar in a warm place. Soon the dough will rise. Remove the lid, puncture the mound of dough, and quickly close the jar again. The gas that caused the bread to rise escapes into the tube that leads to the limewater. Since the gas given off by the yeast is carbon dioxide the limewater will turn milky.

ZONES OF TIME

TELLING TIME AROUND THE WORLD

Materials you'll need:
  tagboard, cardboard, brads, felt pen, globe or good world map

If you were to cross the ocean to visit Europe, you would find that the time changes by one hour in certain special places around the Earth. There are even time changes as you cross the United States. These changes take place as you enter new time zones. The reason for these zones is that the earth spins on its axis from west to east. Man has created zones by drawing imaginary lines called *meridians* from pole to pole. The meridians are fifteen degrees apart. An hour passes as the earth rotates through fifteen degrees of its surface, so each zone marks one hour. The total surface covers 360 degrees.

Greenwich, England, has the zero meridian. Philadelphia is seventy-five degrees west of Greenwich, so there is a difference of five hours (75 divided by 15) between the two cities.

Fasten a small cardboard circle into the center of a large tagboard circle with a brad which permits the inner circle to rotate. Draw lines through both circles representing the twenty-four lines of longitude. They must be equally spaced and pass through the centers of the circles.

Number the lines on the inside circle with the times from noon to midnight on one half of the circle and back to midnight again on the other half.

Use the globe or map to locate large cities all over the world. Start with Philadelphia. Determine how many lines of longitude away San Francisco is and put it at the appropriate line. Write in London the correct degrees of longitude away from Philadelphia in the other direction. Write in other big cities. By spinning the time circle you can find what time it is all over the world when it is a certain time in your own city.

215

ZOO

WHITE MICE

OPOSSUM

KEEPING A BACKYARD ZOO

If you are the kind of boy or girl who likes animals and always has a few around the house, a backyard zoo would be a good summer vacationtime activity for you. In some climates, you can leave your animals out all year. You might even make it a neighborhood project with you and several friends pooling animals and cages. Of course the cages need frequent cleaning and the animals need feeding and care, and you must be willing to spend the time and effort necessary.

If you plan to catch animals especially for the zoo, make sure you have their homes ready for them. Arrange the cages so that the animals which need shade have it and others have some sunlight available to them. The cages must be tightly closed so that unwelcome animal visitors cannot disturb your pets. Warn human visitors not to feed or tease the animals.

Make small signs telling the animals' names and something about them. Be

216

ZOO   ZYGOTE

on hand during visiting hours to talk to visitors.

Be sure to read the instructions for making cages on page 28 and for feeding your animals on page 24.

WATCHING THE DEVELOPMENT OF A FERTILIZED EGG

Materials you'll need:
   amphibian eggs, hand lens

A zygote is a fertilized egg cell. The male and female germ cells have fused to form a zygote. The zygote then goes through cell division and the many-celled embryo develops.

Since the covering of amphibian eggs is transparent, you can watch the frog or toad zygote develop.

Follow directions on page 22 for collecting the eggs. The early stages of frog or toad development can be followed by watching the collected eggs with a hand lens or microscope. Later stages can be seen with the naked eye.

A new zygote is a single cell. Then a furrow forms on top and grows down, dividing the cell in two. A second furrow at right angles divides it into four parts. Each division takes about an hour. This division or *cleavage* continues until the egg has turned into a hollow ball of cells. Then the eyes, ears, and tail of the tadpole are formed.

The process can be stopped at any time by refrigerating the eggs. When they are warmed up to room temperature again, the development goes on.

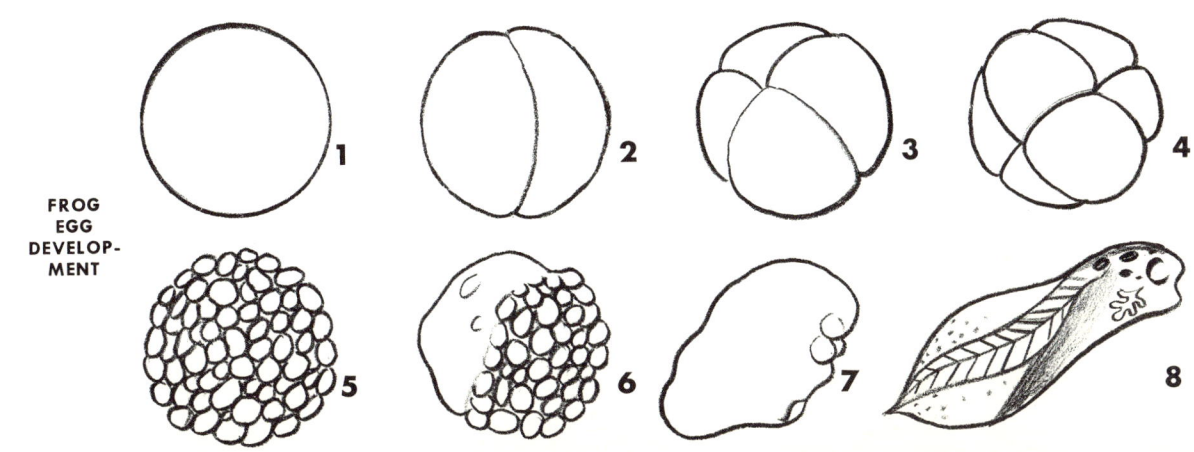

FROG EGG DEVELOPMENT

INDEX

Absorption, 16, 64
Acid test, rocks, 166
Acids and bases, 16, 114
Aeronautics:
  Bernoulli's principle, 19
  controls, 20
  jet model, 117
  jet propulsion, 117
  wind tunnel, 210
Air:
  Bernoulli's principle, 19
  cloud, 62
  condensation, 67
  current, 70
  fog, 92
  gases, 100
  measurement, 24, 38
  space, 17
  thermometer, 196
  weight, 18
Air pressure, 18, 38, 48, 122
Airfoil, 19, 210
Airplane, 19, 20, 21, 117
Alternation of generations, 90
Amphibian, 22, 26, 107, 189
Anemometer, 22, 210
Aneroid barometer, 38
Animal: ant, 30
  baby, 35
  bird, 41
  breeding, 26
  cage, 28
  cat, 56
  caterpillar, 55
  chicken, 62
  dog, 75
  earthworm, 79
  feeding, 24
  fossil, 93
  fruit fly, 94
  hibernation, 107
  mealworm, 132
  paramecia, 150
  planaria, 152
  protozoa, 146, 158
  rabbit, 35, 162
  silkworm, 173
  skeleton, 174
  spider, 33
  taxidermy, 190
  track, 28, 93
  trap, 52, 197
  tropical fishes, 32, 104
  turtle, 200
  wildlife, 27

Animal (*cont.*)
  zoo, 216
Annual ring, 29
Ant colony, 30
Antenna, 29
Antiseptic, 30, 37
Ants, 30
Aquarium: fresh-water, 31
  salt-water, 32
  tropical fishes, 104
Arachnida, 33, 183
Astronomy:
  constellation, 68, 69
  day and night, 73
  earth's rotation, 73
  magnetic field, 127
  moon, 141
  planet, 153
Atom: model, 34
  numbers, 34
  radioactive, 162
  splitting, 33

Baby animals, 35
Bacteriology:
  antiseptic, 30
  bacteria, 37
  culture, 36
Ball bearing, 94
Barometer, 38
Battery, electric, 40
Battery, storage, 40
Beaufort wind scale, 208
Beetle, 132
Bernoulli's principle, 19
Bird: chicken, 60, 113
  feeding station, 44
  food, 24, 35, 44, 45
  house, 41-43
  parakeet, 149
Blood, 46
Blueprint, 47, 128
Bog terrarium, 90, 195
Boiling point, 48
Bone, 48, 49
Botanical press, 50
Breeding, animal, 26, 104
Brooder, 60
Buoyancy, 50

Cages, 28, 115, 197
Camera, 51, 134
Capillarity, 53
Carbon dioxide, 54, 76, 157

Cat, 56
Catalyst, 54, 86
Caterpillar, 55
Cell: animal, 57
  plant, 155, 158
Centrifugal force, 58
Charcoal, 58
Charge, electric, 84, 185
Chemical change, 54, 59, 86, 91, 139, 149
Chemical gardening, 109
Chemistry:
  acids and bases, 16, 114
  blueprint, 47
  carbon dioxide, 54
  crystals, 72
  diffusion, 73
  distillation, 74
  equilibrium, 86
  mixture, 139
  osmosis, 148
  oxidation, 149
  precipitation, 157
  purification, 203
Chemotropism, 199
Chicken: brooder, 60
  embryo, 62, 85
  incubator, 113
Chlorophyll, 61, 152
Circuit, electric, 165, 173
Circuit, parallel, 80
Circuit, series, 80, 96, 160
Circulatory system, 46, 61, 159, 187
Cleavage:
  embryonic, 62
  rock, 167
Cloud chamber, 162
Clouds, 62
Collections: caterpillar, 55
  fungus, 96
  insect, 115
  leaf, 119
  plant, 50, 92
  rock, 165
Color, 16, 64, 77, 89, 183
Communication, 71, 191, 19?
Commutator, 142
Compass, 66
Compost heap, 66
Condensation, 67, 92, 162
Conduction, 67, 106
Constellarium, 68
Constellation, 68, 69

Convection, 70
Crystal radio, 71
Crystals, 72
Culture, bacteria, 36
Current, air, 70, 87
Current, electric, 67, 80, 97, 142, 160, 165, 173
Current, liquid, 70

Day and night, 73
Desert terrarium, 195
Diffusion, 73, 148
Digestion, 86
Dip net, 74
Distilled water, 74
Dog, 75
Dry cell, 80
Dry ice, 76
Dye, 77

Ears, 78
Earth:
   magnetic field, 127
   day and night, 73
   rotation, 73
   time zones, 215
Earthworm, 79
Egg: amphibian, 22
   chicken, 85, 113
   cleavage, 62
   zygote, 218
Electric cell, 82
Electric lighting, 81, 123
Electric motor, 142
Electric switch, 188
Electrical wiring, 80
Electricity: charge, 84
   circuit, parallel, 80
   circuit, series, 80, 96, 160
   conduction, 67
   current, 82
   electrolyte, 83
   electromagnet, 84
   fuse, 96
   galvanometer, 82, 97
   insulation, 105
   light, 105
   light system, 81
   rheostat, 165
   short circuit, 173
   static, 185
   switch, 188
   telegraphy, 191
Electrolyte, 83

Electromagnet, 84, 129, 131, 142
Electroscope, 84
Elements, 34
Embryology, 22, 62, 85, 113, 217
Energy: conduction, 106
   electrical, 83
   light, 123
   sound, 179
   steam, 186
Enzymes, 86
Equilibrium, 86
Erosion, 87
Evaporation, 87, 110
Expansion, 88
Eye, 89, 146

Feeding station, bird, 44
Fern, 90
Fertilizer, 66
Filter, 203
Fingerprints, 91
Fire extinguisher, 76, 91
Fish: aquarium, 31
   goldfish, 32
   guppies, 104
Flatworm, 152
Flowers, 92, 98, 109, 201
Fog, 92
Footprint, 92
Force:
   centrifugal, 58
   friction, 94
Fossil, 93
Fracture test, rocks, 167
Freezing point, 112
Friction, 94
Frog: egg, 22
   hibernation, 107
   tadpole, 189
Fruit fly, 94
Fungus, 96
Fuse, 96

Galvanometer, 82, 97
Gardening: fertilizer, 66
   flower, 98
   garden flats, 98
   grafting, 102
   greenhouse, 100
   hydroponics, 109
   seeds, 171
   vegetable, 98, 201

Gases, 74, 76, 100
Genetics, 94, 107
Geology: fossil, 93
   hardness scale, 105
   rocks, 165-168
   soil, 154, 177-179
   stalagmite, 184
   volcano, 202
Geotropism, 199
Germination, 98, 101, 169, 171
Grafting, 102
Gravity, 103, 108
Greenhouse, 100
Guinea pig, 26, 28, 104
Guppy, 104

Hair hygrometer, 110
Hardness scale, 105, 168
Hearing, 78
Heart, 61, 187
Heat: absorption, 16
   conduction, 68, 106
   electricity, 105
   evaporation, 87
   expansion, 88
Heredity, 26, 95, 107
Hibernation, 107
Humidity, 110
Hydrometer, 108
Hydroponics, 109
Hydrotropism, 199
Hygrometer, 110

Ice, 76, 112
Igneous rock, 167
Inclined plane, 112, 170
Incubator, 113
Indicator, 117
Ink, 59
Insect: ant, 30
   cage, 55, 115
   caterpillar, 55
   collection, 115
   dip net, 74
   fruit fly, 94
   killing jar, 115
   mounting, 116
   relaxing jar, 116
   spreading board, 116

Jet propulsion, 117

Kaleidoscope, 118

Killing jar, 115
Knife switch, 129, 188

Leaves, 50, 119, 120
Lens, 134, 151, 193
Lever, 121
Lift (aero.), 19
Lift pump, 122
Light: absorption, 16
  color, 64
  eye, 89
  photometer, 151
  reflection, 124
  refraction, 125
  spectrum, 183
  speed, 126
Lightning, 126
Litmus test, 16, 114
Loam, 177
Lung capacity, 164

Machines, complex, 126, 186
Machines, simple, 126
  inclined plane, 112
  lever, 121
  pulley, 159
  screw, 170
  wheel and axle, 211
  windlass, 211
Magnet, 66, 83, 128-131, 142
Magnetic crane, 129
Magnetic dip circle, 127
Magnetic field, 127, 128, 131
Magnetic pole, 84, 127, 130, 142
Mammal trap, 197
Matches, 132
Mealworm, 132
Measurement:
  air pressure, 38
  humidity, 110
  rain, 163
  snow, 176
  temperature, 196
  weight, 170
  wind, 24
Mercurial barometer, 38
Metals, 106, 133
Metamorphic rock, 167
Metamorphosis, 22, 55, 132, 173
Meteorology, 207
Mice, 28, 133
Microphotography, 134

Microscope: blood, 46
  cell, 155, 158
  paramecia, 150
  parts, 135
  slide, 134, 137
  tissue, 57
  use, 134
  waterdrop, 138
Microscopic slide, 134, 137
Mineral, 105, 165
Mirror, 118, 151
Mixture, 139
Mold, 140
Molecule, 88
Momentum, 140
Moon, 141
Morse Code, 191
Moss, 141
Motor, 142
Muscle, 49
Mushroom, 96, 184
Musical instruments, 144, 180, 212

Nature trail, 145
Nervous system, 145, 146, 163
Nutrition, 24, 157

Optical illusion, 146, 147
Oscillation, 147
Osmosis, 148, 155
Overshot water wheel, 205
Oxidation, 54, 149

Parakeet, 149
Paramecia, 150
Periscope, 151
Pet food, 24, 56, 75, 132
Photography, 51, 134
Photometer, 151
Photosynthesis, 152, 158
Phototropism, 199
Physics: absorption, 16
  air, 18
  atom, 33, 34
  buoyancy, 50
  capillarity, 53
  centrifugal force, 58
  convection, 70
  electricity, 80-84
  electromagnet, 131
  expansion, 88
  friction, 94
  gravity, 103

Physics (cont.)
  heat, 68, 106
  light, 123-125
  machines, 126
  magnetism, 127-131
  momentum, 140
  motor, 142
  sound, 179
  spectrum, 183
  static electricity, 185
  surface tension, 188
Physiology: blood, 46
  bone, 48, 49
  circulation, 61
  digestion, 86
  ear, 78
  eye, 89, 146
  heart, 187
  muscle, 49
  nervous system, 145
  protein, 157
  pulse, 159
  respiratory system, 164
  senses, 163, 189
  skeleton, 174
Pitch, 180
Planaria, 152
Planets, 153
Plant: anatomy, 57
  aquatic, 32
  chlorophyll, 61
  drying, 92
  fern, 90
  fungus, 96
  garden, 98, 108
  germination, 101
  grafting, 102
  hydroponics, 109
  leaf, 119
  mold, 140
  moss, 141
  mushroom, 184
  oxygen, 155
  photosynthesis, 152
  press, 50
  pollen, 156
  propagation, 101
  root, 169
  seed, 98, 101, 109, 169, 171, 172
  transpiration, 196
  tree, 29, 198
  vegetable, 201
  yeast, 214

Pollen, 156
Precipitate, 157
Precipitation:
  rain, 162
  snow, 176
Preservative, 37
Protein, 157
Protoplasm, 158
Protozoa, 146, 150, 158
Psychrometer, 111
Pulley, 159
Pulse, 159
Pump, 122
Purification, 74, 203

Quiz board, 160

Rabbit, 35, 161
Raccoon, 27, 52
Radio, 71
Radioactivity, 162
Rain, 162
Reactions, 145, 146, 163
Reflection, 123, 124
Reflex, 145
Refracting telescope, 193
Refraction, 125, 193
Regeneration, 152
Relative humidity, 110
Relaxing jar, 116
Reproduction:
  amphibian, 22
  animal, 26, 62, 85, 95,
    104, 113, 132, 218
  plant, 90, 141
Reptiles, 132, 175
Resonance, 179
Respiration, in plants, 155
Respiratory system, 164
Rheostat, 165
Rocks, 105, 165-168
Roots, 169

Salamander, 22
Scales, 170
Screw, 170
Sea water, 32
Sedimentary rock, 167
Seed, 98, 99, 101, 109, 169,
  171-172
Semi-aquatic terrarium, 195
Short circuit, 173
Sight, 89
Silkworm, 173

Simple machines, see
  Machines, simple
Skeleton, 48, 174
Skin, 91, 190
Smoke box, 124
Smoke prints, 120
Snakes, 175
Snow gauge, 176
Soil: air content, 17
  composition, 66, 176
  erosion, 87
  water retention, 177
  types, 178
Solar system, 141, 153
Sound, 78, 126, 144, 179-182
Sound pipes, 181
Sound wave, 29, 182
Spatter prints, 120
Specific gravity, 103, 108
Spectrum, 183
Spider, 33, 183
Spreading board, 116
Stalactite, stalagmite, 184
Stars, 68
Static electricity, 185
Steam, 168
Stethoscope, 187
Storage battery, 40
Streak test, rocks, 168
Sundial, 187
Surface tension, 188
Switch, 188

Tadpole, 22, 32, 189
Taste buds, 189
Taxidermy, 190
Telegraphy, 80, 191
Telephone, 181, 192
Telescope, 183
Temperature, 196
Tension, surface, 188
Terrarium, 90, 96, 194
Thermometer, 196
Thigmotropism, 198
Thyroid, 189
Time, 187, 215
Tin-can telephone, 181
Tissue, 48, 57, 137
Tracks, animal, 28, 93
Transpiration, 196
Trap, 52, 197
Tree, 29, 198
Tropical fishes, 32, 104
Tropism, 198-200

Turbine, 186
Turtle, 200

Undershot water wheel, 201

Vegetables, 201
Velocity, 22
Vibration, 180
Volcano, 202

Water: air content, 17
  condensation, 67
  convection, 70
  filter, 203
  purification, 203
Water filter, 203
Water purification, 74, 203
Water wheel, 201, 205
Wave motion, 29
Weather chart, 206
Weather instruments:
  anemometer, 24, 210
  barometer, 38
  rain gauge, 163
  snow gauge, 176
  thermometer, 196
  wind sock, 209
  wind vane, 209
  wind vane-anemometer, 210
Weather station, 207
Weight: of air, 18
  oscillation, 147
  scales, 170
Wet-and-dry-bulb
  hygrometer, 111
Wheel and axle, 211
Wild flower, 50, 194
Wildlife, 27
Wind, 22, 209, 210
Wind tunnel, 20, 210
Wind vane-anemometer, 210
Windlass, 129, 211
Wiring, electrical, 80
Wood, 212
Woodland terrarium, 194
Worms, 79, 152

Xylophone, 212

Yeast, 214

Zones of time, 215
Zoo, 216
Zygote, 217